Educational Policies and Inequalities in Europe

Educational Policies and Inequalities in Europe

Edited by

Marc Demeuse
University of Mons, Belgium

Daniel Frandji
Ecole Normale Supérieure de Lyon, French Institute of Education, Triangle, France

David Greger
Charles University in Prague, Czech Republic

and

Jean-Yves Rochex
Paris 8 University, France

First published 2012 by
PALGRAVE MACMILLAN

Palgrave Macmillan in the UK is an imprint of Macmillan Publishers Limited, registered in England, company number 785998, of Houndmills, Basingstoke, Hampshire RG21 6XS.

Palgrave Macmillan in the US is a division of St Martin's Press LLC, 175 Fifth Avenue, New York, NY 10010.

Palgrave Macmillan is the global academic imprint of the above companies and has companies and representatives throughout the world.

Palgrave® and Macmillan® are registered trademarks in the United States, the United Kingdom, Europe and other countries.

ISBN 978–0–230–30203–7

This book is printed on paper suitable for recycling and made from fully managed and sustained forest sources. Logging, pulping and manufacturing processes are expected to conform to the environmental regulations of the country of origin.

A catalogue record for this book is available from the British Library.

A catalog record for this book is available from the Library of Congress.

10   9   8   7   6   5   4   3   2   1
21 20 19 18 17 16 15 14 13 12

Printed and bound in Great Britain by
CPI Antony Rowe, Chippenham and Eastbourne

Contents

Portugal

Czech Republic

Romania

Sweden

Figures and Tables

Figures

Tables

Foreword

This book represents a timely and important contribution to ongoing attempts to understand and intervene in the reproduction of social and educational inequalities.

Around the world, nations are placing education at the heart of their social and economic policy. Education, it is claimed, is crucial for the development of active citizenship, social cohesion and international economic competitiveness. Rather than the wealth of nations being based on 'old' forms of capital, it is argued that we now live in a 'knowledge economy' in which the development of human capital through ongoing education is the priority. The importance placed on education is evident from the increasing levels of investment. Education now embraces more learners at more stages in their lives. Many governments now have extensive programmes of preschool education and almost all countries are expanding provision at the higher levels and exhorting citizens to engage in lifelong learning. Without such investment, it is argued, nations will 'fall behind' in the global marketplace.

However, while education systems may be required to gear themselves up for the new global knowledge economy, their ability to meet its challenges is blighted by widespread and enduring educational inequalities. These inequalities are generally associated with other inequalities, particularly those of socio-economic status and ethnicity, and are evident throughout all areas of education systems. Not only do these inequalities persist, but they can even increase as children progress through school. At higher levels, they are evident in variable participation rates, transitions to work and involvement in lifelong learning.

Governments are not blind to these problems. Since the 1960s, many countries have put in place programmes designed to address these inequalities, particularly those associated with socio-economic deprivation. As this book reveals, these programmes vary widely in focus, scale and nature. However, they have generally shared a common fate – they have had, at best, only limited impact.

The persistence of education inequalities in the face of these interventions confronts education researchers, policy makers and practitioners with some difficult dilemmas. One response is to concede defeat – to accept that educational inequalities are a 'fact of life' and that it is a waste of time and money to try to eliminate them. Another response is to keep on trying to intervene, to hope that next time the right policies will be found and educational inequalities will be eliminated.

Clearly neither response is adequate. The first will deny millions of young people – those most in need – the opportunities which their more affluent peers enjoy. The second is the naive assertion of hope over experience. Such naivety will not help the intended beneficiaries and will ultimately lead to the first response in any event.

The third response, and the one to which this book can make an important contribution, is to try to unravel just why strategies designed to reduce inequalities in education do not appear to work. Cross-national comparison clearly has a central role to play in this unravelling. In order to understand why some policies succeed and others fail, it is necessary to look at education provision in terms of systems – and the best way of understanding the characteristics of any one system is through comparison with others.

Cross-national comparison has been facilitated hugely by the increasing availability of data sets, such as that of the Programme for International Student Assessment (PISA), which have enabled comparative analysis of the scale and locus of educational inequalities. However, useful as these data sets are in illuminating patterns, they are not particularly helpful in revealing the processes underlying the patterns. What is needed is a cross-national comparison that is also based on an appreciation of the *specificity* of national systems – a specificity that statistical analyses inevitably have to gloss over. It is increased understanding of this dimension that this book offers.

One of the repeated themes running through the chapters in the book is the context specificity of concepts, data, provision and the nature of learning itself. This context specificity should, however, not be seen as 'interference' but as a source of illumination. As this book reveals, the differences between education systems reflect not only contrasting amounts of resource investment and labour market opportunities – although these factors are important – but also, more significantly, that the differences arise from the sedimentation of different values, priorities and cultures. In order to understand system- (and within-system-) level variables in educational processes and outcomes, we need to explore the various meanings, values and significance that various communities attach to education.

In providing detailed accounts of different countries' attempts to solve their enduring inequalities, this book enriches our understanding of the limits and possibilities of educational reform. The illumination of different strategies and their contexts can actually undermine pessimistic assertions of the inevitability of educational failure for some social groups. Certainly, unless we grasp the complexity of the socio-cultural dimensions of education and the specificities of the context in which policies are inserted, reforms will be weak and ineffectual.

In conclusion, overcoming educational inequalities will be neither easy nor quick. And the development of a solid and scholarly knowledge base is not sufficient in itself – but it is a necessary condition. For these reasons, this book may provide an important step in interrupting some of the patterns of social disadvantage and educational failure.

Sally Power

Acknowledgements

This book presents the first results of the EuroPEP research project, which received the support of the European Commission within the framework of the Socrates 2 programme (actions 6.1.2. and 6.2 'General activities of observation, analysis and innovation'). The success of our application in response to the 2006 call for proposals issued by the Directorate General for Education and Culture (DG-EAC) allowed for the constitution of the EuroPEP research consortium and the effective birth of a research project that was one of the Centre Alain Savary's scientific objectives, at the Institut national de recherche pédagogique (INRP), the co-ordinating institution of the project.

Twelve partner institutions contributed to the study:

- The Centre for Equity in Education, School of Education, University of Manchester (UK);
- The School Administration Institute, University of Mons-Hainaut (INAS-UMH), and the Higher Institute for Labour Studies, Catholic University of Louvain (HIVA-KU Leuven) (Belgium);
- The ESSI-ESCOL research team, Paris 8 University – Vincennes-Saint-Denis (France);
- The Faculty of Early Childhood Education, National and Kapodistrian University of Athens and the Laboratory of Continuing Education and Training, University of Patras (Greece);
- The Centre for Educational Research and Intervention (CIIE), University of Porto, and the Coimbra High School of Education (Portugal);
- The Faculty of Education, Charles University in Prague (Czech Republic);
- Intercultural Institute of Timisoara (IIT) (Romania);
- The Education Department of Uppsala University and the Education Department of Örebro University (Sweden).

Contributors

Lia Antoniou works in the School of Social Sciences, Södertörn University, Sweden. Her current research, funded by the Baltic Sea Foundation, Sweden, considers migrant integration policies in seven EU countries. She has published on integration, migration and citizenship policies; social policy; educational policy; social inequality; social and civic integration; identity; and the boundaries of knowledge.

Angeline Aubert-Lotarski has a PhD in education and works on the methodology of institutional evaluation (quality systems, organisations, programmes and policies). She is a quality co-ordinator in the Faculty of Engineering and researcher at the School Administration Institute, University of Mons, Belgium.

José Alberto Correia is Professor of Education and is currently Dean of the Faculty of Psychology and Education Sciences at the University of Porto, Portugal. Until 2010 he was Director of the Centre for Research in Education (CIIE) at the University of Porto, and he has led several extensive research studies. In particular, he has carried out studies on educational policies, social mediation and community development.

Inês Cruz has a degree in sociology from the University of Coimbra, Portugal, and pursued graduate studies in criminology at the University of Dublin. She is currently a professor in the Superior School of Education of Coimbra (ESEC) and is doing her PhD.

Marc Demeuse is a professor at the University of Mons, Belgium, in the Faculty of Psychology and Education, where he heads the School Administration Institute. A psychologist and statistician, he notably devoted his doctoral dissertation to analysing the choice of schools that would benefit from priority education policy in French speaking Belgium.

Alan Dyson is Professor of Education and Co-director of the Centre for Equity in Education at the University of Manchester, UK. His research focuses on the relationship between social and educational disadvantage, particularly in urban contexts. His extensive studies of school–family–community relations have recently been published in Cummings, Dyson and Todd's (2011) *Beyond the School Gates: Can Full Service and Extended Schools Overcome Disadvantage?*

Guadalupe Francia is Associate Professor in Education at Uppsala University, Sweden. Her research field covers comparative education policy, equity, free choice, cultural and social justice and education reforms.

Daniel Frandji is *Maître de conférences* in sociology at the Ecole Normale Supérieure de Lyon, the French Institute of Education (IFE) and the laboratory Triangle, France. His research topics are sociology of education, sociology of knowledge, school inequalities processes, educational policies.

Nathanaël Friant is a doctoral assistant at the School Administration Institute, Faculty of Psychology and Education, University of Mons, Belgium. His doctoral research analyses educational systems from an equity point of view and studies school segregation in French-speaking Belgium.

David Greger is a senior researcher at the Institute for Research and Development of Education in the Faculty of Education, Charles University, Prague, Czech Republic. He holds a doctoral degree in education science from Charles University, and his research activities are oriented especially towards the fields of comparative education, educational policy and sociology of education. He was a coordinator and member of several national as well as international research projects; currently he leads the first large-scale longitudinal study in education in the Czech Republic. His main research activities concern these topics: equity and quality in education, priority education policies, educational transitions and school choice, and the use of early tracking.

Lázaro Moreno Herrera is an associate professor in the School of Humanities, Education and Social Sciences at Örebro University, Sweden. In addition to the theme of priority education policies, his research interests include practical-aesthetical education, cultural-historical theory and the different dimensions of education at the international level. He is the author of several publications in the above disciplines.

Chryssa Kassimi has a PhD in educational sciences (Paris 8 University – Vincennes-Saint-Denis) and is Research and Studies Officer at the National Centre for Public Administration and Local Government (EKDDA Ministry of Interior, Greece). For over ten years she participated in research projects conducted by several institutions (National Centre for Social Research, University of Athens, University of Patras, University of Thessaloniki) on educational issues affecting the children of immigrants, and students' difficulties and different educational policies affecting them.

Markéta Levínská is a doctor of education, specialising in the ethnography and philosophy of education. She is a member of the research group in the

Department of Psychology, Faculty of Education, Charles University, Prague, Czech Republic. She has recently completed a research project entitled 'The function of cultural models in education'.

Idesbald Nicaise is a professor in the Department of Education Sciences and Head of the research group Education and Lifelong Learning at HIVA (Hoger Instituut voor de Arbeid), both at the Catholic University of Leuven, Belgium. He specialises in the economics of education, with a focus on equality of opportunities. His publications include *The Right to Learn. Educational Strategies for Socially Excluded Youth in Europe* (2000) and *A Social Inclusion Roadmap for Europe 2020* (2010).

Carlo Raffo has a doctorate in education and is a lecturer at the University of Manchester, UK. He taught for 12 years in schools and colleges in the Manchester area. He conducts research in the field of educational equity in urban areas. He focuses on the relationship between education and poverty, the theme of social inclusion and issues of institutional governance in 'difficult environments'. He recently led a review of the literature on education and poverty for the Joseph Rowntree Foundation.

Jean-Yves Rochex is a professor in the Department of Education Sciences, Paris 8 University, France, and a member of the research team ESCOL-CIRCEFT. He is also one of the two chief-editors of the *Revue française de pédagogie*. His research topics are sociology of education, school inequalities processes, educational policies, teaching and learning activities in poor urban schools.

Calin Rus is a sociologist and psychologist, Director of the Intercultural Institute of Timisoara in Romania and expert at the Council of Europe on intercultural education, education for democratic citizenship, education for Roma and intercultural dialogue.

Lucilia Salgado has a PhD in educational sciences and is a professor in the Graduate School of Education in Coimbra, Portugal. His research focuses on the causes of school failure at the elementary school level, including educational and organisational conditions that limit learning to read and also education alternatives in non-formal educational contexts.

Irena Smetáčková is a sociologist and psychologist with a doctorate in educational psychology. She teaches in the Department of Psychology, Faculty of Education, Charles University, Prague, Czech Republic. Her research concerns are focused on equality in education (mainly gender equality) and on the relationships between school and family.

Gella Varnava-Skoura is Professor of Psychology at the National and Kapodistrian University of Athens, Greece. Her work focuses on the prevention of and fight against illiteracy, logical mathematics and the structure and learning of written language by children. She has published works in Greek, French and English.

Dimitris Vergidis is Professor of Adult Education and Educational Policy at the University of Patras, Greece. He studied education science at the Paris 8 University – Vincennes-Saint-Denis and the University Charles-de-Gaulle-Lille 3. He is the author of more than 100 papers in Greece and in other countries (in French and in English) on adult education, illiteracy and evaluation in education.

1
Introduction: Towards a Comparison of Priority Education Policies in Europe

Daniel Frandji

The project

This book aims to present the first series of results from the EuroPEP research project, a collaborative study including 13 partner institutions within 8 member states (England, Belgium, France, Greece, Portugal, the Czech Republic, Romania and Sweden), supported by the European Socrates[1] programme. The objective of this research group is to lead a comparative analysis of priority education policies (from here on referred to as PEPs) within these countries. Although the study is focused on populations of 'compulsory education', it may also include preschool institutions when these do not fall under the period of compulsory education.[2] The research teams involved in this study have shared, some for a long time, a certain number of questions on these policies, including such key issues as the democratisation of access to knowledge and inequalities in learning, expulsion and drop-out rates. Each team, however, examines these issues in different ways, depending on national context and specific fields of study (sociology, psychology, education, statistics and so on). It is this diversity of approach, combined with the diversity of the policies themselves and of the ways in which they are implemented, that gives this work its value.

The goals of the European Commission (EC), as they were outlined in the Socrates Request for Proposal, held particular appeal to us. As is indicated by the title of this proposal, *Towards an Improved Evaluation of the Educational Policies Focusing on the Needs of At-Risk Groups*, the EC sought to foster a series of studies examining the various programmes of the member states that addressed the problem of students who were not fully benefiting from school. Reference here is due to what was done in the 1960s, in the well-known Coleman (US) and Plowden (UK) reports, regarding the implementation of 'compensatory policies' designed to distribute educational funds unevenly, so as to improve the chances of success of students coming from the least privileged backgrounds. In these cases, funds are granted to specific schools or districts rather than to individuals (e.g. in the form of scholarships, loans or free meals).

The study proposal is justified first and foremost by the absence of general knowledge, assessment and understanding of these policies, which seem nonetheless to have given rise to multiple realisations – in Europe as in the rest of the world (French Ministry of Education, 2003). It is further justified by the gap between these policies' goals and their results, which is a cause of concern: the results indicate no significant improvement among the least privileged within the school systems as a whole. The 2005 report by the Commission sur le Progrès regarding the Lisbon objectives notes the importance of certain key skills and well-functioning schools – without early drop-outs – for the proper development of knowledge-based economies. This report also underlines the importance of effective resource management in ensuring quality education – an education that should allow everyone the possibility of reaching a high level of competence. And yet, within every school system, to a greater or lesser degree, a considerable proportion of 17-year-olds (the percentages vary between 4.9 per cent and 48.2 per cent) find themselves out of school and with no secondary school diploma (Eurostat, 2004). The report further emphasises the troubling nature of the phenomenon of students who quit school unqualified, increasing the risk of unemployment, and how differences in education remain strongly correlated to social class. The children from less privileged social backgrounds – regardless of how these groups are defined – always produce the major part of what is known as 'at-risk groups' (from the viewpoint of school failure and its social consequences).

If these findings are at odds with the convictions of certain leaders and citizens, it is important to note – and indeed this will be a main focus of our analyses – how these 'less privileged' populations are defined, as well as the specific details of the policies designed to help them. This book thus includes eight chapters examining such policies – grouped together under the description 'priority education policies' – in each of eight countries. Each chapter examines the research question through an analysis that includes a description of the PEPs within their respective political, social and educational contexts, and a synthesis of the different issues that have arisen, knowledge that has been acquired and research results that have been found. In this introduction we clarify the method used in developing these analyses and the research questions and issues examined. A concluding chapter will expand upon the results of the comparative analysis by taking into consideration the historical and social foundations of the policies in question and by opening up the enquiry to thematic cross-national analyses, to be examined in greater depth and developed in the second step of the EuroPEP study.

Definition and study questions

The phrase 'priority education policies' refers to

> policies designed to have an effect on educational disadvantages through systems or programs of focused action (whether the focus be determined according to socioeconomic, ethnic, linguistic, religious, geographic, or educational criteria) by offering something more (or 'better' or 'different') to designated populations.

We came up with this definition hoping to take into account the diversity of situations studied. The countries involved in this project have had, for varying lengths of time and under different forms, policies of this kind. The definition struck us as being sufficiently broad to take into account the differences among the various programmes, while being sufficiently narrow to apply to a coherent group. The range of situations, however, did not make the task of definition an easy one, and we did not want to produce a fixed definition, frozen in time. We view, then, the one given above as an operational definition, one that is revisable, a working tool with which we would like to have a dynamic relationship: the definition itself should not prevent our reflection on what it includes and what it leaves out.

Three lines of discussion and reflection accompanied the development of this definition and, with them, the questions and issues of the study.

'Priority education policies?'

The first line of discussion refers to the act itself of designating a joint subject of study: 'priority education policies'. This phrase often remains vague and is not used in the same way by all the countries involved in the study. For our purposes, the phrase was used as a matter of convention; we wanted neither to restrict nor to polarise the study by appealing to other concepts and phrases used in work addressing these questions – such as 'compensatory policies', 'affirmative action', or *discrimination positive* (in French) and 'positive action' (in other parts of Europe). One of the main problems – besides translation issues – lies in the absence of a commonly held definition, not only on a legal basis, but on an operational basis for research as well. The above phrases are sometimes treated as synonyms, and sometimes distinguished; the same name may refer to quite different practices, depending on different national contexts and languages.

Gwénaële Calvès (2004) has shown, for example, how at least three possible meanings of the phrase *discrimination positive* are employed in French[3] in current public discourse. The first appears to simply identify a practice – that of a quota – mainly used in admission procedures to universities and institutions of higher learning. This phrase may at other times be used to designate – simply by emphasising the energetic and wilful way it is often implemented – a political objective, namely that of the 'integration of immigrants and their children, women, or people with special educational needs'. Lastly, according to the third and broadest definition, the phrase applies to any rule of selective application, even one of simple differentiation:

> *Discrimination positive* means treating those who are different differently, or – for a narrower variant of the definition – 'to give more to those who have less.' We try on the one hand to take into account the inequality of the situation, while on the other hand, reduce this inequality.
>
> (Calvès, 2004, pp. 3–4)[4]

This third meaning of the phrase *discrimination positive* could perhaps be appropriate, and this is in fact the official phrase used regarding policies implemented in some of the countries included in this book, such as francophone Belgium. That being said, its multiple meanings, coupled with risks of confusion with the practice of quotas, did not grant it a very favourable status from an international and comparative perspective.

The phrase 'priority education' also has its share of history. It echoes most notably the model of the Education Priority Areas in Britain (implemented in 1967 and afterwards discontinued in favour of other plans, which will be discussed later). This model could have influenced, at least in part, the Zones d'éducation prioritaires (ZEP) implemented in France in 1982,[5] the ZEP programmes in the French community of Belgium put into place in 1989 as well as the Territórios Educativos de Intervenção Prioritària (TEIP) in Portugal. All were measures originally used as area-based educational policies, which in the meanwhile have gone through various changes that will be discussed. The use of the noun 'priority' in the adjectival position seems to connote urgency and importance from a public action point of view. The problem of 'school failure' or educational inequalities that are seen as concentrated in specific urban areas seems to have taken priority as a social and public problem to solve, justifying collective action on these questions and an investment of public power: funding scientific research, giving financial and human resources to the institutions concerned, experimental programmes and the like. The phrase 'priority education policies' is no less nebulous than the problems that the concept itself aims to solve, and such policies are often disputed for the way the various funds are allocated.[6]

If we are reconstructing a genealogy, we must also consider the influence of the 'strategies of compensation for the disadvantaged', born in the United States in the wake of the 'war on poverty' launched by the Johnson administration at the beginning of the 1960s. Considerable action was initiated here, with several different programmes supported by the federal government (*Elementary and Secondary Education Act*, 1965). Some of these programmes are still in existence today, albeit having also seen many changes.[7] The connections, however, between these first programmes in the United States, the British Educational Priority Areas and the different policies currently in place in our different countries are not always obvious. And if a 'genealogy' – or at least a history – of the PEPs is possible, there is nothing that should force our thinking along the logic of a linear continuity, or of a simple 'diffusion' of models. The various policies need to be considered and analysed within their specific contexts, so as to minimise the potential cancelling-out effects of the particularities involved in a comparative analysis.[8]

Diversity and delimitation of the subject of study

The second line of analysis concerns issues related to the different forms the various PEPs may take. Such differences may be due to several reasons, including the level of national and local investment, how the targeted populations are defined, how the resources are distributed, different types of organisation, the degree of autonomy of the schools, the kind of actions taken and the curricula and different teaching methods adopted. The main subject of EuroPEP is to examine with rigour these differences and similarities. Can we regroup some of the policies according to certain features? Can we distinguish common practices among some school systems? Do some models of organisation produce more favourable results?

This diversity required a careful selection of the questions to be asked, as well as encouraging reflection about the subject of study itself, insofar as, within any given school system, there may be a number of programmes that could fit our definition. This is clearly the case in England for example, despite flagship programmes such as Education Action Zones, or Excellence in Cities. It is also the case, albeit in different ways, in Sweden, Greece, the Czech Republic and Romania. In these countries our definition of PEPs corresponds to many different programmes and school structures. Our contributors thus had to focus their investigations on some practices and not others; an exhaustive analysis would have exceeded the means of the study. Although such choices may seem arbitrary, the programmes of these countries also fostered considerable reflection from researchers coming from those countries that have policies already clearly separated and explicitly labelled 'priority education' (France, Belgium and Portugal). In these three countries, the label 'priority education' comes under a political–administrative grouping that was brought into question when compared with the experiences of other member states; it does not include, for instance, some programmes that may well merit to be examined under our first definition. We came face to face, in other words, with one of the traps of ethnocentrism, all the more evident perhaps in 'innovative' and 'progressive' policies, which aspire to serve as a model. Such traps are not always easy to avoid, but we must nonetheless at least acknowledge them and be mindful of them.

An opposite trap, however, also threatens researchers adopting the comparative approach – that of diluting the subject itself.[9] It is important to keep in mind both what distinguishes and what is shared. One point of convergence that defines the subject of study is the idea of targeting certain populations, thus making a preliminary categorisation of the 'beneficiaries'. If such targeting is at the heart of priority policies, several types of categories can be identified and called into question. This targeting may involve geographical areas, institutions or students. It may sometimes rely on 'external' or social criteria. The three most common means of targeting in such cases are identifying the recipients on the basis of their belonging to certain minority groups (ethnic, linguistic or religious); identifying them on the basis of certain socioeconomic or sociocultural criteria; and identifying them on the basis of belonging to a specific geographical area. The targeting may also rely on 'internal' school-related criteria, such as progressing within a certain curriculum or accessing different levels of schooling or degrees. Alternatively, it could rely on academic performance (norm-referenced or standard-based), on behavioural criteria (absenteeism, violence, incivility) or on 'well-being'.

One criterion that was agreed upon at the beginning of the project was not to include policies specifically targeting schools for children with special educational needs (referred to as 'special schools' in the United Kingdom). Targeting populations with special educational needs on the basis of medical diagnoses was thus excluded. This choice, which is tied to a categorisation found both in the scientific literature and in the political landscape – the field of physical and cognitive impairments often comes under a different ministry than that of education – should not, however, be interpreted as a sign of lack of interest on the part of the EuroPEP team. Indeed, special education has been the subject of much discussion within our team. In effect, several special education programmes appear to serve roles related to educating children from underprivileged or socially and culturally stigmatised backgrounds, even if this is not their official mission. Conflicts that have arisen from the over-representation of Romani children in the Czech special education system, for example, attest to this fact.[10] Many studies indicate that the development of categories from the special education sector is 'inextricably linked to institutional positions and the seizure of power', and thus not exclusively due to a real division according to purely scientific criteria (Plaisance and Gardou, 2001). Finally, it should be added that the question of whether or not to integrate the special education sector has been the subject of so much debate that the different classifications in the field of school policies are in a state of constant reconfiguration. The field has restructured itself today around the concept of 'inclusive education', enlisting new heterogeneous categories, such as 'students with specific needs' or 'students with particular needs', or even simply 'at-risk groups', which we will encounter on our way. In other words – and we will discuss this further in the conclusion – the current developments raise questions about the borders between what is priority education (in the countries where the field seems independent) and what is special education. The countries arriving later to the PEPs clearly demonstrate this new separation, while also influencing other countries and their original categories.

What objectives?

The third line of questioning concerns the objectives of these policies and their meaning. From the definition itself, it would have been possible to conclude that these objectives include in part fighting educational inequality and school success for children from disadvantaged backgrounds, following the tradition of increased democratisation of school systems throughout the twentieth century. Such a definition, however, would have limited the investigation process: to what degree is this about policies designed, organised, evaluated and modified in order to produce a more equal distribution of the results?

Our comments, though critical, do not come from a paradigm of denunciation or of exposure, as often used in critical analyses (Boltanski, 1990). Rather, we simply aim to take seriously the complexity apparent in each country, a complexity that requires a dose of scepticism towards the official lines of discourse and encourages listening to both the defences and the criticisms surrounding these policies.

For example, as the Belgian team points out in its chapter, implementing the PEPs could be considered as a kind of culmination of a grand and historical 'walk towards equity' (see also Demeuse, 2005). More specifically, the PEPs will join a succession of movements, the first one of which is seen mainly as equal access to the school system (or 'quantitative democratisation' – Step 1), to equal treatment (or 'qualitative democratisation' – Step 2) and finally to equal results at the end of school, or even to an equal level of social achievement beyond school. This model thus demonstrates the importance of synthesising an official discourse, shared by the different countries involved, while also taking into consideration the expectations invested in the success of these policies and thus also the disappointments regarding the results.[11] The model does not, however, allow a full grasp of the complexity of the situation. For instance, in countries where such policies appear to be most explicitly maintained (in England for example), the equality of the results is accompanied by a redefinition of the curriculum itself, perhaps going as far as a redefinition of the concept of knowledge itself. The unintended effects of transforming knowledge and education into 'evaluatable' skills are open questions (Bernstein, 2007; Frandji & Vitale, 2008).

In any case, the meaning of these policies rarely reaches unanimous agreement within any one school system. Are these policies about tackling the sources of school failure and the inequality of school programmes? Are they about fixing the effects of unequal prior treatment 'at the margin'? Or are they perhaps about 'making do' with situations of acknowledged and expected failure (and thus about managing them on a social level rather than about trying to reduce or prevent them)? In reality, priority education policies find themselves pulled between educational, socioeconomic and political objectives: guaranteeing everyone's right to knowledge; protecting the opportunities of the most 'deserving'; working towards professional or 'employable' qualifications; or even insuring a degree of 'peaceful' cultural integration for those at the bottom of the ladder of school competition. The question of the meaning of the policies and of their aims should be asked not only at the level of what is officially stated but also on the level of what is actually *done*, even though the two may be quite different. Therefore, to examine fully what is meant by the relatively neutral phrase 'policies designed to have an effect on educational disadvantage', the definition must take into consideration this complexity and diversity.

A new age of PEPs?

We will come back to these different lines of reflection in the conclusion; some have taken on such increased significance as this research has evolved that we find ourselves faced with a study in a state of constant transformation. Between the time this research began and the publication of this book there have been policy reforms and new programmes put into place, all the while transforming and revising, completing and interrupting previous systems and policies. These changes have been due to various reasons – and not necessarily to poor results – but they have been influenced by political changes, budgetary constraints and national and international interests.

The issue at the beginning was one of methodology: how to circumscribe our subject of study to ensure an adequate comparison. The theoretical and societal issues inherent in this question came quickly to the surface: to what point can we maintain the original borders, so as to have a common subject of study and of comparison? Beyond simple issues of definition – and beyond the risks of polarisation, even perhaps reification, of political–administrative categories specific to certain countries – what reality do we grant this object other than that of a methodological artefact? While staying mindful of the diversity of national contexts and emerging dynamics, we found ourselves sharing the concern that we might be swept away by the spirit of the times, or might settle for a relativist position of adopting, without detachment, new forms of burgeoning politics and their policies.

One line of enquiry: The ambiguities of compensation

This investigation, like the first results, leads to developing a line of analysis about these policies that has been around for quite some time, and in fact involves not only developing it and completing it but perhaps even revising it, given that our observations allow seeing historical changes in the meaning of the PEPs and of the issues involved: changes from the first formulations in the 1960s and 1970s, as 'compensatory policies', to the current implementations in our different countries. Some of these countries implemented the policies in question later, in different sociopolitical contexts, and therefore they have not experienced directly the different steps of this transformation, showing straightaway what seems to be a new political reference point. Here we are thinking particularly of the Czech Republic, Romania and Greece. Portugal is a special case insofar as it took its first steps with the TEIP (which operated similarly to the original PEPs) in the mid-1990s, so these policies quite quickly became a subject of reform.

The history of the PEPs is a good reminder of their complexity and their initial ambiguity: the policies were most certainly born in a period of optimism, as schools were positioning themselves as vehicles for a more egalitarian society (Canário, 2003). The first formulations of the PEPs as 'compensatory policies' set themselves as part of a line of political reforms aiming to shift schools from being elitist institutions to becoming schools for everyone. The creation of a 'comprehensive school' was meant to guarantee equal opportunity in the name of the welfare state. For their promoters, 'compensatory' systems could provide this levelling of educational paths, whereas equal access – simply opening the schools' doors to everyone – had apparently not been enough to offer this guarantee.

Considerable analyses on these systems have demonstrated, however, the range of objectives and inadequacies, the difficulties and dead ends of the adopted modes of action. It is true that the ambiguities observed at the level of action are already apparent at the level of designation: on the semantic level, *compensation* connotes both the act of fixing or neutralising a wrong and that of *comforting* (Frandji, 2008). As such, the exhaustive report produced for the Organisation for Economic Co-operation and Development (OECD) describing the results of the first policies carried out in the United States during the 1960s and 1970s stresses the imprecision of the aims of schooling practices for disadvantaged populations. These practices could be divided between the very broad objective of breaking the cycle of poverty and the very specific goal of improving a particular domain of knowledge (Little and Smith, 1971, pp. 31–37). If the practices are this difficult to evaluate, it goes without saying that evaluating the results, even on the strict basis of whether they helped to equalise academic performance, is not an easy task. Some practices yielded positive, but isolated results; but the overall results were deemed 'unsatisfactory'.

The apparent failure of a number of these projects was thus used as further evidence to reopen the debate on the role of possible genetic factors in the development of intelligence.[12] Essentialism and the justification of unequal social exchanges are often arguments used to close debates on the potential for change. For this weakness in the results is related to the inadequate hypotheses and poorly articulated theories (Little and Smith, 1971) that create the terms of compensatory action.[13] The 'ambiguity' of these policies is thus related to the 'deficit' and *misérabiliste* theories of school failure so often cited – theories that consist in explaining learning difficulties by reference to causes external to the school itself: in this case, to student shortcomings or failures within the familial and social environment of the students.

Many scholars have stressed the significance of this kind of 'legitimacy' interpretation and of the problems that result. Research begun in the 1960s demonstrates how inequalities in school success are complex phenomena, related less to simple causes like student weakness or other factors independent of school than to the broader ways in which school policies are implemented and operated in a selective and socially privileging way. The power relationships and the unequal social relationships that are in place outside of school influence and provide an arbitrary framework for the organisation, the distribution and the evaluation of knowledge by the school. The need for the 'democratisation of the teaching system' comes from this fact. And yet, in the logic of compensation?, it is about

> making up for deficiencies in the cognitive development of children that are causally attributed to social and familial environments.
>
> (Marquer *et al.*, 1975)

Hence the strong criticisms of compensatory policies, judged to be 'paternalist and reductionist' (Isambert-Jamati, 1973), or possible contributors to a shift in attention away from the school's internal organisation and thus, justifiably, from future possibilities of democratisation (Bernstein, 1970).

The British sociologist Basil Bernstein stated the problem clearly:[14]

> The concept, 'compensatory education', serves to direct attention away from the internal organization and the educational context of the school, and focus our attention on the families and children. 'Compensatory education' implies that something is lacking in the family, and so in the child. As a result, the children are unable to benefit from schools.
>
> It follows, then, that the school has to 'compensate' for the something that is missing in the family, and the children are looked at as deficit systems. If only the parents were interested in the goodies we offer, if only they were like middle-class parents, then we could do our job. Once the problem is seen even implicitly in this way, then it becomes appropriate to coin the terms 'cultural deprivation', 'linguistic deprivation', and so on. And then these labels do their own sad work. [...] We should stop thinking in terms of 'compensatory education' but consider, instead,

most seriously and systematically the conditions and contexts of the educational environment.

(Bernstein, 1975, pp. 252–254)

And yet, Bernstein reminds us, the way in which research is carried out tends to confirm, or even to justify, 'the beliefs underlying the organization, transmission and evaluation of knowledge by the school' (Bernstein, 1975, p. 254).

A new point of reference?

Almost 40 years later, the ambiguity does not seem to have disappeared, as we will see through studying the systems and actions taken today. It has in fact doubtlessly been accentuated with regard to significant economic, social and educational changes, whereas the term 'democratisation' seems to have almost disappeared from the lexicon of international educational policy in favour of ideas about modernising the educational system, improving its quality and effectiveness, or adapting it to special needs (European Commission, 2000, 2004, 2006). Several phenomena underline the importance of reopening and revising the first PEP analyses; these phenomena include the questioning of the welfare state, changes in the business world and its relationship to the educational system (needs of adaptability and employability), the emergence of a market logic and new forms of management in the regulation of school policy, and concerns about social stability and demands for group recognition.

Thus, if the eight countries differ in the extent to which they are involved in these changes, one of the main study questions could well be about the relative loss in momentum of the compensatory model in favour of 'inclusive school' models, 'recognition' issues (of difference, of diversity, of multiculturalism) and an individual action rationale. We can only moderate the interpretation of these changes, though many have noted the risks inherent in new forms of 'essentialisation' of school difficulties: fragmenting the idea itself of schooling, protecting access to the elite, fighting against exclusion by ensuring the social and professional integration of students or limiting learning horizons in the name of adapting to specific 'needs' rather than tackling issues of access to knowledge for all within the framework of a knowledge-based society. In fact these issues are fuelled less by a critical sociological analysis of the compensatory policies than by a kind of retranslation of community criticisms (denouncing '*misérabilisme*' in the name of homogenised difference) or of principles involved in the search for greater effectiveness from an instrumental or managerial perspective.

These issues – we'll address them in greater detail in the conclusion – structure several changes in explaining the problem and in targeting populations.

These include an apparent decline in area-based targets or targets based on socioeconomic criteria in favour of socioethnic or linguistic criteria, a trend towards dividing students into new categories – the advent of the 'dys' (learning disabilities, e.g., dyslexia, dysgraphia, dyscalculia) – or the inflation of the 'special'. This is followed by changes in practices based on these categories: cuts and curricular divisions, heavy investment in maternal language teaching, enthusiasm for multiculturalism, motivational teaching, a generous regard for life experience, individualised work, even 'student-guided curricula' and so on. At times, what appears to be new adds up, ironically, to reinvented modes of inspiration that are in fact classically more compensatory: an increase in regular school time, 'cultural enrichment' activities, emphasis on socialisation, 'parent education' programmes and so on. But where talk of compensation ends the discourse on the relational complexity of school inequality – following a *misérabiliste* perspective – the practices that take its place depend more on cultural relativism, utilitarianism and the search for adapting to certain labour markets.

The lack of debate, or the lack of integrating aspects of the scientific debate into the political and social debate, is certainly noteworthy, whether due to haste to get programmes started or to the strength of the new criticisms. And there, too, is a change. The creation of the first PEPs happened in tandem with important debates about the need for, and difficulties of, an 'emancipatory' educational mission for all. A not insignificant part of the criticism of the 'deficit' approach accompanied the first steps towards looking for changes in educational practices that took into consideration cognitive and social issues involved in learning, using pedagogical practices in existing social relations, thinking about writing and the language practices at the heart of school learning: all questions that current problems seem at times to minimise.

Of course, these issues also integrate concerns beyond the field of education, all the while justifying themselves through the results of a culture critical of the standardisation of educational policies and of normalisation, of their lack of effectiveness and of the social and identity consequences of the meritocratic direction of educational policies – for example discrimination, a social hierarchy of cultural differences and the lack of attention to community development. And yet, as has been already emphasised with substance by Viviane Isambert-Jamati, if it remains so much more difficult, on these bases, to think of issues of access for all in terms of 'compensation', the solution is far from being settled (Isambert-Jamati, 1973).

This, however, does not prevent the PEPs from remaining places of investment and of mobilisation (mobilisation of key players, of parents, communities, researchers), places of emerging ideas demanding to be better recognised, shared and questioned. The goal of this comparative analysis is to make progress in asking these questions: to describe, examine and confront these policies; to clarify the debates, analyses and criticisms they have generated; and, finally, to contribute to their evaluations in discovering their limits and their potential in light of the social issues invested in these educational systems.

Methodological concerns

The project EuroPEP was in part motivated by the relative lack of comparative international studies examining the PEPs; there are very few comparisons, even on a simple, broadly descriptive perspective. On the one hand, this stems form the lack of a commonly accepted definition of these policies (notably due to their complexity and to the haste with which they are developed); on the other hand, this stems from the diversity and strong contextual effects, at least in appearance, of the resulting programmes. The problem is compounded by the difficulty of accessing official and scientific literature in the different languages involved and by the lack of broadly distributed monographs, not to mention the lack of synthesis at the supra-national level. And yet each policy and each system is accompanied by its own discourse, analyses, tentative assessments and sometimes national debates that it would be valuable to examine. This, then, is the ambition of the present study. As such, it does not directly rely on an empirical field study, but on the analysis of the variety of discursive material that accompanies these policies, both defending and criticising them, and on a secondary analysis of the data.

The choice of the eight countries involved stems from concerns about representative sampling. This is more at the level of different political and educational contexts of implementations than at the level of the variety of the PEPs themselves – a confirmation that we could not, and would not, argue for without a more thorough investigation at the project's beginning. Among these countries are England, Belgium, France and Sweden – all established parliamentary democracies and heirs to a long history of democratisation of the educational system. The Czech Republic and Romania broke away from communist regimes at the beginning of the 1990s. Both Portugal and Greece were under military dictatorships until 1974. The school structures, educational issues, expectations and concerns of each of these countries remain, of course, intimately tied to these different political histories. They inevitably interact, as assets or impediments, with the directions of European educational policies that now serve as a unifying framework, as well as with the recommendations of other international organisations. They work as translators of all these prescriptive, informative and provocative elements of the PEP implementations. This does not, however, prevent one from seeing that they share the dynamics of operation, redefinitions and convergences.

The school systems of these countries also seem different in their degree of inequality and inequity (Maroy, 2006). We are not able – nor do we claim – to argue further about this point, or to synthesise the different attempts at comparison taken from this perspective. Such a task is complex and would require further research: even the way the factors are operationalised is simultaneously a function of the theories of justice in place and of the quality of the data collected, which itself could lead to changes in the position of each country in relation to the others, as has been well demonstrated by the different reports of the European Group for Research on Equity in Educational Systems (EGREES, 2005) and in other works (Duru-Bellat *et al.*, 2004; Gibson & Meuret, 1995; Mons, 2007). Despite such observed differences – including in more specific and defined domains, like that of academic and/or social segregation assessment between schools (Demeuse and Baye, 2008) – the relative position of the countries at the extremes is, however, rather stable. It is the relative positions of the countries in the middle that varies the most.

Organisation of the study

The present comparative study includes two steps.

The first step was to establish an overview of the state of affairs of the various policies of priority education in the eight countries involved. Each partner was thus asked to provide, using a common question template, contextualised analyses of their policies, including a description of how they worked and a synthesis of the debates and knowledge surrounding them. It is the results of this step that are the subject of the present book. We deemed this step fundamental insofar as it allows defining the outlines and issues of policies, which are often unknown even to specialists working in the domain.

The second step is structured around an analysis of common themes and questions and of the way they are treated by the different countries involved. The aim of this second step is thus not to provide a description of each country's PEPs, as is done here, but rather to develop the comparative analyses involved through more specific themes and to integrate them with each other. More specifically, the researchers examined questions relating to the three following topics:

- justification of the PEPs, targeting of the populations and criteria of the beneficiaries (for whom? why?);
- the kinds of action taken in the PEPs and the ways they are organised (what to do? how to do it?);

– the evaluation of these policies and of the results, as well as the use and abuse of these evaluations (for what results? how are they produced? what are they used for?).

Although the results concerning these topics will be the subject of a second book, the questions that underlie them are addressed in each chapter of this first one.

Comparative method

Needless to say, the present study was subject to all the issues inherent in carrying out comparative studies in general, as well as to those involved in international comparisons in particular (with linguistic differences rendering the task all the more difficult). Cécile Vigour (2005) denounces the proliferation of 'false comparisons', one form of which would be 'contrasting monographs without any attempt of an in-depth synthesis'. Likewise, Marilyn Osborn (2007) notes how comparative international research, by its very nature, can be subject to more methodological compromises than single studies, creating the tendency for many researchers to adopt either a 'safari' approach or that of the 'lonely horseman'. In the first, 'one scholar or one nation's team of scholars formulate the problem, create the research methodology, and carry out the study in more than one country'. In the second, 'the data are collected by individuals and teams in each country and then presented side by side without being compared in any systematic way, followed by the researchers taking their separate ways as the sun sets' (Osborn, 2007).

The first step of our analysis may at first glance raise concerns about a lonely horseman approach, where different countries are presented side by side – though this should not lead one to underestimate the nature of the difficulties inherent in this first step of analysis (difficulties no doubt shared by all comparative international policy research). We deemed this step necessary in light of the diversity of forms these policies take and in a search for the common elements of the issues at hand. An in-depth synthesis and an understanding of what the PEPs are constitute indeed the goal of our research, and not its point of departure. And yet we must stress that an analysis of the PEPs gains nothing by being decontextualised or removed from the broader workings of school systems and from the historical, social and political particularities of each country involved. This is because, as previously explained, one of the central themes of this research is a better understanding of the relationship between these specific and targeted policies and regular school systems. Indeed, we are well aware of the limits of a comparative research that claims to identify 'good practices' and would be easily separated from their contexts and exported. This is a model we cannot adopt: namely the so-called 'benchmarking' approaches, like those developed by some 'peer pressure' international organisations ('international comparisons and performance assessments of public systems aiming to detect and impose good practices on member states by peer pressure', Mons, 2007, pp. 13–14). The comparative approach adopted here does not claim to identify these supposed good practices that are assumed to be as valuable out of context, nor does it aim to reach a single-system convergence. Rather it seeks to increase reflexivity around these contexts by making one think about how they influence defining problems and conceptualising policies and practices on the basis of a shared concern for educational inequality.

To avoid the pitfalls described by M. Osborn (2007) – where one falls either into the 'safari' approach and examines different systems from a single, and perhaps 'exotic' perspective, or into the 'lonely horseman' approach, where different teams, individually, throw together articles without any collective effort – the EuroPEP project specifically devoted some crucial time to creating a team and a subject of study. The different lines of study and the questions accompanying the work on issues of definition, as well as the joint discussions regarding the resulting analyses, allowed developing common reference points, an initial revision and questioning of a set of perceptions, categorisations, expectations and assumptions nationally and internationally shared.

This does not mean that an infinite number of authors wrote these words, but that a significant degree of coordination was accomplished. The chapters went through several back-and-forths between the authors and the coordinators, after which a common framework for writing was defined, one that was neither too inflexible (each chapter retains its uniqueness) nor too independent (similar themes are treated, to different degrees, in all of the chapters).

One final remark: the complexity of the educational situations described, as well as the wealth of analyses, makes any attempt at grouping national studies according to similar modes of operation extremely difficult. Several lines of grouping are possible – and we will address this in the book – but that is a crucial issue for the second step of the EuroPEP work, and it will be the subject of another publication. For this book, therefore, we opted simply to present the chapters about each country, in alphabetical order. The concluding chapter sums up and compares the results of the national analyses presented here for an evaluative reflection on the set of priority education policies and on their developments.

Notes

1. Within the framework of acts 6.1.2 and 6.2 of the Socrates programme: general activity of observation, analysis and innovation (request 2006).

2. The period of compulsory education varies between member states. For further information, see the Eurydice site (http://www.eurydice.org), and more specifically the Eurybase database.

3. We have chosen to leave the term 'discrimination positive' in its original French.

4. Unless indicated otherwise, in the English version of this book, articles appearing originally in French have been translated into English under the editors' responsibility.

5. In discussing word choice for these policies, it should be noted that in French, the term 'education' is used for both the English word 'upbringing' as well as 'education'; the term *scolarité* is more exclusive to schooling.

6. Thus we note a shift in the terminology in France: the first policies in 1981 were called ZP *Zones prioritaires* (Priority Areas), followed by ZEP (*Zones d'éducation prioritaires*, or Education Priority Areas), two names where the word 'priority' referred to areas, and hence was in the plural form in French. The measure is designed to act on areas socially defined, and the institutions within them. Over time and with policy revisions, the term 'priority' lost its plural form, and (beginning in 1998) began to refer to the word 'education' instead. Many judge this lexical shift far from innocent, and see it as related to political developments, though it is difficult to know whether or not the shift was intentional (cf. Armand & Gille, 2006). After considerable hesitation, we also opted for the use of the singular in the French version of this book, insofar as we are using the term in a generic sense.

7. We are thinking particularly of the early childhood Head Start programme. The programme Better Schooling for Educationally Deprived Students, also called Title 1 (because of its place in the Elementary and Secondary Education Act), has seen many changes since 1965, and a revision in 1994, leading to its re-establishment under the dynamics of No Child Left Behind of 2002. See Bénédicte Robert's doctoral thesis (2007) for further discussion on the development of these policies in the United States.

8. This risk can also arise from a position favouring a macro-social analysis or one concentrating on the official prescriptive discourses of the policies rather than how they are actually implemented.

9. This has already been emphasised by P. Fauconnet and M. Mauss (1901): serious research either joins what common sense separates, or highlights differences in what common sense merges together.

10. This phenomenon is not, of course, exclusive to this country, but has been particularly noticeable due to a formal complaint and trial, followed by a conviction for discrimination (in violation of Article 14) before the Grand Chamber of the European Court of Human Rights – EctHR (*Case D.H. et al. v. The Czech Republic*). The complaint concerned 18 Czech nationals of Romani origin who were educated in special schools. In the inferior court, the Czech Republic acknowledged that certain schools designed for children with learning difficulties could have as many as 80–90% of Romani children.

11. In several countries, such 'disappointment' represents a major element in the evaluation of these policies.

12. Notably by Jensen (1968, cited in Little & Smith, 1971, p. 14).

13. This is already the case, for example, with the 'cycle of poverty' theory regularly put on the table at the time, and the subject of much criticism. This theory highlights the psychological factors involved in preventing progress of the poor, to the detriment of economic and social factors.

14. Basil Bernstein (1970) provided one of the most pertinent critical analyses of compensatory policies and the theoretical assumptions that form the theory. This critique was all the more important insofar as the first formulations of Bernstein's work had been at times abusively recruited to justify this argument. This refers to his thesis on language codes that had been reinterpreted in terms of deficit and *misérabiliste* paradigms, far from the original intentions and arguments of its author who was constructing a relational sociological analysis about school inequality.

Bibliography

Scientific documents

BERNSTEIN B. (1975). 'Enseignement de compensation'. In idem, *Langage et classes sociales. Codes socio-linguistiques et contrôle social.* Paris: Les Éd. de Minuit, pp. 249–262. Initial version in English: 'Education cannot compensate for society', *New Society*, 1970, vol. 387, pp. 344–347.

BERNSTEIN B. (2007). *Pédagogie, contrôle symbolique, identité. Théorie, recherche, critique.* Québec: Presses Universitaires de Laval. French translation by G. Ramognino and P. Vitale of the revised edition (London: Rowman & Littlefield, 2000) of *Pedagogy, Symbolic Control and Identity: Theory, Research, Critique* (first edition London: Taylor & Francis, 1996).

BOLTANSKI L. (1990). *L'Amour et la justice comme compétences. Trois essais de sociologie de l'action* [*Love and Justice as Forms of Competence. Three Essays in the Sociology of Action*]. Paris: Métailié.

CALVÈS G. (2004). *La Discrimination positive* [*Positive Discrimination*]. Paris: PUF (Que sais-je? series).

CANÁRIO R. (2003). 'Politiques de discrimination positive: perspective historique' ['Positive discrimination policies: a historical perspective']. In Ministère de l'Éducation nationale, *La Discrimination positive en France et dans le monde* [*Positive Discrimination in France and in the World*]. Proceedings of the convention of March 2002. Paris: CNDP, pp. 15–25.

DEMEUSE M. (2005). 'La Marche vers l'équité en Belgique francophone' ['The move towards equity in French-speaking Belgium']. In M. DEMEUSE, A. BAYE, M. H. STRAETEN, J. NICAISE & A. MATOUL (eds) (2005), *Vers une école juste et efficace. 26 contributions sur les systèmes d'enseignement et de formation* [*Towards Fair and Efficient Schooling. Twenty-Six Contributions on Teaching and Training Systems*]. Brussels: De Boeck University, pp. 191–216.

DEMEUSE M. & BAYE A. (2008). 'Measuring and comparing the equity of education systems in Europe'. In N. C. SOGUEL and P. JACCARD (eds), *Governance and Performance of Education Systems*. Dordrecht: Springer, pp. 85–106.

DEROUET J.-L. & NORMAND R. (eds) (2007). *L'Europe de l'éducation: entre management et politique* [*Education in Europe: Between Management and Policy*]. Lyon: INRP.

DURU-BELLAT M., MONS N. & SUCHAUT B. (2004). 'Academic organisation and social inequality of performance. Findings of the PISA survey'. *Éducation et formations*, no. 70, pp. 123–131.

FAUCONNET P. & MAUSS M. (1901). 'Sociologie'. In *La Grande Encyclopédie*, vol. 30. Paris: Société anonyme de la Grande Encyclopédie.

FRANDJI D. (2008). 'Compensation (politiques de)' ['Compensation (policies of)']. In A. VAN ZANTEN (ed.), *Dictionnaire de l'éducation*. Paris: PUF, pp. 72–75.

Daniel Frandji

FRANDJI D. & VITALE P. (eds) (2008). *Actualité de Basil Bernstein. Savoir, pédagogie et société* [*Basil Bernstein today. Knowledge, Pedagogy and Society*]. Rennes: PUR.

GERESE (2005). *L'Équité des systèmes éducatifs européens. Un ensemble d'indicateurs.* Report available on the Internet: <http://www.mag.ulg.ac.be/schoolequity/docpdf/2005FRANCAIS.pdf> (consulted on 26 June 2008). Document available in English: EGREES (EUROPEAN GROUP FOR RESEARCH ON EQUITY IN EDUCATIONAL SYSTEMS) (2005). 'Equity in European Educational Systems: a set of indicators'. *European Educational Research Journal*, vol. 4, no. 2, pp. 1–151. Article available on the Internet: <http://www.wwwords.co.uk/eerj/content/pdfs/4/issue4_2.asp> (consulted on June 26, 2008).

GIBSON A. & MEURET D. (1995). 'The development of indicators on equity in education'. In OECD, *Measuring the Quality of Schools*. Paris: OECD, Centre for Educational Research and Innovation, pp. 121–131.

ISAMBERT-JAMATI V. (1973). 'Les Handicaps socio-culturels et leurs remèdes pédagogiques' ['Socio-cultural handicaps and their educational remedies']. *L'Orientation scolaire et professionnelle*, no. 4, pp. 303–318.

LITTLE A. & SMITH G. (1971). *Stratégies de compensation: panorama des projets d'enseignement pour les groupes défavorisés aux États-Unis.* Paris: OCDE (translated from English in the same year, *Strategies of Compensation: A Review of Educational Projects for the Disadvantaged in the United States*. Paris: OCDE).

MAROY C. (2006). *École, régulation et marché. Une comparaison de six espaces scolaires locaux en Europe* [*School, Regulation and Market. A Comparison of Six Local School Areas in Europe*]. Paris: PUF.

MARQUER J., CARLIER M. & ROUBERTOUX P. (1975). 'Les Mesures éducatives compensatoires' ['Compensatory educational measures']. In M. REUCHLIN (ed.), *Milieu et conduites cognitives*. Paris: PUF.

MINISTÈRE DE L'ÉDUCATION NATIONALE (2003). *La Discrimination positive en France et dans le monde* [FRENCH MINISTRY OF EDUCATION, *Positive Discrimination in France and in the World*]. Proceedings of the international convention organized on March 5 and 6, 2002 in Paris. Paris: CNDP.

MONS N. (2007). *Les Nouvelles politiques éducatives. La France fait-elle les bons choix?* [*The New Educational Policies. Is France Making the Right Choices?*] Paris: PUF.

OSBORN M. (2007). 'Promouvoir la qualité: comparaisons internationales et questions méthodologiques' ['Promoting quality: international comparisons and methodological questions']. *Éducation et sociétés*, no. 18, pp. 163–180.

PLAISANCE E. & GARDOU C. (2001). Presentation of the project: 'Situations de handicap et institution scolaire' ['Handicap situations and academic institution']. *Revue française de pédagogie*, no. 134, pp. 5–13.

ROBERT B. (2007). 'De l'apprentissage au changement. Les politiques scolaires de compensation en France et aux États-Unis (1965–2006)' ['From learning to change. Compensatory education policies in France and the USA (1965–2006)']. Doctoral thesis (supervised by Agnès van Zanten), Political Science, IEP Paris.

VIGOUR C. (2005). *La Comparaison dans les sciences sociales. Pratiques et méthodes* [*Comparison in Social Sciences. Practices and Methods*]. Paris: La Découverte (Guides repères).

Legal references and official documents

ARMAND A. & GILLE B. (2006). La Contribution de l'éducation prioritaire à l'égalité des chances des élèves [The contribution of priority education to equal opportunity for pupils]. Report to the Minister for State Education, Higher Education and Research, IGEN and IGAEN.

EUROPEAN COMMISSION (2000). Rapport européen sur la qualité de l'éducation scolaire. Seize indicateurs de qualité [European report on the quality of education in schools. Sixteen quality indicators]. Report available on the Internet: <http://ec. europa.eu/education/policies/educ/indic/rapinfr.pdf> (consulted on June 27, 2008).

EUROPEAN COMMISSION (2004). Progress towards the common objectives in education and training. Indicators and benchmarks. Report available on the Internet: <http:// ec.europa.eu/education/policies/2010/doc/progress_towards_common_objectives_ en.pdf> (consulted on June 26, 2008).

EUROPEAN COMMISSION (2006). Moderniser l'éducation et la formation: une contribution essentielle à la prospérité et à la cohésion sociale en Europe [Modernising education and training: an essential contribution to prosperity and social cohesion in Europe]. Joint progress report by the Council and the Commission on the implementation of the work programme 'Éducation et formation 2010' ['Education and training 2010']. Report available on the Internet: <http://ec.europa.eu/education/ policies/2010/doc/progressreport06_fr.pdf> (consulted on June 26, 2008).

EUROSTAT (2004). The statistical guide to Europe, Brussels: European Commission.

England

2

Policy Interventions to Reduce Educational Inequalities – The Case of England, 1997–2010

Lia Antoniou, Alan Dyson and Carlo Raffo

This chapter offers an overview of the priority policies in the English education system, focusing on the period of New Labour governments in England between 1997 and 2010. This was a period in which broadly centre-left governments, following an uneasy mixture of centrally driven interventions and market solutions, undertook intensive – some might say, frenetic – policy activity. Much of this was directed at overall 'improvement' of the education system, but much was also directed at tackling endemic problems of low achievement and educational failure as they manifested themselves amongst particular groups of learners and in particular schools and places. New Labour lost power in 2010 and was replaced by a centre-right Conservative-Liberal Democrat government. Whilst it is certainly the case that the new government has a distinctively different 'style' (most notably in an avowed mistrust of centrally driven initiatives), it continues to profess a commitment to tackling educational inequalities, and the policy landscape remains – for the time being, at least – essentially that laid out in the previous thirteen years.

Although the term 'priority policy' is not one that is commonly used in England, the multiple interventions aimed by New Labour governments at improving the poorest educational outcomes can usefully be labelled in this way. By no means all of these were embodied in legislation, and many of them lasted no more than a few years. Nonetheless, for the purposes of this chapter we regard all of these programmes, initiatives and schemes as priority policies. Moreover, a distinctive characteristic of the New Labour approach – one that is being continued to some extent by the current government – was a focus on tackling poor outcomes not only during the school years, but through 'early intervention' before children enter school. As a result, there was a significant expansion of early years provision and programmes during the New Labour period, and therefore we pay equal

23

attention in this chapter to developments in this sector. Given the high level of activity across these two sectors, it is impossible here to document all of the priority policies introduced by New Labour, let alone the changes to those policies that are currently taking place. Instead, therefore, we focus on a sample of policies which reveal the distinctive features of the New Labour approach, and survey some of the evidence as to its effectiveness. We argue that most of the interventions of this period produced results that were, at best, mixed, and we attempt to analyse why that might be the case. It remains a moot point whether the modest outcomes of New Labour policy justify the approach that was taken, but, we suggest, it may be necessary to see the outcomes from the alternative that is now on offer before reaching a final judgment.

Priority policies – Recent influences and directions

The relationship between educational achievement and social disadvantage has long featured in the minds of English policy makers and successive UK governments. In policy thinking, educational failure has often been understood as a key factor in the production and reproduction of social, occupational and economic disadvantage, and 'priority' policy formulation, therefore, has been seen as having an important preventive role beyond the education system itself. The policy process has also been typified by frequent experimentation, in part due to the varying degrees of success in reducing educational inequalities and in ensuring satisfactory educational outcomes for particular population, area or learner groups. While the links between disadvantage and educational failure, and the subsequent policy activities, are relatively long established, in recent years – predominantly since the election of successive New Labour governments from 1997 onwards – policy activity has been both intensified and widened in focus and outlook.

This intensification can be seen in the tendency towards central intervention. Since the late 1980s an English educational tradition and organisational structure of local control and (largely) local policy formulation, particularly with regard to targeted policies and initiatives, has been systematically challenged, with control for development in particular shifting to the centre. This marked shift to the centre still requires activity from local stakeholders (local authorities, schools, early years centres), in part because local stakeholders are responsible for delivering targeted and non-targeted educational provision and implementing central government initiatives and schemes. Since 1997, however, new central government policies, schemes, initiatives and structural reforms have been proposed and implemented with astonishing rapidity. This has had the (indirect) consequence of fuelling confusion among, and on occasion antagonism from, educational professionals on the ground and other key stakeholders, notably local authorities.

A growing intensification is also evident in the results-driven focus – which has led to an increase in target-setting and a need for educational providers to meet these targets – and the focus on delivering a 'quality-' driven educational system. The use of the amorphous term 'quality' captures a large array of elements: at once referring to curricular and pedagogical developments; the implementation of structural and workforce reforms; ever-rising demands from the government's education inspectorate, the Office for Standards in Education, Children's Services and Skills (Ofsted); and educational providers' successful meeting of targets for children's educational outcomes.The wider focus and outlook in recent years is best typified by the increasing policy interest in the early years, which has become an arena for what are, effectively, priority 'educational' policies. The idea of early intervention is now seen as an essential part of the educational policy jigsaw if the goal of a reduction in educational and other inequalities, especially for children identified as most socially marginalised, is to be realised. The increasing importance given to the early years should not be viewed as replacing recent governments' ongoing interest in schools. Rather, in priority policy formulations the early years have featured as an additional and critical policy arena – as well as a stage in a child's educational life cycle – which (theoretically at least) helps ensure that the twin goals of raising educational achievement and enabling social inclusion for those most disadvantaged can be achieved.

Early intervention has also been closely aligned with the development of policies to promote multi-agency working, which is conceived as beginning in the early years and continuing over the course of a child's educational life cycle. Multi-agency working in effect attempts to link educational and care services (schools, early years centres, health and social services, etc.) and their respective professionals. In policy thinking this has been deemed critical for helping increase the life chances of all children, but particularly so for children most socially marginalised (determined by area, institution or population group) and therefore the emphasis has been on these children. These two developments have been coupled with an assumption that reducing educational failure, and ensuring subsequent educational success, requires broader family and community participation. To this end, a myriad of policy solutions have been proposed and implemented.

Priority educational policies for schools and early years

The English school system is characterised by marked differences in educational outcomes and, arguably, in access to educational opportunities and resources. These differences relate – albeit in complex ways – to social class, ethnicity and gender, and also have a spatial dimension, with access and outcomes being distributed differently across more and less affluent parts of the country (see, for instance, Cassen & Kingdon, 2007; Fabian Society, 2006). In the face of these inequalities, successive governments have engaged in a series of structural reforms – for instance, the tripartite system introduced by the 1944 Education Act, the comprehensive school reforms of the 1970s and the Education Reform Act of 1988 – aimed at improving the performance of the system overall and/or at enhancing access and outcomes for disadvantaged groups. At the same time, there has been a recurrent interest in targeting policies and initiatives at the most disadvantaged groups, institutions and areas – for instance, through the Educational Priority Areas of the 1970s (Halsey, 1972) or the Lower Attaining Pupils Programme of the 1980s (Department of Education and Science, 1989).

Nonetheless, it is probably true to say that the balance of the policy effort historically has been towards structural change. This is in part because central government's responsibility for education has traditionally been shared with local education authorities (LEAs – now, simply local authorities), and it is they who have taken the lead in addressing educational inequality through local initiatives and, particularly, through targeting additional resources at the most disadvantaged schools and children. However, the wave of reforms initiated by the 1988 Education Reform Act severely limited the freedom of action of LEAs whilst strengthening central government control over the school system. The implication is that the capacity for targeting and prioritising has passed increasingly from the local to central level. At the same time, the election of successive New Labour governments from 1997 onwards brought to power a political party with a historical commitment to tackling disadvantage and ensuring equality of opportunity, however much that commitment may have been modified by what many see as a marked shift to the political right.

Amongst other things, that shift saw traditional concerns with equality replaced by a concern with 'social inclusion' and 'exclusion' (Giddens, 1998). While it is beyond the scope of this chapter to trace the complexities and ambiguities of this concept as used by policy makers, it has considerable significance for prioritising and targeting policies. In particular, while earlier priority policies were couched in the language and ideology of compensatory politics (and hence desires to create a more equal society), these more recent formulations accepted a level of inequality as inevitable, and focused instead on offering all citizens guaranteed access to minimum levels of social goods (income, opportunity, health and so on) so that they feel themselves to be included in a common social enterprise.

This change of emphasis was signalled almost immediately upon the first New Labour government taking office by the creation of a Social Exclusion Unit (latterly the Social Exclusion Taskforce) to co-ordinate policy in this area. Social exclusion, governments argued, happens when people experience barriers to their access to common social goods. Such barriers – lack of employment, lack of income, poor health, poor services – are multiple, interact with each other and are capable of producing concentrations of exclusion amongst particular groups and in particular places. Education then plays a crucial role in promoting social inclusion because it is the principal passport to opportunity. As the Prime Minister, Tony Blair, once put it:

> Why are we so keen to raise standards in our schools? Because the quickest route to the workless class is to fail your English and maths class. In today's world, the more you learn, the more you earn.
>
> (Blair, 1997)

The United Kingdom, the argument went, is transforming itself from an economy relying on manufacturing industry – and hence on un- or semi-skilled labour – to a 'knowledge economy' which survives through the value added by the high skills level of its workforce. It follows that high levels of educational achievement are the basis of economic development for the country and of opportunity for the individual. By the same token, low levels of achievement depress the economy and are the major cause of social exclusion at the level of the individual.

On the basis of this analysis, New Labour's schools policy had two major thrusts. One was a drive to enhance system and school performance, and so raise levels of student achievement overall. This 'unprecedented crusade to raise standards' (Blair, 1999) – the so-called 'standards agenda' – involved a powerful cocktail of target-setting, curriculum and pedagogical development and high-stakes accountability measures that were rolled out across the system as a whole. The second thrust was to target resources, initiatives and attention towards those parts of the system and those groups of students where performance and achievement lagged behind the levels that were seen as appropriate. In particular, there was a focus on those learners who were seen as being at risk of social exclusion by virtue of their poor achievements and/or their disengagement from education, and on the schools and other parts of the system serving those learners.

Enhancing system performance and learners' outcomes, as well as focusing on particular groups of at-risk learners, has been critical in stimulating a renewed policy interest in the early years. In England, Early Childhood Education and Care (ECEC) provision has become significantly 'schoolified' (Bennett, 2006; OECD, 2006). This has largely been due to its conceptualisation as a form of pre-primary educational provision, rather than from a social pedagogical perspective, which tends to focus on the social development of the child (the model that dominates in the Nordic countries and in most of continental Europe). This was not always the case; in the 1970s and for most of the 1980s ECEC was largely established and run by parents, overwhelmingly mothers. Parents accessed community and voluntary buildings and created playgroups in order to provide and facilitate opportunities for their children to participate in group-play and to socialise.

In the late 1980s and early 1990s a combination of factors – policy (the introduction of the nursery voucher scheme), economic and socio-political (largely the advent and rise of the 'professional woman') – provided the backdrop for both an expansion in the number of ECEC providers (statutory, voluntary and private) and an increasing acknowledgment of the importance of a 'good start' and of 'early intervention'. By the late 1990s and with the election of the New Labour government, these notions had become the new political orthodoxy – one which now spans ideological and political divisions and has cross-party support. The systematic expansion in the universal entitlement to nursery education (the former nursery voucher scheme) since 1997 is indicative of this – an expansion not questioned or challenged by any opposition party and instrumental in creating a non-compulsory but state-funded early education entitlement. In 2006, free early education funding for 12½ hours was extended from 33 weeks to 38 weeks – mirroring the school year – for all 3- and 4-year-olds; in 2007, the minimum free entitlement was extended to 15 hours per week for 38 weeks a year for the first cohort of children; and by 2010 the minimum entitlement of 15 hours per week for 38 weeks per year was in place for all 3- and 4-year-olds.

The new political orthodoxy surrounding a 'good start' and 'early intervention' was, to some extent, instigated by a range of research studies, many of which received funding from the government's education department. For instance, a research study on the 1970 British cohort identified divergent developmental paths predictive of later attainment in children as young as 22 months, and more clearly at 42 months, as being attributed to family socio-economic status (Feinstein *et al.*, 1999). It suggested that attainment paths, while not fixed at 22 or 42 months, are 'substantial signals representative of the educational progress of children, indicating that differences in the early years are not entirely off-set by the schooling system' (Feinstein *et al.*, 1999, p. 3). The aim of drawing on studies of this kind to inform policy formulation – what was initially labelled 'evidence-based policy' – became a New Labour mantra post-1997, and this was evident across education and other social policy fields. As Norman Glass, Deputy Director of the Treasury (until 2001), stated when describing the newly conceived Sure Start initiative (see below):

> [It] represents a new way of doing things both in the development of policy and in its delivery. It is an attempt to put into practice 'joined-up thinking' but it is also an outstanding example of evidence based policy and open, consultative government.
>
> (Glass, 1999, p. 264)

While it is not within the scope of this chapter to consider the idiosyncrasies of the concept of 'evidence-based policy', findings from large-scale, longitudinal studies on the social and educational benefits of children from disadvantaged families accessing ECEC provision (Farrel & Taylor, 2004; OECD, 2001, 2006; Pascal *et al.*, 1999; Sammons *et al.*, 2004; Schweinhart & Weikert, 1997) did more than just stimulate targeted policy activity in the ECEC field. They also hastened the implementation of whole-system structural, curricular and pedagogical reforms, led to the standardisation of developmentally appropriate early learning attainment goals and created a rationale for new funding streams for priority ECEC provision.

Based on emerging evidence, the categories of at-risk early learners also expanded beyond just those situated in the bottom socio-economic quintiles and were increasingly identified also by gender, ethnicity and early learning difficulties. These groups of at-risk early learners tended to mirror those identified at the school level and policy drew heavily on longitudinal studies indicating a powerful relationship between ECEC access and future school performance. As one study argued, 'pre-school can play an important part in combating social exclusion by offering disadvantaged children, in particular, a better start to primary school' (Sammons *et al.*, 2004, p. 69). As a result, ECEC provision, like school provision, became subject to concerns about 'standards' and was seen as an important means of promoting social inclusion. As the then Prime Minister, Tony Blair, put it:

> Good quality early years education and care is the key to unlocking the cycle of poverty and reducing inequalities in educational achievement...including children with a disability or special needs. We know that the impact of good quality early years provision on children's attainment and social development lasts well into primary school.
>
> (Blair, 2004)

These wide-ranging efforts to tackle 'social exclusion' through successive reforms and initiatives in early years and school provision form the core of priority policies in England. Because of the supposed multiple forms of social exclusion and the interactions between those forms, these policies have also been multiple and rapidly changing. In general terms, however, it is possible to see them as constituted by three broad types of intervention: those focused on groups of 'at-risk' students; those focused on areas where overall levels of education achievement are low; and those focused on poorly performing educational institutions.

Group-focused interventions

These are interventions targeted at groups of learners who are or might be at risk of underachievement, and hence of social exclusion. A report on 'Evaluating Educational Inclusion' by Ofsted identified a wide range of such groups:

- girls and boys;
- minority ethnic and faith groups, Travellers, asylum seekers and refugees;
- pupils who need support to learn English as an additional language;
- pupils with special educational needs;
- gifted and talented pupils;
- children 'looked after' by the local authority;
- other children, such as sick children; young carers; those children from families under stress; pregnant schoolgirls and teenage mothers;
- any pupils who are at risk of disaffection and exclusion.

(Ofsted, 2000, p. 4)

At various points in the New Labour years there were initiatives targeted at all of these groups. Some of these have simply taken the form of funding streams directed towards schools or local authorities to enable them to set up their own programmes of development and provision. For instance, the Vulnerable Children Grant (VCG) directed funding to local authorities so that they could make provision for children who might otherwise be out of school (DfES, 2003c). In other cases, there were more structured national 'strategies' or programmes of work, in which a series of activities have been set up to stimulate provision for particular groups:

- Work with 'gifted and talented pupils', for instance, involved the founda-tion of a 'National Academy for G&T Youth (NAGTY)', the development of a series of networks of local authorities to develop work at regional level, and investment through the Excellence in Cities programme (see below) in areas of disadvantage.
- Work with learners regarded as having special educational needs was catalysed through the Raising Barriers to Achievement Programme (DfES, 2004).
- Work on gender issues was initially focused on boys. The Raising Boys' Achievement Project sought to identify and transfer strategies for clos-ing the gender gap without depressing the (superior) attainment of girls (Younger et al., 2005). Latterly, the focus shifted to embrace girls, but the underlying model of identifying and disseminating 'good practice' has remained the same.

Other group-focused interventions, however, attempted to establish new policy frameworks within which vulnerable and underachieving children could be targeted. The most significant of these was the Every Child Mat-ters (ECM) policy (DfES, 2003a). ECM aimed to create integrated child and family services in each local authority through the structural integration of what were previously separate education and social care functions, through the establishment of children's trusts bringing together all agencies involved with children and their families (including health), and through the articulation of five 'outcomes' – being healthy, staying safe, enjoying and achieving, making a contribution and achieving economic well-being – which all those working with children were expected to pursue. At one level, the scope of ECM was universal since its concerns were with all children and all professionals working with children. In practice, however, most of the services subsumed within the new structures were either focused on children at risk or made additional provision for such children over and above what was provided for all. The policy conceptualised this situation in terms of a pyramid of risk and provision, with universal services providing a base upon which targeted and specialist services can offer provision for those at increasing levels of risk (DfES, 2003a, p. 26).

The education service in general, and schools in particular, was seen as full partners in the ECM agenda, and following some area-based pilots (see below) all schools were required to develop 'extended' provision within the ECM framework (HM Government, 2007). In practice, this meant that they had to offer before- and after-school childcare, a varied menu of extra-curricular activities, community access to school facilities, parenting support and 'swift and easy access' to other agencies for children with difficulties. As with ECM as a whole, this policy was universal in its remit, but with the clear expectation that some of these new forms of provision – for instance, parenting support and referral to other agencies – would be accessed predominantly by children at risk and their families.

The ECM framework had particular resonance for the early years. One of the five outcomes from the ECM policy – 'enjoying and achieving'– was translated in the Children Act (2004) (see http://www.legislation.gov.uk/ukpga/2004/31/contents) into 'education, training and recreation', and a 'ready for school' aim was articulated as a major rationale for ECEC provision in the framework of the Act. Indeed, as early as 1998, a 'Meeting the Childcare Challenge' green paper had given explicit consideration to the issue of raising educational outcomes for all children, and particularly for those deemed at risk of future educational failure (DfEE and DSS, 1998). This goal was preserved in a Ten Year Childcare Strategy (2004), which, amongst other things, focused on ECEC workforce development and reform – especially the introduction of the aim of Qualified Teacher Status for ECEC practitioners – illustrating the importance attached to higher attainment for young children, particularly those identified as most at risk of educational failure.

Elements of the childcare strategy – notably the focus on learning outcomes for those children most at risk of early years and school 'failure' – were subsequently embodied in a Childcare Act (2006) (see http://www.legislation.gov.uk/ukpga/2006/21/contents). This act can be conceived as a pioneering piece of legislation, setting out to transform ECEC services for generations to come and raise outcomes for children most at risk of educational failure and social exclusion. The Act formalised the strategic role of local authorities, whose new duties included pursuing the five ECM outcomes for all pre-school children and reducing inequalities in these outcomes for the most disadvantaged pre-school children; securing sufficient childcare for working parents; and providing a better parental information service. It also led to the creation of new funding streams for the development of ECEC services, targeting children identified as being the most vulnerable to educational failure and social exclusion. The Act laid the basis for the establishment of an Early Years Foundation Stage (EYFS), aimed at creating a 'coherent and flexible approach to care and learning' that focuses on the raising of outcomes for all children, but with extra provision for those most at risk of early years and school failure.

Following on from the ECM document and picking up on one of its key themes – supporting parents – the 'Every Parent Matters' policy (DfES, 2007b) was launched in March 2007 by the Department for Education and Skills (DfES). Alan Johnson, the Secretary of State for Education, stated:

> The evidence that good parenting plays a huge role in educational attainment is too compelling to ignore. It outstrips every single other factor: including social class, ethnicity or disability – in its impact on attainment.
>
> (Johnson, 2007a, p. 1)

'Every Parent Matters' addressed both the vital role parents play in improving their children's life chances and educational attainment and the role of government in helping parents achieve this aim. Despite the universalist language of the policy document, it focused particularly on parents believed to require extra support and assistance to help their children succeed educationally; the key features of the document that developed support for this particular group of parents include:

- Piloting a new family learning course for those parents/carers of children with pre-school children who have literacy and numeracy needs to help them support their children's learning and development up to the age of five.
- Supplying parents with numeracy and literacy needs who have children in year 7 (the start of secondary schooling) with a pack encouraging them to participate in learning activities with their children.
- Offering training to help all local authorities deliver information sessions for parents whose child is entering primary or secondary school. These sessions aim to increase parental understanding of the challenges that their children will face and boost parental confidence and willingness to engage with their child's learning and school.

It also discussed the implementation of parent councils in schools to give parents a voice, the development of a Parent Support Advisor role and a relaunch of Home School Agreements, which provide information on the agreed responsibilities of schools and parents.

Area-focused interventions

Other interventions targeted areas where learners at risk of underachievement and social exclusion were held to be concentrated – typically, urban areas marked by significant disadvantage and low educational achievement. An early version, building to some extent on the experience of Educational Priority Areas in this country (Halsey, 1972) and ZEPs in France (Hatcher & Leblond, 2001), were Education Action Zones (EAZs) (DfEE, 1999a). Seventy-three EAZs were established by a small number of 'partners', including local authority, business, the voluntary sector and community representatives. It was hoped that EAZ partnerships would draw in local and national agencies and charities involved in, for example, health care, social care and crime prevention, and that EAZs would 'link up' with similarly focused Health and Employment Zones and projects funded by the 'Single Regeneration Budget'. A typical EAZ consisted of around 20 schools (usually two or three secondary schools plus their feeder primaries). Although EAZs were managed on a day-to-day basis by an appointed director, each EAZ was formally governed by an Education Action Forum (EAF). EAFs each had a statutory responsibility for formulating, implementing and monitoring a detailed local action plan. To support them in this task, EAZs received government funding of up to £750,000 per annum for 3–5 years, which they were expected to supplement with £250,000 per annum sponsorship in cash or 'kind' from the private and/or voluntary sector. They were usually located in areas of disadvantage within LEA areas, brought together a range of stakeholders under a management structure that was distinct from that of the LEA and (in principle, at least) used additional funding to develop innovative ways of tackling educational problems.

In time, EAZs were supplemented and replaced by Excellence in Cities (EiC) areas, which shared many features in common with its predecessor (NFER, 2007). The EiC programme was launched in September 1999 to raise standards and promote inclusion in inner cities and other urban areas. It focused on leadership, behaviour and teaching and learning, and to this extent was more tightly focused and more prescriptive than earlier phases of the EAZ programme. Initially based solely in secondary schools, the programme quickly expanded to include primary schools. By April 2006, over 1300 secondary schools and 3600 primary schools in 57 Local Authorities had been involved in the EiC programme. The programme tackled underachievement in schools through specific strands targeted at underachieving or disadvantaged groups. Thus, Learning Mentors worked with underachieving students in schools; Learning Support Units were established to provide for students at risk of exclusion from school for disciplinary reasons; a Gifted and Talented pupils programme was developed (see above); and City Learning Centres were established to enhance adult learning opportunities (particularly through information technology) for local people.

Over time, EiC began to act as an umbrella programme within which other initiatives could be located. So, the Behaviour Improvement Programme (BIP) sought to develop common approaches to the management of student behaviour in EiC areas, chiefly through the creation of integrated teams of professionals known as Behaviour and Education Support Teams. As part of the Government's Street Crime Initiative, the DfES funded 34 local education authorities to support measures to improve pupil behaviour and attendance in 2–4 selected secondary schools and their feeder primary schools. Phase 1 of the BIP was set up in July 2002 and involved over 700 schools.

In turn, the Full Service Extended Schools (FSES) initiative (DfES, 2003b) was located initially in BIP areas. The FSES initiative ran from 2003 to 2006, funding 148 schools (at between £93,000 and £162,000 per annum, decreasing annually). The schools were expected to provide a comprehensive range of services on a single site, including access to health services, adult learning and community activities, as well as study support and 8 a.m. to 6 p.m. wrap-around childcare. The initiative introduced a particular emphasis on the co-location of services provided by other non-educational agencies and by early years providers. Structures were loosely developed to foster greater interaction and exchange of information (child- and family specific) between different agencies and providers co-located on school premises to facilitate, for example, 'smoother' educational and social transitions between levels of schooling. In 2005, a national roll-out of the extended schools programme was launched, requiring every state school to offer at least some of the provision made by full service schools by 2010. Like the Every Child Matters policy (with which it was closely allied), the extended schools roll-out was universal in that it involved all schools and aimed to benefit all students. In reality, however, schools serving disadvantaged areas tended to make the highest levels of provision, and that provision was targeted at children and families judged to be in greatest need (Cummings et al., 2010).

Whereas all of these initiatives were available to targeted areas across the country, the City Challenge (DfES, 2007a) recognised the distinctive difficulties facing schools in London and other major conurbations – in terms, for instance, of low levels of achievement, high levels of disadvantage, the problems and benefits of a multi-ethnic population, and the balkanisation of governance in these areas, which tend to be divided between a number of local authorities. Like EiC, the Challenge deployed a range of strategies to address these issues, including targeted intervention in low-performing

schools, programmes aimed at increasing teacher recruitment and reten-
tion, a gifted and talented programme and support to local authorities in
improving their education systems.

In the early years sector, the Sure Start (SS) programme (DfEE, 1999b) was
also conceived initially as an area-based initiative, acting as a cornerstone in
the government's drive to tackle child poverty, educational failure and social
exclusion. By 1997, anxieties about the social and educational exclusion of
poorer families prompted the Chancellor of the Exchequer, Gordon Brown,
to consider policies and initiatives for breaking the cycle of deprivation that
trapped generation after generation. Norman Glass, the Deputy Director of
the Treasury, was asked to investigate. He was persuaded that intervention in
the early years was a cost-effective way to ensure that disadvantaged children
were socially and educationally ready for school.

The initial response took the form of the development of Early Excellence Centres aimed at bringing together ECEC, social support and adult
learning. By autumn 2003, 107 centres were running. At about the same
time, a Neighbourhood Nurseries Initiative sought to expand the availability of high-quality childcare in disadvantaged areas. However, this initiative
was succeeded by the more wide-ranging Sure Start initiative, originally run
through local programmes in the 20 per cent most deprived wards (effectively, neighbourhoods) of England. It aimed to achieve better outcomes
for children, parents and communities by increasing the availability of
childcare for all children; improving children's health, education and emotional development; supporting parents; and developing parents' employment aspirations. Launched in 1999, the Sure Start Unit was an integral
part of the Children, Young People and Families Directorate in the government's education department. The unit worked with local authorities,
Primary Care Trusts (with responsibility for health provision), Jobcentre Plus
(working on supporting people into employment), local community and
voluntary and private sector organisations, and schools to develop in the
first instance around 520 local programmes in England aimed at families
with children under 5, covering around 800 children in each area. Each
programme was managed by a partnership of statutory agencies (including
health and education professionals and institutions – schools, Primary Care
Trusts), ECEC professionals and voluntary and community groups, as well
as parents, who worked together to develop – in theory at least – an integrated approach for families. Partnerships differed in each programme, and
this was seen as being a crucial factor in the scheme's success (Turnstile et al.,
2005).

Children's early language development was singled out as a key deter-
minant of future educational success, and a government target was introduced to cut by 5 per cent the number of 4-year-olds needing specialist help with speech and language development by 2004. A number of
related programmes and schemes were developed to help achieve this goal,

implemented to varying degrees across the SS local programmes. As one Secretary of State for Education, Alan Johnson, explained:

> The gap in achievement opens up at a startlingly young age. A child from a deprived home has on average heard just 13 million words by the age of four, compared to 45 million in a more affluent home. What starts as a problem with vocabulary rapidly turns into a problem with reading, writing and comprehension, leading to poor exam results.
>
> (Johnson, 2007b)

Sure Start expanded rapidly over the New Labour years. Its budget, for instance, rose steadily to £1.5 billion in 2005–2006. The then chancellor's Child Poverty Review, closely aligned to the broader efforts to reduce social exclusion among children, stated that 'child poverty is more than about income' and that in addition to eradicating child poverty, 'the government wants to support parents in their parenting role ... [and] improve services for children living in deprived areas, including targeted programmes' (HM Treasury, 2004, p. 5). The Review provided for additional investment in ECEC for disadvantaged children of £699 million in 2007/2008. These figures were increased almost immediately after publication, and by the time New Labour lost office, the budget for Sure Start was well in excess of £2 billion. With this expansion, Sure Start began to incorporate other programmes in the early-years sector. In March 2003, the government announced plans to rebrand Early Excellence Centres, Sure Start local programmes and Neighbourhood Nurseries as Sure Start Children's Centres. The aim was to build on these earlier programmes to raise standards and integrated services for young children and their families in England. In July 2004 a cash injection of £100 million increased the number of children's centres from the planned 1700 to 2500 in the 30 per cent most deprived communities. By March 2006, there were 650,000 pre-school children benefiting from the programme with the aim of having a centre in every community by 2010. In this way, Sure Start eventually transformed itself from an initiative focused only on the poorest areas to a programme available everywhere – albeit still with a focus on disadvantaged families.

This concern with the area-focused interventions was repeated across many aspects of government social policy. Schools and early years centres in disadvantaged areas also participated in interventions that were developed by government departments and agencies other than the Education ministry. For instance, the early experiments with extended schools arose out of the cross-departmental National Strategy for Neighbourhood Renewal (Social Exclusion Unit, 1998). Likewise, the Single Regeneration Budget and the New Deal for Communities managed by the Department for Communities and Local Government had dedicated education strands and were often a source of funding for schools and early years centres.

Institution-focused interventions

Much of New Labour's mainstream education policy was concerned with driving up standards of achievement by improving the performance of schools and other educational institutions. Governments tended to operate with a 'carrot and stick' approach, offering incentives and rewards for improvement on the one hand, but punishing poor performance on the other. In effect, this resulted in a targeted approach, with institutions regarded as underperforming being singled out for special attention on the grounds that their ineffectiveness threatens the educational and life chances of their students. Thus Ofsted was charged with identifying 'schools causing concern', which were then monitored more regularly than others, were likely to receive heavy intervention from their local authorities and were required to formulate plans to meet demanding targets and ensure their improvement. This approach was mirrored in the early years: early years centres regarded as failing their early learners were more closely monitored by Ofsted, had more frequent inspections and were required to formulate, implement and successfully achieve the jointly developed plans for improvement.

Most schools identified as causing concern rapidly moved out of that category in response to intensive intervention. However, some did not, and might find themselves being closed down and replaced by a new school (albeit, sometimes in the same buildings). As time went on, governments developed a range of so-called 'structural solutions' to deal with low-performing schools. Two programmes of particular note were Fresh Start and the Academies Programme. The assumption in both cases was that interventions to improve the existing school had failed repeatedly, and that fundamental changes were needed in facilities, staffing (usually including the head teacher) and governance arrangements. Fresh Start schools reopened with refurbished facilities and major changes or additions to staff. Establishing a Fresh Start school cost on average around £2.2 million (a mixture of capital and revenue costs). They might be designated as 'Collaborative Restarts', meaning that they were reopened with support from another school – usually one judged to be more successful – with which they may be linked formally as a pair of federated schools. The Academies Programme was a later version of this approach. It went through a number of transformations, but in its initial form typically involved, like Fresh Start, the replacement of one or more existing schools, judged to be beyond intervention, by a new school with new governance arrangements and changes of staff. The programme was controversial because academies were removed from the control of local authorities and instead were effectively run by private sponsors, often from faith groups, business or voluntary groups (see Gunter 2011).

Each of these approaches had a punitive element in that they involved placing existing managers and governors under strict control, or removing them entirely. As such, they reflected a long-standing conviction amongst governments from both major parties that many of the problems of the educational system were attributable to the inadequacy of professionals and local decision makers. In contrast, however, many of the area- and group-focused interventions described above recognised that schools and early years centres serving highly disadvantaged populations and areas might need additional support. The 'schools facing challenging circumstances' programme was an institution-focused example of this approach. In common with many of the initiatives we have already described, it offered a mixture of additional funding, intervention and encouragement to innovate, but in this case to schools with particularly low levels of performance and with highly disadvantaged populations. From 2001 to 2004 the DfES funded an action research project with eight such schools, exploring innovative ways to raise attainment such as the use of school improvement groups in each school; a new literacy programme for pupils unable to access the curriculum on entry because of low literacy levels; the use of interactive whiteboards to develop new approaches to teaching and learning; and the sharing of materials, policies and good practice online (Macbeath et al., 2005).

Evidence of impact

New Labour governments, as we have seen, made much of a commitment to evidence-informed policy and commissioned large numbers of policy evaluations. However, assessing the impact of prioritising policies is not easy, for a number of reasons:

– Not all policy interventions are evaluated.
– Evaluations tend to focus on the multiplicity of individual interventions rather than on the impact of overall policy approaches.
– Interventions frequently overlap with each other, and disentangling the effect of one intervention from all the others is difficult.
– Evaluations tend to be short-term, taking place as the initial funding comes to an end rather than when the policy has had time to bed down and longer-term effects have become apparent.
– Policy moves more quickly than the evaluation process, and interventions are commonly changed or abandoned before a full evaluation has been possible.

It would be impossible in this brief report to present all of the evidence available, even on those interventions that have been properly evaluated. However, it is possible to identify some common themes:

Stimulating activity

There seems little doubt that priority policies of the sort described above were effective in focusing attention on particular groups, areas and institutions, and in stimulating activity in relation to them. For instance, the VCG (Kendall *et al.*, 2004) and strategies to raise the achievement of boys (Younger *et al.*, 2005) and of students from minority ethnic backgrounds (Cunningham *et al.*, 2004) were each successful in directing attention to groups that might easily have slipped beneath the radar if government had concentrated solely on whole-system reform. Similarly, area-focused initiatives such as Excellence in Cities (Kendall *et al.*, 2005), FSES (Cummings *et al.*, 2007) and Sure Start (Anning *et al.*, 2005; Sammons *et al.*, 2004; Turnstile *et al.*, 2005) seem to have acted as catalysts for considerable activity on the ground that might otherwise not have occurred.

In one sense, this is not surprising. As we suggested above, New Labour governments moved beyond their traditional role of establishing broad policy frameworks, and became much more involved at the delivery level. Their interventionist stance typically involved a fund-and-monitor approach, whereby local authorities, schools and early years centres had access to additional funding, but were held to account for the ways in which they used that funding and for the outcomes it generated. Often, as we have seen, this was accompanied by more supportive kinds of intervention on the one hand (the creation of networks, or the publication of guidance) and by the ever-present threat of punitive responses to inadequate performance on the other. This cocktail of measures created strong incentives for early years providers, schools and local authorities to respond to national initiatives, and left little room for them to be ignored.

Producing outcomes

Similarly, there is little doubt that priority policies generated some of the improved outcomes at which they were targeted. For instance, the rate of increase in GCSE (national examination) performance for EiC areas was around twice that of non-EiC schools for a number of years in succession (Kendall *et al.*, 2005). This meant there was a narrowing of the achievement gap between EiC and non-EiC areas, from 12.4 per cent in 2001 to 6.9 per cent in 2005. Moreover, there were improvements for groups of young people targeted by the programme. Similarly, the City Challenges have produced evidence of improved outcomes. Although there was no large-scale independent evaluation, official reports suggested that results at GCSE in London, for instance, improved faster than in England as a whole, and that these improvements were evident in terms of performance at the level of individual students, schools and local authorities (see, for instance, Ofsted, 2006).

This too was evident with the speech and language initiatives directed at parents and children with particular language and communication needs and rolled out in Sure Starts (Roy *et al.*, 2005). In terms of the early years, results indicated that particular groups of at-risk early learners had improved outcomes, including children from ethnic minority groups (primarily Black Caribbean and Black African) and children for whom English is an additional language (Sammons *et al.*, 2004, 2007). These outcome gains seem all the more significant given that parental education, income and occupation are critical factors in determining ECEC use (George & Hansen, 2007). By and large, families accessing formal ECEC provision are typically educated to degree level and in employment; this use then translates into an intergenerational transmission of social advantage (George & Hansen, 2007). However, Millennium Cohort Studies (MCS) data suggest that the relatively high percentages of children from the most disadvantaged groups using ECEC provision indicate that central interventionist policies went some way to achieving their aims of enabling ECEC access to the poorest and most socially excluded children.

The limits of what was achieved

Despite these encouraging signs, however, and despite repeated government claims to be transforming the education system, there are a number of reasons for being cautious about what was really achieved through the intensive priority policy activity of the New Labour years. Despite the intensity of that activity, the reality is that, by the end of the New Labour period, England continued to be scarred by educational inequality (Schools Analysis and Research Division, 2009), and, moreover, by a wider range of social inequalities (Equality and Human Rights Commission, 2010). Indeed, by the middle of the New Labour years, policy makers were already well aware of this, and ministers regularly bemoaned their failure to overcome the endemic inequalities in the education system (see, for instance, Kelly, 2005). A Schools White Paper in 2005 (which paved the way for yet further reform) acknowledged these persistent problems in somewhat gloomy tones:

> Despite the sharp improvement in the number of good schools, there are too many children being let down by schools that are coasting, rather than striving for excellence.

> ... despite the progress that has been made, at every stage of our education system, parental background still plays too important a role in determining attainment and life chances: those from better-off families do better than those from less well-off families.

> Despite all the progress we have made in improving the basics, it is still the case that almost a quarter of children leave primary school without the necessary skills in literacy and numeracy to make a success of the secondary curriculum.

Our participation rate for 17 year-olds in continued education and training is ranked 27th out of 30 industrialised countries.

(HM Government, 2005)

Whatever else the New Labour approach achieved, it did not transform the educational and social landscape of the country. The obvious question is why this should be the case. Any answer to this question is likely to be complex, but we wish to point to three characteristics of New Labour's priority policies that seem likely to form at least part of that answer. It is the tendency of these policies to foster instrumentalism, the contradiction within those policies between central control and local innovation and the depth (or, more accurately, lack of depth) at which policy makers sought to intervene.

Instrumentalism

One reason for being cautious about apparent improvements is that it is clear that the highly interventionist and high-stakes approach used by New Labour governments generated instrumental responses on the part of schools and local authorities (Dyson, 2007). Put simply, where schools and authorities are held accountable for continuous improvements in outcomes, and where these improvements are measured in somewhat crude ways through national assessments, they are likely to do whatever they need to do to produce the results that are expected. For instance, secondary schools soon learned that they could improve their performance figures by switching students from mainstream examinations (GCSEs) to vocational 'equivalents', which were easier to pass. As a result, the government was forced to close this loophole by reporting performance on core subject GCSEs separately. Similarly, primary schools routinely engaged in coaching children prior to taking their national assessments, and/or in focusing on children whose performance is on the borderline of national threshold levels (Richards, 2005). Again, government was forced to consider measuring performance in a different way to try to close this loophole (Johnson, 2006). In each of these cases, improvements in measured performance may have resulted, but it is not clear that these bear much relationship to genuine improvements in students' underlying capacities or in the quality of their schools.

This seems to be a phenomenon that was widespread across the education system, and was certainly not generated only by priority policies. However, the sorts of targeted interventions favoured by New Labour governments tended to exacerbate the problem. Targeted initiatives created extra pressure to produce results and, moreover, to do so within the timeframe of the initiative. Often, professionals on the ground would be torn between a recognition of the need for long-term strategies to address deep-seated educational problems and the imperative to produce quick results, even if this meant resorting to instrumental means (Cummings *et al.*, 2006, 2007; Dyson *et al.*, 2007). Moreover, the response to need could easily give way to a more instrumental response to external imposition of targeting criteria, so that schools, areas and populations with apparently similar levels of need nonetheless received very different levels of provision (Ainscow *et al.*, 2007).

Central control and local innovation

As we have seen, the policies favoured by New Labour depended heavily on central control as government identified priorities, targeted resources and set targets. At the same time, they typically sought to foster innovation and enable professionals on the ground to find solutions to local problems. These two imperatives appeared to be clearly in tension with each other, and each had its own dangers. Centrally driven interventions might not be sufficiently well tuned to local conditions, whilst local responses might be ill-focused or ill-equipped to bring about the radical changes needed.

This was most evident in the Education Action Zone policy, which was noticeably less successful than some other area-focused approaches. The initiative certainly generated a considerable amount of activity, but this was only very loosely directed by central government, at least in the first instance. It is far from certain that the activities undertaken by EAZs targeted the most difficult educational issues in their areas, or that they were implemented in a rigorous manner (Ofsted, 2003). Perhaps not surprisingly, then, there was little evidence of improved outcomes from EAZ areas. One analysis by Power *et al.* (2004) used regression modelling to examine whether the schools in six case-study zones had done better or worse than those in their LEAs. In 2001, the performance of zone schools was lower than that of non-zone schools. When the 2001 results were regressed against pre-zone performance and LEA variables, there was no indication of a narrowing gap since the start of the zone.

In other cases, results were mixed as centrally directed policy seems to have been insufficiently sensitive to local variations. So, for instance, although the impacts of the Gifted and Talented strand of EiC were positive overall, they varied considerably in relation to students' prior level of attainment, attitudes to education, behaviour and ethnicity (Kendall, 2005). Similarly, evidence on the outcomes from the Schools Facing Exceptionally Challenging Circumstances programme is equivocal (MacBeath *et al.*, 2005). Although it seems to have generated some specific improvements in these schools, these were more or less matched by a group of comparison schools. There would seem to have been a mismatch between the centrally directed nature of the intervention and the need to promote innovation, ownership and deep cultural change at school level. As the evaluation report argues:

> The balance between innovation and accountability has been a tension throughout the project, in part due to pressure of examinations and

monitoring visits by HMI [school inspectors] which have constrained more adventurous curriculum initiatives. An innovative culture of change in schools is most likely to be created in a climate where authorities allow schools to take risks without fear of failure.

(MacBeath *et al.*, 2005, p. 5)

Sure Start local programmes were undoubtedly successful in developing local partnerships sensitive to local context and in developing a climate that promoted innovation; indeed this has been seen as one of the key achievements of the initiative (Anning *et al.*, 2005). Nonetheless, evaluations also identify tensions between the two imperatives of central control and local innovation, particularly on a day-to-day basis (Turnstile *et al.*, 2005). Designing services with 'restrictive' boundaries (on the basis of child/pupil age, area or population group) contributed to a failure to meet the needs of children across their developmental life course, especially beyond 4 years of age, and increased the risk of associated stigma, which in turn deterred those most in need from utilising the service. Furthermore, centrally developed, area-based initiatives potentially excluded children and families, despite their individual/family needs, due to boundary rigidity.

Deeper change

Many of the issues raised above return ultimately to the question of how far the sorts of priority policies favoured by New Labour proved capable of addressing the educational problems at which they were targeted. Certainly, there seems to be a contradiction between the fundamental problems of underachievement and disadvantage which characterise the English education system, and the tightly focused, time-limited and results-led interventions that were the preferred means of tackling those problems. Sometimes this contradiction surfaced in evaluations of particular priority policies. For instance, the FSES initiative had as much success as any policy in targeting children and families facing difficulties and bringing about improvements in their achievements and well-being. However, professionals on the ground claimed that its reliance on short-term funding and rapid results has made it more difficult for them to tackle the real problems local people face. In the meantime, evidence for wide-ranging effects was scant, and professionals argued that it would take many years for their work to bear fruit (Cummings *et al.*, 2007; Dyson & Raffo, 2007).

This mismatch between problem and intervention might also explain the decidedly mixed character of the results that priority policies generated. For instance, it seems that the academies and fresh start programmes had some success in 'turning round' schools in difficulties. However, it is also clear that these programmes did not work in every case and that this may be because some schools are located in such difficult contexts that school-focused interventions of this kind were unable to overcome the problems those contexts

generate (National Audit Office, 2006a). A notorious example of this phenomenon is The Ridings School, which hit national headlines in 1996 as a
school that was out of control. Thereafter, it was subject to a succession of
interventions, including being fresh-started. However, it remained a 'failing'
school – a fate that is perhaps not unconnected to the very high levels of disadvantage in the area it served and the negative impact of being surrounded
by selective and other 'high status' schools (Reed, 2007) – and was ultimately
closed down as being beyond redemption.

The story in early years provision was much the same. Despite all the high
hopes for, and undoubted achievements of Sure Start, the overall impacts on
outcomes for children appear to have been modest and patchy rather than
transformational – at least in the short to medium term (National Evaluation of Sure Start, 2008; 2005). For non-compulsory 'educational' services,
like ECEC, one problem appears to be that of ensuring adequate outreach to
those groups least likely to access the educational and social schemes and initiatives developed. Put simply, the groups of families and early learners that
stand to gain most in the immediate and longer term by accessing ECEC
are the least likely to use it (Anning *et al.*, 2007; George & Hansen, 2007;
National Audit Office, 2006b). Whilst this may in part be due to boundary rigidity (Turnstile *et al.*, 2005), it may also relate more concretely to
broader issues of social participation and engagement in deprived communities and the particular exclusion of some population groups from social and
educational services (Antoniou & Reynolds, 2005).

Some concluding thoughts

Looking beyond the surface features of New Labour's approach, it is possible
to identify a more fundamental stance towards the problem of educational
disadvantage and the patterns of social inequalities within which that problem was embedded. We might characterise that stance as being based on
three broad principles:

1. *Optimism.* These policies were characterised by a conviction that all – or
   nearly all – learners can achieve to an acceptable standard, regardless of
   the 'barriers to learning' that they may face. At one point, ministers were
   fond of arguing that 'poverty is no excuse' (National Literacy Trust, 2006)
   for low achievement, and, while this naïve view may have mellowed over
   time, there remained a strong sense that the right sorts of interventions
   can produce dramatic changes in the performance of individual learners
   and of institutions, and of disadvantaged areas.
2. *Relentlessness.* This optimism led to a 'relentless' (DfEE, 1997) pursuit of
   interventions. The failure of one policy intervention to solve a problem
   tended to lead not to the abandonment of the whole approach but to
   the formulation of a further intervention which might (or might not)

learn from the first. So, EAZs were followed rapidly by EiC, Fresh Start by academies, FSES by the national extended schools roll-out, Sure Starts by Children's Centres and so on. Within a broadly stable policy approach, therefore, there was a succession of short-lived interventions.

3. *Innovation.* Priority policies under New Labour were rarely simply about targeting resources and energies onto problematic situations. Given that educational problems were regarded as inherently soluble, the policy assumption was that the historical failure to find these solutions can be attributed to the structures and practices of the past. Innovation was therefore essential, and priority policies typically embodied innovations or, more likely, sought to create the conditions under which innovation was possible. So, for instance, EAZs and EiC created governance structures for area approaches outside the traditional structures of the local authority; academies were 'new' kinds of schools, again operating outside traditional structures; Every Child Matters created new organisational structures within local authorities, and then between local authorities and other agencies.

This stance perhaps explains both what the New Labour approach achieved and what it failed to achieve. It undoubtedly encouraged policy makers to assume that problems of inequality and disadvantage were inherently soluble, and therefore to continue to target energy and resource at those problems, in a constant effort to find the 'right' solution. A continued commitment to prioritisation within the context of whole-system reform would, it was argued, eventually remove – or ameliorate to an acceptable level – the persistent inequalities in the English school system. As the then Prime Minister Tony Blair famously put it:

> Every time I've ever introduced a reform in Government, I wish in retrospect I had gone further.
>
> (Blair, 2005)

There is undoubtedly an argument to be made, therefore, that if the New Labour approach were to be pursued with equal optimism and relentlessness for a further decade or so, the accumulation of modest results would begin to look decidedly more impressive, and that the long-term impacts of early-intervention programmes in particular would begin to be felt.

However, there is also an argument to be made that the New Labour stance encouraged policy makers to focus on a succession of relatively small-scale initiatives rather than considering the more fundamental educational and social changes that might be necessary. On this argument, New Labour's approach was inherently incapable of tackling the problems at which it was directed. On the one hand, priority policies, targeted simply at the manifestations of social and educational inequality, had little hope of addressing its fundamental, structural causes (Dyson & Raffo, 2007; Raffo *et al.*, 2007).

On the other hand, the sort of system reform favoured by New Labour governments, with its emphasis on standards, targets and choice, exacerbated the very inequalities which priority policies were attempting to address. As Hulme and Hulme (2005) point out, there were:

> ...tensions and contradictions evident in a platform of education reform that is couched in the language of social inclusion, yet extends the market in education and regulates this through ever more intrusive instruments of 'governmentality'.

> (Hulme & Hulme, 2005, p. 33)

It is also just possible, however, that it is simply too early to reach a final judgment on the New Labour years. Despite the limitations of what was achieved, New Labour secured a lengthy period in office, during which time substantial effort and resource were targeted at the problems of educational inequality and disadvantage. Whether more might have been achieved by a more radical approach, and whether such a radical approach was politically feasible, are moot points. Whatever the answers, it seems likely that, in the context of the even more avowedly market-oriented government that is now in office, and of the economic shocks to which the United Kingdom like the rest of Europe is now subject, the era of frenetic policy activity to tackle educational disadvantage is at an end. It may yet be that New Labour's approach, for all its 'tensions and contradictions' and all the patchiness of its results, will nonetheless come to seem distinctly preferable to what is about to follow.

Bibliography

AINSCOW, M., CROW, M., DYSON, A., GOLDRICK, S., KERR, K., LENNIE, C., MILES, S., MUIJS, D. & SKYRME, J. (2007) *Equity in Education: New Directions* (Manchester: Centre for Equity in Education, The University of Manchester).

ANNING, A., CHESWORTH, E., SPURLING, L. & PARTINOUDI, K.D. (2005) *The Quality of Early Learning, Play and Childcare in Sure Start Local Programmes* (London: DfES).

ANNING, A., STUART, J., NICHOLLS, M., GOLDTHORPE, J. & MORLEY, A. (2007) *Understanding Variations in Effectiveness Amongst Sure Start Local Programmes* (London: DCSF).

ANTONIOU, V.L. & REYNOLDS, R. (2005) 'Asylum-seeking Children in English Pre-schools: Inclusion and Support in the New Policy Climate', in *The Asylum-seeking Child in Europe* (H.E. Andersson *et al.*, eds) (Gothenburg: CERGU).

BEATTY, C., FODEN, M., LAWLESS, P. & WILSON, I. (2007) *New Deal for Communities National Evaluation: An Overview of Change Data: 2006*, Research Report 33, Centre for Regional Economic and Social Research, Sheffield Hallam University, Department for Communities and Local Government.

BELL, D. (2003) 'Access and Achievement in Urban Education: Ten Years on'. Speech to the Fabian Society by David Bell, Her Majesty's Chief Inspector of Schools (London: Ofsted).

BENNETT, J. (2006) 'Policy Lessons from the Thematic Review', in *Early Childhood Education: Major Themes* (R. Parker-Rees & J. Willan, eds) (London: Routledge).

BLAIR, T. (1997) Speech by the Prime Minister on Monday 2 June 1997, at the Aylesbury Estate, Southwark (London, Social Exclusion Unit, http://www.socialexclusionunit.gov.uk/downloaddoc.asp?id=59, consulted 4 July 2005).

BLAIR, T. (1999) Speech by the Prime Minister Tony Blair about Education Action Zones – 15 January 1999 (London, 10 Downing Street, http://www.number-10.gov.uk/output/Page1172.asp, consulted 24 May 2004).

BLAIR, T. (2004) Speech by the Prime Minister about the early years at the Daycare Trust's Annual Conference, http://www.number10.gov.uk/output/Page6564.asp.

BLAIR, T. (2005) *We Are the Change-makers* (London: The Labour Party), http://www.labour.org.uk/index.php?id=news2005&ux_news[id]=ac05tb&cHash=d8353c3d74, consulted on 25 November.

CASSEN, R. & KINGDON, G. (2007) *Tackling Low Educational Achievement* (York: Joseph Rowntree Foundation).

CHITTY, C. (2002) 'Education and Social Class', *The Political Quarterly*, 73(2), pp. 208–210.

CUMMINGS, C., DYSON, A., JONES, L., LAING, K., SCOTT, K. & TODD, L. (2010) *Evaluation of Extended Services: Thematic Review: Reaching Disadvantaged Groups and Individuals* (London: DCSF).

CUMMINGS, C., DYSON, A., MUIJS, D., PAPPS, I., PEARSON, D., RAFFO, C., TIPLADY, L., TODD, L. WITH CROWTHER, D. (2007) 'Evaluation of the Full Service Extended Schools Initiative: Final Report'. Research report RR852 (London, DfES).

CUMMINGS, C., DYSON, A., PAPPS, I., PEARSON, D., RAFFO, C., TIPLADY, L. & TODD, L. (2006) *Evaluation of the Full Service Extended Schools Initiative*, Second Year: Thematic papers (London, DfES).

CUMMINGS, C., DYSON, A., PAPPS, I., PEARSON, D., RAFFO, C. & TODD, L. (2005) 'Evaluation of the Full Service Extended Schools project: End of first year report'. DfES Research Report, Research report RR680 (Nottingham: DfES Publications), http://www.dfes.gov.uk/research/data/uploadfiles/RR680.pdf, consulted on 26 April 2006.

CUMMINGS, C., DYSON, A. & TODD, L. (2004) 'Evaluation of the Extended Schools Pathfinder Projects'. DfES Research Report, Research Report RR530 (Nottingham: DfES Publications), http://www.dfes.gov.uk/research/data/uploadfiles/RR530.pdf, consulted on 26 April 2006.

CUNNINGHAM, M., LOPES, J. & RUDD, P. (2004) 'Evaluation of EiC/EMAG Pilot Project', DfES Research Report RR583.

DEMIE, F., BUTLER, R. & TAPLIN, A. (2002) 'Educational Achievement and the Disadvantage Factor: Empirical Evidence', *Educational Studies*, 28(2), pp. 101–110.

DEPARTMENT OF EDUCATION AND SCIENCE (DES) (1989) *The Lower Attaining Pupils Programme, 1982–88* (London: DES).

DEPARTMENT FOR EDUCATION AND EMPLOYMENT (DfEE) (1997) *Excellence in Schools* (London: The Stationery Office).

DEPARTMENT FOR EDUCATION AND EMPLOYMENT (DfEE) DEPARTMENT FOR SOCIAL SECURITY (DSS) (1998) Meeting the Childcare Challenge: A framework and consultation document. Cm3959. (London, DfEE).

DEPARTMENT FOR EDUCATION AND EMPLOYMENT (DfEE) (1999a) *Meet the Challenge: Education Action Zones* (London: DfEE).

DEPARTMENT FOR EDUCATION AND EMPLOYMENT (DfEE) (1999b) *Sure Start: Making a difference for Children and Families* (London: DfEE).

DEPARTMENT FOR EDUCATION AND SKILLS (DfES) (2003a) *Every Child Matters. Cm. 5860* (London: The Stationery Office).

DEPARTMENT FOR EDUCATION AND SKILLS (DfES) (2003b) *Full Service Extended Schools: Requirements and Specifications* (London: DfES).

DEPARTMENT FOR EDUCATION AND SKILLS (DfES) (2003c) *Vulnerable Children Grant Guidance.* http://www.education.gov.uk/standardsfund/VCG02rev3lmc7.htm, consulted on 19 October 2011.

DEPARTMENT FOR EDUCATION AND SKILLS (DfES) (2004) *Removing Barriers to Achievement: The government's strategy for SEN,* (London, DfES).

DEPARTMENT FOR EDUCATION AND SKILLS (DfES) (2005) *Has the Social Class Gap Narrowed in Primary Schools? A Background Note to Accompany the Talk by the Rt Hon Ruth Kelly MP, Secretary of State for Education and Skills, 26 July 2005* (London: DfES).

DEPARTMENT FOR EDUCATION AND SKILLS (DfES) (2007a) *City Challenge for World Class Education* (London, DfES).

DEPARTMENT FOR EDUCATION AND SKILLS (DfES) (2007b) *Every Parent Matters* (London, DfES).

DYSON, A. (2007) 'Education in the 2007 CSR', in *The Alternative Comprehensive Spending Review 2007* (M. Baker, ed.) (Manchester: University of Manchester).

DYSON, A., GALLANNAUGH, F. & HOWES, A. (2007) *Pupils First Evaluation: Final Report* (Manchester: University of Manchester).

DYSON, A. & RAFFO, C. (2007) 'Education and Disadvantage: The Role of Community-oriented Schools', *Oxford Review of Education,* 33(3), pp. 297–314.

EQUALITY AND HUMAN RIGHTS COMMISSION (2010) *How Fair is Britain? Equality, Human Rights and Good Relations in 2010. The First Triennial Review* (London: Equality and Human Rights Commission).

FABIAN SOCIETY (Great Britain). Commission on Life Chances and Child Poverty (2006) *Narrowing the Gap: The Final Report of the Fabian Commission on Life Chances and Child Poverty* (London: The Fabian Society).

FARREL, A. & TAYLOR, C. (2004) 'Building Social Capital in Early Childhood Education and Care: An Australian Study', *British Education Research Journal,* 30(5), pp. 623–632.

FEINSTEIN, L. & DUCKWORTH, K. (2006) *Development in the Early Years: Its Importance for School Performance and Adult Outcomes* (London: DfES).

FEINSTEIN, L., ROBERTSON, D. & SYMONS, J. (1999) 'Pre-school Education and Attainment in the NCDS and BCS', *Educational Economics,* 7(3), pp. 209–234.

GEORGE, A., HANSEN, K. & SCHOON, I. (2007) *Millennium Cohort Study: Cognitive Development* (London: CLS).

GEORGE, A. & HANSEN, K. (2007) *Millennium Cohort Study: Childcare* (London: CLS).

GIDDENS, A. (1998) *The Third Way: The Renewal of Social Democracy* (Cambridge: Polity Press).

GLASS, N. (1999) 'Sure Start: The Development of an Early Intervention Programme for Young Children in the United Kingdom', *Children and Society,* 13(4), pp. 257–264.

GLENNERSTER, H. (2002) 'United Kingdom Education 1997–2001', *Oxford Review of Economic Policy,* 18(2), pp. 120–137.

GUNTER, H.M. (ed.) (2011) *The State and Education Policy: The Academies Programme* (London: Continuum).

HALSEY, A.H. (ed.) (1972) *Educational Priority: EPA Problems and Practices* (London: HMSO).

HATCHER, R. & LEBLOND, D. (2001) 'Education Action Zones and Zones d'education prioritaires', in *Education, Social Justice and Inter-agency Working: Joined up or Fractured Policy?* (S. Riddell & L. Tett eds) (London: Routledge).

HIGHAM, J. & YEOMANS, D. (2005) 'Collaborative Approaches to 14–19 Provision: An Evaluation of the Second Year of the 14–19 Pathfinder Initiative', DfES Research Report RR642.

HM GOVERNMENT (2005) *Higher Standards, Better Schools for all: More Choice for Parents and Pupils*, Cm 6677 (London: HMSO).

HM GOVERNMENT (2007) *Extended Schools: Building on Experience* (London: DCSF).

HM TREASURY (2004) *Child Poverty Review* (London: HM Treasury).

HOGGART, L. & SMITH, D.I. (2004) *Understanding the Impact of Connexions on Young People at Risk*, DfES Research Report 607.

HULME, R. & HULME, M. (2005) 'New Labour's Education Policy: Innovation or Reinvention?', in *Social Policy Review 17* (M. Powell, L. Bauld & K. Clarke, eds). Bristol: The Policy Press, pp. 33–49.

JOHNSON, A. (2006) Speech from Rt Hon Alan Johnson MP, Secretary of State for Education and Skills, The National College for School Leadership New Heads Annual Conference, 16 November 2006 (London: DfES).

JOHNSON, A. (2007a) Letter accompanying the Every Parent Matters Document, 15 March 2007, http://www.teachernet.gov.uk/_doc/11184/AJ_parenting_letter.pdf.

JOHNSON, A. (2007b) Speech from Rt Hon Alan Johnson MP, Secretary of State for Education and Skills, titled: 'Education the Key to Promoting Social Mobility', The Institute of Public Policy Research, 17 May 2007 (London: DfES).

KELLY, R. (2005) *Education and Social Progress. 26 July 2005* [Online]. (London: DfES). http://www.dfes.gov.uk/speeches/speech.cfm?SpeechID=242 consulted on 4 August 2005.

KENDALL, S., JOHNSON, A., GULLIVER, C., MARTIN, K. & KINDER, K (2004) 'Evaluation of the Vulnerable Children Grant, National Foundation for Educational Research', DfES Research Report RR592.

KENDALL, L., O'DONNELL, L., GOLDEN, S., RIDLEY, K., MACHIN, S., RUTT, S., MCNALLY, S., SCHAGEN, I., MEGHIR, C., STONEY, S., MORRIS, M., WEST, A. & NODEN, P. (2005) 'Excellence in Cities: The National Evaluation of a Policy to Raise Standards in Urban Schools 2000–2003', DfES Research Report, Research Report RR675A (Nottingham: DfES Publications), http://www.dfes.gov.uk/research/data/uploadfiles/RR675A.pdf, consulted on 26 April 2006.

MACBEATH, J., GRAY, J., CULLEN, J., CUNNINGHAM, H., EBBUTT, D., FROST, D., STEWARD, S. & SWAFFIELD, S. (2005) 'Responding to Challenging Circumstances: Evaluation of the 'Schools Facing Exceptionally Challenging Circumstances' Project' (Cambridge: University of Cambridge Faculty of Education).

MIDDLETON, S., PERREN, K., MAGUIRE, S., RENNISON, J., BATTISTIN, E., EMMERSON, C. & FITZSIMONS, E. (2005) 'Evaluation of Education Maintenance Allowance Pilots: Young People Aged 16 to 19 Years', DfES Research Report RR678 (London: DfES).

MORTIMORE, P. & WHITTY, G. (1997) *Can School Improvement Overcome the Effects of Disadvantage?* (London: Institute of Education, University of London).

NATIONAL AUDIT OFFICE (2006a) 'Improving Poorly Performing Schools in England', http://www.nao.org.uk/publications/nao_reports/05-06/0506679es.pdf.

NATIONAL AUDIT OFFICE (2006b) *Sure Start Children's Centres* (London: NAO).

NATIONAL EVALUATION OF SURE START (2005) 'National Evaluation Report: Early Impacts of Sure Start Local Programmes on Children and Families', Research Report NESS/2005/FR/013 (London: DfES).

NATIONAL EVALUATION OF SURE START (2008) *The Impact of Sure Start Local Programmes on Three Year Olds and Their Families*. Research Report NESS/2008/FR/027 (London: DCSF).

NATIONAL LITERACY TRUST (2006) 'Views on 'Poverty Is No Excuse' ', http://www.literacytrust.org.uk/Database/divided.html, consulted on 25 May 2005.

NFER (2007) *National Evaluation of Excellence in Cities 2002–2006*. Research Report DCSF-RR01 (London: DCSF).

OECD (2001) *Starting Strong: Early Childhood Education and Care* (Paris: OECD).

OECD (2006) *Starting Strong II: Early Childhood Education and Care* (Paris: OECD).

OFFICE OF THE DEPUTY PRIME MINISTER (2005) *Mainstream Public Services and Their Impact on Neighbourhood Deprivation*, http://www.neighbourhood.gov.uk/document.asp?id=1044.

OFSTED (2000) *Evaluating Educational Inclusion* (London: Ofsted).

OFSTED (2003) 'Education Action Zones: Tackling Difficult Issues in Round 2 Zones', Ref HMI 1711 (London: Ofsted), http://www.ofsted.gov.uk/assets/3414.pdf, consulted on 18 May 2007.

OFSTED (2005) 'Excellence in Cities: Managing Associated Initiatives to Raise Standards', HMI Reference no. 2595.

OFSTED (2006) *Improvements in London Schools 2000–06* (London: Ofsted).

PASCAL, C., BETRAM, T., HOLTERMAN, S., GASPER, M. & BOKHARI, S. (1999) *Evidence from the Evaluation of the EEC Pilot Programme* (Worcester: Centre for Research in Early Childhood).

PENNELL, H., WEST, A. & HIND, A. (2005) 'Evaluation of Aimhigher: Excellence Challenge Survey of Higher Education Providers 2004', DfES Research Report RR644.

POWER, S., WHITTY, G., GEWIRTZ, S., HALPIN, D. & MARNY DICKSON (2004) 'Paving a 'Third Way'? A Policy Trajectory Analysis of Education Action Zones', *Research Papers in Education*, 19(4), pp. 453–473.

RAFFO, C., DYSON, A., GUNTER, H., HALL, D., JONES, L. & KALAMBOUKA, A. (2007) *Education and Poverty: A Critical Review of Theory, Policy and Practice* (York, Joseph Rowntree Foundation).

REED, J. (2007) 'The Ridings' Rollercoaster Years', *Yorkshire Post*, 5 March 2007, http://www.yorkshiretoday.co.uk/ViewArticle.aspx?sectionid=55&articleid=2096437, consulted on 28 May 2007.

RICHARDS, C. (2005) *Standards in English Primary Schools: Are They Rising?* (London: ATL).

ROY, P., KERSLEY, H. & LAW, J. (2005) *The Sure Start Language Measure Standardisation Study* (London: DfES).

SAMMONS, P., SLYVA, K., MELHUISH, E., SIRAJ-BLATCHFORD, I. & TAGGART, B. (2004) *The Effective Provision of Pre-school Education (EPPE) Project: Final Report* (London: DfES).

SAMMONS, P., SLYVA, K., MELHUISH, E., SIRAJ-BLATCHFORD, I., TAGGART, B., BARREAU, S. & GRABBE, Y. (2007) *Influences on Children's Development and Progress in Key Stage 2: Social/Behavioural Outcomes for Year 5* (London: DCSF).

SCHWEINHART, L.J. & WEIKERT, D.P. (1997) *Lasting Differences: The High/Scope Pre-school Curriculum Comparison Study through Age 23* Paper No. 12 (Michigan: Monograph of the High/Scope Educational Research Foundation).

SCHOOLS ANALYSIS AND RESEARCH DIVISION, DEPARTMENT FOR CHILDREN SCHOOLS AND FAMILIES (2009) *Deprivation and Education: The Evidence on Pupils in England, Foundation Stage to Key Stage 4* (London: DCSF).

SOCIAL EXCLUSION UNIT (1998) *Bringing Britain Together: A National Strategy for Neighbourhood Renewal*, Cm. 4045 (London: The Stationery Office).

TURNSTILE, J., MEADOWS, P., AKHURST, S., ALLNOCK, D., CHRYSANTHOU, J., GARNERS, C. & MORLEY, A. (2005) *Implementing Sure Start Local Programmes: An Integrated Overview of the First Four Years* (London: DfES).

YOUNGER, M., WARRINGTON, M., GRAY, J., RUDDUCK, J., MCLELLAN, R., BEARNE, E., KERSHNER, R. & BRICHENO, P. (2005) 'Raising Boys' Achievement', DfES Research Report RR636.

Belgium

3
Priority Education Policies in Belgium: Two Modes of Regulation of the Effects of a Market Logic

Nathanaël Friant, Marc Demeuse, Angeline Aubert-Lotarski and Idesbald Nicaise

Introduction

An important feature of the Belgian context is the *'communautarisation'*[1] of education policies. Since 1989 teaching has fallen within the competence of the communities, whereas until then it came under the Federal state. It is the three language-based communities (the French-, Flemish- and German-speaking communities) that manage similar but completely independent education systems, each covering part of the country.[2] In this chapter we will base our account on the French and Flemish communities. The first part deals with the general context of the education systems of these two communities and recounts their joint move towards equity up to 1989. The second part is centred on the priority education policies in the French Community. The targeted populations and the actions prescribed are analysed on the basis of official documents. Their effective implementation and the evaluation of their effects (whether desired or not) is then discussed on the basis of research and the scientific literature available. The third part of this chapter analyses, in the same way, the priority education policies in the Flemish Community. The chapter concludes, as a summary, by examining the similarities and divergences which exist between the two communities.

In Belgium, schooling is compulsory and free for a period of 12 years, which begins in the school year in which the child reaches the age of 6 and ends when the pupil reaches the age of 18.[3] Pre-school (optional, and for a duration of three years) and primary education (between ages 6½and 12) are grouped together under the term 'fundamental education'. Secondary education, lasting six years, is made up of three 'degrees', each lasting two years. The first degree in theory provides a common structure for all pupils (Demeuse & Lafontaine, 2005). Regarding the second cycle, secondary education is divided into courses[4] with different objectives and opportunities, but also with a marked social and academic recruitment (Demeuse, Lafontaine & Straeten, 2005; Demeuse *et al.*, 2007). At the base of the education system is the freedom of education, written into Article 24 of the Belgian Constitution. This freedom applies to two aspects: (1) freedom, for pupils and their family provided by the law dated 29 May 1959, to choose the educational institution that they want;[5] and (2) freedom to organise schools. There are a number of consequences to this freedom of education, and it will be seen that they are related to the priority education policies followed in Belgium. The first consequence is the organisation of the education system into various networks,[6] each with its own educational project, and in which schools and teachers enjoy freedom as to how teaching is carried out. All the various organising authorities are given public finance established on an equal footing, except for the school infrastructures. Community decrees define the missions of fundamental and secondary education, the objectives of each type of teaching and the core competencies[7] which all pupils must be attain, while leaving a free choice of the teaching methods to be used. Consequently, pupil evaluation depends on the school and the teacher. At the present time in Belgium there are no certifying external evaluations providing a comparable measurement of pupils' attainments at any level, thus making comparison among schools impossible, except in the French Community at the end of primary education.[8]

The freedom of teaching also results in a *per capita* funding system for each school. This has led to an education system qualified as 'quasi-market' (Vandenberghe, 1996). This concept reflects the situation of an education system characterised by the simultaneous presence of public funding, a free choice of school and a way of calculating the budget of each school according to the number of pupils registered (Delvaux, Demeuse & Dupriez, 2005). There consequently exists an issue surrounding the way pupils are distributed around the schools, which structures competitive, asymmetrical and territorialised relations of interdependence (Maroy & Delvaux, 2006). They are competitive, not only in relation to the number of pupils registered in the school (first-order competition), but also in regard to pupils' academic and socio-economic characteristics (second-order competition). They are asymmetrical because, on the basis of both the type of pupils they take in and the movement of these pupils between schools, schools can be ranked, some receiving mainly pupils that the others do not want. Finally, these interdependences are territorialised: geographically close schools are interdependent, whatever their network or their offer. While these competitive interdependences structure the way schools act, they also contribute to producing significant inequalities by establishing a cleavage between selective schools and 'ghetto' schools.[9]

A number of studies (Vandenberghe, 2000; Dupriez & Vandenberghe, 2004; Dupriez & Dumay, 2006) have shown that the educational quasi-markets in Belgium lead, by the segregations that they imply, to significant inequalities in school results. The two surveys of 2000 and 2003 by the Organisation for Economic Co-operation and Development Programme for International Student Assessment (OECD PISA) showed a major difference in scores, ranging between the 25 per cent of 15-year-old pupils whose socio-economic index was the highest and the 25 per cent of pupils whose socio-economic index was the lowest. They also underlined the role that secondary schools play in the measured differences in pupils' attainments, these differences themselves being mainly explained by the average socio-economic level of the schools (Baye *et al.*, 2004). This segregation effect is illustrated in 3.1, where the variance of the results in the 2003 PISA mathematics survey is analysed on a country-by-country basis.

The total variances were standardised in relation to the OECD average. A figure higher than 100 means than the variance is higher than the average of the participating countries and, conversely, if the figure is lower than 100. Figure 3.1 illustrates firstly the fact that the total inequality (reflected by the rate of variation) between 15-year-olds is higher in Belgium than in all the other countries studied.

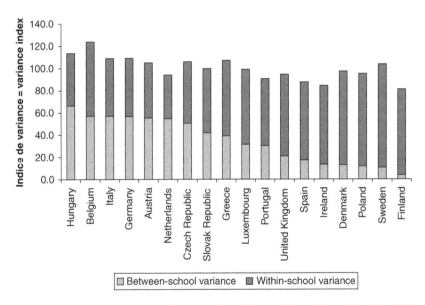

Figure 3.1 Performances in mathematics by 15-year-olds, reflected in the 2003 PISA survey: Variances between and within schools

Figure 3.1 also illustrates the breakdown, by means of a multilevel analysis, of the total variance in results according to school or individual. The lower (lighter) section of each bar represents the variance between schools (the amount variation that can be allotted to the differences between schools), while the upper (darker) section reflects the variance between pupils within a school. Once gain, Belgium finds itself in an unenviable position, because no country except Hungary does worse in terms of inequalities between schools. In other words, this graph shows the enormous impact of the competition generated by the quasi-market system: the Belgian education systems are characterised by large inequalities between schools – whether because of the composition of their pupil population (social and academic segregation) or because of other factors. The causal relationship between competition and social and academic segregation in education was analysed in depth by V. Vandenberghe (1996) and was illustrated for several countries by A. Björklund *et al.* (2006), S. Bradley & J. Taylor (2000) and N. Hirtt (2002).

This, then, is the educational landscape, marked by strong social inequalities, reinforced by the structures and the rules of funding, which forms the backdrop against which priority education policies aim to make corrections. They are, in fact, the current result of a 'move towards equity' in education (Demeuse, 2005). From 1830 until the present, the progressive appearance and coexistence of a certain number of moves towards greater equity can indeed be identified, at different times according to the levels of education. A certain amount of regularity can be perceived in the progression of these moves forward. Whether they relate to fundamental education initially, then to secondary or finally higher education, they progress in three stages:

- quantitative democratisation: this involves opening up access to education for all;
- qualitative democratisation: this involves equalising access to the most prestigious courses of study, in particular by systems of individual assistance based on merit;
- setting up priority education policies to ensure equality of results.

These three stages correspond to various models of justice shared at a given time for a given level of education. In this sense, the move towards greater equity in the Belgian education system can be traced by referring to the four conceptions of equity presented by A. Grisay (1984) and by Demeuse, Crahay & Monseur (2001, 2005): equal access to an equality of social realisation, via the stages of equality of treatment and equality of results. These various stages may coexist at a given time because the democratisation of the various levels does not take place at the same time. Moreover, the changes that determine the move from one stage to another act gradually.

PEPs in the French Community of Belgium

The parallel pursuit of a move towards equity

As of 1989, the French Community and the Flemish Community have been continuing separately, but in parallel, their move towards equity, in particular by implementing priority education policies. These policies are underpinned by two fairly similar conceptions of equity: equality of attainments and equality of social realisation.

These conceptions of equity are characterised by the denunciation of all situations in which the unequal quality of teaching[10] amplifies initial inequalities (Grisay, 1984). They preach equality of attainment for essential competencies, or equal possibilities of using the acquired competencies and social realisation. In this way they accept and encourage unequal treatment according to the principle of 'giving more to those who have less'.

This desire for equity features in the 'Missions' decree, promulgated in July 1997. It is particularly in evidence in the fourth objective pursued by teaching (decree dated 24 July 1997, chapter III, Article 6):

- Promote the self-confidence and personal development of each pupil.
- Help all pupils to appropriate knowledge and to acquire competencies for lifelong learning and to take an active part in economic, social and cultural life.
- Prepare all pupils to be responsible citizens, able to contribute to the development of a united, democratic, pluralistic society open to other cultures.
- Provide all pupils with equal opportunities for social emancipation.

While the principle of equality of attainment and social realisation is behind the priority education policies in the French Community of Belgium, the conception and implementation of these policies are subordinated to the context where strict formal equality is constitutionally guaranteed between citizens (Articles 10 and 11 of the Belgian Constitution) and between pupils (Article 24 of the Belgian Constitution). They are governed by certain conditions:

- accurate and objective identification of the beneficiaries;
- the definition of an action plan aiming at correcting initial objective disadvantages;
- limiting additional resources in order not to encroach on fundamental freedoms of others, and make these additional resources proportional to the damages suffered;
- limiting the range of action to the objectives set.

As can be seen, these policies go beyond the principle of just, formal equality in the field of education, inherited from democratic ideals developed during the 18th century. This approach refers to the current of thought about compensatory learning approaches, according to which it is better to treat those who seem to start out with poorer chances differently because they belong to categories whose results are generally lower, rather than to offer a single and identical service that is known would widen the inequality gap still further because of undifferentiated treatment. The thinking behind such compensatory action therefore aims at substituting, for pupils whose personal 'unchangeable' characteristics[11] are said to be too unfavourable, more advantageous educational characteristics, in order to reach a level of attainment comparable with that of pupils who start off with more going for them (Demeuse & Nicaise, 2005).

And yet, these principles run up against the notion of freedom of choice for pupils and their parents, which accentuates the difficulty of planning and organising a compensatory system that must be able to adapt to rapidly changing school populations and that struggles to keep pace with the acquisition of statistical information. Finally, they must not conflict with other principles, such as the protection of private life: the acquisition and the use of the necessary data must respect these basic rights and not pose more problems than they solve (Demeuse & Nicaise, 2005).

It is in this context that priority education policies, mainly centred on the socio-economic background of pupils, were introduced in the French Community of Belgium. These policies, whether they were the *priority education zones*, inspired by the French ZEPs and founded in 1989, *positive discrimination policies*, which replaced the ZEPs in 1998, or the *Encadrement différencié*[12] (ED) policy, which will replace *positive discrimination* in 2009, use mechanisms that vary the allocation of resources to schools. They stand out from other contexts, where the expression 'positive discrimination' refers to the concept of priority granted to people belonging to underprivileged groups.

Priority education zones

In 1989 the priority education zones (ZEPs) were founded. Unlike the solution adopted in France, the selection of schools was centralised. It was based on education criteria (course of study, orientation, number of school years repeated, etc.) and socio-economic criteria (poorly educated parents, unemployment rate, poverty, etc.) that were identical for all schools. The ZEPs were marked out by the commission for selection, assistance and evaluation of the projects for promoting academic success, and did not correspond to an administrative breakdown but to provisional zones according to the value of the criteria at any given time. There was then no mechanical system for attributing additional resources: they were subject to prior registration of a project by the school. The philosophy behind the way ZEPs were set up was to implement a principle of positive discrimination by measures that would be specific (i.e. directed specifically towards the underprivileged public), preventive, pupil-centred (no segmentation according to the levels of learning, nor according to networks) and open to the environment (parents, community life, etc.) (Conseil de l'Éducation et de la Formation, 1994). The French-speaking Belgian ZEPs, unfortunately from the standpoint of fundamental teaching, gave way to political pressure in favour of the inclusion or otherwise of schools within the zones, and suffered from resources being spread too thinly between many schools (Demeuse, 2005). Also, the idea of zones was badly suited to the context of free choice of school. Certain very old schools educating privileged pupils were located in disadvantaged urban areas, which poses a problem in regard to the specific nature of the action and population targeting. No data are available for the French Community to provide a solid evaluation of the results of the ZEP policy, which was replaced in 1998 by *positive discrimination*, still in force today.

Outside the ZEPs, and before the decree dated 30 June 1998 founding the positive discrimination policy, a series of mechanisms for solidarity between schools was set up in order to rebalance the budgets. The decree dated 14 March 1995 relating to the promotion of a successful school in fundamental teaching identifies 'priority' schools according to objective criteria such as a high percentage of pupils repeating a year, a large number of foreign pupils and unfavourable socio-economic situations. Additional resources are provided to support these schools. In addition, there are also mechanisms for solidarity between schools in the same network, which involve taking away certain resources and redistributing them to the least privileged schools.

Positive discrimination

The 'Missions' decree established equality of social emancipation as one of the aims pursued by the education system in the French Community. For this purpose, a decree aiming at ensuring equal opportunities for social emancipation for all pupils, in particular by implementing positive discrimination, was voted in on 30 June 1998. It defined the term *positive discrimination* in the French-speaking Belgian context as a

> distinction made for the benefit of ordinary, fundamental education and secondary schools, organised or subsidised by the French Community, on the basis of social, economic, cultural and educational criteria.
>
> (decree dated 30 June 1998, Article 3.1°)

The positive discrimination mechanism consists of a modulated allocation of resources to schools according to the socio-economic background of the pupils who are enrolled there. This allocation of additional resources to schools identified as providing education for an underprivileged population is performed mechanically, by ranking the qualifying schools according to an objective criterion, an average *socio-economic index*, and allocating additional means to the least privileged schools according to this criterion. In 2002, another decree completed and clarified the 1998 decree, while preserving similar ways of identifying the beneficiaries. The socio-economic index was again to be used as a basis for a mechanism for modulated allocation of additional resources (for operating only) in 2004, when differentiated funding for schools was implemented, following the refinancing of teaching.

In 2009, the *encadrement différencié* (ED) decree will replace the existing *'positive discrimination'* decree, by allocating additional resources to more schools. This decree also preserves a similar way of identifying the beneficiaries.

Calculating a socio-economic index

In order to implement the positive discrimination policy (and later, the ED policy), an objective socio-economic status indicator, based on the district[13] from which the pupil comes, has been created and is updated at least every four years by a team from several universities (Demeuse *et al.*, 1999; Demeuse & Monseur, 1999). A comprehensive socio-economic index was initially allotted to each district of the Kingdom, on the basis of 12, then 11 variables,[14] taking into account both the requirements imposed by the decree dated 30 June 1998[15] and the scientific literature that finds them reliable as indicators for academic and/or social success. Each pupil is allotted the socio-economic index of the district he/she lives in. This index is a normal distribution metric variable that varies between –3.5 and +3.5. It is recalculated every three years on the basis of the latest statistical data available.

The average of the socio-economic indices of the pupils is taken at the level of the site.[16] The schools are then ranked from the least to the most privileged. The most underprivileged schools, until they cumulatively total approximately 12% of the pupils, receive positive discrimination. In secondary education, *priority* positive discrimination schools receiving additional resources can also be distinguished.[17] In addition, other schools and/or sites can be added, according to objective criteria, to the lists drawn up using the procedure described above (decree dated 27 March 2002). The modulated assignment of resources to schools within the framework of positive discrimination in the French Community is therefore a dichotomous mechanism, defining a border between positive discrimination schools – which involve approximately 12% of pupils and benefit from additional resources – and schools of ordinary status.

The ED decree will soften this dichotomy. Indeed, 25 per cent of the most underprivileged schools will receive additional resources and the mechanism will use five levels of disadvantage, with a proportional resource allocation to each level.

Criticism of the method of identification

M. Demeuse (2002) identifies the main arguments justifying such a method for calculating the socio-economic index from the district where the pupils live and for determining the schools that will benefit on the basis of their population rather than the zones where they are located. The fact that the socio-economic index is not created from data collected directly from the pupils in the schools is because this approach was rejected by the legislator for at least two reasons. The first is related to respecting the private life of the pupils and their parents: both the law[18] restricting individual collection of information about the characteristics of the family environment, and educational staff, are particularly reticent about putting on record information about pupils' socio-economic background. The second is related to how such data are encoded: this is expensive and relatively unreliable.[19] This solution was selected on the basis of the results of former scientific studies (Ross, 1983; Demeuse, 1996, 2002), which show that an indirect indicator of the socio-economic status 'predicts' pupils' educational difficulties as well as the variables collected directly from families.

The fact that schools are identified on the basis of their population and not on the zone in which they are located is, above all, due to the lack of sectoring: that each family can freely choose a school means that the pupils do not inevitably attend the school in their sector, and that populations in a school may fluctuate from one year to another. Identification on the basis of the actual school population was chosen because it makes it enables these constraints to be taken into account, to monitor changes in the population of a school and avoid once-and-for-all cataloguing of schools (Demeuse, 2002).

T.-M. Bouchat, B. Delvaux & G. Hindryckx (2005) note, however, the sometimes debatable character of the way the 'positive discrimination' category is constructed from the administrative standpoint. In addition to the fact that these schools cannot inevitably be identified in the field, they do not form a homogeneous whole by either their population or their context, and do not take in pupils that are clearly more underprivileged than do other schools with an index only just higher than the admission threshold for that category.

The current situation in the French Community of Belgium

It was the decree dated 24 July 1997 that defined the priority missions for education in the French Community, among which can be found that of providing all pupils with equal opportunity for social emancipation, and preparing pupils for becoming citizens in a society open to other cultures. The Contract for the School, proposed by the Government of the French Community in 2005, also defines political guidelines with its '10 priorities for education', including a reassertion of the equality of attainment concerning basic competencies[20] and a determination to fight against educational segregation.[21] Concerning priority education policies, various methods may coexist. There are, for example, at least two types of targeting.[22] Targeting of a linguistic or ethnic nature: pupils are targeted individually because they are from immigrant families or because their native tongue is not the language taught. Socio-economic targeting: allotting additional means to educational sites, and not to the pupils themselves: whatever his/her socio-economic status, a pupil enrolled in the targeted 'positive discrimination' school benefits from additional resources implemented at the level of the site.

Measures based on socio-economic targeting

Positive discrimination objective and means

Positive discrimination (and its successor, the ED policy) mainly involves assigning additional resources to identified schools; these additional resources representing approximately 0.45 per cent[23] of the total teaching budget (with an increase up to 1.35 per cent of the total budget for the ED policy). The objective is to promote educational action in these schools designed to ensure that all pupils have equal opportunity for social emancipation. These additional resources are of three types (decree dated 27 March 2002):

- human resources assigned in the form of 'teacher-periods'.[24] These resources in practice mean additional teachers. These teachers cannot, however, be granted permanent employment, given the deliberately transitory nature of positive discrimination;
- operating resources, allowing non-teaching staff to be employed (youth workers, social workers, nursery nurses, etc.), equipment to be purchased, cultural or sports activities to be organised and funded, or buildings to be fitted out;
- the modification of certain charts for converting the number of pupils into a number of supervisory staff.

The use of additional teachers is not governed by unbending rules defined on an *a priori* basis. In fundamental education, the decree dated 27 March 2002 nevertheless specifies that these additional human resources must be used 'in particular to implement differentiated learning' (Article 8, 3°).

It is a little more verbose with regard to secondary education, for which it indicates that the additional supervision must be assigned

> in particular when implementing differentiated learning, when making small groups, when organising special courses for pupils who do not speak French, for the prevention of violence, the prevention of dropping-out, remedial classes. . . .

(Article 11, 2°)

In reality, while the procedure for identifying potential schools that will benefit from the measures is automatic, the assignment of additional means is subject to the introduction and approval of a positive discrimination action project for each school. In other words, while schools do not need to do anything in order to be identified, they must deliver a project if they want to receive additional resources. An action project must therefore be introduced each year. It must include a maximum of three parts, each one specifying an objective to be attained, presenting the concrete actions under consideration over a period of three years, and explaining how the extra budget is assigned and broken down.

The action project approval procedure differs according to the level of teaching. In fundamental education, it is carried out by a 'local commission', released from the segmentation of teaching in networks. In secondary education, the distribution of resources is performed within the teaching networks, but is subject to approval by the government and a central 'positive discrimination commission'. This distribution of resources within the networks may open the door to distributing resources in a way not in keeping with the initial objectives.

To offer a complete picture of socio-economic targeting, and although this measure does not, in our opinion, really come within the scope of the definition of the priority education policies adopted, mention should also be made of the differentiation policy for school funding. This process was set up in 2004 and relates only to allocations that schools receive to cover their various expenditures, in other words their operating resources. It involves using a continuous mathematical formula weighting the assignment of these allocations to the schools according to their average socio-economic index.[25]

What action?

Few scientific studies have attempted to describe the types of action carried out, or teaching practices used, in positive discrimination schools. We are in the context of an educational quasi-market founded on the principle of pedagogical freedom, the consequence of which is little control over results, little control over method, and teaching staff that are unaccountable[26] for their actions and not very inclined to be evaluated. So it is difficult to know what action has been undertaken in the classroom and to describe or categorise it, not to mention evaluate it. Rey and his colleagues (Coche *et al.*, 2006) may, however, be quoted here. With a view to locating in primary school education those teaching practices that encourage the success of pupils from disadvantaged backgrounds, they studied classes in positive discrimination schools. The aim of this research and the sampling performed do not make it possible to draw any conclusions on the teaching practices being used in positive discrimination schools. T.-M. Bouchat and her colleagues (2005) described the action projects and teaching practices in 12 fundamental positive discrimination schools on the basis of discussions with head teachers. Although most agree that the resources are insufficient and often inadequately assigned, the researchers note certain constant features in the projects:

- remedial work, leading to smaller class sizes, certain classes split into two or 'needs groups';
- social assistance and mediation with the families;
- cultural awakening through excursions;
- the purchase of books and computer equipment.

Among the teaching practices used, they mention work in cycles,[27] classes grouped together, teachers who 'go up' a level with their class, projects and excursions, the organisation of 'needs groups' according to pupils' difficulties, discussion between teachers or meeting the families in school.

Issues surrounding the definition of the socio-economic index

In the French Community of Belgium, the positive discrimination policy refuses any ethnic or linguistic targeting: there are other types of targeted policies that deal with the specific needs of these populations.[28]

In the definition of the socio-economic index used within the framework of positive discrimination, taking into account variables referring to nationality is the subject of much debate. These variables were actually deliberately ruled out, both by the legislator and by the inter-university team in charge of calculating the index (Demeuse *et al.*, 1999). When thinking first began on the variables to be taken into account, it was shown that for an equivalent income level, foreigners of various nationalities do not succeed any less than Belgians (Ouali & Réa, 1994, quoted by Demeuse, 2002), and that while the children of certain nationalities are more prone to educational failure, it is often because they are on average from a less favourable socio-economic status. In addition, there are many nationalities in the French-speaking area of Belgium, in which great economic as well as linguistic and cultural differences exist. From a political point of view, the question of nationality has also been set aside, in order to avoid moral condemnation of populations of immigrant origin, that is not to create 'natural' and final categorisation of groups encountering school difficulties *de facto*. The proportion of pupils of immigrant origin attending a school site is nevertheless an indicator chosen as a *detrimental factor* for the site, and may be used in determining sites with priority positive discrimination.

The scientific arguments against taking into account migratory origin in setting up a priority education policy are, at the present time, disputed by researchers drawing on the model used in the Flemish Community of Belgium (Jacobs, Réa & Hanquinet, 2007). These researchers, by counting out the 'socio-economic status' factor of pupils' results provided by the PISA 2003 study, observe that pupils of immigrant origin still obtain lower scores than other pupils. They therefore argue in favour of policies explicitly targeting pupils of immigrant origin. But the results of this study and their interpretation are far from enjoying unanimous backing (Hirtt, 2007).

Measures based on linguistic and/or ethnic targeting

During the 2004–2005 school year compulsory education in French-speaking Belgium took in a little over 10 per cent of pupils of foreign nationality. Aside from positive discrimination, various structures have been organised to allow these pupils, newly arrived in French-speaking Belgium, and pupils whose native tongue is not French to join the French-speaking Belgian education system to achieve the goals pursued by the 'Missions' decree.

The 'bridge class' (*classes-passerelles*) measure, adopted in 2001 to counter the difficulties encountered by schools located near refugee candidate centres, was set up to meet the particular needs of newly arrived pupils, or, in other words, refugees or refugee candidates.[29] The creation of the 'bridge class' structure depends on the number of these pupils within a school. The pupils concerned are grouped together with their pairs and benefit from special teaching for a limited time period, before joining a class corresponding to their level. This structure may be organised only in certain schools, mainly if they are located near a candidate refugee centre.[30] The fact that the bridge classes are organised within the schools themselves and not in the centres for refugee candidates, and the short amount of time actually spent by the pupils in this system, show a conception of equity towards these children that is like equal access, but which first puts them through a 'passageway', to make effective access easier.

A decree dated 14 June 2001 specifies the competencies aimed at in a bridge class:

- everything that contributes to meeting the general objectives defined (by the Missions decree);
- intensive learning of French for those who do not have a sufficient command of this language;
- suitable remedial training so that the pupil can go back into the appropriate level of studies as soon as possible.

In order to achieve these goals, schools that organise a bridge class receive a little more than the equivalent of one additional teacher. They must submit a report showing that they are really using these additional resources, in particular by means of qualitative and quantitative evaluation of what they are doing towards helping newly arrived pupils to integrate and what guidance they are providing. Learning French is the main activity carried out in the bridge class. These 'French as a second language' courses do not meet with any particular need and do not really correspond to learning French as a foreign language, or to mother-tongue French lessons either. They have no particular curriculum, nor any specified methods. Teachers may, however, take a course in teaching French as a second language organised by the in-service training institute (IFC).[31]

The courses for adapting to the language of teaching (ALE) are based on the same idea, but unlike the bridge class, they involve integrating the pupil directly into a class corresponding to their school level, with special language support. This can be organised in each primary school that has at least ten pupils of foreign nationality (or Belgians of foreign origin) who have no command of the language in which lessons are taught. This course is entrusted to a class teacher specialised in helping pupils to adapt in this way. According to the decree dated 13 July 1998, the Government is responsible for evaluating the relevance of this measure every two years.

Finally, in the French Community there is a policy targeting pupils of immigrant origin, but which is not compensatory in nature: the *language and culture of origin* (LCO) programme, organised by partnership charters signed with Greece, Italy, Morocco, Portugal and Turkey. It allows volunteer schools to host one or more teachers from these countries, with the aim of encouraging children of immigrant origin to integrate into society while safeguarding their original identity, and of helping all pupils to be more receptive to other cultures (the French Community of Belgium, 2007). The programme makes provision for organising lessons in the language and culture of origin, outside school hours and only for the pupils concerned, and also intercultural courses to help all pupils in the class, whether or not they are from the country concerned, to become more receptive to the culture of origin.

What is known about the effects of these policies?

The quasi-market educational situation and the principle of freedom of teaching, as implemented in French-speaking Belgium, make it difficult, at the present time, to study the effects of the priority education policies. We have only scant information on teaching practices, and there are no outside evaluations relating to all the schools and how they teach. As we are not able to come to a rigorously scientific conclusion about the effects of these practices, we will restrict our conclusions, in this section, to identifying the features of the positive discrimination schools, without being able to allocate them to particular teaching practices.

External, non-certifying evaluations in primary and secondary education make it possible to compare the performances of pupils between positive discrimination schools and the other schools in an overall way. Such a descriptive comparison, taking only this variable into account, was carried out by a working group within the general piloting department of the education system (Ministry of the French Community, 2007). In the second year of general secondary education, the results are scarcely encouraging: pupils in positive discrimination schools do less well in the test, with an average score of 50 per cent, than the other pupils, who on average score 59 per cent. But simply comparing these results from the standpoint of whether the pupil does or does not benefit from positive discrimination does not really make it possible to understand the effectiveness of the measure, since it does not take account the influence of related variables such as the social background of the pupils, and therefore does not allow any *ceteris paribus* reasoning.

Evaluations not attempting to study priority education policies can be used to provide another type of answer, albeit one that is not very subtle: in spite of the priority education policies in force in the French Community of Belgium, the ideals of equality of results and equality of social emancipation are a long way from being realised. The 2003 PISA study still shows that the French Community of Belgium has some of the largest variations in results between privileged and underprivileged pupils (Baye *et al.*, 2004). However, it is difficult to determine to what extent, if at all, priority education policies are reducing these variations.

Instructions for following up and evaluating positive discrimination do, nevertheless, exist. The decrees dated 30 July 1998 and 27 March 2002 created a Commission for positive discrimination, responsible, *inter alia*, for giving recommendations on the implementation of the positive discrimination policy and co-ordinating a three-yearly evaluation plan starting in 2003. The first governmental decree setting up such an evaluation plan is dated 9 June 2004 and gives the following objectives:

- Analyse the impact of the positive discrimination policies on pupils' school careers and results.
- Evaluate the effects these policies have on the image of the schools, the transfer of school populations and the effects on the teaching profession.
- Analyse the process of implementing the projects.
- Examine how the organisations for supervising and assisting positive discrimination work.
- Evaluate the means by which resources are allocated.

Within the framework of this plan, a research report was submitted by T.-M. Bouchat and her colleagues (2005). Their aim was to check the hypothesis that positive discrimination schools are morally condemned by studying school mobility in fundamental education. Many observers in the French-speaking Belgian education system in fact fear that the positive discrimination measure leads to condemnation of the schools that benefit from it, or gives them the image of schools specialised in handling difficult situations. This condemnation of positive discrimination schools could lead other schools to offload their responsibility with regard to the students in difficulty onto them, which would exacerbate school segregation still further.

In fundamental education, at any rate, the results obtained by analysis of the movements of pupils between schools do not seem to confirm the researchers' initial assumption. Firstly, most movement observed between positive discrimination schools and the others takes place between schools close to the threshold at which resources are allocated, i.e. between underprivileged schools. Secondly, the number of pupils moving from positive discrimination schools to other types is not inconsiderable. This observation, in conjunction with the fact that the positive discrimination schools are an important port of entry for non-Europeans, may lead them to be seen as a kind of springboard. The question may consequently be asked as to whether this function taken on by the positive discriminations measure really corresponds to its main mission. The authors can nevertheless conclude from their observations that assigning the positive discrimination label to a school seems less to influence parental strategies than other indicators, such as the visible characteristics of the public or the reputation of the school. They observe, finally, that positive discrimination schools provide a significant way of moving towards specialised education. This observation confirms still further the close link between socio-economic background and the move into this type of education.

Other research was centred on how schools are identified for being awarded positive discrimination status by analysing the situation of those schools not on the list but which believe that they should be given additional resources. The results of a study undertaken by M. Demeuse and his colleagues (2006) show firstly the weaknesses of automatic identification by means of the district of origin of the pupils. It appears that the population of the schools studied comes from non-homogeneous districts and does not disperse in a random way throughout the districts, but is concentrated mainly in certain streets. However, this observation runs up against the absence of statistical data at a level lower than that of the district and that can be used to identify schools benefiting from positive discrimination status. As in the study by T.-M. Bouchat *et al.* (2005), this study calls for thinking to be continued as to how resources can be allocated on the basis of a continuous function and not on that of the current dichotomous mechanism.

The study by M. Demeuse *et al.* also looks at formalising new objective indicators in decisions regarding additional schools being listed as having positive discrimination status. The conclusions of this study recommend taking into account pupils' mobility and absenteeism, and the internal and external backwardness[32] of the schools. In this way, it could be considered that a school in which enrolments are late, in which absenteeism is high and in which most pupils are already lagging behind those in other schools, should be able to benefit from additional resources. Taking these last two indicators into account raises several questions, however. Should schools where pupils are often absent be 'rewarded'? Should a financial advantage be awarded to schools taking in pupils who are already lagging behind those in other schools without penalising the latter schools, at the risk of having selective schools offload their students in difficulty to other schools that would be 'paid' to look after them?

It will be seen that one of the most important problems facing the education system of the French Community is the large amount of segregation that remains within it. The government is well aware of this problem, and, via the Contract for the school published in 2005, has shown itself determined to come to grips with it. The priority education policies currently in force do not solve this problem. It will be noted on this subject that they are designed with a view to compensate for, and not to fight against, segregation. M. Demeuse (2002) also shows that groups of pupils within schools may exist, such as level classes or separation between courses. In the same way, the large degree of educational mobility in the French Community remains a factor leading to segregation, and makes it difficult to draw up reliable, up-to-date statistics for allocating additional resources. Little is in fact currently known about the specific impact that the positive discrimination policy may have had on educational segregation.

Flemish Community

Despite more than 25 years of separation between the education systems of the language communities, many similarities persist, even in recent measures aimed at addressing educational priority objectives. We will not, therefore, discuss all the primary education policy (PEP) measures of the Flemish Government in depth. Let us just mention, for the sake of completeness, measures such as 'bridging classes', Dutch as a second language courses, education in the mother tongue and home culture for immigrants, or inclusive education for children with special needs, without entering into a detailed analysis. In what follows, we will discuss the key programmes that have been successively introduced since the late 1980s.

PEP for children from an immigrant background

The first measure relating to PEPs in Flanders dates back to 1989, when *educational priority areas* were established in the Province of Limburg, in a context of economic restructuring. As the coal mining industry went bankrupt and the government decided to stop subsidising it, a 'social investment trust' was created, whose remit was to help the region remedy the social consequences of the closure. One of the priorities of the trust was to raise the educational attainment of children in five municipalities with a high concentration of immigrant workers (most of whom were employed in the coal mines).

At the level of the Flemish Community, a more generic *Priority Education Policy* came into effect in 1991. This policy was targeted at pupils from (relatively disadvantaged) immigrant families[33] across Flanders, in primary and secondary education. Schools were granted additional funding for each target group pupil beyond a minimum threshold, provided they could clearly indicate in a utilisation plan how they intended to spend these resources. Three broad priorities were prescribed:

- the pupils' command of the Dutch language;
- prevention and remediation of learning and developmental problems;
- involving parents in the education process, for example through school community action.

A scientific evaluation of the PEPs for immigrants started after two years of operation (Vanhoren *et al.*, 1995). In this evaluation, the critical success factors and the initial effects on the learning progress of the target group were investigated.

Only in the third year of operation was significant progress observed in the *implementation* of the innovations. With the increasing availability of didactic materials and experience in the schools, the process had acquired its own momentum and in most of the schools innovations were being implemented in all three fields of activity. At all educational levels the 'command of the language' priority turned out to be the most fully developed field of action. One of the reasons for this was the fact that its importance was accepted by all parties and that specific materials had been made available for it. Further, intensive support by an external expert, who at the same time was accepted by the school team, appeared to be of key importance in the introduction and implementation of innovations. Finally, a well-functioning core team of teachers operated as a motor for co-ordinating innovations, transferring them to the entire school level and keeping them going.

The *effects of PEPs on educational performance* have been checked only for the regular primary education system (Schrijvers *et al.*, 2002). This was done by testing the language and arithmetic skills of some 1500 PEP and non-PEP pupils at different points during the second/third and fourth/fifth grades, respectively. From a methodological point of view, this approach cannot be considered very valid, as no comparison could be made with the performance gap(s) before the implementation of PEPs. Nevertheless, the evaluation pointed out that the performance gap between the native and immigrant pupils increased steadily in the fourth grade compared with the second grade. Here, even the pupils from Southern Europe no longer scored significantly better than the North African pupils. Regression analysis was then used to check whether significant differences in progression could be observed between PEP and non-PEP schools. The results were negative.[34] Depending on the test applied or the study year, the effects of the implementation characteristics studied (implementation level of the different fields of intervention) varied in different directions.

Extended Care

In 1993 a legal framework for Extended Care was introduced into the primary education system. Under certain conditions, this policy enabled schools to obtain extra staff and resources to develop an educational approach geared to the specific needs of children (poor and non-poor, native as well as immigrant) with 'social, emotional and learning problems'. These funds must be used for additional educational staff and activities in the transition period from nursery (mainly third year) to primary school (first year).

Despite criticism about the vague definition of target groups, practice focused mainly on pupils from underprivileged families. After five years of operation, the Department of Education also imposed some precise socio-economic criteria to define the target group: children with poorly educated mothers, children from jobless households and/or from single-parent families. Schools could submit action plans for the implementation of four objectives:

- at the level of school organisation: broadening the range of materials and activities available to the pupils and developing multidisciplinary consultation;
- at the level of the class: working on differentiation and individualisation;
- introduction of a pupil monitoring system;
- developing support for developmentally endangered children and children with socio-emotional problems.

Evaluation of the Extended Care practice in schools has yielded mixed findings. Bollens *et al.* (1998) found a significant positive effect of the number of teacher-hours spent on Extended Care on learning progress in the first two grades of primary school. However, it also appeared that schools were now able to detect learning problems earlier, but were unable fully to prevent or remedy such problems: the proportion of children referred to special education increased (and has kept increasing until today), despite the fact that the reduction of referrals was among the primary objectives of Extended Care (Ruelens *et al.*, 2001; Van Heddegem, Douterlungne & Van de Velde, 2003). This suggests that the additional resources were insufficient to remedy problems. Moreover, a mere quantitative investment may yield unsatisfactory results if it is not accompanied with better (initial as well as in-service) training of teachers.

All in all, both PEP and Extended Care failed to reduce educational disadvantage in any substantial way. They seem to have contributed to a better understanding of problems, without resolving them across the board. This is quite understandable, taking into account that the budget invested in both policy strands together did not exceed 1 per cent of the overall education budget.

The Equal Educational Opportunities Act

As from 2002, PEP and Extended Care were merged into a single, more ambitious framework, which is still operational today. The new law introduced several innovations.

First of all, the targeting of resources is now based on *objective and measurable criteria*:[35] the number of poorly educated mothers, jobless households, travelling households, children placed in institutional or foster care, and non-Dutch speaking households.[36] All these criteria refer to the socioeconomic background of pupils, which means a shift of emphasis to a more social and preventive approach. For this purpose, an extensive registration and control system has been developed at pupil level.

In order to minimise the paperwork, the needs of schools are measured every *three years* and the additional funding is kept constant for the same period. Moreover, the specific EEO funding has been increased to 4 per cent in basic education.[37]

The third innovation in EEO is the *increased autonomy* of schools in setting their own priorities. Schools are now supposed to analyse the context at the start of every three-year cycle, and to evaluate their own progress, using their own criteria, during the cycle. The inspectorate mainly evaluates the effects by the end of the third year and thus establishes whether schools are allowed to apply for further extra funding in the next period. Whereas a 'menu' of recommended actions is still provided by the Government, schools are given more degrees of freedom as they need to select one of three priority fields, supplemented with their own priorities. The three priorities put forward by the law include: preventing and remedying learning/behavioural problems; developing language skills; and boosting pupils' self-confidence and independence in determining their educational career.

The financial weighting of students occurs as follows: pupils who meet the criteria listed above are given an additional weighting which varies between 0.4 and 1.2, depending on the nature and cumulation of indicators of disadvantage. Figures 3.2 and 3.3 give an idea of the actual funding per pupil in primary and secondary schools, respectively – in relation to the proportion of target group pupils within the school population.

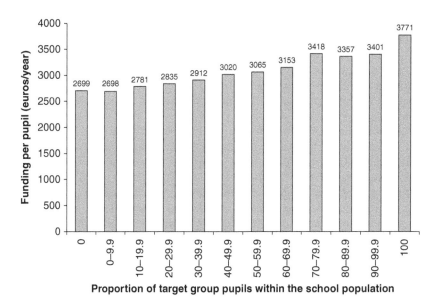

Figure 3.2 Public funding per pupil (€/year) in Flemish primary education, school year 2007–2008, by share of EEO target group
Source: Department of Education.

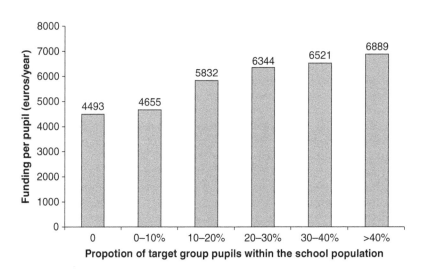

Figure 3.3 Public funding per pupil (€/year) in Flemish secondary education, school year 2007–2008, by share of EEO target group
Source: Department of Education.

Several qualifications must be borne in mind in interpreting these figures. To begin with, the share of the target group is seldom higher than 60 per cent in primary schools. This means that a concentration school (with 50–60 per cent disadvantaged pupils) gets, on average, 14 per cent more per pupil than a 'white' school.[38] There is a general consensus that this does not fully compensate for the additional 'burden' on the former type of school.

Secondly, the actual differences in funding are only partly driven by the EEO funding as such. This is most flagrant in (upper) secondary education, where the EEO budget is minimal compared with regular subsidies. The main reason why Figure 3.3 shows an increasing pattern is the underlying correlation between social background and educational career paths: most disadvantaged students end up in vocational schools, which benefit from higher teacher–student ratios. It is unclear to what extent these higher ratios are justified by technical or organisational arguments (such as the need to split into smaller groups for practical subjects). Some insiders believe that the better staffing in vocational schools can also be seen as a PEP measure – *'avant la lettre'*. Whatever the explanation may be, the present redistribution effect appears to be more intimately connected with social stratification mechanisms (tracking of disadvantaged students to vocational schools) than with the proper social background of students. In fact, this means that disadvantaged students are better funded only if they opt for vocational careers – which obviously goes against the spirit of PEP.

After five years of operation (2002–2007), broadly speaking, all parties tend to agree that the EEO Act has contributed to further improvements in the professionalism of teachers and the schools' capacity to manage their social policy. However, some problems have been identified that motivate further reforms.

First of all, there is some dissatisfaction about the paperwork involved in assessing the needs of schools. A *dilemma between target effectiveness and complexity* characterises the present legislation. Evaluation research had demonstrated that, even when resources are aggregated at the school level, the use of geographical or 'approximate' indicators resulted in a substantial margin of error in targeting resources (Bollens *et al.*, 1998).[39] This explains why a rather complex individual registration system has been developed. Nevertheless, some parents have criticised the intrusive nature of the questionnaires concerning their social background. At the same time, schools complain about the burden of the paperwork, and the ministry is suspicious about the fraud sensitiveness of the system, as the number of subsidised students tends to increase. An expert group is currently examining whether individual electronic records owned by the government, such as census data or data on students benefiting from student grants, can yield similar information with the same degree of precision and without necessitating extensive paperwork. The Department of Education should be able to link existing electronic information concerning individual students and their parents to the school attended by each student.

One of the key issues in defining the target group(s) relates to *ethnicity*. Given the wide gap in educational performance between native and immigrant youth, it is essential to target EP funding at the latter (second-generation Moroccan and Turkish youth in particular). However, unlike countries such as the United Kingdom, Belgium has no tradition of registering information about citizens' ethnic background. Moreover, in a climate of fairly strong xenophobia, the Flemish Government is reluctant to prioritise immigrants. Language would be a straightforward alternative, but this is not evident in a trilingual country.[40] Additional subsidies for non-Dutch speaking students would also favour high-socio-economic status (SES), French-speaking Belgian students.[41] This issue is as yet unsettled. Research has emphasised the necessity of specific measures for children with an immigrant background, as their underachievement can not be explained by socio-economic characteristics alone (Hirtt, 2006).

Most importantly, experts and policy makers agree that a *more powerful redistribution* is needed in the funding per pupil, in order to make a decisive impact on equal educational opportunities. Not only should more weight be given to SES criteria, but the funding should also be (partly) disconnected from the present tracking system in secondary education: disadvantaged students should also be better subsidised if they manage to remain in general or technical education. In other words, a shift needs to be made from study field-related criteria to student-related criteria.

Towards a structural reform

The ambition of the present Flemish Government is to carry through such a structural reform, starting gradually from 2008, in which pupil characteristics were awarded greater weighting in the distribution of resources among schools. The objectives of the reform are twofold: firstly, subsidies differentiated by social background aim to compensate for the higher cost involved in teaching students from lower socio-economic strata. In this way, the latter will receive better-quality education and will hopefully be able to overcome social obstacles. And secondly, the differentiated funding should make low-SES students more attractive to schools, and thus attenuate the selectivity of schools in the 'quasi-market' environment that characterises the Belgian educational landscape.

The present context is quite favourable for such a reform, as overall subsidies per pupil are on the increase: in such a context, it is politically more feasible to redistribute resources.

Not only will the system become more redistributive, according to the social mix within schools, but the redistribution will also be mainstreamed, as the EEO funding will no longer be separated from the regular funding mechanisms. Apart from the overall budget increase, some shifts will also be operated to attenuate the 'tracking' of students (by reducing the differences between general, technical and vocational education) and to encourage economies of scale in secondary education. Public and private schools will also be funded on an equal footing. It goes without saying that such a comprehensive reform involves considerable negotiation and strategic analysis.

Conclusions and perspectives

Throughout this chapter, we have looked at the similarities and the differences in priority education policies of two of the three Belgian education systems. The policies set up on both the Dutch-speaking and the French-speaking sides try mainly to counter the major inequalities that are largely due to the educational quasi-market. While policies such as 'positive discrimination' in the French Community and the *Equal opportunity in education* in the Flemish Community consist above all of a modulated assignment of resources to the schools, they are different in the way they target pupils.

In keeping with research results (Bollens *et al.*, 1998), the Flemish Community chose direct, but voluntary, data collection in the schools, but is confronted today with problems of the protection of private life, administrative complexity and sensitivity to fraud. The French Community, also basing its actions on research results (Demeuse, 1996; Demeuse & Monseur, 1999), opted for indirect data collection based on pupils' place of residence, and has not therefore encountered the same problems as the Flemish community. But this indirect measurement poses problems of fine targeting in certain districts, mainly in the urban environment.

On a more basic level, the French and Flemish communities are notably different in the way they define the population targeted by priority education policies. On the one hand, in the French Community, action taken to deal with a linguistic disadvantage is clearly separated from action on a socio-economic disadvantage, even though the various policies may relate to the same schools. Taking into account information on nationality or the language spoken at home is systematically ignored, both by researchers and decision makers, in regard to the positive discrimination policy. In contrast, in the Flemish Community, this information concerning language is included in the identification of populations targeted by the *Equal opportunity in education* policy. In this context, while researchers have also identified ethnically based target groups (Turkish and Moroccan second-generation immigrants) for which additional resources should be provided, the decision makers continue to have reserves with regard to priority measures likely to worsen the climate of xenophobia reigning in the north of the country.

The Belgian educational quasi-markets are the cause of inequalities, and also create difficulty in any serious evaluation of the effects of priority education policies. In the French Community, in the absence of any currently usable data on external evaluations, the effectiveness of the positive discrimination measures cannot truly be estimated. As for their effects as a system, in particular the fear that the schools benefiting from the measure would be condemned, these have been tempered in the case of fundamental education (Bouchat *et al.*, 2005). In the Flemish Community, the effects of *Priority teaching* and *Extended care* have been evaluated and found wanting. The *Equal opportunity in education* policy, with its objective targeting, larger budget and autonomy granted to the schools, aims to be more ambitious. It is nonetheless difficult to evaluate its effects, firstly because additional subsidies are associated with an unfavourable context in the targeted schools and therefore their net effect cannot really be isolated. Secondly, since the additional funding is identical in all schools with an identical public (within the same community), it is almost impossible to define a control group that would be an exception to the rule. The main question posed by priority education policies in Belgium is that of educational segregation. In an educational quasi-market characterised by a system of courses that are not perceived as being of equal value, for a socially marked and diversely financed public, significant relegation and segregation mechanisms come into being. There is currently nothing to counter these: the priority education policies were drawn up not as an incentive for social diversity, but from a compensatory point of view. Without claiming that social diversity alone would entirely solve the problems of educational inequality, it does appear essential to take action on the segregation phenomena that accentuate them. So in both the French and the Flemish communities, the move is towards the development of policies that encourage greater social diversity by regulating the quasi-market. The question may be asked as to whether the objective of social diversity could not be attained by measures other than the additional subsidies granted as a result of the priority education policies. If need be, these more efficient (because they are less expensive) alternatives would undoubtedly deserve to be implemented first, taking into account not symptoms, but causes.

In the Flemish Community, the *Equal opportunity in education* decree also contains a ruling aimed at limiting the concentration of underprivileged people in ghetto schools. When that concentration is 10 per cent above the average for schools in the area, the school concerned can legally give priority to candidates coming from more privileged backgrounds. This ruling was revised several times since it came into effect in 2002, and it remains disputed: a thorough evaluation of its effects would be welcome.

In the French Community, two academic prospective studies[42] have been carried out in this direction, rooted in a conception of equity as equality of social realisation. The first (Delvaux *et al.*, 2005) studies the feasibility of the creation of 'school catchment areas' in which the schools could work in collaboration whatever their network, especially from the point of view of the teaching offer. It also proposes a system of collective treatment of preferences in choosing schools, in order to further regulate the quasi-market, while respecting parents' freedom of choice. The authors believe that such actions could limit the phenomenon of educational segregation and provide all pupils with equal opportunities for social realisation. The various tensions arising from these proposals do, however, make it difficult to continue along this path.

A second study (Demeuse *et al.*, 2007) considers the possibility of a way of funding schools according to a general formula for allocating resources according to needs (Ross & Levacic, 1999) based on objective indicators including socio-economic indices, but also on information of an educational nature, such as taking into account the external backwardness handled by each school.[43] Such a formula could be used to encourage schools to be less selective, while allocating additional resources to those schools in difficulty. It could also replace the dichotomous positive discrimination mechanism by a form of distribution that is modulated according to a continuous function. Nevertheless, it still runs up against certain perverse effects of incentives and penalisation in a system primarily governed by the law of the market.

Acknowledgements

We would like to thank Bernard Delvaux (UCL) for his critical reading of this text.

Notes

1. See official web site of Belgian Government: http://www.belgium.be/en/about_belgium/government/
2. As from 1989, the legislation of teaching has developed separately in the different Communities, and is implemented on the basis of decrees from the Communities which, as regards education, have the force of law. Each community has a parliament which legislates by decree, mainly for cultural matters and teaching (Beckers, 2006). The reader interested in a short presentation of the Belgian political system can consult the website of the centre for socio-political research and information: <http://www.crisp.be> (consulted on 4 July 2008).
3. Here already there is a slight difference in interpretation between the two communities: on the 18th birthday day in Flanders; at the end of the school year during which the young person reaches 18 in the French Community.
4. Secondary education is structured into three principal courses, both in the Flemish Community and in the French Community: general education, technical education and vocational training.
5. Philosophical convictions, the initial reason for this freedom of choice, weighs today less and less heavily in families' decisions.
6. Three educational networks coexist in Belgium: the Community network, organised and financed by the respective communities; the official subsidised network, organised by an organising authority (town or province) and subsidised by the relevant community; and the free subsidised network (denominational or not),

organised by a private organising authority (diocese, religious congregation, non-profit-making association) and subsidised by the relevant community.

7. The core competencies are indicated as the 'frame of reference presenting in a structured way the basic competencies to be practised until the end of thee first eight years of compulsory education and those which are to be mastered at the end of each stage of these because they are regarded as necessary for social integration and continuation of studies' (Decree 'Missions' dated 24 July 1997 in the French Community, Article 119. A similar definition is included in a Flemish decree).

8. An external certifying evaluation system at the end of primary school education was set up by decree in 2006. All schools are now required to take part since June 2009. Nevertheless it is forbidden to publish or compare results at the school level.

9. This was the term used by the government of the French community itself (Contrat pour l'École – Contract for the school, – 2005).

10. The term 'teaching' does not indicate only the act of teaching but also refers to all the parameters (work conditions, etc.) that make up the process of teaching.

11. As Carroll (1963) understands it, the means really devoted to learning are partly provided by the school (teachers, quality of teaching, quality of the teaching materials, etc.) and therefore 'changeable', and partly provided by the pupil (prerequisites, help at home, etc.), and therefore 'unchangeable' by any thing that is done to change school.

12. There is no adequate English translation of this expression ED. It approximately means 'differentiated funding', although it has a broader meaning, including pedagogical aspects.

13. The notion of district is taken to mean a statistical division of the region: 'a statistical sector, as defined by the Institut National de Statistique, in particular for general population censuses' (Demeuse, 2002, p. 219).

14. The 11 variables currently used to calculate the socio-economic index, subject to government approval, come under the following six fields (Decree dated 27 March 2002):

    – per capita income;
    – level of education;
    – unemployment rate, percentage of activity and percentage people receiving the guaranteed minimum monthly income;
    – professional activities; and
    – housing comfort.

15. According to the decree, an underprivileged district is one where (1) standards of living are low; (2) the level of unemployment is high; and (3) there is a high percentage of families receiving social welfare.

16. In the French Community of Belgium, an educational school may be made up of several distinct sites on different locations, sometimes several kilometres apart. A school is defined as a 'pre-school and/or primary or secondary teaching unit, located in one or more places, directed by the same head-teacher' whereas a site is part of a school defined as a 'building or set of buildings located at a single address…' (Decree dated 30 June 1998, Article 3).

17. The priority positive discrimination sites account for 45 per cent of pupils benefiting from positive discrimination.

18. Law dated 8 December 1992.
19. According to M. Demeuse (2002), many problems may occur throughout the socio-economic status data collection process: inaccurate answers from young pupils or parents, the informant or the person in charge of encoding overestimating his profession, poor knowledge of the nomenclatures used, etc.
20. Priority 2: lead each young person to master basic competencies.
21. Priority 9: 'no' to ghetto schools.
22. For the sake of completion, it may be mentioned that there also exists a third type of targeting: assumption of responsibility for pupils suffering from handicap, but this is does not specifically relate to priority education. In the French Community, since 1971, there has existed specialised teaching, organised in structures distinct from ordinary teaching (in special schools), and providing education for both children suffering from physical handicaps or deficiency and those suffering from intellectual deficiency. Approximately 4 per cent (4.9 per cent for primary schools, and 3.9 per cent for secondary schools) of all pupils in compulsory education attended these structures during the 2004–2005 school year (Etnic, 2006a). This figure, higher than in the other European countries (less than 3 per cent according to Eurydice, 2005), suggests that the criteria of guidance towards specialised education include a larger population.
23. This percentage is determined as follows: A is the 'teachers' pay' budget; B is the 'school subsidies' budget; C is the 'positive discrimination' budget (pay + subsidies): $C/(A + B) = 0.0045$. The 'pay' budgets include employer contributions but not pensions because these come under jurisdiction of the Federal state.
24. The teachers are paid directly by the French Community of Belgium, whatever the teaching network. For this purpose, the schools do not receive a sum of money enabling them to pay the teachers' wages, but a certain number of 'teacher-periods' representing the number of teachers to be engaged according to the number of pupils enrolled in the school. Charts exist for converting the number of pupils into the number of teacher-periods granted.
25. The average socio-economic index is not actually the only parameter weighting the assignment of allocations. It counts for 80% of the weighting, the remaining 20% depending on the size of the school, in order to compensate for the costs inherent in managing a small school.
26. The dimension of *accountability*, used in English, is far from present in the French-speaking Belgian education system. A certain change does, however, seem to be taking place, with the arrival of external evaluations, some of which lead to qualifications (decrees dated 2 June 2006).
27. The 'Missions' decree established cycles for the first eight years of compulsory schooling, seen as a teaching continuum in five cycles: the start of nursery school at age 5; from five years to the end of the second year of primary school; the third and fourth years of primary school; the fifth and sixth years of primary school; and the first two years of secondary school.
28. And yet there is the case of newly arrived pupils (see below) who obtain a score of –2.7 on a scale that ranges between –3.5 and +3.5.
29. 'Newly arrived pupils' are pupils living in the region for less than one year and who are recognised as refugees or stateless people, or who have requested such recognition; are minors accompanying a person recognised as a refugee or stateless person or who has requested such recognition; or are nationals of a developing country or a country of transition (Decree dated 14 June 2001, Article 2, 1°)

30. Schools where a bridge class can be organised must meet the following conditions:

    For the Walloon region: be located in a town where there is a candidate refuge centre, with at least eight children aged between 5 and 12 years for the primary level, or 10 children aged between 12 and 18 years for the secondary level.

    For the Brussels-Capital region, a bridge class can be created in a maximum of 14 schools in the primary sector, and a maximum of 16 schools in the secondary sector.

    Have filed a request to organise the bridge class, including a project for receiving, guiding and integrating newly arrived pupils.

31. Teachers in the French Community must follow six half-days of training a year, organised by the in-service training institute.

32. External backwardness refers to how far behind the pupil is lagging, cumulated over one or more other schools, before he/she enrolled in the school under consideration. Internal backwardness expresses how far behind the pupil is lagging within the school under consideration (Demeuse *et al.*, 2006).

33. The target group was defined on the basis of two criteria:

    – the pupil's grandmother on the mother's side did not have Belgian nationality at birth and was born outside Belgium;
    – the pupil's mother did not attend school past age 18.

34. Again, the methodology cannot be considered very orthodox, as non-EPP schools must differ from EPP schools on some points (e.g. the overall share of the target group in their student population).

35. The five criteria listed here apply to basic education and the first two grades of secondary education. More restrictive criteria (based on previous educational achievement) are used in the upper grades of secondary school. As a consequence, the impact of EEO is secondary education is much smaller.

36. The linguistic criterion applies only in combination with other criteria to determine the EEO-weight of a pupil. In practice, only pupils from immigrant families are being targeted.

37. EEO funding in (upper) secondary education has remained marginal. This is partly the result of a deliberate option to concentrate resources at the start of the school career.

38. This Dutch expression 'witte school', literally translated here, denotes schools comprising almost exclusively native middle- and upper-class pupils.

39. For this reason, unlike the French community, the socio-economic index based on pupils' district of residence had been rejected as a basis for the calculation of subsidies.

40. In addition to the Flemish and French communities, Belgium also comprises a small German-speaking community.

41. For this reason, the mother tongue of students is currently subordinated to other social criteria: in EEO funding, non-Dutch speaking pupils attract higher subsidies only if they also meet other criteria of social disadvantage.

42. Within the framework of educational policies, university teams are more and more involved in proposing prospective analyses and not simply evaluating existing situations. From this point of view, the very nature of researchers' work has been modified (Aubert-Lotarski *et al.*, 2007).
43. That is how pupils who are lagging behind in other schools are dealt with when they join the school under consideration.

Bibliography

Scientific documents

AUBERT-LOTARSKI A., DEMEUSE M., FRIANT N. & DEROBERTMASURE A. (2007). 'Conseiller le politique: des évaluations commanditées à la prospective en éducation' [Advising the politician: evaluations commissioned from educational research]. *Les Dossiers des Sciences de l'Éducation*, no. 18, pp. 121–130.

BAYE A., DEMONTY I., FAGNANT A., LA FONTAINE D., MATOUL A. & MONSEUR C. (2004). 'Les compétences des jeunes de 15 ans en Communauté française de Belgique en mathématiques, en lecture et en sciences. Résultats de l'enquête PISA 2003' [The competencies of fifteen-year olds in the French Community of Belgium. Results of the PISA 2003 survey]. *Les Cahiers du Service de pédagogie expérimentale*, no. 19–20.

BECKERS J. (2006). *Enseignant en Communauté française de Belgique: mieux comprendre le système, ses institutions et ses politiques éducatives pour mieux situer son action* [A teacher in the French Community of Belgium: gaining a better understanding of the system, its institutions and its educational policies to gain a better grasp of ones role in the system]. Brussels: De Boeck.

BJÖRKLUND A., EDIN P. A., FREDERIKSSON P. & KRUEGER A. (2006). *The market comes to education in Sweden. An analysis of Swedish school reforms during the 1990s.* New York: Russell Sage Foundation.

BOLLENS J., VAN DE VELDE V., CNUDDE V., VANOBBERGEN B., VANSIELEGHEM N., DOUTERLUNGNE M., NICAISE I. & VERHAEGHE J.-P. (1998). *Zorgverbreding in het basis- en secundair onderwijs: een zoektocht naar financieringscriteria* [Reinforced supervision in basic and secondary education: looking for funding criteria]. Louvain: HIVA/RUG, Vakgroep Onderwijskunde.

BOUCHAT T.-M., DELVAUX B. & HINDRYCKX G. (2005). *Discrimination positive et mobilité scolaire. Rapport de recherche remis à la Communauté française dans le cadre du plan d'évaluation des politiques de discrimination positive* [Positive discrimination and educational mobility. Research report delivered to the French Community in the context of the evaluation scheme for positive discrimination policies. Unpublished research report].

BRADLEY S. & TAYLOR J. (2000). *The effect of the quasi-market on the equity-efficiency trade-off in the secondary school sector.* Working Paper no. 2000/008. Lancaster: Lancaster University Management.

CARROLL J. B. (1963). 'A model of school learning'. *Teachers College Record*, 64, pp. 723–733.

COCHE F., KAHN S., ROBIN F., REY B. & GENOT P. (2006). *Pratiques pédagogiques à l'école primaire et réussite des élèves venant de milieux défavorisés* [Educational practices in the primary school and success of children from underprivileged backgrounds]. A research report available on the website of Enseignement en Communauté française de Belgique: <http://www.enseignement.be/@librairie/documents/ressources/110/rapfin_2006.pdf> (consulted on 3 July 2008).

CONSEIL DE L'ÉDUCATION ET DE LA FORMATION (CEF) (1994). *La discrimination positive, moyen de favoriser la réussite scolaire des enfants issus de milieux défavorisés* [Positive discrimination as a means for encouraging academic success in children from under-privileged backgrounds] (16 September 1994). Brussels: Communauté française de Belgique, Conseil de l'éducation et de la formation. Document available on the CEF website: <http://www.cefcfwb.be/biblio_file_get.phpPdf_id=67&df_check=> (consulted on 3 July 2008).

DELVAUX B., DEMEUSE M. & DUPRIEZ V. (2005). 'En guise de conclusion: encadrer la liberté' [By way of conclusion: managing freedom]. In M. DEMEUSE, A. BAYE, M. H. STRAETEN, J. NICAISE & A. MATOUL (éds.), *Vers une école juste et efficace. Vint-six contributions à l'analyse des systèmes d'enseignement et de formation.* [Towards fair and efficient schooling. Twenty-six contributions to the analysis of education and training systems]. Brussels: De Boeck.

DELVAUX B., DEMEUSE M., DUPRIEZ V., FAGNAN A., GUISSET C., LAFONTAINE D., MARISSAL P. & MAROY C. (2005). *Les bassins scolaires: de l'idée au projet. Propositions relatives aux domaines d'intervention, aux instances et aux territoires.* [School catchment areas: from idea to project. Proposals on scope, authorities and regions]. Research report available on the FTP server of the Institut d'administration scolaire – Université de Mons-Hainaut: <ftp://ftp.umh.ac.be/pub/ftp_inas/bassins> (consulted on 3 July 2008).

DEMEUSE M. (1996). *Mise au point d'un dispositif d'évaluation des performances « objectives » des établissements scolaires dans l'enseignement fondamental de la Communauté française* [Developing an 'objective' system for evaluating the performance of schools in basic education in the French Community]. Final report – Phase III. Liège: Université de Liège, Service de pédagogie expérimentale. Unpublished report.

DEMEUSE M. (2000). 'La politique de discrimination positive en Communauté française de Belgique: une méthode d'attribution des moyens supplémentaires basée sur des indicateurs objectifs [The positive discrimination policy in the French Community of Belgium: a method for allocating additional resources based on objective indicators]'. *Cahiers du Service de pédagogie expérimentale*, nos. 1–2, pp. 115–135.

DEMEUSE M. (2002). Analyse critique des fondements de l'attribution des moyens destinés à la politique de discrimination positive en matière d'enseignement en Communauté française de Belgique [Critical analysis of the fundamentals of allocating resources for the positive discrimination policy in the French Community of Belgium]. Doctoral thesis, psychological sciences, Liège University.

DEMEUSE M. (2005). 'La marche vers l'équité en Belgique francophone [In pursuit of equity in French-speaking Belgium]'. In M. DEMEUSE, A. BAYE, M. H. STRAETEN, J. NICAISE & A. MATOUL (éds.), *Vers une école juste et efficace. Vingt-six contributions à l'analyse des systèmes d'enseignement et de formation* [Towards fair and efficient schooling. Twenty-six contributions to the analysis of education and training systems]. Brussels: De Boeck, pp. 191–216.

DEMEUSE M., CRAHAY M. & MONSEUR C. (2001). 'Efficiency and equity'. In W. HUTMACHER, D. COCHRANE & N. BOTTANI (eds), *In pursuit of equity in education. Using international indicators to compare equity policies.* Doordrecht: Kluwer, pp. 65–91.

DEMEUSE M., CRAHAY M. & MONSEUR C. (2005). 'Efficacité et équité dans les systèmes éducatifs. Les deux faces d'une même pièce?' [Efficiency and equity in education systems. Two sides of the same coin?]. In M. DEMEUSE, A. BAYE, M. H. STRAETEN, J. NICAISE & A. MATOUL (eds.), [Towards fair and efficient schooling. Twenty-six contributions to the analysis of education and training systems]. Brussels: De Boeck Université (Economie, Société, Région), pp. 391–410.

DEMEUSE M., DEROBERTMASURE A., FRIANT N., HERREMANS T., MONSEUR C., UYTTENDAELE S. & VERDALE N. (2007). Étude exploratoire sur la mise en œuvre de nouvelles mesures visant à lutter contre les phénomènes de ségrégation scolaire et d'inéquité au sein du système éducatif de la Communauté française de Belgique [Exploratory study on implementing new measures in the fight against educational segregation and inequity within the education system of the French Community of Belgium]. Brussels: Gouvernement de la Communauté française de Belgique (unpublished research report).

DEMEUSE M. & LAFONTAINE D. (2005). 'L'orientation scolaire en Communauté française de Belgique' [School guidance in the French Community of Belgium]. *Revue internationale d'éducation de Sèvres*, no. 38, pp. 35–51.

DEMEUSE M., LAFONTAINE D. & STRAETEN D. (2005). 'Parcours scolaire et inégalités de résultats' [School career and unequal results]. In M. DEMEUSE, A. BAYE, M. H. STRAETEN, J. NICAISE, A. MATOUL (eds), *Vers une école juste et efficace. 26 contributions sur les systèmes d'enseignement et de formation* [Towards fair and efficient schooling. Twenty-six contributions to the analysis of education and training systems]. Brussels: De Boeck Université (Economie, Société, Région), pp. 259–273.

DEMEUSE M. & MONSEUR C. (1999). 'Analyse critique des indicateurs déterminant l'attribution des moyens destinés à la politique de discrimination positive en Communauté française de Belgique' [Critical analysis of the indicators determining the allocation of resources for the positive discrimination policy in the French Community of Belgium]. *Mesure et Évaluation en Éducation*, 22, nos. 2–3, pp. 97–127.

DEMEUSE M., MONSEUR C., COLLARD A., MARISSAL P., VAN HAMME G. & DELVAUX B. (1999). *La détermination des quartiers devant être pris en compte pour l'établissement de la liste des établissements et implantations à discrimination positive* [Determining the districts to be taken into consideration in drawing up the list of positive discrimination establishments and sites]. Inter-university study commissioned by the Ministry of the French Community of Belgium in the framework of the decree dated 30 June 1998 aiming to ensure that all pupils have equal opportunity for social emancipation, especially for the implementation of positive discrimination measures. Unpublished report delivered to the government of the French Community of Belgium.

DEMEUSE M. & NICAISE J. (2005). 'Discriminations et actions positives, politiques d'éducation prioritaire...vers une rupture de l'égalité formelle en éducation' [Discrimination and positive action, priority education policies...towards a break with formal equality in education]. In M. DEMEUSE, A. BAYE, M. H. STRAETEN, J. NICAISE & A. MATOUL (eds), *Vers une école juste et efficace. Vingt-six contributions à l'analyse des systèmes d'enseignement et de formation* [Towards fair and efficient schooling. Twenty-six contributions to the analysis of education and training systems]. Brussels: De Boeck, pp. 233–257.

DEMEUSE M. *et al.* (2006). 'Behind positive discrimination in the French Community of Belgium: central criteria vs. local actions'. In L. MORENO HERRERA, G. JONES & J. RANTALA (eds.), *Enacting equity in education: Towards a comparison of equitable practices in different European local contexts.* Helsinki: Research Center for Social Studies in Education – University of Helsinki.

DE WINTER L., DIERYNCK R., GOMMERS E., MEEUSEN S., VAN DE VELDE J., VERHESSCHEN P., VAN DEN BERGHE R. & SMEYERS P. (1997). *OVGB: een uniek samenspel met vele partners. Evaluatie van het onderwijsvoorrangsgebiedenbeleid in Limburg* [Priority education zone policy: co-ordination of multiple partners. Evaluating priority education zones in Limbourg]. Louvain: Centrum voor Onderwijsbeleid en – vernieuwing, Université catholique de Louvain.

DUPRIEZ V. & DUMAY X. (2006). 'Élèves en difficulté d'apprentissage: parcours et environnements éducatifs différenciés en fonction des structures scolaires' [Pupils with learning difficulties: educational careers and environments differentiated according to school structures]. *Les Cahiers de la recherche en éducation et formation*, no. 51.

DUPRIEZ V. & VANDENBERGHE V. (2004). 'L'école en Communauté française de Belgique: de quelle inégalité parlons-nous?' [Schooling in the French Community of Belgium: what kind of inequality are we talking about?]. *Les Cahiers de recherche en éducation et formation*, no. 27.

ETNIC (Entreprise des technologies nouvelles de l'information et de la communication) (2006a). *Statistiques de l'enseignement de plein exercice et de promotion sociale (2005–2006)* [Statistics on full time and in-service education (2005–2006)]. Document available on the ETNIC website: <http://www.statistiques.cfwb.be/publicationsDetails.php> (consulted on 3 July 2008).

ETNIC (2006b). *Les indicateurs de l'enseignement, numéro 1, édition 2006* [Indicators of Education, number 1, 2006]. Electronic document available on the website of Enseignement en Communauté française de Belgique: <http://www.enseignement.be/prof/dossiers/indicateurs/index.asp> (consulted on 3 July 2008).

EURYDICE (2004). *L'intégration scolaire des enfants immigrants en Europe. Belgique-Communauté française* [Educational integration of immigrant children in Europe]. Electronic document available on the Euridyce website: <http://www.eurydice.org/ressources/eurydice/zip/0_integral/044FR.zip> (consulted on 3 July2008).

EURYDICE (2005). *Chiffres clés de l'éducation en Europe 2005* [Key figures for education in Europe 2005]. Luxembourg: Office des publications officielles des Communautés européennes.

GRISAY A. (1984). 'Quels indicateurs pour quelle réduction des inégalités scolaires?' [What indicators for what reduction in educational inequality?]. *Revue de la Direction générale de l'organisation des études (Brussels)*, no. 9, pp. 3–14.

GROOTAERS D. (1998). *Histoire de l'enseignement en Belgique* [A history of teaching in Belgium]. Brussels: Éditions du Centre de recherche et d'information sociopolitiques (CRISP).

HIRTT N. (2002), 'Marchés scolaires, filières, sous-financement: la catastrophe scolaire belge' [Educational markets, courses of study, under-funding: the Belgian educational catastrophe]. *L'École Démocratique*, no. 9.

HIRTT N. (2006). *PISA 2003 et les mauvais résultats des élèves issus de l'immigration en Belgique. Handicap culturel, mauvaise intégration, ou ségrégation sociale?* [PISA 2003 and the poor results obtained by children from immigrant backgrounds. Cultural handicap, poor integration or social segregation?] Brussels: Aped.

HIRTT N. (2007). *Performances scolaires des élèves allochtones et origine sociale: notes marginales auprès du rapport de la Fondation Roi Baudouin* [Academic performance of native-origin pupils and social origin: marginal notes to the report by the Fondation Roi Baudoin]. Electronic document available on the Aped website: <http://www.ecoledemocratique.org/IMG/pdf/Discussion_FRB.pdf> (consulted on 3 July 2008).

JACOBS D., RÉA A. & HANQUINET L. (2007). *Performances des élèves issus de l'immigration en Belgique selon l'étude PISA. Une comparaison entre la Communauté française et la Communauté flamande* [Performance of children from immigrant backgrounds in Belgium according to the PISA study. A comparison between the French Community and the Flemish Community]. Electronic document available on the

Fondation Roi Baudouin website: <http://www.kbs-frb.be/uploadedFiles/KBS-FRB/Files/FR/PUB_1665_E&JA_PisaFr.pdf> (consulted on 3 July 2008).

MAROY C. & DELVAUX B. (2006). 'Multirégulation et logique de quasi-marché: le bassin de Charleroi en Belgique' [Multi-regulation and the quasi-market logic: the Charleroi region in Belgium]. In C. MAROY (ed.), *École, régulation et marché: une comparaison de six espaces scolaires locaux en Europe*. Paris: Presses universitaires de France, pp. 315–351.

MINISTÈRE DE LA COMMUNAUTÉ FRANÇAISE: SERVICE GÉNÉRAL DU PILOTAGE DU SYSTÈME ÉDUCATIF (2007). *Évaluation externe non certificative, deuxième année de l'enseignement secondaire: lecture et production d'écrit: résultats et commentaires* [Non-certifying outside evaluation, year two of the secondary school: reading and writing: results and comments]. Electronic document available on the website of the Ministry of the French Community of Belgium: <http://www.enseignement.be/@librairie/documents/outileval/evalext/2007_2S-RC.pdf> (consulted on 3 July 2008).

ROSS K. N. (1983). *Social area indicators of educational need*. Hawthorn (Victoria): Australian Council for Educational Research.

ROSS K. N. & LEVACIC R. (1999). *Needs-based resource allocation in education*. Paris: International Institute for Educational Planning.

RUELENS L., DEHANDSCHUTTER R., GHESQUIÈRE P. & DOUTERLUNGNE M. (2001). *Op de wip. De overgang van het gewoon naar het buitengewoon basisonderwijs: analyse van de verwijzingspraktijk in Centra voor Leerlingenbegeleiding* [The bird on the branch. Transitions from basic education to specialised education: analysis of reference practices in pupil support centres]. Louvain: HIVA.

SCHRIJVERS E., HILLEWAERE K., VAN DE VELDE V. & VERLOT M. (2002). *Evaluatieonderzoek van het onderwijsvoorrangsbeleid* [Research-evaluation of the priority education policy]. Louvain: HIVA.

VAN HAECHT A. (1985). *L'enseignement rénové de l'origine à l'éclipse* [Renovated education from its beginnings to its eclipse]. Brussels: Éditions de l'université de Bruxelles.

VANDENBERGHE V. (1996). *Functioning and Regulation of Eductional Quasi-Markets*. Louvain-la-Neuve: CIACO (New series, no. 283).

VANDENBERGHE V. (2000). 'Enseignement et iniquité: singularité de la question en Communauté Wallonie-Bruxelles [Education and iniquity: a singular question in the Walloon-Brussels Community]'. *Les Cahiers de recherche du GIRSEF*, no. 8.

VAN HEDDEGEM I., DOUTERLUNGNE M. & VAN DE VELDE V. (2003). *Mag het iets méér zijn? Evolutie van het project zorgverbreding in het basisonderwijs* [Can one ask for a little more? Development of the 'extended care' project in basic schooling]. Louvain: HIVA.

VANHOREN I., VAN DE VELDE V. & RAMAKERS J. (1995). *De evaluatie van het onderwijsbeleid voor migranten* [Evaluation of education policies in favour of immigrant populations]. Louvain: Hoger Instituut voor de Arbeid.

Legal references and official documents

BELGIQUE (1959). Law dated 29 May 1959 modifying certain provisions of the legislation relating to teaching (Moniteur: 19 June 1959).

COMMUNAUTÉ FRANÇAISE DE BELGIQUE (2007). Circularn° 1841 dated 18 April 2007 pertaining to the language and culture of origin. Document available on the website of the French Community of Belgium: <http://www.adm.cfwb.be/index.php?m=doc_view&do_id=2028> (consulted on 4 July 2008).

GOUVERNEMENT DE LA COMMUNAUTÉ FRANÇAISE DE BELGIQUE (1995). Decree dated 14 March 1995 pertaining to the promotion of a school for success in fundamental schooling (Moniteur: 17 August 1995).

GOUVERNEMENT DE LA COMMUNAUTÉ FRANÇAISE DE BELGIQUE (1997). Decree dated 24 July 1997 defining the priority missions of fundamental and secondary education and providing the organisation required to carry these out (Moniteur: 23 September 1997).

GOUVERNEMENT DE LA COMMUNAUTÉ FRANÇAISE DE BELGIQUE (1998). Decree dated 30 June 1998 aiming to ensure that all pupils have an equal opportunity for social emancipation, particularly by the implementation of positive discrimination (Moniteur: 22 August 1998).

GOUVERNEMENT DE LA COMMUNAUTÉ FRANÇAISE DE BELGIQUE (2001). Decree dated 14 June 2001 dealing with the integration of newly arrived pupils into education organised or subsidised by the French Community (Moniteur: 17 July 2001).

GOUVERNEMENT DE LA COMMUNAUTÉ FRANÇAISE DE BELGIQUE (2002). Decree dated 27 March 2002 modifying the decree dated 30 June 1998 aiming to ensure that all pupils have an equal opportunity for social emancipation, particularly by the implementation of positive discrimination and including various modified measures (Moniteur: 16 April 2002).

GOUVERNEMENT DE LA COMMUNAUTÉ FRANÇAISE DE BELGIQUE (2004a). Decree dated 28 April 2004 pertaining to the differentiation in funding of fundamental and secondary schools (Moniteur: 28 June 2004).

GOUVERNEMENT DE LA COMMUNAUTÉ FRANÇAISE DE BELGIQUE (2004b). French Community government order defining a plan for evaluating and following up positive discrimination, in application of Article 5, §2, of the decree dated 10 June 1998 aiming to ensure that all pupils have an equal opportunity for social emancipation, particularly by the implementation of positive discrimination.

GOUVERNEMENT DE LA COMMUNAUTÉ FRANÇAISE DE BELGIQUE (2006). Decree dated 2 June 2006 pertaining to the outside evaluation of the attainments of pupils in compulsory education and to the basic school certificate at the end of primary education (Moniteur: 23 August 2006).

France

4
Twenty-Five Years of Priority Education Policy in France: Dubious Specificity and Disappointing Results

Jean-Yves Rochex

Priority education policies, such as they are defined in this book,[1] are essentially synonymous in France with the creation of priority education zones (ZEPs) and, with the backing for the projects therein, policies that are implemented, financed and run by the minister for education and his agents. This is why most of this chapter will be devoted[2] to an analysis of these policies, to which we will add some analysis of other policies and measures that come under the state education ministry (fighting violence in school, setting up 'relay classes or measures'), or other ministries, in particular the ministry for the town, or the ministry for social cohesion (measures known as 'educational watch' and later 'educational success').

In France the creation of ZEPs was one of the very first measures taken and announced, as of July 1981, by Alain Savary, then minister for education of the first government resulting from the political change which saw the left returning to power for the first time since the advent of the Fifth Republic in 1958. The ZEP policy came into force at a time when completion of the implementation of unselective secondary schools and access to secondary education for all, far from making social inequalities disappear from schooling, reconfigured them by transforming the methods by which they were produced, making their most visible manifestations appear both later in schooling and socially more unacceptable. It also happened after critical sociology work had contributed not only to highlighting the persistence of these inequalities but also to questioning the part played in their production by school culture and how this was transmitted, and the operating processes of the education system. Finally, it happened in a context in which concern – which was to grow, and to which the ZEP policy would contribute – for those socio-geographical zones ('districts') and schools; these are where one finds concentrations of the working-class, the most downtrodden populations, the most underprivileged and those worst hit by the return of, and increase in, unemployment and insecurity. It inaugurated – along with other related policies, in particular that which would become the urban policy – a major change in public policies and approaches, and the sociological theories they took as a starting point. This development, which saw the themes of exclusion and social bonding supplant those of inequality and social conflict, was to consider and present the 'districts', the 'zones' and the schools or institutions targeted by these public policies, not only as being places where the difficulties and contradictions proper to the social structure and its education system concentrate and appear most strikingly, but also as being configurations that are themselves sources of difficulties, requiring specific treatment targeted at these territories (Tissot, 2007).

A policy of increasingly dubious specificity

The ZEP policy, the first French example of so-called 'positive discrimination', set itself the objective, according to the terms of the first circular which founded it in July 1981, 'of contributing to correct social inequality by the selective reinforcement of educational action in the zones and social environments with the highest level of learning difficulties' and, to achieve this, 'to subordinate an increase in resources to their expected yield in terms of democratisation of education'. For its promoters, it was not merely a question 'of giving more to those who have the least', according to the concise formula to which this policy is often reduced. It was also about targeting regions (rather than populations), selected according to the socio-economic and educational characteristics of the populations that lived and attended schools there (all the schools in these regions and all the pupils who attend them being likely to be involved), and to call on the involvement and thinking of the people concerned. These were encouraged, collectively, to work out and implement educational and school projects appropriate to the difficulties they were encountering within these regions, without actually prescribing directions to take or methods of work, the development of such projects being, in theory, a prerequisite for the schools and institutions concerned to be provided with additional resources. Making a break, therefore, with the political principle of formal equality (which was and remains far from being effective), the implementation of ZEPs was also the first French example of a policy aiming at 'regionalising educational policies' and at 'diversifying the educational offer', problems which have gradually applied to all the political decisions taken in education since the 1980s. It oversaw a very significant reorientation of public school policies that were now supposed to correct the deficiencies in the policies followed in the 1960s and 1970s, which had been drawn up and were controlled at state level, and which expressed the social battles and contradictions concerning democratisation in terms of unification of the education system and school culture, and of equal access to this culture and at different levels of this system. This reorientation would thereafter be interdependent with a development that was just as sensitive of political discourses and objectives, in which the themes of the fight against social exclusion, innovation and modernisation were to prevail over those of democratisation and the fight against inequalities.

For the time being, statistical criteria and categories used to argue for the implementation of such a policy and to define the regions and the schools that it would target primarily concerned learning difficulties and having to repeat a school year, on the one hand, and socio-economic disadvantage on the other. The asserted aim was explicitly to fight against socially determined learning difficulties and to democratise the education system; certain researchers, deeply involved in its implementation, would consequently not hesitate to affirm that the ZEP policy was a 'laboratory for social change in education' (CRESAS, 1985). From both a political and scientific standpoint, little attention was then given to sexual inequalities, while sociologists and promoters of the ZEP policy stressed, going against common opinion, statistical data showing that, all things being equal, children from immigrant families were not more subject to learning difficulties than their peers from the same socio-economic background. The republican political heritage and the critical sociological tradition came together to give thought to, and to target, the fight against educational failure and inequality in terms of socio-economic background (more than of social relations) rather than in terms of ethnic, cultural or linguistic minorities, as do many English-speaking countries; dealing with newly arrived non-French-speaking migrant pupils (who represent less than 5 per cent of the school population) was not regarded as coming under ZEP policy. It was only later on – with the assertion of the 'crisis of the suburbs' – that the processes of ethnic categorisation, attribution or claims would continue in the social and educational arena, in the media and in political debates and discourses, that research work would take an interest in the concept of ethnicity and in the processes or feelings of ethnic segregation, and that the fact that administrative statistics can deal only with nationality or birthplace (of the pupils or their parents) and not with their belonging to an ethnic or linguistic minority would be blamed (cf. Payet & van Zanten, 1996; Lorcerie, 2003).

Set in motion in 1981, the ZEP policy is now more than 25 years old. And yet, in spite of a certain official continuity, it is far from having benefited from constant political and administrative concern and support by the various ministries which followed one another during this period: on the contrary, it went through an alternation of phases of ministerial silence, or even hibernation, and phases of 'revival', in 1989–1990, then in 1997–1998, and again in 2005–2006. While the first two revivals were due to Socialist ministers, the third was down to a 'right-wing' minister. Each revival phase resulted in a reworking of the ZEP map and a more or less significant and explicit reorientation of its objectives.

When this policy was implemented, the ZEP catchment areas were defined and budgets allocated at the level of each local education authority, and without common criteria being defined nationally. This was the cause of the heterogeneous nature of the ZEPs defined in this way and also of the major disparities between authorities and *départements*, which resulted not only from the socio-economic and educational characteristics of the regions concerned alone, but also from the complexity of local arbitrations and political and administrative processes, and which in some cases led to the schools and institutions of a ZEP, or even of the ZEP considered as one of the most 'difficult' by a local education authority, not taking in a clearly more 'under-privileged' population than their counterparts who did not come under the ZEP policy in a neighbouring authority. Combined with these disparities, concerning the processes involved in defining ZEPs were details of implementation that were highly disparate between one authority, *département* or zone and another. While the ZEP policy generally had positive connotations, at a time when the change of government raised hopes for social and educational change, the ministerial incentives that made project and partnership the key words for a regionalised educational policy adapted to pupils' difficulties gave rise, from those whose involvement was required locally (teachers and other school staff, head teachers, councillors, welfare workers, pupils' parents), not only to uneven means of involvement, but also to individual and collective interpretations and strategies, the supposed convergence of which was far from being a foregone conclusion, and which were the source of more or less fierce and overt compromise, misunderstanding, dissension and conflict of interests or legitimacy (Henriot-van Zanten, 1990).

The number of ZEPs underwent little change during the earliest years of this policy: there were 363 in September 1982 and 390 in 1984–1985 – each corresponding in the very great majority of cases to one or more secondary schools and the primary schools that supplied them with pupils – which concerned 6.5 per cent of schools and 8.5 per cent of primary pupils, and 10.5 per cent of secondary schools and pupils (in the range 11–15 years: vocational training and the final years of secondary education were always and remain today, though to a lesser extent, largely untouched by the ZEP policy). The first revival, in 1989–1990, was marked, *inter alia*, by a systematic determination to link the ZEP policy with urban policy, mainly involving problems arising from the concentration of social and economic difficulties – particularly unemployment, insecurity and the development of juvenile delinquency – in the working-class collective housing districts in towns: all schools located in the districts embracing the latter were then classified as ZEP. The number of ZEPs then rose to approximately 530: 9.6 per cent of primary schools and 12.4 per cent of their pupils;

14.2 per cent of secondary schools (11–15 years) and 14.9 per cent of their pupils. The proportion of pupils in ZEPs was still very variable from one education authority to another – from 5 to over 20 per cent, with these variations, however, not giving a true picture of the variations in the social and educational characteristics of the authorities concerned (Moisan, 2001).

Several studies and publications advocated the need for rationalising and harmonising the criteria by which the catchment areas of the priority areas were defined, and the allocation of resources reserved for them. In a report ordered from them by the minister but which was never made public, two inspectors stressed 'the limits of an approach based only on local decisions and criteria' and the need for 'clear political instructions at a national level to reorganise the ZEP catchment areas'. Arguing in favour of catchment area redefinition being accompanied by a revival of the projects, they asserted that 'disproportionate extension of ZEPs would cause a formula which must be targeted to lose its effectiveness' and concluded from this that 'the percentage of pupils in ZEPs throughout the country as a whole should, if anything, be reduced, and in no circumstances increased' (Moisan & Simon, 1996). In spite of this, it was exactly the opposite that happened and, following a second revival, the priority education policy, in 1999, would concern 770 zones or networks, providing education for nearly 1,700,000 pupils, or approximately 18 per cent of primary schoolchildren and over 21 per cent of pupils in secondary (11–15) schools. There is a parallel between this, with some slight differences in timing, and what was happening at the same time to urban policy: the number of districts impacted by this policy also kept growing, from several dozen districts at the beginning of the 1980s to several hundred by the end of the decade, and over 1000 ten to twelve years later. A number of observers and analysts then deplored what seemed to them to be a dilution of the priority education policy, 'the ill-considered extension' of the ZEP catchment area making it the case that

> extreme cases, those where the public service cannot perform its mission normally, are no longer distinguished from the bulk of primary and secondary schools which take in mainly working-class children.
>
> (Bourgarel, 1999; OZP, 2002)

A third revival, begun in late 2005 by a 'right-wing' government, and partly basing its argument on such criticisms, would introduce differentiation and ranking at three levels to the priority education policy, and to the schools and institutions concerned. The first level concerns approximately one third of ZEP secondary schools and primary schools in their sector recruiting from the most underprivileged backgrounds and in which the social and learning difficulties were most acute. Approximately 250 secondary schools were chosen by the statistical services of the ministry, according to common criteria; renamed, together with the primary schools supplying them, as 'success ambition' networks (RAR), they had the additional resources allo-cated to them reinforced. The second level concerns schools and institutions characterised by a greater social diversity than their 'success ambition' coun-terparts. These, according to the ministerial texts, are destined to remain in priority education, and must continue to receive the same assistance as before. Finally, the third level concerns schools and institutions, intended, according to the ministry, 'to gradually leave priority education', a prospect which obviously caused a lot of opposition from teachers and local offi-cials, for whom it would mean a financial loss and a worsening of their work conditions, and which, as this chapter is being written, is a long way from having been (or even being able to be) actually implemented. Quite the reverse: the number of ZEPs has continued to grow and was, in early 2008, very close to 1200.

In addition to these developments and analyses concerning districts, cate-gories of pupils, schools and institutions, targeted by the priority education policy, are those that deal with their objectives and conceptions which, offi-cially or otherwise, have helped to orientate their various inflexions. Denis Meuret has pointed out that such a policy may be subject to two approaches and two different aims; one, that he describes as social or redeeming, con-siders ZEPs as a policy aiming at significantly reducing the inequalities of academic success between social categories or groups, and thus at improv-ing the academic results of the most underprivileged pupils (an approach more in keeping with targeting based on populations than on regions); the other, which he describes as liberal, appears more in keeping with target-ing of regions, considers ZEPs as a policy aiming at helping pupils' educated in disadvantaged socio-geographical and institutional environments to suc-ceed, all other characteristics being equal (sex, social origin, initial level, etc.), in equal measure to their counterparts educated in more favourable conditions. These conceptions were doubtless both present at the beginning of the ZEP policy, but the second has surreptitiously taken over from the first and has pushed it into the background, in parallel with the assertion of pragmatism to the detriment of political resolve and with the dispelling, in the guidelines and the measures implemented by the different ministries that have followed one another since 1981, of the theme and the objective of democratising the education system before those of modernising it: 'The objective of compensating for social disadvantage has given in more and more to that of compensating for a local disadvantage' (Meuret, 2000). This deflection has led various observers and analysts of the ZEP policy and its developments to write of, or even deplore, how the latter is now more like a policy for social management of educational inequality and segregation than a marked policy in the fight against their main causes, and against the social and educational processes that produce them (Glasman, 1992; Rochex, 1997; van Zanten, 2001).

The beginning of the 21st century and the latest revival of the ZEP policy saw another reorientation assert itself, as political discourses and objectives began more and more to stress individualised courses and encourage 'talents', which now aim at giving priority to pupils rather than to 'zones'. Pupil characteristics are, more and more often, presented in terms of diversity of talents, pace, interests, aptitudes or forms of intelligence, to which schools are invited to adapt, and which are less and less thought of in connection with an analysis of the social and educational processes that give them form and content. This move towards individualisation is interdependent with measures of growing significance, aiming both to promote actions and measures for 'individualised assistance' and to help the best pupils from ZEP schools and institutions to enter institutions considered as being of a higher level, even to institutions and courses known to be 'prestigious' (certain *lycées* and universities). This seems to be harking back to a 'meritocratic' ideology, casting little doubt on the way the education system works and its responsibility for constructing educational difficulties and inequalities, essentially blaming these on the pupils and their families, while aiming at widening the recruitment of the 'elite' to include the most deserving pupils or the most promising from working-class backgrounds and districts. The objectives aiming at reducing the difference between schools by improving 'educational quality' for the most underprivileged fade into insignificance compared with that of enabling their best pupils having access to 'excellence', the model for which scarcely bears critical examination any more (Oberti, 2007); the perspective for democratisation is overshadowed in favour of a goal of diversification and broadening the recruitment of the 'elite' and of giving each pupil, considered above all as an individual, the best chance of success. A significant political development on the left as on the right, to which the ideological discrediting of critical approaches and the theories of reproduction in the sociology of education, or even a relative de-sociologising of theoretical thought and educational research, contributes, and to which it contributes, in return, to fuel, in favour of approaches and aims considered to be more 'pragmatic' and more likely to lead to professional qualifications.

These evolutions and reorientations of the ZEP policy and its objectives did not, however, take place in an unchanged institutional environment. Quite the reverse, and while the terms project and partnership have been, from the very start, the key words of this policy, they were gradually to become those of educational policies and, more broadly, of the policy of 'modernising the public service', begun during the 1980s, and about which Luc Rouban (1990) could write that they 'are put forward as an answer to a situation considered to be 'problematic' without the nature of the problem being really made cleared [*sic*]'. So a great number of educational or institutional innovations – for which the ZEP policy was the testing ground, in the name of the real or supposed specific nature of the problems and difficulties with which school and its professionals were confronted, and according to procedures calling on the initiative and the commitment of those involved and the 'partners' of the school – gradually came to make up a pedagogical and politico-administrative *doxa* that successive changes of government have not, in spite of some reorientations, called into question. They then came under the umbrella of regulations or more-or-less restrictive incentives (in particular via funding procedures) that contributed appreciably to modification of the education system as a whole and the work of its staff. Consequently, the very great diversity of the choices made, actions carried out and actual involvement in ZEPs, and the extension to all or part of the education system of the principles and regulations of which it was the testing ground mean that it is today extremely difficult to define what are the specific features of the ZEP policy, from national down to local level, and thereby attempt to evaluate its effects. The most eloquent example is undoubtedly the obligation under which each primary and secondary school has been, for the last ten years or so, to have their own 'project' adapted to the characteristics of its pupils.

Such an undertaking is made all the more difficult by the fact that various plans and measures initiated by either the state education minister or other ministries were added to the ZEP policy and partially superimposed on it; these often concern a large proportion of schools and their pupils, targeted by the ZEP policy, but may not concern some of them, while they include certain districts, and certain secondary or primary schools not concerned by the ZEP policy. The state education minister therefore set up various plans and measures aiming at reducing the mobility of teachers working in 'difficult environments' and at providing support for them as they begin teaching, at promoting assistance with school work for pupils whose home environment does not provide the necessary resources to do this, and at fighting against violence in school or against the processes of 'dropping out'. New ways of targeting and new categories were created, in particular the 'sensitive schools' category denoting schools in which the phenomenon of violence in school appears to be highest, and which receive additional resources to cope with this. While this category concerns a large proportion of ZEP secondary schools, these two categories and the measures they denote do not overlap, as a considerable percentage of 'sensitive' schools are not classified as ZEPs, and vice versa. As for the 'local educational contracts' created in 1998 aimed at combining the efforts of state education and those of the municipalities, primarily around extra-curricular cultural activities and assistance with pupils' work, these were, from the outset, presented as having a general-purpose vocation aiming at the whole of the country, but also as needing to be set up specifically and initially in the ZEPs. Finally, the measures known as 'educational watch' (*Veille éducative*), then 'educational success' (*Réussite éducative*), launched in 2002 and 2005, respectively by the ministry for the town and for social cohesion, were placed under the responsibility of the mayors and had to associate the various social services and schools to be targeted, in the urban areas concerned by the urban policy, individuals aged between 2 and 16 years in socially 'fragile' situations. The approach that these measures promoted was intended to be 'global' and not just academic, and broke with the region-based approach that was integral to ZEP policy. According to the terms of one of the founding texts of the 'educational success' measure,[3] this was

> a personalised support policy which aims at providing educational assistance adapted to each individual and/or family situation, and continuing over time, with performance targets which are evaluated annually on the basis of national and local indicators.

Such an individualised or individualising policy appears very significant in regard to the developments in progress, to which we will return, in that it aims at individuals, identified from particular difficulties or weakness and monitored individually by a 'referent'. It goes against an approach by 'zones' or 'target public', defined on the basis of where they live or to what social or cultural group they belong (for some initial results deriving from the analysis of this measure, cf. Joly-Rissoan *et al.*, 2006).

This has led to a situation today that is paradoxical to say the least, in which the need for a positive discrimination policy in favour of the zones and the schools where the conditions of teaching and learning are regarded as being the most difficult – or in favour of the populations that are the most underprivileged from the socio-economic and educational standpoints[4] – no longer seems to be disputed in the educational arena or in French political debate (which was not the case in the 1970s and 1980), while at the same time the objectives, the specific features and, as we shall see, the effectiveness of such a policy appear increasingly dubious.

An under-administered policy, with limited means and disappointing results

All the available statistical indicators show that, as a whole, it is indeed the most socially and educationally underprivileged populations that were concerned by the ZEP policy (and by the measures mentioned above). The schools designated as being 'priority' are characterised by a strong over-representation of pupils from working-class backgrounds, foreign pupils, those belonging to families hardest hit by insecurity and by the largest percentage of pupils who have repeated one or more school years.[5] Statistical data show also – even if their lack of accuracy underestimates this development – that the social make-up of 'priority' schools has changed unfavourably since the beginning of the 1980s. The very significant deterioration in the social and economic situation in a number of urban districts concerned, combined with an increase in 'avoidance strategies' used by the least underprivileged families in these districts (so that their children are not educated in schools they consider as going downhill), is seen as not being very effective, or even dangerous. Many ZEP schools are consequently experiencing an increasingly strong concentration of pupils encountering social and educational difficulties, and are suffering from a situation in which the processes of academic segregation are intensifying the processes of social segregation.

The overall statistical data nevertheless subsume and mask a significant internal diversity between zones, schools or classes. This means that ZEP secondary schools vary considerably from each other; while the proportion of children of workers or the unemployed is lower than the national average (42.3 per cent) in one ZEP secondary school in ten, it is greater than 80 per cent in 10 per cent of ZEP secondary schools. Many ZEP schools, therefore, appear as victims of ways of thinking which have led, over the last few decades, to an increased social polarisation of the educational arena, to growing disparities between state secondary schools and to a concentration in some of these of the poorest and most insecure pupils. Various studies have also shown that educational segregation is not only the effect of urban segregation, but that schools and those in charge of them, anxious to attract and keep good pupils, transform the restrictions resulting from the local environment, which generally lead to a reinforcement of educational, social or ethnic polarisation between schools, but also between classes within the same school (Payet, 1995; van Zanten, 2001); and also lead to internal disparities within secondary schools becoming more important in a ZEP or in a socially underprivileged environment than elsewhere (Giry-Croissard & Niel, 1997). The significant heterogeneity between zones and ZEP schools obviously weakens and makes difficult comparisons between ZEP zones and non-ZEP zones – including situations concerning pupils with similar social and academic characteristics. This type of comparison, which has many defects, is nevertheless almost the only means that the statistical services of the ministry use to try to evaluate the ZEP policy quantitatively and to assess the results in the light of the stated objectives.

Although it benefits from increasing political legitimacy, the ZEP policy nevertheless remains under-managed and very poorly controlled and regulated at the various levels of the education system; this bears witness to both its very variable status and its low visibility in the various flow charts of the administration, the ministry, the education authority or the *département*, and also to the minor role that inspectors play within it, particularly in secondary education. While the incentive towards involvement for school staff, who are invited collectively to draw up and implement projects aiming at improving pupils' schooling, is one of the fundamentals of the ZEP policy and of similar measures, very few specific measures have been implemented to assist and direct the educational and professional involvement so recommended, in order more accurately to target the types of pupils concerned or the types of action or expected measures. The role of the ministry and its representatives is much more concerned with providing an incentive – particularly via funding procedures – than giving instructions, and the methods of incentive, regulation and control deal more with intentions and very general topics (mastery of language, reading and writing, the fight against violence and incivility, education in citizenship, to mention only the most frequently occurring examples), or with measures, than with teaching methods or results. This carries the risk that the professionals concerned will be guided by their own conceptions of collective interest, or even by their own interest or habitus, and by their representations of working-class environments, than by common, clearly discussed and established political and educational objectives (on these various aspects, cf. Lorcerie, 2006).

Spread over several hundred zones or networks and, within these, to a large extent devoted to both improving the degree of pupil supervision and recognising the difficulties of the job by providing better remuneration for staff working in ZEPs, the resources available for this policy are dispersed, little known and not very specific. In fact, no overall financial results for this policy existed until recently, and those that have since been drawn up (Armand & Gille, 2006) take into account only the budgetary resources that the state education minister devotes to it, and exclude further funding provided by the various local authorities, or those coming under other ministries. The additional resources provided by the state education system consist mainly of staffing resources (teaching, education, health, social work), compensatory funding and educational funding. Nearly 15,000 full-time equivalent jobs – roughly half of which are for primary education and half for secondary – are devoted to the ZEP policy. In primary schools, these resources, which are almost exclusively teaching posts, are devoted essentially to lowering the number of children per class and to the assignment of 'classless' teachers for support or co-ordination tasks. In secondary schools, 61 per cent of these full-time equivalent jobs are teaching posts (or hours), 24 per cent concern educational staff and 15 per cent other staff categories (mainly health and social work). Such an over-representation of non-teaching staff (education, health and social work) in the resources reserved for the ZEP policy testifies both to the needs perceived and the increasing importance of concerns about problems of violence in school, the climate in schools and 'socialisation' of the pupils (cf. below); certain analysts fear that this is to the detriment of dealing with difficulties and inequality in regard to learning and school culture.

Approximately one-third of the compensatory funding is devoted to career improvement and two-thirds (approximately €110 million) to allocating a special bonus to all staff working in ZEPs (a little more than €1000 per year for each member). This bonus, begun during the first revival, aimed at reducing instability and staff turnover, an objective it did not help in achieving, nor even approaching. In regard to educational and social funding, this represents only an extra €25 per pupil in ZEPs, to which must be added funding – often 3–4 times greater (Lorcerie, 1993) allotted by the local authorities or obtained as part of urban policy.

On the whole, the available data enable one to estimate that a pupil educated in a ZEP benefits from financial help 10–15 per cent greater than that allocated to a non-ZEP pupil, an extra cost that is devoted to reducing the number of pupils per class, which is lower by about two in ZEPs compared with non-ZEPs. These resources, and the priority to which they bear witness, do not seem today to be more marked than in the mid-1980s, whereas ZEPs are experiencing an increasing concentration of the poorest and most insecure populations, and the socio-economic and education situation has notably deteriorated in that area (Trancart, 2000). In such a context, the question of the means devoted to the ZEP policy has always caused tension and controversy between those who are in favour of a primarily qualitative approach – putting forward the need for coherent projects and a major transformation of the way the education system works and how its staff works, and even deploring the fact that the budgetary issue is pushing the teaching debate all the more into the shade as the latter is limited (Moisan & Simon, 1997) – and the partisan approach, while if not exactly of a quantitative logic, is at least in favour of significantly greater budgetary support for the most 'difficult' schools (Thélot, 2001) and for improving the living conditions of the pupils and families concerned (Maurin, 2004). These are tensions and debates that cut across those which take shape between the temptation to think or let it be believed that the processes that produce educational difficulty and inequality, or 'the determinants of academic success in ZEPs', might be only academic, or even educational or professional, and the temptation to think or let it be believed that they might be concerned with only social processes prior to, and outside of, schooling, and might owe nothing to the way the education system and its staff operate.

Two types of statistical data enable attempts to evaluate the effects of the ZEP policy: firstly, those that concern the characteristics and the careers of pupils (number of pupils repeating a school year, access to the various levels of the syllabus and the various courses of study, etc.); secondly, those that concern their attainments in the various disciplines, assessed on the basis of standardised tests that all pupils undergo when they enter the third year of primary school (CE2) and the first year of secondary school ('sixième') in mathematics and French, or from the marks they obtain in the *brevet* examination that marks the end of the first four years of secondary school. As will be seen, the relationship between these two types of data appears increasingly dubious, the first being much more sensitive than the second to national or local policies for the management of flows, such as the reduction in the numbers of pupils repeating a school year, or the abolition of early subject choices at secondary school. These surveys show, as stated above, that pupils in ZEPs are indeed those who have the greatest socio-economic and educational problems. Concerning the percentage of pupils who have repeated one or more years in school and the amount of streaming, the available figures do not show any reduction in the differences between the situation in ZEPs and that overall, but they do show that data from ZEP schools have not been omitted from the reduction in the number of pupils repeating a school year and the general raising of academic courses which the whole of the education system has experienced, while at the same time the social and economic situation of the districts concerned has significantly deteriorated. Longitudinal surveys following up cohorts of pupils provide complementary data on the careers of pupils educated both within and outwith ZEPs. Thirteen per cent of pupils who entered secondary school in 1995 were educated in a ZEP, having encountered difficulties in primary school; 53 per cent of these either had attended one or more classes twice before entering secondary school or obtained an overall assessment score in French and mathematics that put them among the bottom 25 per cent pupils nationally; 21 per cent combined both characteristics (as against 30 and 9 per cent, respectively for their peers who were never educated in a ZEP). If their secondary school careers were more problematic than those of their peers not educated in ZEPs, this variation is due to differences in the home environment and success at primary school. On the other hand, with equivalent characteristics at the outset, the difference is reversed, and ZEP pupils more often reach the fifth year of secondary schooling (general and technological subjects) without having to repeat a year than their non-ZEP counterparts.[6] However, quantitative data (Murat, 1998; Caille, 2001; Stefanou, 2001), corroborated by a number of more qualitative investigations (Broccolichi, 1995; Bautier & Rochex, 1998; Broccolichi & Ben-Ayed, 1999; van Zanten, 2001; Beaud, 2002) allow one to believe that such an improvement in the school careers of pupils educated in ZEPs is not necessarily due to an improvement in their school attainments, but rather, to a considerable extent that is difficult to assess, to a lower level of selectivity of the criteria and practices of evaluation and guidance applied to them. Performance evaluation tests in French and mathematics taken by pupils in all third year primary classes and first year secondary classes show that (1) those in ZEPs obtain lower scores than their peers; (2) the variations have hardly lessened since these tests have been in existence (they vary between 8 and 13 per cent from one year to the next); and (3), contrary to common opinion, including that of teachers, scores are higher in mathematics than in French. In addition, a more detailed analysis, dealing not only with overall scores but presenting results according to the various types of item, shows that the variations in regard to ZEP pupils are greater in proportion to the degree of complexity of the skills required to answer these, whereas they are not very great for items requiring more restricted skills, accessible through mechanical training. Such an observation – and we will return to this – makes one wonder about the teaching carried out in ZEPs, and how this is adapted to the real or assumed characteristics of pupils: do ZEP teachers not tend to favour training their pupils in 'basic' skills and giving them parcelled-out and repetitive technical teaching, to the detriment of intellectually and culturally richer, but more demanding, competencies and learning? (Andrieux *et al.*, 2001). At the end of the day, it seems that Denis Meuret's observation made in 1994 still applies: he wrote that the ZEP policy has not made it possible

> to create a situation where, on average, pupils educated in these zones would succeed better than their characteristics would lead one to hope for.... Actually, they even succeed a little less well than they would succeed elsewhere, the difference proving larger for pupils who were initially in a difficult educational or social situation.

> (Meuret, 1994)

Studies making it possible to go beyond the overall results discussed above and to present them according to sites, *départements* or education authority are rare indeed. Such is the explicit objective of the report drawn up in September 1997 by the inspectors Moisan and Simon, who made it clear that they did not so much seek to evaluate the ZEP policy as to identify how and why certain ZEPs 'succeed' while others are in danger and in an emergency situation. Their work combines a statistical survey aiming at calculating the 'added-value' of more than 400 ZEPs (the difference between the performances observed in pupils in the first year of secondary school in these zones and the performances one might expect to observe there given the characteristics of the pupils) and a monographic-type study of 36 ZEPs, and highlights the great disparity existing between the zones, while endeavouring to understand why certain ZEPs turned out to be particularly efficient whereas others obtained results well below their expected performance. The authors see the success factors identified in this way in terms of multiple recommendations for a revival of the ZEP policy: the fight against 'ghettoisation' and strategies for avoiding ZEP secondary schools; the rigorous development, implementation and evaluation of learning-centred projects; followed-up and durable measures for assisting, giving recognition to and stabilising teachers; the development of schooling at age two and initiatives to help families; the choice of qualified persons in charge at various levels; the need for a strong political message and effective and durable piloting at all levels (Moisan & Simon, 1997). These conclusions, which converge on those that can be drawn from the majority of the research work dealing with the details of implementing the ZEP policy, are found in a report, drawn up nearly ten years later by two other inspectors, who observed that the ZEPs with the best results are those that encourage and are able to implement the continuity of learning, a high degree of structuring of teaching to preserve learning time, a high standard, collective work and a relationship with the environment of the school that is attentive to ensuring that the means of relating to the environment is not detrimental to learning (Armand & Gille, 2006, p. 47). And yet, such a state of affairs tends rather to be less common, and the authors conclude from their examination of the ZEP policy that

> as the essential has not been dealt with – a quality external and internal diagnosis and the adaptation of teaching practices – the effectiveness and the efficiency of this policy could not be in keeping with the means made available.
>
> (Armand & Gille, 2006, p. 115)

All the data and analyses presented above do not allow us to make a clear assessment of the ZEP policy, and lend themselves to different interpretations. Some, tending towards a 'social' definition of this policy (according to the terms used by D. Meuret) would deem this assessment disappointing (cf. for example Rochex, 1997; CÈBE, 2000) while others, tending more to give it a 'liberal' definition, believe that 'this policy has partly attained its initial objective' (Caille, 2001), helping to ensure that the educational situation of the pupils and schools concerned can withstand the deteriorating socio-economic conditions of the districts and the families concerned. Over and above these differing appraisals, which are partly concerned with different conceptions of the ZEP policy, it should be remembered that it is extremely difficult to distinguish and evaluate one specific effect of this policy, because the comparison between ZEPs and non-ZEPs is too inexact – the statistical indicators used are multiple and sometimes divergent (cf. the dissociation mentioned above between the progression of pupils' careers and the evaluation of their academic attainments), and also because this policy has resulted in a great diversity of actions and projects. We may nevertheless wonder whether the reasons for such a relatively disappointing appraisal are not, in addition to the deteriorating socio-economic environment and that of the conditions for learning and teaching resulting from it, related to these actions and projects, to the ways that teaching activities and the contents implemented therein are redefined, and to the ways of adapting the teaching offer and the teaching practices in ZEPs to the characteristics of the pupils and the classes, which might in fact prove to have a lesser democratising effect than their promoters think. This is a hypothesis that is corroborated by the majority of the work that has attempted to describe and analyse the details of implementing the ZEP policy in the various sites and schools.

Projects and actions whose effects are proving to have less of a democratising effect than was hoped for

Begun at a time of optimism and determination, the ZEP policy was based on providing school staff (and their partners) with the incentive for change and the development of projects, without any experimentation, method or contents for teaching or organisational change being officially prescribed, or even promoted. This confidence in the reflection and initiative of those involved – extended a few years later to the entire education system, at the same time as the project rhetoric – could hardly be said to have been accompanied by any significant work aimed at providing those involved with improved skills for diagnosing and analysing the causality and the ways in which learning difficulties and educational inequality are produced and the most likely means of making them regress, no more than any specific research programme to examine these questions. It nevertheless progressively shifted in emphasis with the rise of social, political and institutional concerns about certain questions or themes (reading and the fight against illiteracy, violence in school, assistance with homework, absenteeism or dropping-out, etc.), which were to be the subject of incentive measures via the methods of selection and funding of actions and projects that those involved locally offered to carry out.

All the work relating to the details of implementing the ZEP policy has shown that the latter has been, since the beginning, overwhelmingly backed by a logic of action more than by a real project logic; those who believe that it would be worthwhile and advantageous to implement such action argue *a posteriori* to justify and legitimate it and, very often, to obtain funding or institutional recognition for it. This observation led Dominique Glasman to write that the ZEP projects

> may also be interpreted as *the answer justifying the question*, in other words the action under consideration moving towards the problem to which it is supposed to provide a solution. To the extent where – if we allow ourselves to exaggerate a little – one sometimes wonders if it is not the answer which gives legitimate existence to the question, or which at least determines the way of asking it.
>
> (Glasman, 1992, p. 69; author's italics)[7]

This logic of juxtaposing actions bears witness to the difficulty which those involved feel in defining and treating priorities on a hierarchical basis (Moisan & Simon, 1997), in going beyond the representations that they have of their pupils' competencies, but also of the families, their life styles and their educational practices as being globally disadvantaged, in order better to specify and analyse the difficulties of learning and acculturation with which pupils are confronted (Glasman, 1992; Charlot, 1994; Bouveau & Rochex,

1997). It also reflects the multiplicity and the variation in orientations, instructions or incentives of the various authorities likely to provide material or financial support for the actions and projects implemented; these authorities are also having difficulties in defining, co-ordinating and treating priorities on a hierarchical basis because they are subjected to the need for making them visible and promoting them in the eyes of parents, the media or public opinion.

Beyond their apparent diversity, ZEP actions and projects can nevertheless be classified into certain main categories: (1) actions aiming at improving learning, predominantly centred on reading and writing, mastery of language and artistic and cultural activities, but which grant only a very limited amount of room for mathematics and, more generally, scientific and technical culture (whereas the evaluations discussed above show that the difficulties of ZEP pupils are greater in mathematics than in French); (2) measures for assistance or tutoring, help with homework, in or out of school (cf. Glasman, 2001 for a summary of this question); (3) actions – in ever-increasing numbers – aimed at reducing violence, 'incivility' or absenteeism, improving the 'climate' in schools and the 'socialisation' of pupils, or promoting 'education in citizenship'; and (4) actions aimed at improving relationships between school and the families. Next – less important in quantitative terms – comes special action for training school staff, actions centred on the use of information and communication technologies, those aimed at improving 'communication' between the various protagonists (teachers at the various levels of the syllabus, parents, welfare workers) or the image of the schools, or concerning the creation of, alterations to or the restoration of premises. In a 1988 study analysing the reports written in 1983 for the ministry by the ZEP co-ordinators, Viviane Isambert-Jamati showed that the objective of reinforcing learning was predominant in the action described and the educational choices made, and that therefore the creation of ZEPs had not given rise to the driving or extra-pedagogical 'drift' that some feared or even denounced in advance (Isambert-Jamati, 1990). But she did observe that the initiatives reported were leading to the development of structures and initiatives complementary to ordinary classroom activity, rather than to work on implementing different teaching methods, while noting that on reading the reports it was not possible to be sure how effective would be the chain of remediation between the actions described and improvement in learning and academic success.

This questioning of the potential or observable effects of ZEP actions and projects on learning, and their democratisation, would be taken up again by other researchers (Bouveau *et al.*, 1992; Fijalkow, 1992; Glasman, 1992; Lorcerie, 1993, 2006; Charlot, 1994; Bouveau & Rochex, 1997), on the basis not only of analysis of documents but also of research undertaken on site. This work highlighted the fact that ZEP action and projects often concern 'cultural' or artistic activities, that they very frequently take place on the

fringe of ordinary class work and are also frequently presented and justified as being more fun, more attractive and more fulfilling than the latter.
On reading or hearing the promoters of such action

> it is exactly as if teachers were making a strict separation between
> school activities considered as tedious by nature, and the more or less
> entertaining or artistic activities used in the projects.
>
> (Fijalkow, 1992)

Just as much as the relevance of these projects, which turned out to be very
variable from one action or site to another, it was now open to question how
these relate to ordinary class work and learning: are they marginal or auxiliary to this ordinary work, with which they are then merely juxtaposed, or
do they even contribute to making the school world less credible and still
more difficult to understand for pupils who are the least familiar with it?
Or do they have a feedback effect on this ordinary work strengthening its
relevance, effectiveness and credibility, particularly for pupils with the greatest difficulty? Do they not merely scratch the surface, rather than getting to
the bottom of things, making school and the activities it proposes attractive
without making them either more effective nor more democratising, even
scrambling some of the objectives and rules for those pupils who are least
able to decipher what is merely implicit, and diluting the exposure time of
such pupils to learning? These questions or concerns are supported by various studies showing that, especially for ZEP pupils, project logic may assert
itself to the detriment of learning logic, and may combine with a logic of
immediate success, leading teachers to parcel out and simplify the tasks they
propose to pupils in 'ordinary' situations and at 'ordinary' times; and also
to the detriment of what is required for effective learning that goes beyond
the mere execution of, or mere success in, partial and very narrowly contextualised tasks (Charlot *et al.*, 1993; Andrieux *et al.*, 2001; Peltier *et al.*,
2004).

As for the various tutoring or assistance measures in existence today in
practically all working-class districts and all ZEP projects, and which are
often an essential feature of the local educational contracts signed between
municipalities and state education representatives, these are open to the
same type of questioning. In the account he gives of the many evaluation and research tasks dealing with these measures, Dominique Glasman
notes that, while their effects are at the very least doubtful, between one
site and another there are great differences in how the public are targeted
and actually reached, in the criteria and evaluation methods implemented
and in their time span; these studies show that the use of assistance or
tutoring measures contributes to improving pupils' behaviour but does not
lead, or only slightly does so, to any marked improvement in their school
results, the progress observed being in addition inversely proportional to

the initial difficulties of the pupils. Observation of sessions reveals recurrent 'wasted opportunities' and the weight of 'educational utilitarianism' leading pupils and group leaders to perform in such a way that the former can get their school work 'out of the way' as soon as possible to be 'in order' with the institution, without being able intellectually to becoming involved in the meaning of the activity proposed, thereby going beyond mere following of instructions and formal execution of tasks (Glasman, 2001).

In the same way, one may wonder about the juxtaposition, or even the cleavage, that ZEP or school projects frequently display between, on the one hand, so-called 'socialisation' actions, aiming to improve the school 'climate', to combat violence, incivility or absenteeism and to make school a pleasant and safe place to be, and on the other, those aimed at a better appropriation by the pupils of the contents of knowledge and intellectual techniques. This type of project and the arguments accompanying them or promoting them – and which can be read or heard in remarks made by teachers, by administrative or political officials or by certain researchers – are mostly underscored by more or less implicit problems according to which the meaning of the school experience and the relation with the educational institution could be (re)built from the outside – or at least on the fringe of pupils' learning and intellectual and cultural activity. So it happened that, as of 1996, the ministry began testing and developing, on the sidelines or even outside schools, structures known as 'relay classes or measures', making it possible to take in pupils causing major disciplinary problems and who were in the process of dropping out or becoming marginalised, while they were assisted in finding an educational or professional solution. The conclusion that can be drawn from these structures, which are not specific to the ZEP policy but which, for the vast majority, target pupils and secondary schools concerned by this policy, shows that while we have been able to reduce lack of discipline, violence and absenteeism and to improve slightly the 'climate' of ordinary classes by removing some of the most troublesome pupils, we are a long way from helping the latter to change the way they relate to knowledge in order that they might enjoy a better situation with regard to learning (Martin & Bonnéry, 2002; Millet & Thin, 2005). Admittedly, it is not easy to contemplate the relationship between 'socialisation' and learning, for both for research and daily action. It may be considered, however, that there is a difficulty that is just as great, and one that carries significant social and institutional risks in ratifying and devoting – even unknowingly – the theoretical and practical cleavage which makes one regard them as two separate and independent fields, and in imagining that learning could take place only on the basis of preliminary socialisation to which it could not itself contribute. In other words, might school be possible and effective providing that children and teenagers have become pupils beforehand? Might not the register of learning and cognitive development itself produce socialisation effects? Is not the avoidance of these questions,[8] which are also political questions, likely to lead directly to a two-speed school where, on the one hand, learning and culture would contribute to the personal development and autonomy of children from privileged backgrounds, while on the other one would attempt to socialise and 'to comfort the poor' rather than provide them with the intellectual tools that would emancipate them, and a loss or a lack of direction for learning and its contents would be countered by the promotion or the development of purposeless sociability and conviviality? Isn't this likely to move towards substituting social pacification for the democratisation of access to knowledge and the fight against academic inequality?

These are questions and conclusions that are very closely related to those presented above, which O. Jolly-Rissoan and D. Glasman derive from examining the details of implementation and an initial evaluation of the educational success measure (*Réussite éducative* – RE). They write that

> in the majority of cases, the fields of curative and preventive action under consideration immediately determine the meaning of the weaknesses which it is intended to cure: part of the solution is to be found in the action plan proposed, before any multi-field analysis of individual situations.... The analysis of the processes leading to educational failure often stays on the surface and is content to describe more or less accurately the economic, social, cultural and family difficulties of the children concerned.

These authors also note that it is quite difficult to ascertain exactly which actions have been carried out, beyond generic headings such as educational support or support for parenting: 'What exactly does one do with the young person? To what extent is what we offer him likely to help him: one scarcely knows?' In the same way, and in line with what has just been said about the ZEP policy, they question the ambiguity of the evaluation methods and objectives of this type of policy:

> Very often, as regards urban policy or measures departing somewhat from common law, evaluation is more focused on the progress made in terms of partnerships which have been achieved, on new collaborations begun, on work relationships made between institutions or professionals who were not accustomed to working together.... It is not unusual, that having congratulated oneself for building partnerships and local arenas for discussion, one neglects to *really* ask, – i.e. instead of just counting up the 'beneficiaries' and the resources employed for them – what the measure has really produced for the people it was targeting. As far as RE is concerned, it should be asked exactly how and to what extent it has enabled a child to progress, and how individualisation has been fruitful for him or

her.... If the results for the children are not there, RE may appear as what it is then likely to be reduced to: a kind of educational support against social exclusion, perhaps locally able to pacify, but not solve anything.

(Joly-Rissoan *et al.*, 2006)

The various questions and analyses presented above are in line with a number of pieces of research concerning more 'ordinary' practices in ZEP classes and schools or those recruiting mainly, or almost exclusively, from working-class environments (for a summary, see Kherroubi & Rochex, 2004). This research is in agreement on two main issues. Firstly, it shows that pupils from working-class backgrounds – who are the most dependent on school and the relevance of the learning and teaching work with which they are there confronted – have, more than others, 'to learn about school in order to learn at school' as Anne-Marie Chartier (1992) puts it; in other words to discover and appropriate invisible knowledge, less related to the content than the form of learning and the study methods specific to school, its operating rules and how its interpersonal relations work (Vincent, 1980). This invisible knowledge is very often required by the school and taken for granted or regarded as self-evident, with hardly any work devoted to providing it for those who do not have it. Children from more privileged backgrounds have already partly discovered and built this knowledge, before school and outside it, within, and thanks to, their home environment. While school work and knowledge, because they are always concerned with literacy, require (and allow) work to pull together, to distance, to decontextualise and recontextualise, to redescribe and reconfigure pragmatic knowledge of ordinary experience in which the goal of success and realisation is paramount in comparison with that of understanding; and while they require (and allow) detours through reflection, doubt and the use of semiotic and linguistic tools of representation and thought, pupils are unequally prepared and disposed, because of the cognitive and linguistic modes of socialisation used in their family and their social experience, for such work, for such a detour, and for the transformations of the relationship with time, language and the world these require. However – and this is a second point – the projects and actions and, more generally, the ways in which the teaching offer and teaching practices used with pupils from working-class backgrounds are adapted and differentiated have a strong tendency, as have the political and administrative instructions and incentives which they meet, to undervalue, ignore or circumvent this sociological and socio-cognitive dimension of the production of educational difficulties and inequalities, in favour of innovation, socialisation, the concern to implement activities considered as more attractive, more 'motivating' for pupils, or the concern to preserve their 'self-image' by proposing tasks in which they can succeed. Such focusing on the success, the variety and the attractiveness of tasks, or on safeguarding order or the 'climate' of the classroom, can consequently be asserted to the detriment of the intellectual relevance and productivity of the ways used to adapt, and therefore to the detriment of the goals of democratisation pursued or stated. These perverse effects are contributed to, in various ways depending on the contexts, by representations too general and vague, unspecified with regard to the difficulties inherent in the intellectual work required, of the characteristics of the pupils that need to be adapted to, and the accumulation of gaps in the knowledge of certain pupils and in certain classes, and the situational constraints that burden the work of teachers and pupils in the most difficult schools.

Such observations and analyses show that it is not enough to break, or to want to break, with 'the indifference to differences' between pupils to which the work of Bourdieu and Passeron alluded and denounced more than 30 years ago in the way the education system works and the ordinary practices of its professionals, to be capable of giving consideration to, and implementing, this 'rational, sociologically-inspired pedagogy' which they then called for (Bourdieu & Passeron, 1970). But all the same, one must be able both to recognise and specify the relevant differences from the point of view of the intellectual work concerned, and to imagine and be able to implement how to adapt and adjust to these most relevant differences to ensure that they are not translated, or as little as possible, into educational difficulties and inequalities. One has to admit that the ZEP policy is as disappointing in this respect as it is for the statistical indicators used to evaluate the attainments and the academic background of the pupils concerned. While such a result cannot entirely be laid at the door of this policy and the way it was piloted and implemented, in a context where the socio-economic difficulties in the populations, districts and schools concerned are getting worse, it may nevertheless be considered that it is not unrelated to the way in which its objectives and orientations were thought up and implemented, and to the way in which they have developed, sometimes in a controlled and explicit way, and sometimes less so.

Conclusion

To conclude, we would like to stress some aspects of the appraisal, questioning and analysis that seem important to us with respect not only to the presentation which has just been made of 25 years of ZEP policy in France but also to the presentations of similar policies in other European countries that can be read in this work.

Our first remark concerns the absence or inadequacy of ZEP policy targeting and piloting. As has been said, the policy targets regions, or more exactly schools located in regions chosen according to socio-economic and academic criteria, but, since it does not choose between prevention and remediation, it does not specifically target any age group or any school level (unlike the insistence on early childhood and pre-schooling that can be observed in other countries); it is scarcely more prescriptive concerning the types of institutional, curricular and pedagogical actions and measures considered as most relevant for promoting effectiveness and fairness, for reducing social and sexual inequality, or concerning the results expected (the concept of *success contracts* that appeared in the administrative vocabulary during the 1997–1998 revival has remained to a very large extent virtual). Consequently, nothing guarantees that the means made available for this policy are, within ZEP schools, focused on the pupils most in difficulty, nor on the levels of the syllabus allowing preference to be given to a goal of prevention rather than remediation; quite the reverse: dispersion, or even dilution, of the efforts and additional resources seems most frequently to be the case. The absence or inadequacy of guidance concerning the expected content, nature and methods for the projects and transformations appears from the very start of the ZEP policy as the counterpart to the confidence shown in those who are active in the field and in teaching staff, those presumed to be in a position to draw up and implement, by themselves, relevant, effective and democratising projects, in a country and an education system both deeply attached to the 'educational freedom' of teachers and marked by an elitist heritage. But neither the political and administrative authorities nor research agencies (who were, moreover, scarcely involved in the design and the implementation of this policy – cf. *Revue française de pédagogie*, 2002) were able to direct the thinking and the action of those involved, who had therefore no alternative but to make use of their own resources and representations of what it was possible, legitimate and relevant to do. This lack of guidance and of tools would in part be compensated by the assertion, particularly via funding procedures or ministerial programmes targeted at a specific question, and on more specific directions: command of language, the fight against violence or absenteeism, etc. Nevertheless, on the one hand these guidelines for work would be formulated in very generic terms, not very likely to be helpful for the daily action of those involved and, on the other, they would generally aim at dealing with the most visible, or even the most spectacular and most politically significant, problems (such was the case with the question of violence in school, which received much media coverage and is a very sensitive issue for the political authorities), which would partly cause attention to be focused on secondary rather than primary schools, on cure rather than prevention, and on treating the consequences rather than the causes of social and educational issues so designated.

In the same way this attention appears increasingly supported by a way of interpreting pupils' difficulties by indexing them mainly on the basis of what their characteristics might be, considered quasi-naturally, and in particular on their ethnic or cultural characteristics or 'origins', in a process that certain authors describe as an 'ethnicising' process of educational or social issues, and which today legitimates or makes licit themes, questionings and scientific or uninformed judgements that were hardly so yesterday. So, in place of the 'explanation' of 'failure' or educational inequality by the social environment at one time dominant in the professional ideology of the teaching world and in social and media-related discourse, we have the 'explanation' by origin. In place of what may look today like a certain concealment of the question of ethnicity behind the social question in the sociology of the years 1979–1980 and statistical reasoning of the type 'all other things being equal', a greater importance attached to this question seems to have been substituted, to the detriment not only of the social question, but of the need for giving more consideration to the relationship between the one and the other.

From this arise certain contradictory or paradoxical characters of the ZEP policy, its developments and implementation. Whereas this policy and the choice of the schools concerned are based essentially on criteria and knowledge of the sociological, or at least at least socio-statistical type, and on a concern for improving the schooling and learning of children from working-class backgrounds, the sociological dimension practically disappears from the work and the educational thinking governing the choice, implementation and promotion of the most symbolic actions and projects of this policy. These actions and projects are overwhelmingly underpinned by pedagogical conceptions, or even dogmas that are insensitive to sociological questioning and are based on a generic, abstract, model of the pupil or learner,[9] by a set of problems, or even rhetoric, that relate more to innovation than democratisation, of the treatment, or even of the recognition, of diversity than the fight against inequality (Bernstein, 2007), without the question of knowing whether the modes of innovation most frequently implemented are not likely to maintain or even reinforce the opacity and implicit nature of educational culture and practices for pupils from working-class backgrounds being considered or even questioned. These actions and projects, and the generic conceptions underpinning them, coexist with others, seemingly more related to sociological questioning and more anxious to take into account pupils as they are. But these actions and projects, these ways of adapting and the arguments behind them or which justify them, may go against the targeted or stated objectives because these often deal with questions of socialisation, improvement or safeguarding of the 'climate' of schools or the self-image of pupils independently or on the fringe of the question of learning and acculturation, or because they contribute, in the day-to-day life of the classroom and generally without those involved being aware of it, to restricting the learning offer and opportunity, and the requirements of intellectual work that pupils are asked to perform.

Far from being the laboratory of social change in education that some wished to see, the ZEP policy and its implementation have hardly provided the opportunity to move forward in the conception and implementation of this 'rational, sociologically-inspired pedagogy', to which the work of Bourdieu, Passeron and Bernstein aimed to contribute. It may even be wondered whether the inflections given, more or less explicitly, to this policy have not turned their back on this direction of work, on the one hand, by developing, during the first 'revivals', from aiming at democratisation, considered as compensation for a social disadvantage, to aiming at the social management of educational inequality, considered as compensation for a local disadvantage; and on the other hand, more recently, by giving priority to individualising courses, recognising and encouraging talents, and promoting excellence, using forms of rhetoric which are today more and more often the rule in political discourse and regulations concerning not only the ZEP policy, but also all the educational policies of the early part of this century. A new inflexion seems be gaining ground, the scope and effects of which are too early to assess, which would tend to redirect the explicit or implicit objectives of these educational policies, and particularly the ZEP policy, towards aiming at maximising the individual potential of each pupil, regarded as a quasi-natural characteristic, without laying down the objective of gaining a better understanding (the better to transform) the social and educational processes which give form and content to this 'potential', to this diversity of talents or the needs to which the education system is invited to adapt. It seems that we are witnessing an increase not only in measures closely adapted to the various categories of 'specific needs' or pupils 'at risk', which are adopted without their being really questioned and very often help to naturalise them, the ways of categorising that designate a particular segment of the population or social arena as posing a 'problem' and calling for treatment (which is what is undoubtedly to be observed concerning the *educational success* measure), but also in the measures aimed at recognising the 'right to excellence' of the most 'deserving' individuals from working-class backgrounds and districts, granting them more opportunity for exemption from the school catchment area and for schooling in institutions that recruit from more privileged social backgrounds, and by making it easier for them to have access to the courses and universities considered as the most prestigious, while reconfiguring the ambitions of pupils who will remain in ZEP districts and schools around the acquisition of the 'common core of knowledge and competencies' established by the reform law voted in 2005.[10] It does seems that an objective of broadening and diversifying the recruitment of 'elites', which differs notably from the objective of reducing social inequality that underpinned the creation of the ZEP policy, is now asserting itself.

The questions raised here do not concern the register of political decision making and analysis alone, but also that of research work. They raise new issues for research while at the same time inviting it to go reconsider some old questions. Among these questions – that we can here only briefly mention, some of which receive more attention in the introductory and concluding chapters of this book – those relating to the need for more consideration to be given to the relationship between the social processes and the educational processes proper that lead to educational inequality, the relationship between social determinants and singular destinies and schooling, or to the relationship between those special academic and social configurations that are ZEPs, or what van Zanten calls 'the school of the periphery', and the generic social and academic logic of domination and segregation which are concentrated and become exacerbated in ZEPs; those questions, too, which subsume the concept of compensatory education or policies and the criticism they have attracted or, even more broadly, those of the conditions for a possible 'sociology of cognitive development which takes the cognitive side of inequalities between social groups seriously' (Duru-Bellat, 2002).

Notes

1. Cf. 'Introduction'.
2. This chapter has benefited from contributions and critical comments by Élisabeth Bautier, Choukri Ben Ayed, Stéphane Bonnéry, Sylvain Broccolichi, Daniel Frandji, Françoise Lorcerie, Benjamin Moignard and Sofia Stavrou. Thanks also go to Dominique Glasman for his critical proofreading of the first version of this text.
3. 1st call for tender by the inter-departmental delegation for the city (Délégation interministérielle à la Ville -DIV), March 2006.
4. If there is any debate today, it relates not to the principle of a so-called 'positive discrimination' social and educational policy itself, but to the relevance of an approach in terms of regions rather than of populations (cf. Maurin, 2004).
5. The French education system is one of the ones which, as of the first years of primary school, has the most children doing a school year again because of learning difficulties.
6. This relatively minor advantage can be observed only for pupils who have done all their primary schooling in a ZEP.
7. This same observation is a recurrent one in the reports that inspectors have devoted for more than ten years to school projects, deploring the fact that they primarily concern fringe aspects of learning and stop at the classroom door, that they are generally limited to a juxtaposition of incomplete and opportunist actions, and are above all perceived as means of obtaining some additional resources and the certification of initiatives whose relationship with national objectives or that of democratising academic success is more proclaimed than proven (cf. for example IGEN, 1997; IGAEN, 1999). It is also to be found in the report that Odile Joly-Rissoan and Dominique Glasman devoted to the first assessments of the 'educational success' programme launched in 2005 by the ministry for social cohesion, then in charge of town policy (Joly-Rissoan et al., 2006).
8. On these questions, cf. Rochex, 2000; on 'relay-classes', cf. Martin & Bonnéry, 2002.
9. The inspector Charles Toussaint wrote in 1986, in connection with the first phase of the ZEP policy, that 'never had so much concern been shown in the French education system about the process of the construction of knowledge by

the learner', before adding that this was 'a minor revolution, almost unnoticed because it was limited to minorities and had no spectacular repercussions', as if it were enough for this underground revolution to become more widespread for the objectives of the democratisation of academic success to move forward (Toussaint, 1986). This appraisal may be seen as a particularly eloquent example of the underestimation of the impact of sociological constraints on the processes of teaching and learning in ZEPs, and the overestimation of the effectiveness and the democratising nature of the projects and actions implemented there.

10. In the 9 October 2007 issue of the national daily newspaper *Le Monde*, in connection with a 'success ambition' secondary school that benefited from the undivided attention of the minister for state education behind the creation of the 'ambition success' networks in 2006, we read that the first area of the project implemented there is entitled 'practices used to help with acquiring the common core'.

Bibliography

Scientific documents

ANDRIEUX V., LEVASSEUR J., PENNINCKX J. & ROBIN I. (2001). 'À partir des évaluations nationales à l'entrée en sixième: des constats sur les élèves, des questions sur les pratiques' [From national evaluations as pupils enter secondary school: observations on the pupils and questions on practices]. *Éducation et Formations*, no. 61, pp. 103–109.

BAUTIER E. & ROCHEX J.-Y. (1997). 'Apprendre: des malentendus qui font la différence' [Learning: misunderstandings that make all the difference]. In J.-P. TERRAIL (ed.), *La scolarisation de la France. Critique de l'état des lieux*. Paris: La Dispute (Taken from J. DEAUVIEAU and J.-P. TERRAIL (dir.) (2007), *Les sociologues, l'école et la transmission des savoirs* [Sociologists, school and the transmission of knowledge]. Paris: La Dispute).

BAUTIER E. & ROCHEX J.-Y. (1998). *L'expérience scolaire des «nouveaux lycéens». Démocratisation ou massification?* [The educational experience of 'new high-school pupils'. Democratization or a mass phenomenon?] Paris: Armand Colin.

BEAUD S. (2002). *80 per cent au bac...et après? Les enfants de la démocratisation scolaire* [80 per cent with a high-school diploma...and then what? The children of academic democratisation]. Paris: La Découverte.

BENABOU R., KRAMARZ F. & PROST C. (2004). 'Zones d'éducation prioritaire: quels moyens pour quels résultats? Une évaluation sur la période 1982–1992' [Priority education zones: what resources for what results? An evaluation over the period 1982–1992]. *Économie et statistiques*, no. 380, pp. 3–29.

BERNSTEIN B. (1992). 'La construction du discours pédagogique et les modalités de sa pratique' [The construction of pedagogic discourse and the modalities of its practice]. *Critiques sociales*, nos. 3–4, pp. 20–58.

BERNSTEIN B. (2007). *Pédagogie, contrôle symbolique et identité. Théorie, recherche, critique* [Pedagogy, symbolic control and identity. Theory, research, critique]. Lévis (Québec): Les Presses de l'Université Laval.

BOURDIEU P. & PASSERON J.-C. (1970). *La Reproduction. Éléments pour une théorie du système d'enseignement* [Reproduction: Factors for a theory of the teaching system]. Paris: Les Ed. de Minuit.

BOURGAREL A. (1999). 'Va-t-on étendre sans fin les ZEP?' [Are priority education zones going to be extended indefinitely?]. *VEI Enjeux*, no. 117, pp. 8–15.

BOUVEAU P., CHARLOT B., ROCHEX J.-Y. et al. (1992). 'Le soutien aux politiques éducatives dans les ZEP-DSQ (1989–1992)' [Support for education policies in priority education and social development zones]. *Report for the Caisse des Dépôts et Consignations*. Paris: Association ANALISE.

BOUVEAU P. & ROCHEX J.-Y. (1997). *Les ZEP, entre école et société* [Priority education zones: between school and society]. Paris: Hachette/CNDP.

BROCCOLICHI S. (1995). 'Orientations et ségrégations nouvelles dans l'enseignement secondaire' [New directions and segregations in secondary education]. *Sociétés contemporaines*, no. 21, pp. 15–27.

BROCCOLICHI S. & BEN-AYED C. (1999). 'L'institution scolaire et la réussite de tous aujourd'hui: "pourrait mieux faire"' [The academic institution and success for all today: 'could do better']. *Revue française de pédagogie*, no. 129, pp. 39–51.

CAILLE J.-P. (2001). 'Les collégiens de ZEP à la fin des années quatre-vingt-dix: caractéristiques des élèves et impact de la scolarisation en ZEP sur la réussite' [Priority education zone secondary school pupils in the late nineties: pupil characteristics and impact on success of schooling in priority education zones]. *Éducation et Formations*, no. 61, pp. 111–140.

CÈBE S. (2000). *Développer la conceptualisation et la prise de conscience métacognitive à l'école maternelle: effets sur l'efficience scolaire ultérieure du CP au CE2. Une contribution à la prévention de l'échec scolaire des élèves de milieux populaires* [Developing conceptualisation and metacognitive awareness at pre-school: effects on the subsequent efficiency of the first years of primary education. A contribution to the prevention of educational failure of pupils from working-class backgrounds]. Doctoral thesis in psychology, Université de Provence.

CHARLOT B. (1994). '"Ce qui se pense" dans les zones d'éducation prioritaires: analyse des demandes de financement' [What is being thought about in priority education zones: analysis of funding requests]. In B. Charlot (ed.), *L'école et le territoire: nouveaux espaces, nouveaux enjeux* [School and region: new areas, new stakes]. Paris: Armand Colin.

CHARLOT B., BAUTIER E. & ROCHEX J.-Y. (1993). *École et savoirs dans les banlieues... et ailleurs* [School and knowledge in the suburbs... and elsewhere]. Paris: Armand Colin.

CHARTIER A.-M. (1992). 'Questions d'apprentissage' [Questions of learning]. *Cahiers pédagogiques*, no. 309, pp. 19–21.

CRESAS (1985). *Depuis 1981, l'école pour tous? Zones d'Éducation Prioritaires* [Since 1981: schooling for all? Priority education zones]. Paris: INRP/L'Harmattan.

DURU-BELLAT M. (2002). *Les inégalités sociales à l'école. Genèse et mythes* [Social inequality at school. Genesis and myths]. Paris: PUF.

FIJALKOW J. (1992). *Rapport à la Caisse des Dépôts et Consignations concernant l'aide à la définition, la conduite et l'évaluation de projets éducatifs* [Report to the Caisse des Dépôts et Consignations concerning help with defining, running and evaluating educational projects]. Toulouse: Université Toulouse-le-Mirail, multigr.

GIRY-CROISSARD M. & NIEL X. (1997). 'Homogénéité et disparité des classes dans les collèges publics' [Homogeneity and disparity in state school classes]. *note d'Information*, nos. 97–30, DEP-MEN.

GLASMAN D. (1992). *L'école réinventée? Le partenariat dans les zones d'éducation prioritaires* [School reinvented? Partnership in education priority zones]. Paris: L'Harmattan.

GLASMAN D. (2001). *L'accompagnement scolaire. Sociologie d'une marge de l'école* [Educational support. Sociology of a side issue of schooling]. Paris: PUF.

HENRIOT-VAN ZANTEN A. (1990). *L'école et l'espace local. Les enjeux des zones d'éducation prioritaires* [School and the local area. The issues surrounding priority education zones]. Lyon: Presses Universitaires de Lyon.

ISAMBERT-JAMATI V. (1990). 'Les choix éducatifs dans les zones d'éducation prioritaires' [Educational choices in priority education zones]. *Revue française de sociologie*, vol. XXI, no. 1, pp. 75–100 (Taken from V. ISAMBERT-JAMATI (1990), *Les savoirs scolaires. Enjeux sociaux des contenus d'enseignement et de leurs réformes* [Academic knowledge. Social issues surrounding educational content and its reforms]. Paris: Éditions Universitaires).

JOLY-RISSOAN O., GLASMAN D. *et al.* (2006). *Le programme* Réussite éducative*: mise en place et perspectives*. Rapport pour la Délégation interministérielle à la Ville, Université de Savoie.

KHERROUBI M. & ROCHEX J.-Y. (2002). Note de synthèse 'La recherche en éducation et les ZEP en France. 1re partie: 'Politique ZEP, objets, postures et orientations de recherche' [Summary report 'Research into education and priority education zones in France. 1st part: 'Priority education zone policy, research subjects, stances and developments']'. *Revue française de pédagogie*, no. 140, pp. 103–132.

KHERROUBI M. & ROCHEX J.-Y. (2004). Note de synthèse « La recherche en éducation et les ZEP en France. 2e partie: 'Apprentissages et exercice professionnel en ZEP: résultats, analyses, interprétations' ». *Revue française de pédagogie*, no. 147, pp. 115–190.

LORCERIE F. (1993). 'Le partenariat et la "relance" des ZEP' [Partnership and 'revival' of priority education zones]'. *Les Cahiers de l'IREMAM*, no. 3.

LORCERIE F. (dir.) (2003). *L'École et le défi ethnique. Éducation et intégration.* [School and the ethnic challenge. Education and integration]. Paris ESF.

LORCERIE F. (2006). 'L'éducation prioritaire: une politique sous-administrée' [Priority education: an under-administered policy]. *VEI Diversité*, no. 144, pp. 61–71.

MARTIN É. & BONNÉRY S. (2002). *Les classes relais. Un dispositif pour les élèves en rupture avec l'école* [Relay classes. A measure for pupils who have rejected school]. Paris: ESF.

MAURIN É. (2004). *Le ghetto français. Enquête sur le séparatisme social* [The French ghetto. An investigation into social separatism]. Paris: Seuil.

MEURET D. (1994). 'L'efficacité de la politique des zones d'éducation prioritaires dans les collèges' [The effectiveness of the priority education zone policy in secondary schools]. *Revue française de pédagogie*, no. 109, pp. 41–64.

MEURET D. (2000). 'Les politiques de discrimination positive en France et à l'étranger' [Positive discrimination policies in France and abroad]. In A. VAN ZANTEN (ed.), *L'école, l'état des savoirs* [School: the state of knowledge]. Paris: La Découverte.

MILLET M. & THIN D. (2005). *Ruptures scolaires. L'école à l'épreuve de la question sociale* [Rejecting education. School put to the test by the social question]. Paris: PUF.

MOISAN C. (2001). 'Les ZEP: bientôt vingt ans' [Almost twenty years of priority education zones]. *Éducation et Formations*, no. 61, pp. 13–22.

MURAT F. (1998). 'Les différentes façons d'évaluer le niveau des élèves en fin de collège' [The different ways of evaluating pupils' level at the end of the fourth year of secondary school]. *Éducation et Formations*, no. 53, pp. 35–49.

OBERTI M. (2007). 'L'école dans la ville. Ségrégation, mixité, carte scolaire' [School in the city. Segregation, diversity, catchment area]. Paris: Presses de Sciences Po.

OZP (OBSERVATOIRE DES ZONES PRIORITAIRES) (2002). *Reconstruire l'éducation prioritaire* [Rebuilding priority education] Preparatory text for the OZP study days on May 8 and 9, 2002, multigr.

PAYET J.-P. (1995). *Collèges en banlieue. Ethnographie d'un monde scolaire* [Secondary school in the suburb. Ethnography of an academic world]. Paris: Méridiens-Klincksieck.

PAYET J.-P. & VAN ZANTEN A. (1996). Note de synthèse 'L'école, les enfants de l'immigration et des minorités ethniques: une revue de la littérature française, américaine et britannique [Summary report: 'School, children from immigrant backgrounds and ethnic minorities: a review of French, American and British literature']'. *Revue française de pédagogie*, no. 117, pp. 87–149.

PELTIER M.-L. *et al.* (2004). *Dur d'enseigner en ZEP* [Hard work teaching in priority education zones]. Paris: La Pensée sauvage Éditions.

Revue française de pédagogie (2002). 'Les ZEP: vingt ans de politiques et de recherches' [Priority education zones: twenty years of policies and research], no. 140.

ROCHEX J.-Y. (1997). 'Les ZEP: un bilan décevant' [Priority education zones: a disappointing result]. In J.-P. TERRAIL (ed.), *La scolarisation de la France. Critique de l'état des lieux* [Schooling in France. A critical inventory]. Paris: La Dispute, pp. 123–139.

ROCHEX J.-Y. (2000). 'Apprentissage et socialisation: un rapport problématique' [Learning and socialisation: a problem relationship]. Address at the summer university of the CRAP-Cahiers Pédagogiques. In M. TOZZI (ed.), *Apprentissage et socialisation* [Learning and socialisation]. Montpellier: CRDP du Languedoc-Roussillon.

ROUBAN L. (1990). 'La modernisation de l'État et la fin de la spécificité française' [Modernisation of the state and the end of French specificity]. *Revue française de sciences politiques*, 40, no. 4, pp. 521–545.

STEFANOU A. (2001). 'Les caractéristiques des collèges de l'éducation prioritaire et le destin scolaire de leurs élèves' [The characteristics of *collèges* in priority education and the academic destiny of their pupils]. *Éducation et Formations*, no. 61, pp. 97–101.

THÉLOT C. (2001). 'Égalité et diversité dans le système éducatif: constats, enjeux et perspectives' [Equality and diversity in the education system: observations, issues and perspectives]. In A. VERGNIOUX and H. PEYRONIE (eds), *Le sens de l'école et la démocratie* [The meaning of school and democracy]. Berne: Peter Lang.

TISSOT S. (2007). *L'État et les quartiers. Genèse d'une catégorie de l'action publique* [The state and city districts. Genesis of a public action category]. Paris: Seuil.

TRANCART D. (2000). 'L'enseignement public: les disparités dans l'offre d'enseignement' [Public education: disparities in the education offer]. In A. VAN ZANTEN (ed.), *L'école, l'état des savoirs* [School: the state of knowledge]. Paris: La Découverte.

VAN ZANTEN A. (2001). *L'école de la périphérie. Scolarité et ségrégation en banlieue* [School around the edge. Schooling and segregation in the suburbs]. Paris: PUF.

VINCENT G. (1980). *L'école primaire française. Étude sociologique* [Primary school in France. Sociological study]. Lyon: PUL.

Legal references and official or administrative documents

ARMAND A. & GILLE B. (2006). *La contribution de l'éducation prioritaire à l'égalité des chances des élèves* [The contribution of priority education to equal opportunity for pupils]. Report to the Minister for State Education, Higher Education and Research, IGEN and IGAEN.

IGAEN (INSPECTION GÉNÉRALE DE L'ADMINISTRATION DE L'ÉDUCATION NATIONALE) (1999). *Rapport général* [General report]. Paris: La Documentation française.

IGEN (Inspection générale de l'Éducation nationale) (1997). *Le collège: sept ans d'observations et d'analyses* [The *collège*: seven years of observations and analyses]. Paris: CNDP/Hachette Éducation.

MOISAN C. & SIMON J. (1996). *Aménagement de la carte des zones d'éducation prioritaires* [Altering the catchment areas for priority education zones]. IGAEN and IGEN, multigr., 20 pages.

MOISAN C. & SIMON J. (1997). *Les déterminants de la réussite scolaire en zone d'éducation prioritaire* [Determining factors for academic success in priority education zones]. Report to the Minister for State Education, IGAEN and IGEN. Paris: INRP (Centre Alain Savary).

TOUSSAINT C. (1986). *Rapport relatif aux zones prioritaires* [Report on priority zones]. MEN-IGEN.

Greece

5
Greece: On Mechanisms and Successive Programmes between Support and Innovation

Gella Varnava-Skoura, Dimitris Vergidis and Chryssa Kassimi

Educational policies designed to address and prevent school failure have a history going back about 25 years in Greece; the first were put into place during the Socialist governments of the 1980s. These policies have not, however, assumed significant importance in the public eye in terms of debates or scientific research, despite efforts by some scholars. Instead, topics at the heart of educational debates in Greece in the last decade have mainly been about access to higher education, the evaluations of universities and the creation of private universities – an initiative that has come up against serious resistance in the name of equal rights to free and public education (Donatos *et al.*, 2006). The last three years have also witnessed lively scientific and political debates generated by the introduction of new history textbooks.

Before concentrating on policies addressing school failure, it is informative to examine the various measures taken towards increasing educational democratisation and improving the quality of compulsory education within a broader context following the fall of the dictatorship (1967–1974) in 1974.

First, a common compulsory education programme of nine years was put into place in 1976 (Law 309/1976), and was extended to ten years in 2007. This includes one year of pre-school, six years of primary school and three years of *gymnasio* (secondary school). In 1984, teacher training for pre-school and primary school became university-level, and regional teacher training centres were then put in place (Law 1566/1985). Textbooks, provided free to all students at all levels in public schools, were redesigned, and for the first time teacher textbooks were provided to teachers for additional pedagogical support.[1] In addition, some simplifications in the written language were adopted, which contributed towards facilitating the learning of spelling.

At the same time, educational policies designed to decrease inequalities produced within the school were implemented with an egalitarian perspective. More specifically, high school (latter part of secondary school) entrance

127

exams were abolished; it is within this context that in 1982 the first tutoring and remedial support practices were organised for students in the first two years of high school (Law 1304/1982, Article 27).[2] In addition, the state gave particular help – in the form of tutoring and remedial support classes ('reception classes') – to students of Greek emigrant parents and political refugees who were repatriated in the 1980s (Law 1404/1983, Article 45).

Following this, towards the end of the 1980s, tutoring and remedial support was opened to all school levels, regardless of student origin (Law 1824/1988, Article 4); this was provided within the framework of a broader programme targeting illiteracy, following a decision by the Council of Ministers of Education of the European Economic Union (EEC) in 1984.[3] The Greek government thus recognised, through various written texts and speeches, the relationship between school failure and features of school functioning and the students, as well as the broader social causes (Vergidis, 1995a, p. 196). During the 1990s, the question of school failure (defined in part by the number of pupils having to repeat a school year, but especially by drop-out rates) took centre stage within both the scientific and the educational arenas. Research carried out by the Pedagogical Institute, a division of the Ministry of Education,[4] and other studies showed a decrease in drop-out rates in the first cycle of secondary school (Lariou-Drettaki, 1993; Vergidis, 1995a; Palaiokrassas *et al.*, 2001; Greece: Ministry of Education and Religious Affairs, 2006a).

In 1997, several significant changes were put into place, including the 'full-day school',[5] a national curriculum reform and the promulgation of new approaches to school knowledge. A reform to the system of access to higher education was also initiated, as was an evaluation procedure for educational practices. These changes were tied to recommendations by the CEE and were integrated within a framework of co-ordinating educational policies among the Member States.[6] Such changes mark a reorientation towards educational policies underlying the objectives of modernisation of the educational system. Nonetheless, it should be noted that during this time no studies examining student learning were carried out by either the Ministry of Education or other national research centres. Some authors have emphasised the absence of official research on knowledge and skill learning, suggesting that such an absence may even be intentional (Evangélou & Paléologou, 2007, pp. 51–52). It should be underlined that the absence of 'national standards' and objective criteria and assessment tests makes the task of evaluating students' skill and knowledge levels throughout their school years quite difficult.[7] This gap has been highlighted to some degree by international research by the International Association for the Evaluation of Educational Achievement (IEA) and by the Organisation for Economic Co-operation and Development's (OECD) Programme for International Student Assessment (PISA).

Understanding the issues tied to priority education policies requires a brief look at certain particularities of the Greek national context in which these policies take place.

The principal characteristics of the Greek educational system

The first publications dealing with the topic of social inequality and school success appeared relatively late, within the socio-political situation created by the fall of the military dictatorship in 1974 (Lambiri-Dimaki, 1974; Tsoukalas, 1975, 1977; Eliou, 1976; Psacharopoulos & Kazamias, 1985; Tzani, 1988; Varnava-Skoura, 1992). Some of these scholars take the critical perspective of theories of social reproduction and find only a reproductive role of the school system in the results, while others emphasise certain particularities of the Greek context that are fundamentally related to a relatively significant representation of the least privileged social classes among institutions of higher learning. These differences are themselves due to a particular feature of the Greek context: Greece is characterised by a level of both over-education (a relatively high rate of graduates from institutions of higher learning) and under-education (a high rate of illiteracy, especially in older populations, high rates of school drop-outs and the low educational level of some students leaving the *gymnasio*) (Vergidis, 1995a; Kortesi-Dafermou, 1998; Kalogridi, 2000; Varnava-Skoura & Vergidis, 2002; Vergidis & Stamelos, 2007; Greece: Ministry of Education and Religious Affairs, 2007b). In particular, the level of over-education increased following the inauguration of new universities following the Socialists' election victory in 1981.[8]

The level of public funding for teaching is very low; in Greece, it is around two-thirds of the average per student of the OECD countries (OECD, 2006, p. 30). The educational authorities themselves acknowledge the low level of public funding in comparison with that of other countries (3.8 per cent of the GNP versus 5.07 per cent for the whole of the EU countries, according to Eurostat), especially with regard to first and second degrees (Greece: Ministry of Education and Religious Affairs, 2007b, pp. 37–38). Furthermore, the highly centralised nature of the Greek state and public services influences the public school system, in which virtually all children in Greece are enrolled. From both a pedagogical and administrative standpoint, the system is highly centralised, long characterised by a common textbook for each subject and highly uniform teaching practices.

Among the system's weaknesses is, according to political leaders, the lack of any evaluation process. The only available data regarding student performance at a national level come from comparative international research, such as the IEA and PISA projects which show a low level of acquisition (in reading/comprehension and in maths) compared with the other countries participating in the research (OECD, 2004, 2006, p. 14; Greece: Ministry of Education and Religious Affairs, 2006b). The main problem, therefore, does not necessarily concern attendance: according to the National Statistical Service, since the year 2000, 99 per cent of students finished primary school. Rather, it concerns improving the level of instruction provided and developing skills, especially in reading/comprehension, as well as in maths. The strong egalitarian tradition of teachers and the absence of national assessment criteria, however, often succeed in 'hiding' the degree of inequality and skills demonstrated by international research (Vitsilaki-Soroniati, 2004, p. 264).

The school population has also changed according to different waves of immigration over recent decades. Greece has thus changed from a mainly emigrant country to – during the 1980s – a host country for immigrants from places such as Albania (57.5 per cent of the immigrant population) and the former Soviet Union, as well as other countries of Eastern Europe, Asia and Africa. A large part of the population coming from Albania and the former Soviet Union are of Greek origin. According to the 2001 census data, immigrants (of which 45.5 per cent are women) account for 7 per cent of the country's total population and about 9.5 per cent of the workforce (Kritikidis, 2004). At the same time, the problem of low birth rate is becoming more acute. In 2005, there were 107,500 births compared with about 148,000 in 1980 (Greece: Athens Academy, 1990, p. 20; Greece: National Statistical Service, 2007). The school population is thus changing according to the low birth rate combined with an increase in the number of students whose first language is not Greek. In the 2004–2005 school year, students with foreign or repatriated parents represented 9.4 per cent of students in the *gymnasio* (Drettakis, 2007, p. 45). This development creates the need to strengthen programmes designed to help integrate these students into the school system.

Within this context, the European policies against social exclusion developed in the 1990s appear to have had considerable impact on the way in which school inequality is approached, not only at the level of educational policy, but also in terms of scientific debates (Tsiakalos, 2004, pp. 42–43). The integration of certain priority education policies by the Greek government in successive Community Support Frameworks, starting in the second half of the 1990s, has played a significant role. This decision has strongly influenced both the political debate and the scientific research regarding how to address school failure. More specifically, the interest taken by the European Union towards populations threatened by social exclusion has led educational authorities to emphasise the needs of certain populations, specifically children of immigration, children of the Muslim minority in Thrace and Romani children. Within the framework of multicultural education, considerable resources are allotted to help these children integrate (EU funding of up to 75 per cent). In addition, other priority policies such as 'full-day school' benefit from this kind of funding. The following section describes the most significant priority education policies.

Priority education policies

Tutoring/remedial support programme

Tutoring and remedial support was instituted by the Socialist government in the late 1980s (Law 1824/1988, Article 4), after a trial period between 1984 and 1988. Regarding remedial support at the level of the *gymnasio*, this law stipulates the application of a previous law for students in the later years of secondary school showing signs of learning difficulty (Law 1304/1982, JO 144, Article 29). In regard to primary school, details of the programme were specified a few years later (Presidential Decree 462/1991, Article 5), in the form of additional instruction in Greek and maths for 'weak' students, and more specifically for 'students who have not acquired the basics in areas of reading, writing, and arithmetic' (Presidential Decree 462/1991, Article 5).

In the most recent ministerial regulations for the *gymnasio* (Ministerial Decree 96734/G2, JO1301/2003: 'Remedial support for students in the *gymnasio*'), there is a reformulation of the objectives and definitions of the targeted population. It is no longer only an issue of children with learning difficulties (weak students), but is also an issue of

> children showing gaps [in different subjects] and who consequently can not follow the programme or participate effectively in the educational process or students who wish to improve their performance.

The new objectives target the reintegration of students in the educational process, a reduction in school drop-out rates and improvement in performance. The practices remain the same, although the disciplines involved have been broadened (to include physics, chemistry and foreign languages). In fact, in practice the reasoning behind putting remedial support and tutoring services into place is linked more to administrative and organisational issues (filling teachers' schedules) than pedagogical ones. How these practices are actually carried out does not depend on identifying the nature of the difficulties of the students involved, making any evaluation of the results difficult. Instead, the teaching follows the 'regular' programme, which is to say traditional teaching methods with a few additional hours of instruction to small groups of students removed from the regular class, which incidentally often produces a degree of stigma, especially at the primary level. These negative effects appeared within the first few years of the programme's implementation (Papaconstantinou, 1986; Varnava-Skoura & Kostaki, 1992).

According to the most recent data, 1.2 per cent of primary school students and 5.5 per cent of *gymnasio* students participated in these programmes,[9] demonstrating low rates of implementation in primary school, the ideal time to target prevention and treatment of school failure. Regarding the rate in the *gymnasio*, although this is higher than that of primary schools, it is nonetheless just below the percentage of students who quit school at this level (6.09 per cent) (Ministry of Education and Religious Affairs, 2006a; Ministry of Education and Religious Affairs, 2007a, p. 35). As far as any evaluation is concerned, there is still no official and systematic assessment. At the same time, the data provided by the annual reports of education advisors – intended as a tool to monitor teaching practices – are not treated in any systematic way, thus preventing any real assessment. The few existing studies rely on data, for the most part, from the beginning of the 1990s and provide a report on primary school practices from the first implementations of the programme (Papaconstantinou, 1986; Manitsa, 1990; Varnava-Skoura & Kostaki, 1992). The data from these studies were re-analysed in a more recent study (Vrettos, 2001) involving a survey of teachers and education professionals (school councillors and supervisors) in a region of Attica. The weak use of this programme was due, according to this study, to the lack of political will and funding on the part of the Ministry of Education, as well as to a lack of pedagogical support.

The common element of all these studies is the emphasis on the programme's weaknesses, such as the lack of training for teachers involved in different teaching methods, organisational problems and lack of funding. According to these analyses, there are no effects on the students from the point of view of academic improvement. Even now there is no information available in relation to school-related characteristics of students participating in the programmes; and yet, remedial support and tutoring continue to be the most widespread programme with a relatively high number of pupils in secondary school. The lack of any qualitative research on the educational process is also important to note; this requires both authorisation from the Pedagogical Institute as well as teachers' consent.

Pilot programmes for remedial support and tutoring

Within the context of the second Community Support Framework (Operational Programme for Initial Training and Teacher's Education), which has facilitated significant support for improving the educational system since 1994, it was decided to explore a different pedagogical approach based on ideas underlying the Educational Priority Areas in England and the ZEPs (Zones d'éducation prioritaire) in France (Varnava-Skoura & Vergidis, 2002, pp. 21–24).[10] Two main initiatives were planned: (1) a study aimed at defining the areas with the greatest educational needs (education priority areas – EPAs); and (2) developing pilot programmes in some schools within a differentiated teaching approach, thus allowing for 'positive discrimination' while nonetheless involving all the students in a school-wide project regardless of their academic performance.

The study aimed at defining EPAs was given to the National Centre for Social Research (EKKE) by the Ministry of Education (Maratou-Alipranti *et al.*, 2006). The University of Thessaloniki directed the implementation of the pilot programmes. To ensure adequate and continuous support at the local level, the universities entrusted with carrying out these programmes then created a network of university teams in three different universities in areas where there were a large number of participating schools.

The schools that participated in the pilot programmes reflected the range of characteristics often associated with areas of special social and educational needs (geographically isolated areas, disadvantaged urban neighbourhoods, rural regions, etc.). During the first year of these pilot programmes (1997), they were put into place in 30 schools at the primary level (including pre-schools for prevention) and the first cycle of secondary school. Following very positive results, the Ministry of Education asked for these pilot programmes to be extended, in two successive phases, up to the year 2000, in 127 schools.

All the schools that participated had serious problems. They were not chosen based on centralised procedures, but were invited in response to a call for candidates. The offer, which appeared in the press, concerned specific regions and defined the participatory criteria for the first phase as the percentage of students with weak performance, as well as the commitment of at least half the teachers and the school director to participate, a commitment which required extension of regular hours. The school was also required to have space to create a teaching resource centre. In a second phase, the elaboration of a school-wide project was required while ensuring support through the co-ordination of teams associated with the universities.[11] When the project was launched, the teachers were surveyed regarding the following issues:

1. school description (socio-demographics, human resources, material resources, teacher profiles, infrastructure, absenteeism, turnover of personnel, other actions put into place, extra-curricular activities, student assessments and school 'climate');[12]
2. their opinions regarding the reasons why their weak students have difficulty in school, as well as their teaching experience and practices.[13]

Primary school teachers attributed students' difficulties to either family background or personal problems, or they gave no response. Secondary school teachers gave largely the same reasons, although they also mentioned learning gaps that had built up since primary school. Regarding student behaviour, all teachers acknowledged that this was characterised by a lack of participation in class. The teaching philosophy underlying the programmes required more open communication within the school. An initial assessment of the activities and programmes was undertaken to examine and modify the activities to better guarantee overall improvement, particularly for students with difficulties.

Teachers underwent professional development programmes, at the individual school level and regional and national levels. These courses provided support for the implementation of each school's project, activities requiring multiple options and the effective collaboration of the teachers, none of which characterise the standard methods practised in Greece. Furthermore, they introduced the teachers to the use of active and differentiated methods, to the use of developed educational material as well as to the initial evaluation procedures that constituted one of the axes of the pilot programme's evaluation.

At the student level, the school project – carried out in the afternoons after regular school hours – aimed to involve the whole school in interesting educational activities for at least five hours per week during the school year, and in the summer (especially for the weaker students) in camps (with educational activities for three hours per day for three weeks). The development of the school project was helped by creating a resource centre to improve school infrastructure in multiple ways. This played an important role in experimenting with new teaching methods and engaging students.

The pilot programmes were evaluated by both internal (Varnava-Skoura & Vergidis, 2002, pp. 245–264) and external (Lazaridis, 1999; Kalavasis, 2000) evaluators. The positive impact of the programmes for the teachers was seen in their evaluation reports, but also in a series of interviews with both teachers and students. The most noteworthy element to emerge from these data is how the teachers' conceptions and attitudes towards the 'weak students' changed. They witnessed very positive changes in these students, within a context of a redefined relationship, guided by the school project and the practice of 'positive discrimination', a change that also reflected a kind of development in their own knowledge and awareness. The teachers involved in these programmes also mentioned positive side effects in 'regular' school activities.

The interviews with the students demonstrated clearly that they were, in general, very happy with their involvement in the school project as well as the other possibilities provided by the programmes. Rates of absenteeism decreased significantly and the rate of student participation was high in each school, despite the fact that the pilot programmes were optional. Compared with the morning school programme, many students spoke about how their relationships had changed with their teachers (Varnava-Skoura & Vergidis, 2002, pp. 256–265). At the end of the period of application of the pilot programmes, statistical analysis of teacher evaluations of student progress indicated significant improvement in all classes and especially in the first class (Varnava-Skoura & Vergidis, 2002, pp. 245–264). Progress made from the students in the *gymnasio* was, however, less striking (*ibid.*, p.246). Although the most significant progress was made by the 'good' students, according to teacher evaluations (293/347) the group of weaker students in primary school showed improved performance; this includes satisfactory improvement (120/347), considerable improvement (100/347) and very considerable improvement (73/347), showing that all students benefited from the programmes (*ibid.*, p. 248).

These programmes were scheduled to end in the year 2000, and the Ministry of Education did not follow up with any area-based priority education policies. No follow-up was offered despite official discourse about adopting the approach within the context of the full-day school that we describe below. The open approach of the pilot programmes was abandoned, because of both the relatively high cost[14] and the broader lack of educational policies targeting school failure on the part of the Ministry of Education, even though the philosophy behind the creation of the PEPs was adopted by the Centre for Education Policy Development and the General Confederation of Labour. Traces of the pilot programmes, however, remain, insofar as the material continues to be used within other programmes. Such is the case, for example, with material developed for the maths programme, later adopted by and applied in the programme for children of the Muslim minority.[15] Similarly, material developed for oral language and early writing skills comprised the basis of the new national programme of pre-school language teaching. Furthermore, the teaching material developed by the pilot programmes for writing was distributed by the Ministry of Education to all teachers in pre-school and primary school for the 1999–2000 school year as support material, with the perspective of creating new teaching methods. Data regarding the distribution of these resources are not currently available, but we consider their continued use a positive indication regarding their quality.

Pre-school and 'full-day school'

Integrated within the framework of modernising the Greek educational system and improving school quality, Law 2525 of 1997 established both pre-school and 'full-day school' as optional programmes for parents who wanted their children to take part. 'Full-day' programmes extended school hours, which had been considered insufficient for some time, especially at the pre-school and early primary school levels. In practice, this meant doubling school hours in pre-school, and adding four hours per day for the first year in primary and three hours per day in the final year.

According to official statements, the pre-school programme aims for:

improving pre-school instruction, complete preparation for children entering primary school, reinforcing the government's role in reducing educational and social discrimination and supporting working parents.

The implementation of the full-day school at the primary level had the same objectives, and went even further. More specifically, the main pedagogical and social objectives were described as the following (Pyrgiotakis, 2001):

- enrichment of the curriculum, both in terms of content and activities;
- redefinition of instruction with new methods based on collaboration and exploration rather than traditional 'frontal' instruction;
- an interdisciplinary approach and improved teacher–student co-operation;
- homework preparation within the larger school framework, and providing extra help if necessary.

The main social objectives were focused on monitoring the students in a constructive and accountable way and decreasing school inequalities through new disciplines and increased support for weaker students; encouraging parents and local authorities to give school a central role in social life; and provide assistance to working parents' needs.

In a first phase, the programme was applied to a pilot group of 28 primary schools. The programme was part of the second Community Support Framework in 1999 and received significant funding support. In the pilot schools, the programme targeted all students. The teaching programme as a whole was reorganised according to the objectives presented above. Computer skills, foreign language (English) and the arts assumed a more important place within the curriculum. The Greek Pedagogical Institute took on both the scientific and management responsibilities of the programme. The teachers received support and participated in different kinds of professional training. There were also changes to the schools' infrastructures to accommodate the longer school days, the need for a place to eat lunch and the need to develop new programme content.

The full-day primary school pilot programmes received very positive evaluations, prompting the ministry to redefine them as experimental schools, which could then begin a process of generalisation (Aggelis, 2005). An investigation of these pilot programmes by the Pedagogical Institute (*ibid.*, p. 25) looked at student performance after moving on to the secondary level as well as how much, and in what ways, they participated in school life. The results showed a higher percentage of students with good performance among those who had attended the experimental schools compared with those who had attended 'regular' schools. Also, students in the pilot programmes showed higher participation in school activities, a greater sense of communication and collaboration, and more developed critical thinking skills.

After the programme was generalised, according to data on the 2003–2004 school year from the Education Research Centre (2005), full-day pre-schools accounted for 24.4 per cent (1203 establishments) of all pre-schools. Full-day primary schools made up 60.2 per cent of all primary schools for the same year (3034 establishments). The percentage of primary students participating in the full-day programmes represented 25.5 per cent of the primary population as a whole.

When considering that participation in the extended hours of the full-day school was optional, the above statistics show that most parents did not opt for this programme. The implementation of the full-day school, outside of the pilot programmes, thus highlights a considerable gap between the objectives and the realisation of the programme. This is also one reason that the rate of student participation is relatively low. The situation is much better at the pre-school level (Patiniotis, 2005). An external evaluation sponsored by the Ministry of Education, and carried out in collaboration with a team of university advisers, describes through both quantitative and qualitative analyses interesting data regarding the opinions of parents of full-day school students, the teachers who work there and educational professionals. As a whole, parents of students in 'regular' school describe themselves as more satisfied with school operations and organisation than do parents of students in the full-day schools. In addition, the students did not stop their extra-curricular activities (foreign languages, dance, etc.) because of the fact that these are also offered within the framework of the full-day schools. Positive results were seen at the level of reinforcing women's employment. The instructors seemed pleased with the way the students participated in the activities that had been developed. At the same time, however, most teachers mentioned that many students withdrew from the programme over the course of the year. Finally, the teachers most satisfied at having participated in the programme were the pre-school teachers.

The main problems associated with the full-day school, according to teachers and other education professionals, include the following: lack of buildings and general infrastructure, problems arising from reorganising the curriculum and issues that teachers confront directly such as delays in nomination procedures, difficulty ensuring collaboration with 'regular' school teachers and high teacher turnover. Other research is consistent with these observations, while nonetheless underlining the positive overall attitudes of those involved (Loukeris *et al.*, 2005; Pamouktsoglou & Nikolaou, 2005). Likewise, outside assessments found an overall positive opinion on the part of participating teachers and education professionals (90.4 per cent positive). It is, however, important to note that this positive opinion comes from the general discourse developed around the programmes and not from its actual realisation, as was indicated by the majority of those interviewed who incidentally stressed the need for greater support for the programme. There are no appropriate data regarding the progress or skills acquired by the students.

Programmes and practices designed to help integrate foreign and repatriated children into the school system

The school-aged population involved in this category has increased progressively as a result of different migratory movements triggered by various causes. This category presently includes children of Greek repatriated parents,[16] children of parents of Greek origin[17] and children of parents immigrating from the Balkans, Eastern Europe, Africa and central Asia. It should be noted that the number of children of repatriated or foreign parents increased by 15 per cent between 1995–1996 and 2004–2005.[18] The first measures regarding children of repatriated parents were in 1983, in connection with the implementation of 'reception classes' – special remedial classes for pupils coming from other languages and cultures – and general remedial classes (Law 1404/1983, JO 173 Article 45 and Law 1894/1990, JO 110). The *reception classes* for children of European or non-European immigrant workers in Greece were also put into place that year (Presidential Decree 494/JO 186/1983). Following demographic changes with different waves of immigration, the targeted population of this programme has increased (Ministerial Decree F2/378/G1/1124/JO 930/1994). However, the explicit reference to the category of 'foreign children' appears in a ministerial order of 1999 that puts the *reception classes* and remedial classes within the context of multicultural education (Ministerial Decree F10/20/G1/708/JO 1789/1999).

It is important to note that in all the official texts governing welcoming and integration, the targeted population is approached in an all-embracing manner; it includes students of both repatriated parents and foreign parents, despite major differences in the socio-cultural characteristics and educational needs of the two groups.[19]

The ministerial order of 1999 mentioned above brought about important changes in terms of how the programmes were organised and how the students were chosen. Two kinds of *reception classes* were introduced (a closed structure and an open structure), as well as a specific teaching programme developed by the Pedagogical Institute and teaching materials developed by the Pedagogical Institute and the University of Ioannina. Regarding selection procedures and classifying the students involved, a diagnostic tool to measure the level of Greek language acquisition was also developed by the Pedagogical Institute, without it being a standardised test. Through the experimental programme tied to these policies, a new diagnostic tool is currently being developed, with standardisation expected.

In regard to recognising the linguistic and cultural capital of these students, optional instruction of their first language and culture has been provided since 1994. Teaching the first language of 'foreign students' in school has, however, been a subject of controversy, with the Ministry of Education having to intervene to stop certain initiatives of teacher groups in primary schools, and this, despite interventions on this subject, even at the parliamentary level, made by opposition parties. Thus, programmes of this kind are not really applied, which means that they rely solely on initiatives taken by the immigrant communities and their associations (Nikolaou, 2000).

In general, educational policies relating to children of immigration swing from those of assimilation to those of multiculturalism, even including the implementation of so-called multicultural schools (26 first- and second-degree establishments) and practices focused on improving the educational and social integration of these students (Law 2413/1996, Articles 34–37, JO 124 on multicultural education).

In general, there is a large gap between what is planned in these programmes (*reception classes* and remedial classes) and what is actually carried out. Many authors express strong reservations about the effectiveness of these programmes (Damanakis, 1997; Nikolaou, 2000; Kassimi, 2003; Nikolaou & Korilaki, 2006; Vasiliou *et al.*, 2007). During the 2005–2006 school year, these programmes involved 5409 students (Ministry of National Education, 2006), which represents 8.9 per cent of students of Greek and repatriated parents in primary school. The limited number of structures – and thus available places – is linked to how the programmes are implemented and how funds are allocated. The most encouraging results come from an experimental programme created by the Ministry of Education through the Community Support Frameworks, the implementation of which was entrusted to the University of Athens and, for the second stage, the University of Thessaloniki for secondary school practices.[20]

This programme puts particular importance on remedial support and language tutoring (especially for newly arrived immigrants) and recognises the necessity of the learning of Greek – both within school and beyond – by children of repatriated and foreign parents, by allotting Greek in 'second-language' or 'foreign language' classes. This programme also developed support material for several subjects at all three levels of instruction (pre-school, primary, secondary), in order to respond to the needs of these groups. As the goal was to apply the principle of 'mainstreaming', issues of original culture and language were never explicitly raised. That being said, creating bilingual teaching material (for some subjects) was considered beneficial for overall performance and thus for the integration of this population into the school system.

Regarding student selection, some of the interventions involve all of the students in a particular school and not exclusively children of immigrant parents. Even some schools with small immigrant populations are involved, though the emphasis is on those with a high percentage of children of immigrant parents. Incidentally, the area-based dimension is also integrated into the school selection process because the geographical distribution of schools covers the whole country, and especially the areas considered 'priority areas' based on high rates of school failure and drop-out.[21]

The experimental programme for children of foreign and repatriated parents was assessed in a study looking at the three programmes targeting minority populations; European funding support imposed internal and external evaluation procedures. The external evaluation occurred at the end of the first phase of application (2004) and relies on both programme factors and survey results from teachers and students in primary and secondary school (Ministry of Education and Religious Affairs, 2005).

The results were very positive, given the progress noted for both school and social integration. According to indicators given to the evaluator by the institution responsible for carrying out the programme, there was improvement in the school situation of students of immigration. The percentage of students of immigration who finished primary school was 95 per cent in 2004, compared with 60 per cent in 2000. Furthermore, the percentage of students enrolled in the *gymnasio*, compared with the number of students who finish primary school, was 80 per cent in 2004 as against 60 per cent in 2000.

The pedagogical material developed in the programme was also highly evaluated by the students. The professional development training programmes were not sufficiently developed however, with 40 per cent of *gymnasio* teachers considering that they need special training.

Teaching children of the Muslim minority in Thrace[22]

The elementary teaching system for the children of the Muslim minority in Thrace (27 per cent of the region's population)[23] is based on the Treaty of Lausanne and differentiates itself from the common law dispositions governing elementary teaching. The children, however, may choose between schooling with the majority in the general school system or being schooled in special 'minority' schools. Most choose the latter. The programmes of these schools have two languages of instruction – Greek and Turkish. Aside from the instruction of these two languages, religious instruction, maths and physics are taught in Turkish, while history, geography, 'environmental studies' and civic education are taught in Greek. The Lausanne treaty makes no mention of secondary schools, and the majority of students reaching this level are schooled in the general instruction *gymnasia* and high schools.[24] According to statistics, the region of Thrace holds the highest number of residents who have not finished (compulsory) school. At the same time, the drop-out rate is very high among minority children. In 1997, a programme to improve the teaching of children of the Muslim minority of Thrace was instituted by the Ministry of Education in integrating successive Community Support Frameworks. The programme was conducted in collaboration with the University of Athens.

This programme was developed at a time of relatively positive political relations between Greece and Turkey, with the goal of improving the teaching of minority children to help them better integrate into the Greek educational system.

One of the first actions taken was to understand the specific needs of the Muslim minority, given the programme's mission of respecting other cultures. Because of unreliable data regarding the drop-out rates of the target population, a study carried out revealed the true nature of the problem

(Askouni, 2006, p. 17). To give a rough idea, of the students enrolled in *gymnasio* in 1997–1998, only 44 per cent finished their studies. Another important element brought to light by this research is that at the end of primary school, these children have not attained a satisfactory level in speaking either Greek or Turkish. One of the reasons suggested to explain this low level of performance is that the textbooks and programmes were designed for children whose maternal language is Greek, and they thus presented considerable difficulties for the children.

Within the perspective that the textbooks be pleasing and familiar to the students, a new series of textbooks and teaching material was developed, with references to the cultural milieu of the Muslim minority of Thrace.[25] The material was adapted to the linguistic characteristics of the students and involved the four subjects taught in Greek. Since the year 2000, following a trial period, these textbooks comprise the official texts of the minority primary schools.

In a second phase, the programme was also applied at the secondary school level, in areas with a heavy concentration of the Muslim minority population. In addition, new pedagogical materials were created for Greek language teaching (based on the main differences between the Greek and Turkish languages), as well as literature, history, maths, physical sciences and geography.

Professional development for teachers assumed a major place in the programme. It was addressed to the voluntary teachers of the minority school and centred on issues of teaching methods to maximise benefits from the new teaching manuals for Greek as a second/foreign language, classroom communication management techniques and an interdisciplinary approach to school knowledge. Within the professional development framework, follow-up and teacher support were also given considerable importance.

As the goal was familiarity with the specificities of the local culture, surveys of local leaders, minority representatives and educational partners were carried out (Askouni, 2006, pp. 17–18). Two programme support centres were also created and managed by local groups. Run by a culturally mixed staff, their objective was to develop support outside of the school (planning summer classes, computer classes in Greek, Greek classes for parents, etc.). These support centres contributed to fostering communication and collaboration with Muslim parents. The increase in the number of parents who enrol their children in various activities and the number of mothers learning Greek are positive indicators of the trust parents have in these centres. The programme represents the most positive intervention in the area of minority instruction today, according to an external evaluation sponsored by the Ministry of Education. It was also well received by members of the Muslim community (Ministry of Education, 2005). Regarding minority student participation in the educational process, available data show an increase of 8.4 per cent in primary school over the period 2000–2004. This number rises to 34 per cent in secondary school, a significant development. It should be noted that a system of quotas was recently planned for minority access to higher education and that this has contributed to such positive development. The positive reactions of the students that led to the increase in the number of schools involved in the programme also deserves mention. In regard to effects on minority student performance, these are seen as generally positive. Ninety per cent of students who participated in the remedial support and tutoring stated that it had helped them a lot. A majority of these students (72 per cent) felt that they were helped not only in regard to Greek language but in all subjects generally.

The teacher survey is consistent with these results. The majority of teachers considered the effects of the remedial courses and tutoring to be positive for the students, not only in regard to making them feel more at ease with the Greek language, but also in terms of developing communication and expression skills. The internal programme evaluations also found a correlation between professional development and improvement in student performance. Students who had teachers engaged in regular professional development showed much better results than students of teachers not involved in professional development. And finally, another positive outcome, albeit more difficult to quantify, is that a large part of the local culture adopted the main goals of the programmes and recognised its worth, not only for the Muslim minority, but for all of Thrace.

Actions for the education of Romani children[26]

Schooling of Romani children has posed problems for several reasons, including the living conditions of part of this population, how the children are represented in society, the stigmatisation of their 'difference' and the ineffectiveness of other actions developed in this area (Vergidis, 1995b; Vasiliadou & Pavli-Korre, 1996; Katsikas & Politou, 1999). According to some estimates, the number of Roma living in Greece is about 250,000. Almost 60 per cent are illiterate, whereas the percentage of those who have settled and lived in the same area for at least 20 years is 50 per cent (Greece: National Committee on Human Rights, 2001). It appears that a large part of the Roma living in Greece have a permanent residence and are starting to support their children going to school. And yet, Romani children are still subject to racism and school exclusion. This exclusion can be either active (enrolment refusal) or passive (their physical presence in class is tolerated but they do not participate in the educational process). Until the mid-1990s, interventions designed to improve living conditions and the integration of the Roma into Greek society were fragmented and characterised by a lack of continuity and coherence.

Progressively, however, Roma families with permanent homes in urban areas and relatively higher financial means started to send their children to school. In some cases, and in areas with a large Roma population, there are a small number of schools comprising only Romani children. Roma representatives, however, have clearly expressed their opposition to this type of school and prefer that their children go to 'regular' schools, with the goal of fostering social integration with the community.

The type of programme adopted was special classes integrated into regular schools. These programmes are quite similar to the *reception classes* put in place for children of immigrant parents and the special education integration classes. In such classes there is a programme parallel to the 'regular' classes, focused in theory on taking care of this group's special needs and language instruction. Despite this programme, the level of school integration for this population has remained relatively low, given that the answers provided, in the form of a specific programme, did not take into account the living conditions and specific educational needs of the Romani children. A programme put in place in 1997, contemporarily with the other programmes targeting special populations, attempted to address in a more thorough manner the issues of this group that are particularly affected by school exclusion.

The University of Ionnina carried out the programme for the education of Romani children from 1997 until 2004. The programme's main objective was to implement conditions that would improve school attendance and integration into the educational system. This objective was pursued through practices that first encouraged enrolment of Romani children, and then encouraged staying on in school (coping with dropping out). It was found that the low educational level of this group is due mainly to the effect of difficult conditions in all areas, especially in housing, health and work. Furthermore, language differences exacerbate the integration difficulties of these children (Vergidis, 1998, p. 65). The programme in question aimed to reduce specific problems in regard to the integration of Romani children into the educational system. More specifically, the actions taken attempted to address school drop-out within the framework of compulsory education, weak performance leading to school failure, unequal teaching treatment and discrimination, and weakness in the administrative system preventing sufficient organisation to apply the institutional framework governing compulsory education.

The various actions taken to achieve the above goals were the following:

– research on living and educational conditions of the Roma in Greece;
– follow-up and teaching support for Romani children and, more specifically, (1) mediation between the school and family to better inform the family about the importance of school and to build a relationship with the school; and (2) educational intervention support from the teaching support centres for school integration, and setting in place music laboratories to increase the value cultural capital and its articulation with language instruction;

- development of a special database to monitor schooling (enrolment, drop-out, specialised knowledge such as music) and children by class, school, town, department and region;
- media intervention to disseminate information and increase awareness of public opinion.

According to the official external assessment, there is a gap between the main goals and how the actions were applied. Some types of action (e.g. a network of collaborators) are more developed than others such as remedial support and tutoring, professional development for teachers and production of support materials. Despite these difficulties, however, authorities maintain the programme's necessity for integrating Romani children into the educational system.

The research team presented a report showing positive results regarding a number of variables including the number of Romani children enrolled in school, the length of their schooling, the percentage of children who move on to secondary school, the percentage of students who complete the compulsory education period of nine years and the number of students who took advantage of the remedial support and tutoring. The same report also states that over the period 2000–2004 there was a considerable decrease in school drop-out rates for Romani children at the primary level. The internal assessment found that the teachers who participated in the programme considered the results regarding school attendance by Romani children to be very positive. Now in its third phase, after a two-year break due to administrative problems (2004–2006), the programme is now being co-ordinated by the University of Thessaly and aims to decrease drop-out rates and improve school integration through development of skills that will allow regular schooling and community awareness programmes concerning issues of prejudice and discrimination.

Conclusions

Following the fall of the dictatorship in 1974, both conservative and Socialist governments – but especially the latter – have sought to ensure the democratisation and modernisation of the educational system within the framework of Greece's membership within the European Community. In particular, the Socialist governments of the 1980s, based on the 1984 decision of the Council of Ministers in Education, adopted specific measures towards improving school standards for working-class children.

As the above description of the various programmes makes clear, financial support from the European Union, and more specifically from the Community Support Frameworks targeting improved instruction, strongly influenced the content and directions of the educational actions taken to deal with school failure and exclusion. The adoption of European policies on social exclusion by the Greek educational authorities resulted in focusing the programmes dealing with school failure and exclusion on classic social groups (children of immigrants, Romani children and children of the Muslim minority). Financing programmes addressing school failure and exclusion, established by the Community Support Frameworks, allowed the educational authorities the potential to allocate considerable funds to this area. Without question, significant knowledge has been developed over the last ten years regarding the integration of these children, as well as the generation of an educational and scientific debate on the implementation procedures and the results of these programmes (see, for example, Varnava-Skoura & Vergidis, 2002; Askouni, 2006; Dragona & Fragoudaki, 2008).

The main feature of these policies, from the planning and application point of view, is their centralised structure. It should be noted that the term 'priority education policies' is not used by Greek educational leaders. And yet, implicitly, the request for financial support from the European Union suggests that the Greek authorities, as well as the community leaders who receive the request, consider these to be priority policies. The priority education policies presented are all defined at the central level by the Ministry of Education and Religious Affairs. There are, however, two major categories: the Ministry of Education and Religious Affairs may apply the policies using its own organisational structure and services, or the ministry delegates the scientific responsibility and application of these policies to research centres such as universities.

The first category includes priority education policies targeting improved school performance for weak students; it is related to remedial support and tutoring. These policies were created, according to the official discourse, on the idea of differentiated and individualised teaching practices; the way in which the programme has been developed and its main features, however, reflect a total accommodation of the methods and contents of the school programme, without any inquiry into the sources of school problems. This explains to some extent the shifting of weight of these practices from the primary level in the first years of its application to the secondary level, or *gymnasio*, and then to high school where school failure is most visible. It is interesting to note that the Ministry of Education and Religious Affairs has performed no systematic evaluation of the programme.

This category also includes policies related to full-day schools. As we have already mentioned, this programme is included in priority education policies co-financed by the European Union largely because they contribute to improving work opportunities for mothers. The data from the evaluation for the Ministry of Education and Religious Affairs clearly show several features in need of improvement. One common feature of these two priority policies managed directly by the Ministry of Education is that they act according to the 'regular' school norms, offering more time for support, introducing new subjects and time devoted to homework study. It appears that no transfer-able educational or scientific know-how has been gained through applying these policies. Rather, it seems to be a quantitative change insofar as more instructional hours have been added for certain students. The *reception classes* and the remedial lessons, operating outside of the multicultural educational programme co-ordinated by the University of Athens and the University of Thessaloniki, follow the same logic.

The second category includes programmes where the development and implementation was entrusted to universities; this category includes the remedial support and tutoring pilot programmes as well as the programmes for specific groups. Within these programmes emerged specific reasoning and practices adapted to the needs of the target population. The effort con-cerned not only the application of modern teaching practices but also the development of scientific knowledge with certain groups, as well as within some programmes with the groups themselves.

More specifically, the following was carried out within the framework of these programmes:

- research on specific educational needs for target populations;
- creation of teaching material;
- professional development for teachers;
- differentiation of teaching practices (e.g. school-wide projects);
- support structures and infrastructures (e.g. a support centre in the pro-gramme for children of the Muslim minority);
- application of teaching innovations (such as music labs, teaching resource centres and summer programmes).

Several teaching practices developed within these programmes appear to have been integrated into the overall rationale of reforming and mod-ernising the school system recently undertaken by the Ministry of Education and Religious Affairs. In our opinion, this creates the knowledge and skills necessary for developing new programmes of study and putting into place more effective teaching practices. At the same time, a scientific debate has begun to develop based largely on the research data gathered from the university-directed programmes. Some of the practices applied in the late 1990s have been adopted as centralised educational policies. Their imple-mentation has, however, faced a number of obstacles insofar as they have been created through various regulations and without any real teacher sup-port, evaluation procedures, professional development, teaching material or continued scientific support.

The only programmes shown to be effective in reducing school drop-out rates by both internal and external evaluators are the programmes managed by the universities. As we have already mentioned, the progress of these interventions, the quality of the teaching material, the improved school performance based on teacher reports, the increase in student participation in school activities and the reduction in drop-out rates have been acknowledged.

It appears that the programmes associated with these priority education policies were not adopted with the rationale of 'compensatory' pedagogy, but were created with the perspective of an overall improvement of the educational context, while nonetheless addressing specific needs of targeted groups. These programmes gave scholars in the educational sciences the potential to develop interventions that brought positive change to specific groups, but also more generally enriched the educational landscape as a whole. These interventions are linked to fundamental changes that need to take place in compulsory education to improve it in a qualitative sense. This process has already begun with the development of new interdisciplinary approaches that characterise the new common school programme. In this way they are precursors of necessary processes in improving the educational system.

Prospects in the fight against school exclusion and school failure seem better than ever, despite both new and old educational problems, given that these are now officially recognised, that programmes are financed to address them and that educational infrastructures now exist with their own pedagogical material. The actions taken by the Ministry of Education on the quantitative level (full-day school and remedial support), combined with a qualitative differentiation of educational practices, could – with the help of research scientists – gain support from the results, the knowledge and teaching material gained from these programmes. For this, however, we must have not only political will but also the will to proceed from rhetoric to practice, as well as the ability to ensure the institutional and material conditions necessary for such a transition. We must nonetheless clarify that, despite the implementation of these programmes and their positive results regarding the respective target groups, as a whole the Greek educational system remains characterised by uniformity, centralisation and considerable learning inequalities (Vosaïtis & Ifanti, 2006; Vergidis & Stamelos, 2007). The institutionalisation of the teaching methods and tools developed within these programmes were not accompanied by training of teachers, in how to take advantage of them, nor by any significant changes in school functioning, in terms of teaching relationships that presuppose infrastructure improvement, teacher supervision or enhanced financial resources.

Acknowledgements

We would like to thank Kostas Lamnias for helpful comments on a first draft of this text.

Notes

1. Successive governments also reinforced a dual educational network through the development of technical and professional instruction in the latter part of secondary school, and the creation of Technological Institutes (higher technical instruction).
2. Centres designed to prepare students for success after high school were created under the same law, as well as high school diplomas to enter into higher post-secondary education (Law 1304/1982, Article 26).
3. Cf. Spinatou (1987).
4. The full name is the Ministry of Education and Religious Affairs.
5. In Greece primary school typically took place only in the morning. The 'full-day schools' carried over until 4 o'clock in the afternoon.
6. An important reference text is: European Commission (1995), White Paper on Education and Training. Teaching and Learning. Towards the Learning Society.
7. There are, however, a few studies by individual researchers; these cannot make up for the lack of systematic study on a national level, which would need the resources of a national research institution.
8. Three new universities were created after the victory of the Socialist party in 1981.
9. These are based on calculations from statistics from the Education Research Centre (Educational Research Centre, 2003).
10. See: http://www.ecd.uoa.gr/prosopikes_selides/gellask/ppstl/Default.htm for a description of the programme (consulted July 11, 2008).
11. For further details about the procedure and accompanying texts, see Varnava-Skoura & Vergidis (2002, pp. 284–286, 304–309).
12. See Varnava-Skoura & Vergidis (2002, pp. 289–297).
13. See questionnaire, *ibid.*, pp. 298–303.
14. This was also pointed out by B. Bernstein, when participating in a conference organised within the framework of teacher training of the pilot programmes in Athens (Varnava-Skoura & Vergidis, 2002, p. 13) where he spoke of the reluctance of many governments to invest in the educational success of all students, particularly that of disadvantaged groups.
15. The programme is presented later in this chapter.
16. This refers to Greeks who immigrated to Western countries – the United States, Canada, Belgium, Germany and Australia – in the 1950s and 1960s and who returned to Greece. This also includes Greeks who immigrated to Socialist countries as political refugees (Hungary, Romania, the Soviet Union, etc.) after the defeat of the Democratic Army of Greece during the Greek Civil War (1946–1949).
17. This includes (1) the Pontioï, who were born and lived in the former Soviet Union and (2) the Greek minority of Albania, settled in the Epirus region in the northwest of Greece that is part of Albanian territory.
18. The strong percentage increase is also related to demographic issues within Greece (the low birth rate means fewer Greek students enrolled in primary school).
19. The implementation of the *reception classes* and the remedial classes comes from the decision of the regional teaching directors, following suggestions from education professionals (directors and heads of school). The financing of these programmes is defined by ministerial orders, though they vary. It was considered important that permanent positions for the *reception classes* be created; however, these positions were most often filled by substitute teachers, a practice which does not encourage continuity and coherency. As far as the remedial courses are

concerned, they were put into place following the model of the tutoring and remedial support programme, where teachers who wished to supplement their income were paid by the hour.

20. For further information, see the website: http://kapodistriako.uoa.gr/stories/109_th_01/index.php?m=2 (consulted July 11, 2008).

21. Regarding the first cycle of secondary school, the criterion for school selection is the percentage of students (over 20 per cent) with repatriated and foreign parents.

22. See the description of the programme at: http://www.museduc.gr/index.php (consulted July 11, 2008).

23. According to government figures, the 'Muslim minority' population is about 100,000. According to these data, the Muslim minority accounts for 27.5 per cent of the total population of Thrace (363,479 residents) and 0.9 per cent of the population of the country. This group is made up of three different ethnic groups: (1) a group of Turkish origin; (2) the Pomakoi; and (3) the Roma. A large proportion of the Roma of the region of Thrace are Muslim; other Greek Roma are Orthodox Christian.

24. There are only two minority schools, and two religious schools at the secondary level.

25. This includes a total of 41 textbooks for the six primary school classes, as well as specific language instruction software.

26. http://www.roma.uth.gr (consulted July 11, 2008).

Bibliography

Scientific documents

AGGELIS A. (2005). *Episkopisi tis pilotikis efarmogis 'Oloimero Sholio'* [An insight into the piloting of the full-day school]. Athens: Ministry for Education and Religious Affairs, Pedagogical Institute.

ASKOUNI N. (2006). *I ekpedefsi tis mionotitas sti Thraki* [Educating the minority in Thrace]. Athens: Ed. Alexandria.

DAMANAKIS M. (1997). *I ekpedefsi ton pallinostounton ke allodapon mathiton stin Ellada. Diapolitismiki proseggisi* [The education of repatriated and foreign children in Greece. An intercultural approach]. Athens: Ed. Gutenberg.

DONATOS G. *et al.* (dir.) (2006). *Metarithmisi stin Anotati ekpedefsi* [Reform of higher education]. Athens-Komotini: Ed. Sakkoulas.

DRAGONA TH. & FRAGOUDAKI A. (dir.) (2008). *Protsthessi ohi aferessi, pollaplassiasmos ohi dieressi. I metarythmistiki paremvassi stin ekpedefsi tis miotitas tis thrakis* [Addition and not subtraction, multiplication and not division. The reforming intervention of education of the minority in Thrace]. Athens: Ed. Metehnio.

DRETTAKIS M. (2005). 'To epipedo ekpedefsis Ellinon kai allodapon stis periferies tis choras to 2001' [The level of education of Greeks and foreigners in the regions of the country in 2001]. *Journal AVGI*, January.

DRETTAKIS M. (2007). 'Kata 150% afxithikan i mathites me pallinostountes ke allodapous gonis ti dekaetia 1995/1996–2004/2005' [The number of pupils of repatriated and foreign parents has increased by 150% during the decade 1995/1996–2004/2005]. *Synchroni Ekpaidefsi*, no. 148, pp. 43–56.

EDUCATIONAL RESEARCH CENTRE (2003). *To elliniko ekpaideutiko systima, synoptiki eikona se arithmous* [The Greek education system: a brief presentation in figures]. Athens: Educational Research Centre.

EDUCATIONAL RESEARCH CENTRE (2005). *Apotiposi tou ekpedeftikou sistimatos se epipedo sholikon monadon* [The profile of the education system at school level] (supervised by V. Koulaidis). Athens: Educational Research Centre.

ELIOU M. (1976). 'Geografiki katanomi ekpedeftikon efkerion' [Geographical distribution of educational opportunity]. *Epitheorisi Kinonikon Erevnon*, no. 28, pp. 259–274.

EVANGÉLOU O. (2005). *I diapolitismikotita sto analytiko programma toy ellinikou dimotikou scholiou. Oi apopseis ton ekpaideftikon* [Interculturality in the primary school curriculum in Greece. The teachers' points of view]. Doctoral thesis in education, TEAPI, University of Athens.

EVANGÉLOU O. & PALÉOLOGOU N. (2007). *Sholikes epidosis allofonon mathiton. Ekpedeftiki politiki-Erevnitika dedomena* [Academic performance of pupils speaking other languages. Educational policy – Resaerch data]. Athens: Ed. Atrapos.

FRAGOUDAKI A. (1985). *Kinoniologia tis ekpedefsis. Theories gia tin kinoniki anisotita sto sholio* [Sociology of education. Theories for social inequality in schools]. Athens: Ed. Papazissis.

GOTOVOS A. *et al.* (1986). *Kritiki pedagogiki ke ekpedeftiki praxi* [Critical pedagogy and pedagogical practice]. Athens: Ed. Gutenberg.

GREECE: ATHENS ACADEMY (1990). *To dimografiko provlima tis Elladas. Ipogenitikotita ke giransi tou plithismou* [Greece's demographic problem. Low birth rate and ageing population]. Athens: Publications by the Centre for Research into Greek Society, no. 2.

GREECE: NATIONAL COMMITEE ON HUMAN RIGHTS (2001). *I katastasi ton Tsigganon stin Ellada* [The condition of the Roma in Greece]. Document available on the Internet at the address: <http://www.nchr.gr/category.php?category_id:61> (consulted on December 6, 2005).

GREECE: MINISTRY OF EDUCATION AND RELIGIOUS AFFAIRS: SPECIAL MANAGEMENT SERVICE EPEAEK (2005). *Axiologissi ylopoioumenon ergon, anichnefssis anagon kai schediasmou mellontikon paremvasseon tis energeias 1.1.1 tou EPEAEK gia ti diapolitismiki ekpaidefsi* [Evaluation of work in progress, detecting needs and conception of future interventions for action 1.1.1 of the EPEAEK for intercultural education]. Athens: Ministry of Education and Religious Affairs.

GREECE: MINISTRY OF EDUCATION AND RELIGIOUS AFFAIRS: PEDAGOGICAL INSTITUTE (2006a). *I mathitiki diarroi sti defterovathmia ekpedefsi (Gimnasio, Enieo Lykio, TEE)* [Dropping out in secondary education (*Gymnasio*, comprehensive schools, technical and professional schools): Research]. Athens: Pedagogical Institute.

GREECE: MINISTRY OF EDUCATION AND RELIGIOUS AFFAIRS (2006b). Comments on PISA.

GREECE: MINISTRY OF EDUCATION AND RELIGIOUS AFFAIRS: OPERATIONAL PROGRAMME FOR EDUCATION AND INITIAL PROFESSIONAL TRAINING (2007a). *Programmatiki periodos 2007–2013. Epihirisiako programa 'Ekpedefsi ke dia viou mathisi'* [Period of programming, 2007–2013. Operational programme 'Lifelong education and training']. Athens: Ministry of Education and Religious Affairs.

GREECE: MINISTRY OF EDUCATION AND RELIGIOUS AFFAIRS (2007b). Information report, 4/1/2007.

GREECE: NATIONAL STATISTICAL SERVICE (2007). *Statistikes fisikis kinisis plithismou* [Statistics on changes in population]. Athens: Press release.

KALAVASIS F. (2000). *Extesi axiologisis gia to Ergo 1.1.d.3 'Exaplosi efarmigis programaton enihitikis didasklalias'* 1998–2000 [Evaluation report for the project 1.1.2d.3 'Extension of the application of support education programmes 1998–2000']. Rhodes: University of Aegean.

KALOGRIDI S. (2000). *I antlipsis gia to sholio ke ti metasholiki tous poria mathiton pou egatelipsan tin enniahroni ipohreotiki ekpedefsi* [Representations of school and the future from pupils who have dropped out of compulsory schooling]. Doctoral thesis in education, directed by G. Varnava-Skoura, Thessalonika, Thessalonika University.

KASSIMI C. (2003). *The greek primary school and teachers facing the immigrants children: Realities and alibis.* Doctoral thesis in education, directed by E. Bautier, University Paris 8-Vincennes-Saint-Denis.

KATSIKAS CH. & KAVADIAS G.-K. (1998). *Krisi tou sholiou ke Ekpedeftiki politiki. Kritiki ton ekpedeftikon allagon 1990–1997* [School crisis and education policy. Critique of educational change (1990–1997)]. Athens: Gutenberg ed.

KATSIKAS CH. & POLITOU E. (1999). *Tsiggani, mionotiki, pallinosountes ke allodapi stin elliniki ekpedefsi. Ektos 'taxis' to 'diaforetiko'?* [Roma, minorities, rapatriated people and foreigners in the Greek education system. Is 'different' still something different to 'class'?]. Athens: Ed. Gutenberg.

KORTESI-DAFERMOU CH. (1998). *Graptos logos ke sholiki exelixi* [Written language and educational career]. Athens: Ed. Ellin.

KRITIKIDIS G. (2004). 'I metanastes stis periferies tis horas' [Immigrants in the regions of the country]. *Information*, Work Institute, General Confederation of Greek Workers, no. 110.

LAMBIRI-DIMAKI I. (1974). *Pros mian ellinikin kinoniologian tis pedias* [Towards a Greek sociology of education]. Athens: National Centre for Social Research.

LARIOU-DRETTAKI M. (1993). *I egatalipsi tis ipohreotikis ekpedefsis ke paragontes pou shetizonte me aftin* [Dropping out in secondary education and the factors related to this]. Athens: Ed. Grigoris.

LAZARIDIS P. (1999). *Extesi axiologisis gia to Ergo 1.1.d.1 'Schediasmos kai amesi efarmogi pilotikon programaton enihitikis didasklalias' 1997–1998* [Evaluation report for the project 1.1.2d.3 'Conception and immediate application of support education programmes 1997–1998']. Volos: Thessaly University.

LOUKERIS D., KAPABATZAKI Z. & STAMATOPOULOU E. (2005). 'Axiologisi tou thesmou tou Oloimerou Dhmotikou Scholeiou. Mia kritiki prosegisi simfona me tis apopsis ton diefthintonkai ton ipodieuthintoni tvn ipefthinon tous [Evaluation of the full-day primary school system. A critical approach according to the opinions of the directors, assistant-directors or officials]'. In D. Loukeris (ed.), *Oloimero sholio: theoria, praxi ke axiologissi* [The full-day school: theory, practice and evaluation]. Athens: Ed. Patakis, pp. 349–397.

MANITSA C. (1990). 'Programata enishitikis didaskalias. Mia prosopiki martiria' [After-school tuition programme: an account]. *Synchroni Ekpaidefsi*, no. 51, pp. 41–48.

MARATOU-ALIPRANTI L., TEPEROGLOU A. & TSIGANOU I. (2006). *To elliniko sholio me tin avgi tou 21ou eona. Ekpedeftikes anagges, provlimata ke prooptikes* [The Greek school at the dawn of the 21st century. Educational needs, problems and perspectives]. Athens: Ed. Gutenberg.

MYLONAS TH. (1982). *I anaparagogi ton kinonikon taxeon messa apo tous sholikous mihanismous* [Reproduction of social mechanisms through educational mechanisms]. Athens: Ed. Grigoris.

NIKOLAOU G. (2000). *Entaxi ke ekpedefsi ton allodapon mathiton sto dimotiko sholio. Apo tin 'omiogenia' stin polipolitismikotita* [Schooling and integration of foreign pupils in the primary school. From "homogeneity" to multiculturalism]. Athens: Ed. Ellinika Grammata.

NIKOLAOU G. & KORILAKI P. (2006). 'I enisxisi tis prospatheias ton allodapon kai palinostoudon mathiton sto dimotiiiko scholio. Empiriki ereyna sxetika me ti litourgia ton taxeon ypodochis kai ton frodistiriakon tmimaton' [Reinforcing the efforts of foreign and repatriated pupils in primary school. Empirical research into the way classes for newly arrived pupils and remedial classes work]. In Th. BAKAS, M. SAKELLARIOU, M. SPANAKIS & S. TSIALOS (ed.), *Théorie pédagogique et Praxis* [Pedagogical theory and praxis]. Ioannina: S. Pantazis/Ioannina University.

OECD (2004). *Learning for tomorrow's world. First results from PISA 2003*. Paris: OECD.

OECD (2006). *Education at a glance. Highlights*. Paris: OECD.

PALAIOKRASSAS S. *et al.* (2001). *Erevna 'Mathitiki diaroi sto gimnasio (fournia mathiton 1997/98)'* [Research 'Dropping out in the *gymnasio* 1997/98']. Athens: Pedagogical Institute.

PAMOUKTSOGLOU A. & NIKOLAOU S. (2005). 'Oloimero scholio ke ikogenia: apotelesmata erevnas–Protaseis ke prooptikes [Full-day school and family: research results–proposals and perspectives]'. In D. LOUKERIS (ed.), *Oloimero sholio: theoria, praxi ke axiologissi* [The full-day school. Theory, praxis and evaluation]. Athens: Ed. Patakis, pp. 319–348.

PAPACONSTANTINOU P. (1981). 'I anisotita stin elliniki ipohreotiki ekpedefsi' [Inequality in Greek compulsory education]. *O Politis*, no. 44, pp. 46–51.

PAPACONSTANTINOU P. (1986). 'Efarmoges tis antistathmistikis agogis sto elliniko sholio' [Applications of compensatory education in Greek schools]. *Synchroni Ekpaidefsi*, no. 26, pp. 33–37.

PATINIOTIS N. (2005). *To Oloimero nipiagogio* [The full-day nursery school]. Athens: Ed. Tipothito Georgios Dardanos.

PSACHAROPOULOS G. & KAZAMIAS A. M. (1985). *Pedeia ke anaptixi stin Ellada: kinoniki ke ikonomiki meleti tis tritovathmias ekpedefsis* [Education and development in Greece: a social and economic study of higher education]. Athens: National Centre for Social Research.

PYRGIOTAKIS I. E. (ed.) (2001). *Oloimero sholio. Litourgia ke prooptikes* [The full-day primary school – functioning and perspectives]. Athens: Textbook Publication Agency.

SKOURTOU E. *et al.* (2004). *Metanastefsi stin Ellada ke ekpedefsi-Apotimissi tis iparhousas katastasis, Proklisis ke Prooptikes veltiosis* [Immigration in Greece and education. An inventory. Challenges and perspectives for improvement]. Athens: Athens University/Immigration Policy Institute.

SPINATOU Athina (dir.) (1987). *La lutte contre l'analphabétisme dans les pays membres des Communautés européennes aujourd'hui* [The fight against illiteracy in member states of the European Community]. *Actes du premier congrès européen* [Proceedings of the first European congress]. Athens, 16–18 September 1987, Ministry of Culture, Ministry of Education and Religious Affairs, the European Commission.

STAMELOS G. (2002). *Prospathia ihnilasias tou ellinikou ekpedeftikou sistimatos* [An attempt at traceability in the Greek education system]. Athens: Ed. Psifida.

TSIAKALOS G. (2004). 'Kinonikos apoklismos: orismi, plesio ke simasia' [Social exclusion: definitions, framework and meaning]. In K. KASIMATI (ed.), *Kinonikos apoklismos: I elliniki empiria* [Social exclusion: the Greek experience]. Athens: Ed. Gutenberg/KEKMOKOP.

TSOUKALAS K. (1975). 'I anotati ekpedefsi stin Elada os mihanismos kinonikis anaparagogis' [Higher education in Greece as a mechanism for social reproduction]. *Defkalion*, 13, no. 4, pp. 18–34.

TSOUKALAS K. (1977). *Exartisi ke anaparagogi; O kinonikos rolos ton ekpedeftikon mihanismon stin Ellada (1830–1922)* [Dependency and reproduction. The social role of the educational apparatus in Greece (1830–1922)]. Athens: Ed. Themelio.

TZANI M. (1988). *Sholiki epitihia; Zitima taxikis poelefseos ke koultouras* [Educational success. Questions of social origin and culture]. Athens: Ed. Grigoris.

VARNAVA-SKOURA G. (1989). *Themata gnostikis anaptixis, mathissis ke axiologissis* [Topics of cognitive development, learning and evaluation]. Athens: Ed. Papazissis.

VARNAVA-SKOURA G. (1992). 'Support de la famille dans l'Éducation: quelques aspects de la réalité grecque' [Family support in education: some aspects of the Greek reality]. *Revue internationale de pédagogie*, 38, no. 5, pp. 535–541.

VARNAVA-SKOURA G. & KOSTAKI A. (1992). *I enishitiki didaskalia stin protovathmia ekpedefsi (1991–1992). Mia proti katagrafi tis litourgias tou thesmou, paratirisis ke protasis* [After-school tutoring in primary school (1991–1992). A first appraisal of how the system works, observations and proposals]. Athens: Pedagogical Institute.

VARNAVA-SKOURA G. (2001). *Antistathmistiki thesmi sto dimotiko sholio. I periptossi tis enishitikis didaskalias. Dierevnisi tis efarmogis tou thesmou-prooptikes* [Compensatory measures in primary schools. After-school tutoring. An exploration of how the system was set up – perspectives]. Athens: Ed. Atrapos.

VARNAVA-SKOURA G. & VERGIDIS D. (2002). *Programata gia ti sholiki epitihia. Apogevmata, nihtes ke dio kalokeria* [Afternoons, nights and two summers. Programmes for educational success]. Athens: Ed. Papazissis.

VASILIADOU M. & PAVLI-KORRE M. (1996). *I ekpedefsi ton Tsigganon stin Ellada* [Education of the Roma in Greece]. Athens: Ministry of Education and Religious Affairs, General Secretariat for Popular Education.

VASILIOU P., YOTI L., DOUKA E., KORILAKI P., LOLIS K., CHRISTOPOULOU E. & NIKOLAOU G. (2007). *Meleti tou vathmou efarmogis ton thesmikon taxeon ipodochis ke ton provlimaton litourgia tous. Oi apopseis ton ekpedeftikon ke ton diefthidon* [A study on the amount of implementation of the institution of classes for newly arrived pupils and their problems: teachers' and head teachers' viewpoints]. Athens: Research Institute – Pedagogical Research/Confederation of Primary School Teachers in Greece.

VERGIDIS D. (1982). 'I paremvasi ton Diethnon Organoseon stin elliniki ekpedeftiki politiki' [The intervention of international agencies in Greek educational policy]. In KMM & KEMEA, *Kritiki tis ekpedeftikis politikis* [Critique of education policy]. Athens: KMM/KEMEA.

VERGIDIS D. (1995a). *Ipoekpedefsi* [Under-schooling]. Athens: Ed. Ypsilon/books.

VERGIDIS D. (1995b). 'Neoratsismos ke sholio. I periptossi ton tsigganopedon' [Neoracism and the school. The case of Romani children]. *Synchroni Ekpaidefsi*, no. 81, pp. 51–62.

VERGIDIS D. (1998). 'Pigenoun i tsiggani sholio? I sholiki entaxi ton tsigganopedon stin Kato Ahaia' [Do the Romani go to school? Educational integration of Romani children Kato-Ahaôa]. *Arethas*, no. 1, pp. 41–69.

VERGIDIS D. & STAMELOS G. (2007). 'I ipoekpedefsi stin Ellada' [Under-schooling in Greece]. *To Vima ton Kinonikon Epistimon*, no. 49, pp. 201–225.

VITSILAKI-SORONIATI CH. (2004). 'I simpliromatikotita piotikon ke posotikon methodon stin kinoniologiki ke ekpedeftiki erevna' [The complementary nature of qualitative and quantitative methods in education and sociological research]. In G. PAPAGEORGIOU (dir.), *Methodi stin kinoniologiki erevna* [Methods in sociological research]. Athens: Ed. Tipothito Georgios Dardanos, pp. 255–289.

VOSAÏTIS G & IFANTI A. (2006). 'Apokentrotikes politikes ke tassis endinamossis tou sholiou kata tin periodo 1985–2003 stin Ellada-Kritiki prosseggissi' [Decentralisation policies and trends for reinforcing schools during the period 1985–2003 in Greece. Critical approach]. In G. BAGAKIS (ed.), *Ekpedeftikes allages, i paremvassi tou ekpedeftikou ke tou sholiou* [Educational change, the intervention of the teacher and the school]. Athens: Ed. Metehmio, pp. 221–227.

Vrettos N. G. (2001). *Antistathmistiki thesmi sto dimotiko sholio. I periptossi tis enishitikis didaskalias. Dierevnisi tis efarmogis tou thesmou-prooptikes* [Dispositifs de compensation dans l'école élémentaire. Le cas du soutien scolaire. Une exploration de la mise en place du dispositif –Perspectives]. Athènes: Ed. Atrapos.

Legal references and official or administrative documents

European Commission (1995). *Livre blanc sur l'éducation et la formation. Enseigner et apprendre. Vers la société cognitive* [White paper on education and training. Teaching and learning. Towards the cognitive society]. Brussels: EC.

Greece. Law 309/1976 JO A100/39-4-1976 ... *Peri organosseos kai dioikisseos tis Genikis Ekpaidefseos* [The organisation of general education].

Greece. Law 1304/1982, JO A144. *Gia tin epistimoniki - paidagogiki kathodigisi kai ti dioikisi sti geniki kai ti mesi texniki epagelmatiki ekpaidefsi kai ales diataxeis* [For the management and administration in professional technical secondary education and other measures].

Greece. Law 1404/1983, JO A173. *Domi kai leitourgia ton technologikon ekpaideftikon idrymaton* [Structure and functioning of technical education institutions].

Greece. Law 1566/1985, JO A167 *Domi kai leitourgia tis protovathmias kai defterovathmias ekpaidefsis kai alles diataxeis* [Structure and functioning of primary and secondary education and other measures].

Greece. Law 1824/1988, JO A296 *Rithmisi thematon ekpaidefsis kai ales diataxeis* [Regulating educational issues and other measures].

Greece. Law 1894/1990, JO A110. *Gia tin Akadimia Athinon kai alles ekpaideftikes diataxeis* [On the Athens education authority and other educational measures].

Greece. Law 2413/1996, JO A124. *I elliniki paideia sto exoteriko, i diapolitismiki ekpaidefsi kai alles diataxeis* [Teaching Greek abroad, intercultural education and other measures].

Greece. Law 2525/1997, JO A188. *Eniaio Lykeion, prosvassi ton apofoiton stin tritovathmia ekpaidefsi, axiologissi tou ekpaideftikou ergou kai alles diataxeis* [Comprehensive schools, graduates' access to higher education, evaluating educational work and other measures].

Greece. Presidential decree 494/1983, JO 186. *I idryssi taxeon ypodochis gia tin ekpaidefsi teknon ypikoon melon i kai mi melon ton Evropaikon Koinotiton* [Opening classes for newly arrived pupils for the education of children of nationals of member and non-member countries of the European Communities].

Greece. Presidential decree 462/1991, JO 171. *Axiologissi kai enischytiki didaskalia mathiton Dimotikou scholeiou* [Evaluation and after-school tutoring of primary school pupils].

Greece: Ministry of Education and Religious Affairs. Ministerial decree F2/378/G1/1124, JO 930/1994. *Idrisi kai litourgia Taxeon Ipodohis kai FrondistiriakonTtmimaton* [Foundation and functioning of classes for newly arrived pupils and remedial classes].

Greece: Ministry of Education and Religious Affairs. Ministerial decree 96734/G2/2003, JO 1301.L. *I enischytiki didaskalia mathiton Gymnasion* [After-school tutoring of *gymnasia* pupils].

Portugal

6
From the Invention of the Democratic City to the Management of Exclusion and Urban Violence in Portugal

José Alberto Correia, Inês Cruz, Jean-Yves Rochex and Lucilia Salgado

The educational policies implemented in Portugal over the last three decades can be understood only in the light of this country's backwardness in this field, as compared with other European countries. Even though the indicators provided by these investigations are open to discussion, Portugal belongs to the countries of the European Union whose average performance in the Programme for International Student Assessment (PISA) surveys is the poorest, these results being counterbalanced by the fact that the variation and the inequalities between pupils or schools are lower there than their median value in all Organisation for Economic Co-operation and Development (OECD) countries. Hence there is the twin political objective of raising the level of education and improving the conditions of learning and teaching for the whole of the population on the one hand, and fighting against educational failure on the other, this second objective giving rise to the implementation of structural efforts and measures aiming at creating the conditions for preventing lasting exclusion, and also at reaching the pupils or young adults already suffering from exclusion. It is this interweaving of different objectives, themselves in the process of change, for which the authors of this chapter[1] would like to provide better understanding.

From the Carnation revolution to the stabilisation of the state

Before this, it should be remembered that Portugal underwent a very long period of dictatorship, which lasted more than 40 years. This dictatorship made the fight against education one of its principal ideological bases, in the name of national 'regeneration' and of the 'innate qualities' of the Portuguese people. The duration of compulsory schooling was reduced, pre-school education done away with, teacher training stopped and the institutions in charge of it closed: all this contributed to create a situation of backwardness, the effects of which can still be felt, in terms of both results and the absence or weakness, in most of the Portuguese population, of an educational culture that would nurture and pass on the motivation neces-sary for the appropriation of learning in families, even though the 1960s did see a set of legislative measures adopted that aimed at widening the recruitment base for secondary education while preserving its elitist char-acter. So not only was the Portuguese education system organised around an authoritative ideology for a considerable time, which weighed on the contents of school culture, the ways in which these were passed on and how the whole system was organised and managed, but when the Carna-tion revolution which put an end to the dictatorship broke out in April 1974, the country had the lowest level of education in Europe. Nearly a quarter of the population aged over 15 was illiterate. Forty-five per cent of pupils did not attend to the end of compulsory schooling, which then lasted six years; almost 70 per cent did not go beyond the ninth year, and less than 10 per cent reached higher education; pre-school education in 1974–1975 concerned only 11 per cent of the 3–6 age range (Teodoro, 1982). Twenty years later, the 1995 national survey on literacy brought to light the fact that 47 per cent of 15–65-year-olds did not use writing in their daily life.

The radical, political and social transformations and mobilisations which accompanied and followed the Carnation revolution led, in the educational field, to a situation in which the problems of democratising access to school were thought of as being closely related to the problems of democratising school as an institution, and to the promotion of its engagement in the construction of a democratic, participative society, firmly committed to the fight against inequality and social injustice. Over and above the changes of an institutional nature, this period was marked by a strong popular engage-ment in the life of schools, and by the development of dynamics founded on the objective of a profound relationship between the democratisation of the access to school and school life, on the one hand, and the transformation of social relations, on the other. According to J.A. Correia (1999), this period saw the search for, and experimentation in, a political redefinition of educa-tional justice where school would be seen not only as a social measure for training the future citizens of a democratic society but as a place for experi-ment in which a participative democracy is experimented on, a democracy which, through the relations it has with the social contexts, helps to trans-form them. The political objective of reinforcing and modifying the relations between school and community led to knowledge of the community and the active intervention of school, with those involved in it being thought of as contributing to

> the liberation of initiative and speech, to an incitement for people and groups to act collectively, to the will to assume individual and collective responsibilities and to the enhancement of the socialist work ethic.
> (Grácio, 1977, quoted by Stoer, 1986, pp. 194–195)

Perhaps through lack of being able to find a lasting translation into institutional terms, these political dynamics and perspectives were to come up against, in the educational field as in the other political and social arenas, a 'standardisation' process and a general movement to stabilise the institutions of the representative democracy, centred on the state. Democracy was then thought of less as the transformation and construction of the social sphere than as the integration of each person into a democratically established legal order. In the field of education, this explains the focus on the objective of equal access to the more or less stabilised public institutions and to educational and cultural knowledge, regarded as axiologically neutral universal commodities, and the retreat, or even disappearance, of co-operative or non-institutionalised, educational forms and processes based on other not exclusively educational conceptions of knowledge and social dynamics. A conception of education as contributing to the construction of the social sphere leaves room for a conception that makes it into a tool for economic development and the modernisation of the country, and a vector for equal opportunity, while integrating school into a homogeneous political area that could essentially be managed by the state and limited to its action and its initiatives (Stoer, 1982). This development was reinforced by the examination of Portugal's educational policies, carried out by the OECD in 1984. This stressed the importance of a scientific and technological education for economic growth, the need for granting absolute priority to professional training and the need to strengthen ties with the socio-economic environments so that the education system is better able to meet their needs.

Organisation of the education system and the first programmes to combat educational failure

This process was to reach a temporary conclusion with the law of October 1986 on the organisation of the education system. This consecrates democratic management styles for schools and institutions as an elected board of management, associating representatives for teachers, pupils and non-teaching staff. The 1986 law extended the duration of compulsory schooling to nine years (from ages 6 to 15), divided into three cycles, lasting four, two and three years, respectively; it established a unified teaching system which put an end to early distinctions between general and technical education, such distinctions being postponed until the end of compulsory schooling. Compulsory education, or basic schooling, was then organised in three cycles, whose curricula were designed centrally. During each of the four years of the first cycle, pupils are assigned to only one general-purpose teacher. Lessons in the two years of the second cycle are organised in a more discipline-based way, and can be dealt with by either one sole teacher or several teachers specialised in the various disciplinary fields. Finally, the third cycle prepares either for the continuation of secondary general or professionally oriented studies in college, or for preparation for the world of work, both disciplines being taught by a specialised teacher. These three cycles of compulsory education can be organised within the same integrated basic school, or spread out over different schools (often between first-cycle schools and second- and third-cycle schools, particularly in rural environments). The move from one cycle to another is conditional upon requirements concerning the acquisition of knowledge taught during the previous cycle and upon conditions of age. The cycle-based organisation has replaced a system in which education was organised, and pupils assessed, year by year, by an organisation in which progression is seen over a two-year period and decisions about moving to a higher level made on the basis of pupil assessment at the end of these two years. This modification, designed to avoid early failure and the need to repeat school years, and also to allow pupils better to adapt to school requirements, did not, however, lead to the administrative changes which should have accompanied it (teachers do not have the same pupils two years running, and textbooks have remained annual). It has also been suspected of enabling certain pupils to progress in basic education without having acquired the necessary skills and knowledge to do so. Finally, significant efforts were made, as of the late 1970s, to develop and promote pre-school education; these efforts took shape along three different paths: the creation of pre-school classes in primary schools, running from 9.00 a.m. to 3.30 p.m.;[2] support for local private structures related to associations, the Church or social solidarity institutions backed by the Ministry for Social Issues;[3] and the development of private nursery schools. These three paths and the institutions to which they gave birth were to be, if not exactly unified, at least made coherent by the Pre-school Expansion Programme begun in 1995–1997, and by the development of curriculum guidelines, making it possible to move towards a national pre-school education system, but not without causing fierce controversy relating to the need and the nature of such guidelines.

The Interdepartmental Programme for Promoting Educational Success

The implementation of the 1986 law was followed one year later by the launch, by a conservative government inspired by social Catholicism, of the first national plan aiming at fighting against educational failure, the

Interdepartmental Programme for Promoting Educational Success (PIPSE), initiated by the resolution of the Council of Ministers dated 10 December 1987. This programme, primarily aimed at the first cycle of basic schooling, was designed to reduce the rates of backwardness and learning difficulties; at the time, close to one pupil in six was lagging behind academically in primary school and pupils took on average 5.1 years to pass through the first four theoretical years of the first cycle; the cost of educational failure during basic schooling was estimated at the equivalent of €9 million. This PIPSE programme aimed, according to the wording of the Council of Ministers' resolution:

> to create conditions such that the generation of pupils entering [in 1988] the first year of primary school to begin nine years of compulsory education, can complete the first cycle of basic schooling without learning difficulties.

This programme was intended initially to impact the material conditions which compromised the academic success of children from underprivileged socio-cultural environments, by assisting with 'food, transport, educational facilities...how spare time is spent and the progressive move towards widespread special education' (Leite, 2000). Nine guidelines were laid down and implemented: health care; teaching, pedagogical, didactic or psycho-socio-educational assistance in schools; special education; food aid; support for families; spare time activities and the development of sport at school; professional or pre-professional initiation; supply of school equipment; and the creation of school transport networks.

The PIPSE programme had a very short lifespan, since it was suspended in 1991–1992, without any local structure being maintained to continue the work begun. This programme was a centralising and transitory initiative (Benavente, 1994) that did not give rise to studies or assessments to take stock of its action, other than the observation that it had little impact on educational failure and the numbers of pupils having to repeat a school year or dropping out of the system (Martins & Parchão, 2000). The national co-ordinator of the PIPSE, however, considered that this programme had helped to bring schools and communities closer together, and provide recognition of the importance of the role and the responsibility of everyone in educating children (Pinto, 1991). For other analysts, the PIPSE also had the positive effect of introducing the problem of educational failure into political and social discourse, and of asserting that this was a problem to be solved within the education system (Salgado, 1991). It led to the implementation of local partnerships and constituted an initial platform for training primary school teachers. It was undoubtedly one of the first political initiatives to associate the rhetoric of compensatory state intervention with objectives of broadening the scope of education, including courses and curricula leading to professional or pre-professional qualifications for pupils. But its transitory nature meant that it was not possible to undertake any detailed work, or to evaluate its impact in comparison with its objectives, which could only be limited if one considers, as does Leite (2000), that the programme was centred 'more on technical and didactic than on structural aspects'. Afonso assesses it differently, stressing the observation that this programme undoubtedly provided the occasion for

> concrete innovations set up by the teachers who committed to the project and who received the local support of committed and motivated teams, [but the programme] did not succeed in carrying out and achieving most of the promises and objectives it had set itself, nor to significantly reverse the trend towards failure or dropping-out, and did not give rise to structures for ensuring continuity of the policies considered to be relevant, or teaching techniques and experiments which were on the way to producing positive results.
>
> (Afonso, 1997, pp. 147–148)

The Education for All Programme

The PIPSE programme, terminated in 1991, was followed in the same year by the launch of a new programme, the Education for All Programme (PEPT), drawn up following recommendations from the world conference on 'education for all' (the Jomtien conference, March 1990) and from the conference of OECD Ministers. According to the resolution of the Portuguese Council of Ministers that established it, the general objectives of this programme were

> to promote equal opportunity by creating the conditions for access to education for all and by improving school attendance and results, to reinforce the quality of teaching … to create the conditions allowing young Portuguese people to become personally and professionally qualified so as to ensure their geographical and professional mobility, and freedom of movement within the European Union.

The aim of the programme was consequently to ensure that, by the year 2000, all pupils had successfully completed the 9 years of compulsory schooling and were able to have access to 12 years of schooling. More than the previous programme, it stressed the action of teachers and strategies specific to school to encourage school attendance and success, completion of compulsory schooling and insertion into the job market. It stresses the importance of taking local characteristics into consideration, and the creation of networks and partnerships between those involved locally and institutional partners (school/community, school/world of work). Like the PIPSE, it makes provision for the possibility of completing compulsory schooling through training courses leading to professional or pre-professional qualifications, a form of diversification put forward in regard to the need for individualising the educational process.

This programme was set up on a candidature basis using one of two methods:

- schools putting forward their application based on an educational project specific to the school but respecting the constraints and requirements specified by the regulations and national programmes;
- research or higher education institutions offering to perform contextualised studies with a view towards building these school projects. These projects were to increase the capacity of schools to act locally to prevent dropping out and failure; to work in partnership with local institutions; and to develop the link between school and the environment in order to ensure that teaching is in keeping with the social, economic, cultural and surrounding reality. While primary schools (in the first cycle) already had experience of this type of work with the community, such was not the case for second- and third-cycle schools, for whom these practices were completely new and who were able, by means of the PEPT project, to perform experiments and teaching that were partly to be reinvested in the implementation of the priority educational regions (TEIP), which we will now describe.

The requirements for implementing the PEPT programme locally were as follows:

- integrate the problems of the PEPT programme into the educational project of the school and mobilise all the administrative bodies along these lines;
- set up a school quality observatory, using a set of indicators worked out by the national leaders of the project by which the state, as appraiser, maintains the means of control and regulation over the increased autonomy of the schools;
- integrate into curricula 'regional and local components' that represent the school's insertion into the environment and how these take into consideration the factors that have an influence on schools confronted with diverse publics;
- promote in-service training for teachers to work with 'at-risk publics'.

Two other non-compulsory components were envisaged or proposed:

- community work based on co-operation between institutions and centred on local or regional resources and competencies;
- differentiated learning techniques centred on the personal and cultural identity of each child likely to drop out or have learning difficulties, with a view to enhancing individual and group differences.

The attempted association with research or higher education institutions made it possible for many researchers to study the everyday life of schools, aiming to facilitate the introduction of scientifically based changes. Research groups throughout the country produced studies on the life of schools, dealing either with specific subjects (e.g. mathematics, reading, natural science) or particular aspects, such as the assessment of learning, curriculum development, the regional and local components of the curricula, the personal and social development of children and young people, and the transitions between pre-school and primary education and between primary school and the other cycles. These studies gave rise to various publications, in a collection of notebooks specific to this programme (the PEPT notebooks) and in reviews or scientific works.

The PEPT programme ended after seven years. It left significant traces in the educational and scientific communities, and a large amount of knowledge produced by the system has, according to certain analysts, been taken into account in subsequent or current reforms. But it was a more sociological perspective, targeted more significantly at specific publics and categories of pupils, that was behind the creation in 1996 of the TEIP, the most symbolic measure in the educational policy of the new Socialist government and its asserted desire to make education a political priority.

Generic measures aiming at improving the quality of the education system

Before approaching the study of this flagship priority education policy measure in Portugal, we must say a brief word about the generic political measures taken in the first years of the 21st century to improve the quality of the Portuguese education system and the effectiveness of the work carried out by its professionals and the learning of its pupils. One of the objectives of these measures was to consolidate the pre-school education system, where attendance was optional, to make it more coherent and to universalise it by an increase in the offer of education and by encouraging families, particularly families from working-class environments who were largely unfamiliar with school, to enrol their children. The pre-school education system consists of two networks, one concerning the public sector, the other the private sector, often related to religious or community institutions. The state, via the Ministers for Education and for Social Security and Work, endeavoured to harmonise these two networks, and to control and guarantee the teaching quality of the services provided – for example, by ensuring that all the teachers (a large majority of whom are women) working in either of the networks are graduates holding a diploma from the first cycle of higher education in early childhood education. The state was also concerned to increase the financial aid provided to institutions for pre-school education, together with assistance for families. Adjusting timetables and supplying meals for the pupils, allowing parents, particularly mothers, to lead a professional life, were one measure that made a notable contribution to increasing the proportion of children benefiting from pre-school education. But for all this, the lack of places still means that today, approximately one quarter of the children cannot be accommodated in the pre-school education system (Fenprof, 2007). Other measures aim at improving learning in basic education. The National Plan for the Teaching of Portuguese aims

> to improve the levels of written comprehension, and spoken and written expression in all first cycle schools, for a period of from four to eight years, through modifications in how the language is taught.
>
> (Decision no. 546/2007)

This directly targets teachers working in this cycle and early childhood teachers, through initial and in-service training, a significant part of which takes place on site, grouping schools together and includes methods of work and assistance in the classrooms. The National Reading Plan ('Ler+'), a government initiative placed under the responsibility of the Minister for Education in collaboration with the Ministry for Culture and the Minister for Parliamentary Affairs, set the objective of raising the literacy level of the Portuguese population, promoting the development of reading and writing skills and creating or developing reading habits. It aims at promoting daily reading and the pleasure of reading for children, young people and adults, in classrooms, nursery schools and libraries and at home, upgrading teaching and consolidating the network of public and school libraries. The objective is ultimately to improve the results attained by Portuguese pupils in national and international literacy surveys (Alçada *et al.*, 2006). Similarly, the Action Plan for Mathematics aims to improve the results in this discipline for pupils in the second and third cycles, by increasing teaching time and strengthening teaching teams, and by calling on the educational boards of the schools to implement strategies such as following up the same pupils by the same teachers throughout a whole cycle. Other programmes concern experimental activities in the teaching of sciences and relating these to domestic or non-educational activities, or implementing new information and communication technologies in the schools. Still others aim at extending school time and at making full-time school more widespread, both to increase the time and improve the offer of learning, and to make school timetables more compatible with the working hours of parents. They also aim to enrich the curriculum, broadened to include the teaching of English and after-school tutoring in order to allow pupils to do their homework and to consolidate their learning by having access to resources – mainly books and computers – available in schools but inaccessible to their family. Some of these measures have undoubtedly benefited, at the administrative and/or teaching levels, from the PIPSE and PEPT programmes described above or from programmes targeted more specifically at regions or types of pupils to which we now turn our attention.

Priority education policies at the turn of the century

Priority education regions

Inspired by the French priority education zones (ZEPs), the priority education regions (TEIPs) were created by a law dated 8 July 1996 and form a measure for priority education targeting geographical and administrative regions undergoing serious social and economic difficulties and suffering from high drop-out and learning difficulty rates. They bring together several schools or institutions that are encouraged to better co-ordinate their actions. This policy, which concerns 34 towns located throughout the country, has set the following general objectives:

> to improve the educational environment and the quality of the pupils' learning; to realise an integrated and linked vision of compulsory schooling which encourages connection between its three cycles, and between these and pre-school education; to create conditions encouraging the relationship between school and 'working life'; to progressively co-ordinate educational policies and the link between the life and the work of schools in a geographical area with the towns in which they are located.
>
> (Law dated 8 July 1996)

Groups of schools where projects are developed that aim to improve the quality of education and the promotion of innovation are considered as TEIPs. The schools and regions concerned will be chosen by the ministry, without any national criteria (socio-economic or educational indicators) being published and are used for this purpose. The schools that comprise a TEIP are to work jointly in the development of such a project, in which teaching and non-teaching staff, pupils, parent–teacher associations, municipalities and cultural and leisure organisations must collaborate. A project of this kind must attempt: (1) to create the conditions for academic and educational success for pupils and young people; (2) to prevent absenteeism and dropping out by diversifying the educational offer, in particular by having recourse to alternative curricula which, without being detrimental to the common core of learning, take into account the specific characteristics of school populations; and (3) to develop innovation in the fields of environment education, artistic and technological education and the experimental teaching of sciences. It must define the training needs for teaching and non-teaching staff, and also those of the community, and propose work to meet these needs. Finally, it must be devised and implemented in close co-operation with the local community, and promote integrated management of the resources made available for the development of educational, cultural, sport and leisure activities, both for children and young people being educated and within the framework of adult education. Each project is negotiated, from both the educational and the financial standpoints, between the groups of schools and the regional education departments, the whole programme being co-ordinated by the government department concerned with basic education, and assessed by the institute responsible for educational innovation. To enable co-ordination of the various aspects and the connection between pre-school education and the different cycles (and even the different schools in charge of these different cycles), a teaching council is created in each TEIP, in which representatives of the various school levels and cycles – and, depending on the specific features of the project, the parent–teacher associations, the health and social services and the municipalities – must be represented in a well-balanced way. Administrative and financial management of the project is performed by either one of the integrated basic schools or a second- or third-cycle school belonging to the TEIP.

The main topics that are used recurrently by the project designers to identify and present the difficulties with which schools and teachers are confronted relate to the gaps in basic learning shown by pupils from working-class environments – in particular in reading and written comprehension – and to the difference between these pupils and the school culture and the meaninglessness of this learning; in combatting this, the designers propose having recourse to differentiated learning that allows children to develop their culture and no longer feel themselves to be in a situation of failure. Consequently, the main strategies suggested and implemented by the schools involved in the TEIP were as follows:

– strengthening human resources, in particular for socio-cultural leaders and staff in psychology and guidance departments;
– improving school results by implementing tutorial, individual or small group assistance measures, aiming not only at the acquisition or the development of competencies (reading, writing, mathematics) but also at restoring pupils' self-esteem and motivation;
– adding extra working time for fundamental subjects such as Portuguese and mathematics, by means of accompanied study or time allocations for schools within the framework of the National Reading Plan or the Action Plan for Mathematics;
– teaching Portuguese as a second language for pupils for whom this is not their first language, in small groups, created on the basis of their language level;
– diversifying and broadening the training offer, in particular for training or professional incentives for young people;
– discussing issues with families, organising meetings for them outside work time, calling on them to participate in school activities, in particular in activities based around reading or presentation of their life history;
– improving safety in schools, particularly by the use of magnetic cards or surveillance cameras.

The complementary resources allotted to TEIP schools have also been used to reduce class sizes, to improve the situation of teachers and to reduce the turnover of those who work in the most difficult contexts, to promote collaboration and assistance between teachers from different cycles and to implement, with collaboration from non-teaching specialists, extra-curricular activities or classes with alternative curricula.

The TEIPs were very well received, and even with a certain amount of enthusiasm in the educational field, both by teachers and militant educationalists and by those involved in educational research. Many schools involved in the PEPT programme were to reuse this experience in the TEIP programme. After giving a reminder that this programme was set up after other one-off 'positive discrimination' educational projects, and recognising 'the need to devote resources and efforts to the fight against inequality, and the importance of relations between school and community and of creating partnerships', A.M. Bettencourt and M.-V. Sousa stressed that TEIPs were the most ambitious initiative of this type, insofar as they more explicitly assume

> a philosophy of education for all, calling for the creation of forms of connection between the cycles of basic education, and support for the integration of pupils and the construction of their school courses.
>
> (Bettencourt & Sousa, 2000, p. 17)

Similarly, M.R. Fernandes and J.A. Gonçalves (2000) consider that TEIPs foreshadow another model of positive discrimination:

> a model for the regionalisation of educational policies founded on the enhancement of the local sphere and the dynamics which are at work there; a model which has proven more effective for solving educational problems than that of centralised and non-interactive decision-making.

For other authors, the importance of TEIPs lies in the fact that they make concrete 'a new form of social preoccupation, appropriate for a new political turning and for the insistence on social policies which is the result of the change of government', and that they pose 'with a great deal of acuity the question of education's contribution to creating social (in)equality' (Sarmento *et al.*, 1999, p. 6); these authors nevertheless stress that such a policy, like other Portuguese educational policies, may perfectly well come under the lineage of European guidelines that are more anxious to manage the detrimental effects of the social crisis in the educational field than to create the conditions for greater social equality, and that it is consequently likely to be only 'the expression, in a particular institutional set-up, of the process of globalization and Europeanization of educational policies' (*ibid.*).

From the same standpoint, S.R. Stoer and F. Rodrigues write that the creation of TEIPs is part of the development of

> new social policies which, while likely to support modes of contextualised and more interactive collective action, may just as well come within structural dynamics that stress individual responsibility and contributing to underestimating the social question.

After stressing that the partnership recommended by TEIPs is today the dominant figure in Europe of a 'new social technology' and a 'new form of control aiming at guaranteeing that the effects of market fragmentation and deregulation do not threaten the "normal" operation of the system', they point out that, in the Portuguese context of an 'unfinished Social state' that still has to call on voluntary help and philanthropy to perform its social protection functions, the legitimisation of partnership actions may contribute to the development of other dynamics, and update alternatives borne by local development and informal solidarity networks (Stoer & Rodrigues, 2000). TEIPs may, when viewed in this way, be regarded as an ideal 'analyser' of the emergence of new conceptions of educational policies and 'justice', of their potential effects, of their ambivalences and ambiguities, and of those of the reorganisation processes of public administration of the educational sector.

This initial phase of the TEIPs, which was to last three years, did not lead to a systematic and longitudinal quantitative evaluation that would make it possible to compare the statistical data concerning pupils and schools involved in TEIPs with those of comparable pupils and schools. But it did give rise to a certain amount of research work that provides a contrasted assessment of TEIPs. Some of this work stressed the fact that one of the essential contributions of this experiment might be in the area of school learning and how it is organised. For one thing, schools and teachers in the various cycles were thought to have learned to work better together, and to collaborate with the staff and institutions working in the pre-school field.[4] Experience with TEIPs may have provided the opportunity to move forward collectively in the development and the implementation of an integrated conception of the educational process and of school courses and requirements. It may have also been the occasion for unprecedented collective thinking and work on teaching innovation, on taking the characteristics of pupils and the communities into consideration in order to diversify the educational offer and teachers' ways of working, and also for a notable increase in the scope for teacher autonomy and in the material and human resources made available to them (cf. Alonso, 2000; Fernandes & Gonçalves, 2000). In this sense, even though the effects concerning pupils' academic success may seem disappointing and contrasted, this experiment is thought to have had 'indirect' effects on the transformation of teachers' conceptions and ways of working, on the creation of teaching materials and the dissemination of positive experiences, and on the development of general educational policies and that of training programmes for teaching and non-teaching staff. And in evaluating it, one should take less interest in pupils' results (especially as the experiment was of short duration) than in the effects of TEIPs in terms of construction and promotion throughout the education system, and of a 'culture of change' (Alonso, 1999).

Other appraisals are more cautious or more critical. Thus, at the end of a piece of 'qualitative' research, A.M. Bettencourt and M.V. Sousa emphasise that the drawing up of the educational project did not involve a significant proportion of the teachers concerned, and that the integration dynamics of schools and cycles often led to childhood education and first-cycle schools becoming subordinated to the organisational model of second- and third-cycle schools; this subordination may have acted to the detriment of relations with the families and the community. They also point out that since the top-down logic according to which TEIP policy was designed and launched 'made a clean slate of the former experiences and commitments of the teachers concerned', these policies were implemented on the sidelines, even sometimes running against pre-existing collaboration dynamics, thereby causing 'a certain indifference or resistance from the very people who were supposed to be driving the project' (Bettencourt & Sousa, 2000, p. 17). Other analysts stress that the *a priori* and administrative definition of TEIPs and the top-down approach that dominated it limited the scope for rallying those involved in the social sphere outside the world of school and the 'creation of local interactive relationships which might have allowed educational practices to take better root in a community-based approach' (Sarmento *et al.*, 2000); they consider it regrettable that such confinement or 'educational ethnocentrism' to some extent led to

> other partners' deferring their participation, leaving it to the initiative of the schools and conferring on this partnership an instrumental support function for the operation of the school system.
>
> (Canário, Alves & Rolo, 2000)

Still other authors, or those above, highlighted the fact that the innovations and action, drawing inspiration from socio-educational guidelines, had been implemented using a primarily cumulative or additive approach between ordinary lessons and curricula and the project activities, to the detriment of an approach where each could have fuelled the others and called them into question. Such a juxtaposition, even fragmentation, between 'time for lessons and time for innovation' (Bettencourt & Sousa, 2000, p. 22), is likely to result in restricting consideration given to 'local knowledge' to 'cultural' or 'project' activities, relatively marginalised and simply added to 'the curriculum school' defined and organised with reference to national programmes, and to structured, standardised and compartmentalised knowledge (Sarmento *et al.*, 1999), to the detriment of a more integrating and/or more critical aim that would question again the school curriculum and culture as a whole and their social relevance for working-class environments and for communities. The innovation borne by the TEIP experience is therefore felt to have remained on the sidelines and even been forgetful 'of the structuring role of fundamental learning that makes up the core of the curriculum in the pupils' course' (Fernandes & Gonçalves, 2000, p. 31).

It would therefore not be surprising to note that the available details of the assessment of the effects of TEIPs show that, even though certain schools can report an improvement in their pupils' results of in terms of learning, the most visible positive effects of the experiment as a whole have much more to do with a reduction in absenteeism and dropping out, and an alleviation of discipline problems, than with improved learning, a reduction in educational failure and a decrease in social differences. The reduction in the drop-out rate has sometimes resulted in an increase in the number of pupils having to repeat a school year, without any notable improvement in results and in learning (Fernandes & Gonçalves, 2000, p. 73). The reasons for such a result are undoubtedly to be sought in the tensions, ambivalences and ambiguities of the TEIP policy, to which we will return in the last part of this chapter. For certain authors, they also concern representations that are at the very least problematical of the populations and regions concerned, and that are an oversimplified diagnosis of the social and educational difficulties attempting to be solved, a diagnosis

> which is mainly based on a set of value judgements, based on non-clarified conservative prejudices, and in which facts ('educational failure') are mixed up with completely subjective appraisals ('lack of patriotism'), poor quality moralising ('difficulties in assuming one's role as a father') and racial prejudice ('ethnico-cultural heterogeneity').
>
> (Canário, Alves & Rolo, 2000, p. 149)

The paradox is that, in spite of these contrasting or even critical appraisals, the suspension of the TEIP programme was presented by the Minister of Education as a consequence of its success, and was announced at the conclusion of a national seminar devoted to assessing it, during which its contradictory and limited effects had been highlighted. It was as if, over and above pupils' results, what signified the success of the experiment for the authorities was as much the dissemination, the vulgarisation and even the naturalisation of the rhetoric and discourse, now mobilised to rethink and reconfigure generic or 'common law' educational policies, among which the figure of the project (in conjunction with those of quality, autonomy, accountability and evaluation), or rhetoric in favour of the adjustment or increased flexibility of curricula (frequently associated with that in favour of the needs of the economy and of bringing school closer to the business world), or that in favour of the fight against exclusion, tend to push that in favour of the fight against educational and social injustice and inequality into the background. So it was that in 2001 the Director of the Government Basic

Education Department was able to declare that the majority of the problems concerning educational failure and learning

> ought to be able to be solved within the framework of the ordinary national curriculum, provided that it is sufficiently flexible and that the schools are managed in a sufficiently flexible way.

And this is only by way of provision, because this flexibility has not (yet) come into effect, the specific projects and alternate *curricula*, 'with their defects, their errors and their variations', may prove to be a necessary recourse, in particular to keep or reintegrate certain pupils in school (Abrantes, 2001).

A second TEIP programme was nevertheless to be launched approximately ten years after the first, in late 2005, under the name of 'New TEIPs', in a changed political and administrative context – changed *inter alia* by the integration of management styles and discourses related to the first TEIP phase. While the stated objective was still to promote education for all as a condition for social cohesion and the possibility of facing up to the challenges of the information society and the knowledge economy, the references to social and educational inequality tended to disappear behind the targeting of 'difficult zones'. The scope of the New TEIPs was therefore to be limited to the urban centres of Lisbon and Oporto, a choice justified by the fact that it was thought to be in these zones that the 'difficult areas' are concentrated, in which 'violence, lack of discipline, dropping out and educational failure' predominate, an assertion which is not based on any study. Thirty-six schools in the urban areas of Lisbon and Oporto would be integrated in these New TEIPs. They were invited by the official documents to engage in the implementation of 'a diversified set of measures, actions and work, in school and in the community, primarily aimed at getting pupils back into school'. They were to work 'at preventing absenteeism and dropping-out' in order to create the conditions for improving academic success, these conditions hardly appearing any longer to be considered, by the initiators of the New TEIPs, as concerning a broader perspective for social and political democratisation of the way school and its curricula operate. They had to commit to bringing down the indicators for dropping out and educational failure, violence and lack of discipline, and sign, for this purpose, a three-year contract with the ministry, which includes teaching and financial aspects. The tension between the logic of democratisation and the logic of managing the most detrimental effects of social exclusion seems to have swung distinctly in favour of the latter. The arguments on which these New TEIPs are based and the way they are implemented contain a mix of references to local development, safety concerns, speeches and initiatives about early professionalisation and a kind of naturalisation of managerial rhetoric. The semantics of partnership, which calls for state interventions to be permeable to local specific features and dynamics or even for the conditions of local production of educational policies to be created, fades into the background behind that of the contract, which restricts representation of the notion of 'local' to that of the institutions that are supposed to represent its interests, and local dynamics and involvement in co-ordinating the action of the various institutions working in the same geographical area, among which is stressed the importance of private social solidarity institutions (in Portugal often related to the Church), companies, employment and professional training centres, organisations for protecting minors and members of the police force engaged in the Safe School programme. The marked insistence on the answers that need to be found to questions of safety, on the development of sport at school and special educational measures illustrates the trend of the New TEIP policy with regard to problems of urban and school violence, and a corresponding thinning-out of the references it makes to the objective of fighting against social injustice and inequality in the field of education; it is consequently hardly surprising to note that measures implemented favour a disciplinary approach over the prospect of trying to transform educational relationships. These trends are still at work as these lines are being written, and at a time when the New TEIP policy has been very slightly extended to some other urban centres.

Alternative courses or Alternative Curricula and the Choice programme

While the TEIPs were created as a region-centred policy aiming at preventing educational failure and exclusion, the Alternative Curricula programme, linked to the previous one and launched in the same year (1996), targeted a population: children or young people who were already in a situation of failure or virtual educational exclusion. It aimed at working out solutions concerning pupils considered as posing problems that could not be solved neither within the framework of the ordinary educational system nor in that of recurring education[5] (Casa-Nova, 2004). This programme was aimed at young people having experienced repeated failure at school, with serious problems of integrating into the school environment and at significant risk of dropping out testifying to their educational failure. It aimed to help substantially decrease drop-out rates and educational failure in the third cycle (from the seventh to the ninth year of compulsory schooling), to ensure that a greater number of these young people in difficulty remain in the education system and complete their compulsory schooling, and to 'reintegrate young people who have been excluded or who are likely to be excluded from the conventional system'.

As its name suggests, this programme dealt to a large extent with redefining the curriculum, but also with the time and the organisation of study, in order to propose a new curriculum, better suited to the needs and motivations of the targeted pupils. This new curriculum was to comprise 'conventional' educational content, artistic content, learning about trades, professionalisation or pre-professionalisation. The latter were not only to be added to the first, but were to be the fulcrum of the Alternative Curricula, and were intended to drive a change in pupils' attitude with regard to school and life, based on their experience and the dynamics of the community. They could be taught by teachers, but also by professionals or technicians in the relevant fields and could give rise to a double qualification: academic and professional. The underlying assumption was that making curricula flexible and individualised in this way would make it possible to counteract the most serious cases of difficulty and failure, those for which the usual responses in terms of reinforced learning proved to be insufficient. The pupils included in this programme (with the agreement of, and if possible, commitment from, their family) were put into classes of no more than 15 pupils, with altered times and timetables, and with teachers and contributors who were advised to avoid expositional methods in favour of more interactive and motivating techniques, in keeping with the following principles: (1) approach general disciplines and complex contents via topics and questions with which the pupils were familiar in order to develop their experience; (2) facilitate group dynamics in the classroom; (3) keep pupils occupied with concrete tasks as far as possible; (4) create situations that make pupils more independent; (5) develop strategies that stimulate observation, curiosity, research, discovery and self-assessment; and (6) use and experiment on objects of study and methods related to the physical and social environment. The necessary transformations that this programme called for were considered in three different registers: the curriculum, the contexts of learning and training, and teachers' ways of working, backed by a rather hazy ideology of innovation or active methods.

A new phase of this type of programme was to be started in 2003, under the name of Alternative Curricula courses, and involved the same publics and the same general objectives, while attaching greater importance to the objective of helping the young people concerned to build a 'life project', being put into earlier and more serious contact with the socio-economic world. In this new phase, classes could be limited to 10 pupils, in an attempt to individualise the learning process. Schools were recognised as having an increased amount of autonomy: while they still had to maintain common objectives, in particular in Portuguese and mathematics, they had greater leeway in the area of the curriculum, with the aim of enabling 'permeability between courses and the transition towards other methods of training, or towards a continuation of studies' (Portugal: Ministério da Educação, 2006a, p. 1). The statutory texts then adopted made it possible for pupils following these alternative curricula courses to enrol in methods of learning other than school learning (most of the time in the world of work), in theory provided they were 16 years old, but in practice as of the age of 14. The teachers working on these programmes welcomed this formula as a practical solution for the young people concerned, considering that school alone was not able to answer their needs and their situation.

And yet the programmes of the Alternative Curricula courses underwent much criticism and were at the centre of fierce controversy in the education community. At the heart of the criticism and controversy was the fact that these programmes introduced differentiation into the ambitions of the basic school and, by particularly targeting young people from the most underprivileged social environments, perpetuated the inequality and social discrimination of which they were victims. Criticism came from three main sources. First, a whole trend in the sociology of education considered that these programmes aimed to integrate or reintegrate the pupils concerned, more than actually integrating them, and that the so-called Alternative Curricula were in fact restricted curricula when compared with the requirements of the national curricula, subordinate curricula and not equivalent to those with which other pupils continued to be confronted. The fact of eliminating or reducing a certain number of subjects or contents seriously compromises, they believe, the potential of pupils' continuing their studies, and for this reason is a means of perpetuating inequality, under the cover of a so-called positive discrimination measure (Stoer, in Put-Nova, 2004, p. 7). Other virulent criticism came from the educationalists of the Modern school (a movement deriving from Freinet techniques and institutional education), which, in the same vein, denounced the uneven effects of these programmes, advocating another model of educational methods. The third source of criticism came from progressive teaching unions, who considered that these programmes were a step backward from what had been achieved in the 1974 revolution. In contrast, teachers confronted with the difficulties of pupils with learning difficulties that risked their removal from school defended this measure, considering that it made it possible to bring to light and take into account the discrimination of which these young people were already victims, and to seek appropriate solutions to their difficulties. At all events, this debate undoubtedly enabled more precautions to be taken in the implementation of these programmes, and meant that the ministry set up a whole set of measures aiming to control and guarantee their quality, and was able to assert that this programme was a major success.

Also targeting young people who were 'excluded' or at risk of exclusion, the Choice programme, launched in January 2001, explicitly set as an objective the prevention of delinquency or criminality, and the social integration of young people from urban areas and in difficulty. This programme was initially limited to the districts of Lisbon, Oporto and Setubal, and was extended to the whole of the country as of its second phase in 2004 (there was to be a third phase in 2007). This programme, conforming as it did to the pattern of the United Nations Guidelines for the Prevention of Juvenile Delinquency (the Riyadh conference in December 1990), inspired by the recommendations and the actions of Canada's National

Crime Prevention Council and the French experience of intervention and creation of social mediators in underprivileged districts, was to lead to the creation of activities for the personal development of young people, encouraging their integration and development within their community. These actions involve selective (they target certain age ranges and the most vulnerable districts), integrated (inter-institutional and interdisciplinary) and partner-based interventions. It is less a question of creating new actions than of bringing together and making mutually coherent pre-existing initiatives, operations and resources, with a view to optimising and reducing costs.

These delinquency prevention programmes also included work with children or young people and their families regarded as particularly vulnerable to the processes of marginalisation, exclusion and incipient delinquency, because of an unfavourable socio-economic environment and/or 'negative' or fragile personal characteristics. The second phase of the Choice programme was to widen the scope of initial delinquency prevention with a view to integration in a spirit of solidarity and social justice, making children of immigrants and ethnic minorities one of the priority targets, and requesting schools, training centres, associations or private social solidarity institutions to propose relevant teaching action. The implementation of these activities was on a voluntary basis and was to be fun and attractive. The approach was mainly along the following lines: (1) training in data processing and new technologies; (2) professional training; (3) designing individual vocational courses; (4) psycho-educational support, school and family mediation; (5) development of relations with families; and (6) occupying leisure time and informal education – objectives and actions that were to be maintained for the third phase of this programme.

Debates and controversies

In Portugal as elsewhere, the conception, implementation, analysis and evaluation of priority education policies gave rise to significant and fierce debate and controversy, in the worlds of both educational research and social and educational action. Three major questions appear to summarise what appeared to us as being the most important debates: (1) that of ethnic minorities at school and multicultural education; (2) that of the relationship between political or educational action and regions or local communities, and the representations that those involved in the former have of the latter; and (3) that of the ambiguities or ambivalence of the very conception and objectives of PEPs in the Portuguese context, itself related to an international context, and particularly to the European context.

To deal with the first question, it is worth recalling that Portugal has, since the Carnation revolution, experienced significant demographic changes, one of the most outstanding features of which is certainly that it is today not only a country of emigration but also one of immigration: the population of foreigners has continued to grow from the 1980s up until today, with an increase of 97 per cent during the decade 1986–1996. And yet, this population, far from being homogeneous, appears to be split into two.

There are people from other European countries or from Brazil who generally perform scientific, technical or managerial activities and therefore tend to belong to the higher socio-professional categories, and who live within the large urban areas where they work. At the other extreme of this foreign population are firstly people from African countries where Portuguese is the official language (PALOP) (Angola, Cape Verde, Guinea-Bissau, etc.), and secondly, people from various Eastern European countries (Ukraine, Moldavia, Russia, etc.) or from non-Portuguese-speaking Africa (Zaire, Senegal, Nigeria), these populations having much greater difficulty with socio-economic, residential and even administrative issues than the first (Baganha, 2007). The growth of the foreign population, and particularly of immigrant categories in the most difficult and most precarious situations, obviously raises the question of how this issue is taken into consideration in the debates and decisions on educational policy: integration and fighting against the educational failure of pupils belonging to these minorities, the battle against racism and intolerance, and intercultural education. As in many other countries, the increasing visibility of the multicultural character of society and the school population produced changes in the way of considering public policies: from a compensatory and integrating aim, primarily targeting children belonging to ethnic minorities, to an intercultural aim seeking to promote cultural and language diversity as being a source not only of recognition for some but of enrichment for all; from a predominating focus on the question of equality to increased importance given to the question of recognition (Verne, 1987; Bernstein, 2007). The law of 1986 stipulates that, amongst its other objectives, the education system has in its principles that of

> guaranteeing the right to be different, founded on the respect for individual personalities and life projects, taking into account and enhancing knowledge and different cultures.

A few years later a Secretariat for the Co-ordination of Multicultural Education Programmes (SCOPREM) was created, along with a Multicultural Education programme.

And yet, this intercultural education dimension or objective does not appear to be a central issue, nor even a very important one in the PIPSE or TEIP programmes, taking into consideration the objectives of fighting against exclusion or dropping out, an undervaluation that has been explicitly criticised by certain authors. M. Casa-Nova, for example, points out that while the 1996 law bringing in TEIPs justifies this in its preface by mentioning the limited chances of academic success 'in zones comprising a significant proportion of pupils of various ethnicities, children of migrants or itinerant families', it no longer refers, in the objectives stated subsequently, to the need for developing intercultural education in the schools concerned. L. Souta also regrets that this law makes

> no explicit reference to intercultural education, whereas out of the 148 integrated schools in the 34 TEIPs defined for the year 1996–1997, 27 had previously been involved in an intercultural education programme.

This makes the absence of this dimension even more paradoxical (Souta, 1997). Both authors note and deplore that this absence goes hand in hand with, and encourages, a conception based on deficiency, belittling to the populations and the families concerned, resulting in the fact that the choice and the marking-out of the regions concerned are based essentially on a negative approach:

> TEIPs were characterised on the basis of a negative approach to the situation of the pupils' families and of the pupils themselves, and never on the potential that this situation might contain. As a positive discrimination measure involving allocating more financial and human resources, [TEIPs] nevertheless did not have, as an ideological base, the objective of taking cultural differences into account positively, without reducing them to academic criteria, in order to involve them in an educational project.

Hence, a certain disappointment is noted with regard to a programme considered as potentially promising as to the possibility of promoting a resolutely intercultural approach (Casa-Nova, 2004, p. 8).

More generally, the same type of question or disappointment is at the heart of other analyses relating to the relation of school to the 'local sphere', that is, the districts or communities (not used here in the ethnic or cultural sense) involved in TEIPs. For certain authors, the TEIP policy could have provided the opportunity to move towards greater democratisation of school and society (in the sense of less inequality and more social justice) and more democracy in school and society, by combining greater autonomy for schools with better integration and co-ordination between schools (in particular schools of different cycles) and taking into consideration the needs and resources of the district and the community. But here too, the tension between a 'mobilising' approach and a 'deficiency-based' approach to regions and communities was reduced in favour of the latter; and equilibrium, difficult to achieve between the various approaches to integration mentioned by M.-L. Alonso (1995) – vertical integration (between cycles and schools), horizontal integration (between the various fields, subjects and times of learning for a given pupil) and lateral integration (between academic experience and that of the 'ordinary' world and life, and between school and social life) – was largely established in favour of the logic and criteria of academic management and effectiveness alone, without the concern of better taking into account the expectations, dynamics and projects of the local community, coming to question them and making them change in a notable way. Therefore, the possibility of building an area and a network for collaborating relations, with no hierarchical relation between the various educational or school structures or between these and their 'partners', was to a great extent reduced to the integration of schools under the domination of second- and third-cycle schools, to which were conferred responsibility for the administrative management of TEIPs, and tended, because of this, to become the leading schools, whereas the bonds between first-cycle schools, families and communities were historically more developed, because these schools were greater in number and were closer both socially and geo-graphically to working-class urban or rural environments. The dominant compensatory and deficiency-based approach led to a narrow and impov-erishing conception of the regions destined to become TEIPs, selected and marked out in a purely top-down way, as areas allowing the state to imple-ment its action more efficiently in areas considered as being difficult. The political arena opened up by the idea of education built locally from the social standpoint was consequently restricted to that of official action, or even to an arena dominated by academic ethnocentrism (Canário, Alves & Rolo, 2000), even to the detriment of the possibility of working on school in a broader, networking-type, social and political arena (Stoer & Rodrigues, 2000). The tension analysed by Correia between the possibility that TEIPs be the tool for an emancipatory construction of the local sphere and that they be merely a more efficient use of local resources at the service of official inter-vention was reduced in favour of this latter approach, to which the move, on a semantic level, from the theme of partnership to that of a contract, would bear witness (Correia, 2004).

But, if such is the case, it is undoubtedly because the very project of cre-ating TEIPs and the way in which it was made a reality through laws and regulations were shot through with ambivalence and possible contradic-tions. R. Canário, N. Alves and C. Rolo highlighted the fact that the law bringing in TEIPs and its accompanying documents stressed different and possibly contradictory objectives: the fight against inequality, equal oppor-tunity, the fight against exclusion, improvement of quality, promotion of innovation. This relative fuzziness is, according to these authors, peculiar to the ambiguities of this policy, which appear related to the difficulty in working out 'a clear, minimal doctrine', but also

> to the rhetorical use of trendy concepts and expressions reflecting more concern with producing political effects rather than with giving an account of reality,

and to

> the profoundly contradictory coexistence between various forms of logic, some referring to the sixties and seventies (equal opportunity logic);

others to the eighties and nineties (the logic of quality or the fight against exclusion).

It is this coexistence between various types of logic belonging to different periods which gives TEIPs, and French ZEPs, a certain hint of anachronism.

(Canário, Alves & Rolo, 2001)

H. Barbieri highlights the multiple meanings and ambivalence of the concepts of partnership, socio-educational project and increased autonomy for schools. In a political context strongly marked by neo-liberalism, all these notions may justify and back up the logic of competition between schools and regulation of the school system by market rules and values, or, on the contrary, reinforce the logic of the promotion of the public school, related to a perspective of greater participation by the local community and finding real expression in an education based on principles of social solidarity, and aiming to create the conditions, not only for more social justice, but also for the democratisation of institutions (Barbieri, 2004). Here too, contradictions and ambivalence seem to have been stacked in favour of a type of logic that the above-mentioned authors would describe as neo-liberal, and where different forms of logic combine and are reinforced: (1) the connection between educational policies and a target of economic development (the construction and reinforcement of vocational training, practically non-existent in Portugal until the 1970s and 1980s, having played a very important role in promoting and legitimising this connection); (2) the reorganisation and legitimising of state intervention using compensatory and pacifying logic against the harmful effects of economic competition; and (3) justification of the themes and measures for diversification and professionalisation of the curricula by those of compensatory education and individualisation of learning.

As a conclusion to this examination of the priority education policies implemented in Portugal over recent years, it can be said that these were initially a set of measures, initiated by decisions and official logic, aimed at involving specific publics or regions delimited according to given socio-economic criteria. Although these policies and the programmes to which they led have always displayed and asserted objectives of equal opportunity as regards compulsory schooling, one can also justifiably regard them as having been an arena for experimentation aimed at educational problems or making it possible to reconsider them, redefining the relationship between state and education in a less conflictual way, and proposing a political redefinition of education that uses the weapons and the vocabulary of criticism from the 1970s and turns these to serve pragmatism according to some, to serve neo-liberal ideology and economy according to others, but in all cases at the service of new standards and forms of normativeness. It can then be understood that the successive reformulations that these policies have undergone owe much less to the evaluations of the effects of the various programmes implemented than to the specific political issues of successive governments, which found, in these policies and rhetoric with which they support themselves, a symbolic arena for the legitimisation – via the compensatory principle and objective – of the promotion and implementation of policies which may go against the stated principles and objectives of a reduction in social inequality affecting school attendance and academic success.

Notes

1. Contributions to this chapter were made by Isabel Almaida and Catarina Ramos.
2. At the beginning, these schools were mainly set in up in rural areas where there were no other answers. Demographic trends then either caused rural areas to be turned into deserts, the villages consequently not having sufficient children to open this type of class, or led to urbanisation of the villages, the timetables of working parents then becoming incompatible with those of these classes.
3. Until 1995 these organisations had no educational guidance from the minister of education even though teachers ('childhood educators', according to the Portuguese terminology) all had a university degree and a special postgraduate qualification.
4. Such a development was to contribute, in March 1998, to the creation of groupings of schools, and administrative and educational management measures, which were to be appreciated with varying degrees of satisfaction.
5. Recurring education is evening school education, outside ordinary class time.

Bibliography

Scientific documents

AAVV (2000). *Territórios Educativos de Intervenção Prioritária* [Edicational regions for priority action]. Lisbon: Instituto de Inovação Educacional.
ABRANTES P. (2001). Interview. *Publico*.
AFONSO A. J. (1997). 'Para a configuração do Estado-providência na educação em Portugal, 1985–1995' [For a configuration of the welfare state in education in Portugal, 1985–1995]. *Educação, Sociedade & Culturas*, no. 7, pp. 131–156.
AFONSO A. J. (1998). *Políticas Educativas e Avaliação Educacional. Para uma análise sociológica da reforma educativa em Portugal 1985–1995.* [Educational policies and evaluating education. Towards a sociological analysis of the education reform in Portugal 1985–1995]. Braga: Centro de Estudos em Educação e Psicologia, Instituto de Educação e Psicologia, Universidade do Minho.
AGÊNCIA L. (2007). 'Governo vai investir 15 milhões em escolas problemáticas' [Government is to invest 15 million in problem schools]. *RTP*. Article available on the Internet: <http://www.rtp.pt/index.php?=266837&visual=5> (consulted on July 16, 2008).
ALÇADA I., CALÇADA T., MARTINS J., MADUREIRA A. & LORENA A. (2006). *Plano Nacional de Leitura*. Relatório Síntese [National reading scheme. Summary report]. Lisbon: Ministério da Educação.
ALONSO M.-L. (1995). 'O design curricular da reforma: que projecto de cultura e de formação?' [Designing the reform curriculum: what project for culture and training?].

In M. L. Couceiro (ed.), *Ciências da Educação: Investigado et Acção*, vol. II. Braga: Sociedade Portuguesa de Ciências da Educação, pp. 139–153.

Alonso M.-L. (1999). 'Inovação curricular, formação de professores e melhoria da escola. Uma abordagem reflexiva e reconstrutiva sobre a prática da inovação-formação' [Curriculum innovation, teacher training and improving school. A reflexive and reconstructive approach to innovation-training practices]. Doctoral thesis, Braga, Universidade do Minho.

Alonso M.-L. (2000). 'Ensino Basico e Integração Educativa nos TEIP' [Basic education and educational integration in TEIPs]. In Ana M. Bettencourt et al., *Territórios Educativos de Educação Prioritária*. Lisbon: Ministério da Educação – Instituto de Inovação Educacional.

Alves N. & Canário R. (2004). 'Escola e Exclusão social: das promessas às incertezas' [School and social exclusion: from promise to uncertainty]. *Análise Social*, vol. XXXVII, no. 169, pp. 981–1010.

Alves N. et al. (1996). *A Escola e o Espaço Local. Políticas e Actores* [School and the local region. Policies and people]. Lisbon: Instituto de Inovação Educacional.

Amaro R. (1990). 'O "Puzzle" Territorial dos anos 90. Uma Territorialidade Flexível (e uma nova base para as relações entre nações e regiões)' [The territorial 'jigsaw puzzle' of the 1990s. A flexible area-based approach (and a new basis for relations between nations and regions)]. *Vértice*, no. 33, pp. 39–48.

Azevedo J. (1994). *Avenidas da Liberdade – reflexões sobre a política educativa* [The avenues of freedom – reflections on educational policy]. Porto: Edições Asa.

Baganha M. (2007). 'Dinâmicas Migratórias' [Migratory dynamics]. Colóquio *Globalização, Pobreza e Migrações* [Conference *Globalisation, poverty and migrations*]. Coimbra: CES/FEUC.

Barbieri H. (2002). *O Projecto Educativo e a territorialidade das políticas educativas* [The educational project and the regionalisation of educational policies]. Tese de Mestrado, Porto, Faculdade de Psicologia e de Ciências da Educação.

Barbieri H. (2004). 'Os TEIP, O projecto educativo e a emergência de "Perfis de Território"' [TEIPs, the educational project and the emergence of 'region profiles']. *Educação, Sociedade & Culturas*, no. 20, pp. 43–75.

Barroso J. (2003). 'Factores organizacionais da exclusão escolar' [Organisational factors of social exclusion]. In D. Rodrigues (dir.), *Perspectivas sobre a Inclusão. Da educação à sociedade* [Perspectives on the subject of inclusion. From education to society]. Porto: Porto Editora, pp. 25–36.

Barroso J. (dir.) (2003). *A escola pública: regulação, desregulação, privatização* [State school: regulation, deregulation, privatisation]. Porto: Asa.

Barroso J. (2004). 'A autonomia das escolas uma ficção necessária' [The autonomy of schools: a necessary fiction]. *Revista Portuguesa de Educação*, vol. 17, no. 2, pp. 49–83.

Barroso J. (2006). 'La régulation de l'éducation comme processus composite' [The regulation of education as a compositite process]. In C. Maroy (ed.), *École, régulation et marché. Une comparaison de six espaces scolaires locaux en Europe* [School, regulation and market. A comparison of six local school areas in Europe]. Paris: PUF, pp. 281–314.

Barroso J. (dir.) (2006). *A Regulação das políticas públicas de educação. Espaços, dinâmicas e actores* [The regulation of public education policies. Spaces, dynamics and people]. Lisbon: Educa & Ui&dCE.

Barroso J. & Viseu S. (2006). 'De la régulation par l'offre scolaire à la régulation par la demande: le cas de Lisbonne' [On regulation by the educational offer and regulation by demand]. *Revue française de pédagogie*, no. 156, pp. 51–61.

BENAVENTE A. (1994). *As inovações nas escolas: um roteiro de projectos* [Innovations in schools: a project report]. Lisbon: Instituto de Inovação Educacional.

BERNSTEIN B. (2007). *Pédagogie, contrôle symbolique et identité. Théorie, recherche, critique* [Pedagogy, symbolic control and identity. Theory, research, critique]. Lévis (Quebec): Les Presses de l'Université Laval.

BETTENCOURT A.-M. & SOUSA M. V. (2000). 'O conceito de ensino básico e as práticas de integração educativa' [The concept of basic education and educational integration practices]. In AAVV, *Territórios Educativos de Intervenção Prioritária*. Lisbon: Instituto de Inovação Educacional (IIE).

CANÁRIO R. (2005). *O que é a escola? Um 'olhar' sociológico* [What is school? A sociological 'view']. Porto: Porto Editora.

CANÁRIO R. (2006a). 'A escola – da igualdade à hospitalidade' [School –from equality to hospitality]. In D. RODRIGUES (ed.), *Educação inclusiva. Estamos a fazer progressos?* [Inclusive education. Are we getting anywhere?]. Cruz Quebrada: Faculdade de Motricidade Humana.

CANÁRIO R. (2006b). *A escola tem futuro? Das promessas às incertezas* [Does school have a future? From promise to uncertainty]. Porto Alegre: Artmed.

CANÁRIO R., ALVES N. & ROLO C. (2000). 'Territórios Educativos de Intervenção Prioritária: entre a "igualdade de oportunidades" e a "luta contra a exclusão"' [Education regions for priority action: between equal opportunity and the fight against exclusion]. In AAVV, *Territórios Educativos de Intervenção Prioritária*. Lisbon: IIE, pp. 139–170.

CANÁRIO R., ALVES N. & ROLO C. (2001). *Escola e exclusão social* [School and social exclusion]. Lisbon: IIE/Educa.

CARAMELO J. & CORREIA J. A. (2004). 'Políticas e Figuras do Local: contributos para a construção de um cosmopolitismo comunitário' [Policies and figures in the local arena: contributions towards building a community cosmopolitism]. *Cadernos do ICE*, no. 7.

CASA-NOVA M. (2004). *Políticas sociais e educativas públicas, direitos humanos e diferença cultural* [Social and educational policies. Human rights and cultural difference], VIII Congresso Luso-Afro-Brasileiro de Ciências Sociais, Setembro, Coimbra.

CASTEL R. (1995). *Les métamorphoses de la question sociale. Une chronique du salariat.* [Metamorphoses of the social question. A chronicle of the wage system]. Paris: Fayard.

CHARLOT B. (dir.) (1994). *L'école et le territoire: nouveaux espaces, nouveaux enjeux* [School and the region: new areas, new issues]. Paris: Armand Colin.

CHARLOT B., BAUTIER É. & ROCHEX J.-Y. (1993). *École et savoirs dans les banlieues…et ailleurs* [School and knowledge in the suburbs…and elsewhere]. Paris: Armand Colin.

CO-ORDENAÇÃO NACIONAL DO PIPSE (1991). 'Combate ao insucesso ou promoção do sucesso?' [Fighting failure or promoting success?]. *Noesis. A educação em revista – o insucesso*, no. 18, p. 17.

CORREIA J. A. (1994). 'A Educação em Portugal no limiar do sec. XXI: perspectivas de desenvolvimento futuro' [Education in Portugal at the threshold of the 21st century: perspectives for future development]'. *Educação, Sociedade & Culturas*, no. 2, pp. 7–30.

CORREIA J. A. (1999). 'Relações entre a Escola e a Comunidade: da lógica da exterioridade à lógica da interpelação' [Relations between school and the community: from the logic of externality to the logic of interpellation]. *Revista Aprender*, no. 22, pp. 129–134.

184 *Portugal*

CORREIA J. A. (2004). 'A construção político-cognitiva da exclusão social no campo educativo' [The politico-cognitive construction of social exclusion in the educational field]. *Revista Educação Unisinos*, vol. 8, no. 15, pp. 217–246.

CORREIA J. A. (2005). 'Contributos para a construção de "narrativas educativas de esquerda"' [Contributions to the construction of left-wing 'educational narratives']. *Perspectiva*, vol. 23, no. 2, pp. 407–426.

CORREIA J. A. & CARAMELO J. (2003). 'Da Mediação Local ao Local da Mediação: Figuras e Políticas' [From the mediation of the local to the local in mediation: figures and policies]. *Educação, Sociedade & Culturas*, no. 20, pp. 167–191.

CORREIA J. A. & MATOS M. (2001). 'Da Crise da escola ao escolocentrismo' [From the crisis of school to 'school-centredness']. In R. S. STOER, L. CORTESÃO and J. A. CORREIA (dir.), *Transnacionalização da educação. De Crisa da Educação a Educação da Crise*. Porto: Edições Afrontamento, pp. 91–117.

CORREIA J. A., STOLEROFF A. & STOER S. R. (1993). 'A ideologia da modernização no sistema educativo em portugal' [The ideology of the modernisation of the education system in Portugal]. *Cadernos de Ciências Sociais*, nos. 12–13, pp. 25–51.

COSTA J. & OLIVEIRA C. (1999). 'Territórios educativos de intervenção prioritária: uma abordagem exploratória de uma realidade em construção' [Priority action education regions: an exploratory approach to a reality under construction]. *Inovação*, vol. 12, no. 2, pp. 113–128. Summary of the Article available on the Internet: <http://www.dgidc.min-edu.pt/inovbasic/edicoes/ino/ino12-2/art8.htm> (consulted on July 16, 2008).

COSTA J. A., SOUSA L. & NETO-MENDES A. A. (2000). 'Gestão Pedagógica e Lideranças Intermédias no TEIP do Esteiro' [Pedagogical management and intermediary leadership in the TEIPs of Esteiro]. In AAVV, *Territórios Educativos de Intervenção Prioritária*. Lisbon: Instituto de Inovação Educacional, pp. 83–104.

COSTA M. J. (2000). 'Apoio Integrado no sistema regional de educação de infância' [Integrated support in the regional education system for children]. *Infância e educação – investigação e práticas*, no. 2, pp. 93–108.

FERNANDES M. R. (dir.) (1999). *Formas de articulação entre os Ciclos Educativos nos Territórios Educativos de Intervenção Prioritária. Um Estudo de Caso Múltiplo. Relatório de Investigação* [Forms of interaction between the educational cycles of the priority education intervention regions. A multiple case study. Research report]. Lisbon and Faro: Instituto de Inovação Educacional et Universidade do Algarve (Doc. Policopiado).

FERNANDES M. R. & GONÇALVES J. A. (2000). 'Os Territórios Educativos de Intervenção Prioritária como Espaço de Inovação Organizacional e Curricular' [Priority education intervention regions as a place for organisational and curricular innovation]. In AAVV, *Territórios Educativos de Intervenção Prioritária*. Lisbon: Instituto de Inovação Educacional.

GRÁCIO S. (1986). *Política educativa como tecnologia social* [Educational policy as social technology]. Lisbon: L. Horizonte.

GRÁCIO S. (1998). *Ensinos técnicos e política em Portugal. 1910–1990* [Technical education and politics in Portugal. 1910–1990]. Lisbon: I. Piaget.

LEITE C. (2000). 'Uma análise da dimensão multicutural no currículo' [An analysis of the multicultural dimension in the curriculum]. *Revista Educação*, vol. 9, no. 1, pp. 137–142.

LEITE C. (dir.) (2005). *Mudanças curriculares em Portugal. Transição para o século XXI* [Changes in the curriculum in Portugal. The transition to the 21st century]. Porto: Porto Editora.

LEITE C. & FERNANDES P. (2007). 'A organização das escolas por agrupamentos – de uma autonomia prometida a uma prática comprometida' [The organisation of schools by groups – from promised autonomy to compromised practice]. In C. LEITE and A. LOPES (eds), *Escola, currículo e formação de identidades*. Porto: Edições ASA, pp. 51–72.

LIMA L. C. & AFONSO A. J. (2002). *Reformas da Educação Pública: Democratização, modernização, neoliberalismo* [Reforms in public education: democratisation, modernisation, neo-liberalism]. Porto: Ed. Afrontamento.

MAGALHÃES A. & STOER R. (2002). *Escola para todos e excelência acadamica* [Schooling for all and academic excellence]. Porto: Profedições.

MAGALHÃES A. & STOER R. (dir.) (2006). *Reconfigurações, educação, Estado e cultura numa época de globalização* [Reconfigurations, education, state and culture during a period of globalisation]. Porto: Profedições.

MARTINS A. M. & PARCHÃO I. (2000). 'Legitimação psicológica do insucesso escolar e a (des)responsabilização dos professores' [Psychological legitimisation of educational failure and increasing or reducing teacher responsibility]. Madrid: Facultad de Educación.

MARTINS M. A. (1996). *Pré-História da aprendizagem da leitura: Conhecimentos Precoces sobre a Funcionalidade da linguagem escrita, Desenvolvimento Metalinguístico e Resultados em leitura no final do 1º ano de escolaridad* [The prehistory of learning to read: early knowledge about the functionality of the written language; metalinguistic development and the results for reading at the end of the first year of schooling]. Lisbon: ISPA.

MATOS M. (1999). 'Autonomia das Escolas: Atribuir ou Construir Novas Competências Profissionais?' [School autonomy: attributing building new professional competencies?]. *Territorio Educativo*, no. 5.

MELO A. & BENAVENTE A. (1978). *Expériences d'éducation populaire au Portugal – 1974–1976* [Experiences of lower-class education in Portugal – 1974–1976]. Paris: UNESCO.

PINTO F. (1991). 'Falando do PIPSE [About the PIPSE]'. *Noesis. A educação em revista – o insucesso*, no. 18, p. 17.

PIRES E. (2000). *Da inquietação à quietude: o caso do PIPSE* [From anxiety to tranquillity: the PIPSE issue]. Lisbon: Colecção Temas de Investigação – Direcção – Geral de Inovação e de Desenvolvimento Curricular.

ROBERTSON S. & DALE R. (2001). 'Regulação e Risco na Governação da Educação. Gestão dos Problemas de Legitimação e Coesão Social em Educação nos Estados Competitivos' [Regulation and risk in the governance of education. Managing problems of legitimization and social cohesion in education in the competitive States]. *Educação, Sociedade & Culturas*, no. 15, pp. 117–147.

ROCHEX J.-Y. (1997). 'Les ZEP: un bilan décevant' [Priority education zones: a disappointing result]. In J.-P. TERRAIL (ed.), *La scolarisation de la France. Critique de l'état des lieux* [Schooling in France. A critical inventory]. Paris: La Dispute, pp. 123–139.

RODRIGUES F. & STOER R. S. (1993). *Acção local e mudança social em Portugal* [Local action and social change in Portugal]. Lisbon: Fim de Século.

RODRIGUES F. & STOER R. S. (1994). 'Acção Local e Cidadania' [Local action and citizenship]. In AAVV, *Dinâmicas Culturais, Cidadania e Desenvolvimento Local*. Lisbon: Associação Portuguesa de Sociologia, pp. 175–188.

RODRIGUES F. & STOER R. S. (2001). 'Partenariat et développement local au Portugal: du localisme globalisé à une forme nouvelle d'action collective' [Partnership and local development in Portugal: from globalised localism to a new form of collective action]. *Les Cahiers Européens de la Sorbonne Nouvelle*, no. 1, pp. 113–135.

SALGADO L. (1991).'Do Insucesso Escolar aos Facilitadores de Sucesso' [From educational failure to the success facilitators]. *Noesis*, no. 18, pp. 34–37.

SALGADO L. (1997). 'Políticas e Práticas de Educação de Adultos em Portugal – Perspectiva Multicultural' [Policies and practices in adult education in Portugal – a multicultural perspective]. In M. B. TRINDADE & M. L. MENDES (eds), *Educação Intercultural des Adultos em Contexto Multicultural*. Lisbon: Universidade Aberta, pp. 185–211.

SALGADO L. (2000). 'Les Compétences en lecture et en écriture et leur apprentissage' [Reading and writing skills, and learning them]. In *Colectânea de Comunicações*, vol. I. Coimbra: IPC, pp. 125–135.

SALGUEIRO G. & ABOOBAKAR F. (s.d.). *Currículos Alternativos – Breve Abordagem*. [Alternative curricula: a brief approach]. Microsoft PowerPoint document available on the Internet: <http://www.proformar.org/teia/tdin/recursos/did_geral/met_ensino/ Curr per centC3 per centADculos per cent20Alternativos.ppt#256,1,Currículos Alternativos> (consulted July 16, 2008).

SARMENTO M. J., PARENTE C., MATOS P. S. & SILVIA O. S. (1999). *Dimensões Organizacionais e Administrativas dos Territórios Educativos de Intervenção Prioritária. Um estudo avaliativo no âmbito da Região Norte. Relatório Final* [Organisational and administrative dimensions of the education regions for priority action. An evaluative study in the North region. Final report]. Braga: Universidade do Minho/Centro de Estudos da Criança.

SARMENTO M. J. *et al.* (2000). 'A edificação dos TEIP como Sistemas de Acção Educativa Concreta' [Setting up TEIPs as concrete educational action systems]. In AAVV, *Territórios Educativos de Intervenção Prioritária*. Lisbon: IIE.

SEABRA T., BENAVENTE A., CAMPICHE J. & SEBASTIÃO J. (1994). *Renunciar à Escola – o abandono escolar no ensino básico* [Giving up school – dropping out of basic education]. Lisbon: Fim de Século.

SOUTA L. (1997). *Multiculturalidade e Educação* [Multiculturality and education]. Porto: Profedições.

STOER S. R. (1982). *Educação, Estado e Desenvolvimento em Portugal* [Education, the state and development in Portugal]. Lisbon: Livros Horizonte.

STOER S. R. (1986). *Educação e Mudança Social em Portugal, 1970–80, uma década de transição* [Education and social change in Portugal, 1970–1980, a decade of transition]. Porto: Ed. Afrontamento.

STOER S. R. (1994a). 'Construíndo a escola democrática através do campo da recontextualização pedagógica' [Building the democratic school via the field of pedagogical recontextualisation]. *Educação, Sociedade & Culturas*, no. 1, pp. 7–27.

STOER S. R. (1994b). 'O Estado e as políticas educativas: uma proposta de mandato renovado para a escola democrática' [The state and education policies: a proposal for a renewed mandate for democratic schooling]. *Revista Crítica de Ciências Sociais*, no. 41, pp. 3–33.

STOER S. R., CORTESÃO L. & CORREIA J. A. (dir.) (2001). *Transnacionalização da educação. Da Crise da educação a educação da crise* [Transnationalising education. From the crisis of education to education of the crisis]. Porto: Edições Afrontamento.

STOER S. R. & MAGALHÃES A. M. (2003). 'A Nova Classe Média e a Reconfiguração do Mandato Endereçado ao Sistema Educativo' [The new middle class and the reconfiguration of the mandate addressed to the education system]. *Educação, Sociedade & Culturas*, no. 18, pp. 25–40.

STOER S. R. & RODRIGUES F. (1998). *Entre Parceria e Partenariado: Amigos Amigos, Negócios à Parte* [What partners?]. Lisbon: Celta Editora.

STOER S. R. & RODRIGUES F. (1999). *As Parcerias nos Territórios Educativos de Intervenção Prioritária* [Partnerships in the education regions for priority action]. Porto: IIE/CIIE.

STOER S. R. & RODRIGUES F. (2000). 'Territórios Educativos de Intervenção Prioritária. Análise do Contributo das Parcerias' [Education regions for priority action. Analysis of the contribution of partners]. In AAVV, *Territórios Educativos de Intervenção Prioritária*. Lisbon: IIE, pp. 171–194.

STOER S. R., STOLEROFF A. & CORREIA J. A. (1990). 'O novo vocacionalismo na política educativa em Portugal e a reconstrução da lógica da acumulação' [The new vocation in the education policy in Portugal reconstruction of the logic of accumulation]. *Revista Crítica de Ciências Sociais*, no. 29, pp. 11–53.

TEODORO A. (1982). *O sistema educativo Português: Situação e perspectivas*. [The Portuguese education system: situations and perspectives]. Lisbon: Estúdios Horizonte.

TEODORO A. (1994). *Política educativa em Portugal – educação, desenvolvimento e participação política dos professores* [The education policy in Portugal – teacher education, development and participation]. Venda Nova: Bretrand Editora.

UNESCO (1981). *Para uma política da educação em Portugal* [Towards an education policy in Portugal]. Lisbon: Estúdios Horizonte.

VERNE E. (1987). *Les politiques d'éducation multiculturelle. Analyse critique* [Multicultural education policies. Critical analysis]. Paris: OCDE.

VAN ZANTEN A. (2001). *L'école de la périphérie. Scolarité et ségrégation en banlieue* [School around the edge. Schooling and segregation in the suburbs]. Paris: PUF.

Legal references and official or administrative documents

CENTRO DE ATENDIMENTO NOVAS OPORTUNIDADES (2007). *Metas e Medidas Novas Oportunidades – Jovens* [Aims and measures of new opportunities]. Available on the Internet: <http://www.novasoportunidades.gov.pt/metas_jovens.aspx> (consulted on July 16, 2008).

FENPROF (2007). *Um quarto das crianças com três anos sem vaga na rede pública do Pré-Escolar* [A quarter of three-year-olds without a place in the public pre-school network]. Document available on the Internet: <http://www.fenprof.pt/?aba=27& cat=61&doc=2289&mid=115> (consulted on July 16, 2008).

PORTUGAL (1984). Decreto-lei no. 102/84 (1984). Lei da Aprendizagem [Law on learning]. In Ministério da Educação (1993). *Cadernos PEPT – Educação para todos: A construção local dos currículos e a relação escola – meio*. Lisbon: Editorial do Ministério da Educação, pp. 122–128.

PORTUGAL (1986). Lei no. 46/86 (1986). Lei de Bases do Sistema Educativo [Fundamental law on the education system]. Available on the Internet: <http://www.sg. min-edu.pt/leis/lei_46_86.pdf> (consulted on July 16, 2008).

PORTUGAL (1991). Decreto-lei no. 383/91 (1991). Lei da Pré-Aprendizagem. In Ministério da Educação (1993). *Cadernos PEPT – Educação para todos: A construção local dos currículos e a relação escola – meio*. Lisbon: Editorial do Ministério da Educação, pp. 129–130.

PORTUGAL (1996). Decreto-Lei no. 205/96 (1996). *Diário da República*, no. 248. I Série A.

PORTUGAL (1997). Lei no. 5/97 (1997). *Diário da República*, no. 34. I. SÉRIE. A.

PORTUGAL (2004). Resolução de Conselho de Ministros no. 60/2004 (2004). *Diário da República*, no. 102 – I série B.

PORTUGAL (2007a). Despacho no. 546/2007 (2007). *Diário da República*, no. 8. II. SÉRIE.

188   *Portugal*

PORTUGAL (2007b). Despacho no. 546/2007 (2007). *Diário da República*, no. 8. II. SÉRIE.
PORTUGAL: MINISTÉRIO DA EDUCAÇÃO (1989). *A reforma educativa em Marcha: balanço de dois anos de governo* [The educational reform in motion: assessment of two years of de government]. Lisbon: Ministério da Educação.
PORTUGAL: MINISTÉRIO DA EDUCAÇÃO (2006a). *Percursos curriculares alternativos* [Alternative curricula]. Available on the Internet: <http://www.min-edu.pt/np3/178.html> (consulted on July 16, 2008).
PORTUGAL: MINISTÉRIO DA EDUCAÇÃO (2006b). *Relançamento do programa dos Territórios Educativos de Intervenção Prioritária* [The revival of the Education regions for priority action programme]. Document available on the Internet: <http://www.min-edu.pt/np3/70.html> (consulted on July 16, 2008).
PORTUGAL: MINISTÉRIO DA EDUCAÇÃO (2007). *Plano de Acção da Matemática regista balanço positivo no seu primeiro ano de execução* [The mathematics action plan shows a positive result in its first year of implementation]. Document available on the Internet: <http://www.min-edu.pt/np3/667.html> (consulted on July 16, 2008).
PORTUGAL: MINISTÉRIO DA EDUCAÇÃO E DA SEGURANÇA SOCIAL E DO TRABALHO (2003). Despacho no. 948/2003. *Diário da República*, 2.a série, n. 7, de 9 de Janeiro.
SISTEMA EDUCATIVO NACIONAL DE PORTUGAL. MINISTÉRIO DA EDUCAÇÃO DE PORTUGAL Y ORGANIZACIÓN DE ESTADOS IBEROAMERICANOS (2003a). *Breve evolução histórica do sistema educativo* [A brief historical evolution of the education system]. Available on the Internet: <http://www.oei.es/quipu/portugal/historia.pdf> (consulted on July 16, 2008).
SISTEMA EDUCATIVO NACIONAL DE PORTUGAL. MINISTÉRIO DA EDUCAÇÃO DE PORTUGAL Y ORGANIZACIÓN DE ESTADOS IBEROAMERICANOS (2003b). *Escolaridade obrigatória* [Compulsory schooling]. Document available on the Internet: <http://www.oei.es/quipu/portugal/esc_obligatoria.pdf> (consulted on July 16, 2008).

Czech Republic

7
Priority Education Policies in the Czech Republic: Redesigning Equity Policies in the Post-Communist Transformation

David Greger, Markéta Levínská and Irena Smetáčková

General context

When reporting on the priority educational policies (PEPs) at the current stage of development of the Czech Republic (CR), it must be taken into account that this is a country which, since November 1989, underwent a transition from a totalitarian political system, and centrally planned, state-owned economy to democratic governance respecting human rights, the restoration of private ownership and a market economy. The implicit or explicit comparison of PEPs before and after 1989 is widely used in this report, in many cases contrasting these two periods. We are aware of the fact that such contrasting of periods requires a high level of simplification; on the other hand it enables the various international readers lacking in-depth knowledge of the Czech national context to better understand the main trends and characteristics of the development of PEPs in our country.

Initially, we will describe the general structure of the education system in the Czech Republic that is the main context for PEPs. The Czechoslovak school structure was basically, and with only moderate changes, inherited from the 19th century, when the 1869 School Act extended compulsory education to eight years. Education was provided by a five-year *obecná škola* (community school), which was the common school for pupils aged 6–11 years. After five years of community school it was possible to choose one of the following three, qualitatively very different, streams: an additional three years at community school, *měšťanská škol* (civic school); secondary school – a seven-year *reálná škola* (secondary technical school); or an eight-year *gymnázium* (upper secondary general school). This school structure, with parallel and separate branches of study for pupils aged 11–14 years, has been widely criticised since the 1920s from the perspective of social justice, in particular by calling on the education system to achieve equality of educational opportunity understood as equality of treatment or conditions. It was argued that only through comprehensive (common) schooling could equality of educational opportunity be achieved. That the same quality of education was to be provided for all was seen as the most democratic nature of education. Discussions on the introduction of the comprehensive school were interrupted by WWII and reopened after 1945. Finally, it was the Communist Party, after it took power and introduced the totalitarian regime, that passed the School Act in April 1948, establishing a comprehensive school model in Czechoslovakia.

The progressive comprehensive school model, with the system of internal differentiation that would allow the maximum development of each child's potential and that has been widely discussed and experimentally tested in several schools since the 1920s, was gradually dismissed and replaced by the unified and collectivist common school, without respect for individual pupil differences. This was the main criticism of the common school introduced in 1948. Critics mainly stressed its unified curriculum and steady-paced progress for all pupils, and the main characteristic of the common school was for them the emphasis on sameness and mediocrity. Even though during more than 40 years of existence of the common schools there have been many reforms attempting to react to the heterogeneity of the student population through the diverse mechanisms of differentiation or extra-curricular activities, this was still seen by many as an insufficient endeavour. This criticism was widely shared by the general public and representatives of the Czech elites after the Velvet revolution in 1989, and it led to a highly articulated demand for a structural reform of the education system. After experiences with common school during the 40-year period of 'real socialism' in Czechoslovakia, they did not believe in the ability of the comprehensive school to respect individual students' learning styles, interests, personal traits and other differences. As a result of this disappointment with the common school, the six- and eight-year *gymnázia*, which had operated in the Czech Republic until 1948, were re-established by a 1990 amendment to the Education Act. The original and publicly proclaimed aim was to provide more demanding education facilitating further academic studies for students as young as 11 showing a higher level of cognitive ability. As reports by the Czech School Inspectorate have repeatedly stated, the segregation of more talented pupils from the rest, who continue attending basic schools, has resulted in a gradual decrease in the standards of educational processes and achievements of the population in mainstream schools. The 1996 recommendation of the Organisation for Economic Co-operation and Development (OECD) examiners in regard to forming a comprehensive lower secondary school was not adopted by the Ministry of Education. The government-promoted White Paper of 2001 reiterated that the two streams of education should be gradually merged and that internal differentiation should take place within basic school. The inclusion of this recommendation in the new Education Bill in the form of the gradual abolition of the lower years of six- and eight-year *gymnázia* prompted public debate, which was dominated by the requirement on the part of parents with higher levels of education and socio-economic status that a more demanding form of education be retained for their children. The pressure exerted by parents, *gymnázia* directors and teachers, and academics in the media, not to mention their political influence, prevented the proposed reform and was one of the reasons the bill was rejected as a whole in 2001. The new Education Act approved in 2004 preserves selectivity in the Czech education system and keeps the separate branches of study at the lower secondary level.

The analyses of the data from international studies on student achievement – mainly the Programme for International Student Assessment (PISA) and Trends in International Mathematics and Science Study (TIMSS) – revealed that the selective entrance examination to multi-year *gymnázia* disfavours children with lower cultural capital (students from the two lowest quintiles of socio-economic status comprised only 15 per cent of the student population in these selective schools – Matějů & Straková 2005). These analyses show that the Czech Republic is one of the countries where the impact of family background on student performance is very high, that the differences between schools are above the OECD average (the differences in results between schools are 1.5 times greater than the OECD average) and that the schools largely differ in their socio-economic background (the socio-economic background of the schools explains 37 per cent of the variance in students' test results, which is the seventh highest value among the countries involved in the 2003 PISA study).

The selective nature of the Czech education system and the existence of the multi-year *gymnázia* are widely criticised by researchers, and quite recently all political parties in the Czech Republic also recognised it as a problem. Nevertheless, the political will to change this status of education is lacking, because, as the political parties repeatedly explain, the 'general public wants to retain these selective schools'. This brings us to the general attitudes of Czech society and its views on education. Eliminating early selection would require a change of culture that believes success in school is more a matter of ability than of effort, hard work or quality education. So the main goal for many is to recognise the ability of every child as early as possible and to provide him/her with a sufficiently challenging education (or, on the contrary, not too challenging for those who are less able). Educational failure is therefore often seen as a lack of ability or of support from the family.

Generally speaking, there is no discussion among the general public on educational failure. One of the reasons might be the lack of data. In the Czech Republic, there is no national testing at any level of education.

Therefore all the above-mentioned data are derived from international large-scale assessments. Even though the Education Act of 2004 prepared by the Social Democrat Party planned to introduce a national school-leaving examination at the end of upper secondary school from the year 2008, this was postponed by the new conservative government led by the Civic Democratic Party until 2010, and some even argue that it should not be introduced at all. The Social Democrat government also started experimentally to implement national testing in the fifth and ninth grades, and this project is currently being gradually phased out by the current government.

The authors of this report believe that one of the important reasons for having the national testing scheme with a strong emphasis on monitoring and diagnostic function of education is the quest for achieving equal educational opportunity in the sense of equality of results. Until now many forms and the real extent of educational failure in the Czech education system have been hidden and identified only at school level. Unmasking the nature and extent of educational failure and educational inequalities is therefore a necessary (and still lacking) first step for opening public debate on the issue of how to cope with it, and for finding the effective policy measures to intervene.

Priority educational policies in the Czech Republic

In the following, we will widely use the term 'priority educational policy' in line with its definitions from the Introduction, even though such an equivalent is not used in the Czech language and in legislative documentation or public debates. Mostly, the political measures in education we are about to describe are referred to as compensatory action, positive discrimination/action or specific measures. In particular, the term 'positive discrimination' is officially rejected on the grounds that any discrimination is not correct, and therefore the term 'positive action' is preferred. But more important than the terminology used is the general characteristic of PEPs in the Czech Republic. By and large we can distinguish three different ways of targeting educational interventions: targeted groups, institutions and areas. In the Czech Republic only group-focused interventions are used, even though some other countries use all three approaches to deal with educational inequalities in their country (see, Chapter 2 for England). There is no national testing in the Czech Republic and therefore no information about academic performance, which might be one of the reasons for the failure to use institutionally focused interventions. In the following, therefore, we will describe PEPs in the Czech Republic by the different groups for which the political measures are implemented.

The other aspect of PEPs to be mentioned is their historical development. For each specific targeted group the historical development is outlined in consequent sub-chapters, so in this introduction we will point only to the general characteristic of the development of PEPs. When analysing the development of social issues in the Czech Republic, there is usually a comparison between the state of affairs in the 'real socialism' era and the development after the Velvet revolution and the demise of the communist regime in November 1989.

From 1948 until 1989 educational policy, together with other spheres of public policy, was formulated in line with the official ideology of communist political elites that aimed to eliminate the mechanisms of social reproduction in education and that emphasised upward mobility. The goal to be achieved was the equality of educational opportunity that was widely understood to be in line with the concept of equality of results. The understanding of equity at that time is characterised by many authors as a 'statistical justice' (e.g. Štech 2008), meaning that the main aim was to achieve the representation of different social groups at upper secondary and tertiary education in a ratio equivalent to their representation in society as a whole – statistically equal representation of all classes and groups. For that purpose many characteristics other than students' ability were checked in the process of admission to upper secondary and tertiary education (so-called *kádrová kritéria*) – for example class origin and socio-economic status of the family, the political affiliations of the parents, rural/urban background or gender. Equality of educational opportunity was to be attained, in particular by the proper selection and control of the student intake at higher levels of education according to pre-set criteria (the quota system). According to this student selection practice, the education system was perceived by communist officials as *a priori* (by definition) equal and fair and, therefore, there was no need for research analysis into educational inequalities. Even though the quota system has led to some positive results (e.g. equalising the opportunity for achieving higher levels of education between women and men), Shavit and Blossfeld (1993) came to the conclusion, based on the international data analysis, that the impact of social background on student attainment in higher levels of education was generally the same in former socialist countries and capitalist countries. The notion that 'communist positive discrimination' applied through the quota systems did not lead to significant results in reducing socio-economic inequality in access to education is also supported by many other researchers (Matějů 1993; Hanley 2001). Kreidl (2006) challenges this conclusion on methodological as well as theoretical grounds, and shows by analysing the data that, in the periods of the most orthodox communist egalitarianism in Czechoslovakia (1949–1953 and 1970–1973), socio-economic inequality of access to secondary and tertiary education declined.

The quota system was therefore the main instrument for achieving equality of educational opportunity in the 'real socialism era', even though there is disagreement on the effects of this policy. We could consider the quota system as a special kind of positive discrimination targeting sub-populations, among whom the main priority was working-class families and women.

According to the official legislation in education from 1948 to 1989, 'students requiring special care' were the main category of students for whom positive discrimination was to be applied and different conditions for their education were to be provided. Under the definitions of students requiring special care were mentioned physically and mentally handicapped students. Experts on the education of physically and mentally handicapped students state that Czechoslovakia had the most elaborate system in the world of special schools for these children (Vocilka 1997). Nevertheless the experts also mention the other, more problematic, side of the coin: the segregated nature of special education. Handicapped pupils (and also adults) were almost entirely isolated from 'normal–healthy society' so effectively that most able-bodied people did not come into contact with the handicapped. The real effort for the social inclusion and educational integration of the handicapped is characteristic, especially for the period since 1989. Even though the integration of the handicapped as a goal was mentioned in some Education Acts even prior to 1989, the real schooling of these children was in sharp contrast to this. The issues surrounding the education of physically and mentally handicapped students are beyond the scope of this book, and we will therefore not go into more detail on the description of positive discrimination towards these children.

Among measures targeted at other groups explicitly mentioned in the Education Acts in the period 1948–1989 were the programmes for talented pupils in the 1984 Education Act § 41–43. For these, schools with special emphasis and extended teaching in specific subjects (e.g. foreign languages, mathematics, science, music, art and sport) were opened, and the opportunity to study according to an individual study plan, and therefore to complete basic school in less than eight years, was to be provided. Nevertheless, this is not to be understood as mirroring educational reality.

Compared with the period 1948–1989, the development started in late 1989 and lasting until the present is characterised by the reformulation of public policies in many spheres of life, including educational policy. The concrete steps in the development of PEPs for each specific group will be described in detail in the sections below; at this point we are simply recording the stronger emphasis on equality of educational opportunity by quoting from the most important documentation from that era.

First of all, significant examples of policy reformulation could be seen in the widening of the category of 'students with special educational needs', in the identification of other targeted groups in legislative documents, and in the formulation of positive action and compensatory measures for these groups. This is especially well documented in the analysis of the first 2004 Education Act in comparison with the 1984 Education Act it replaced.

Following the 1989 political upheaval, the equality of educational opportunity again appeared on the scene and the general argument was in favour of 'the interpretation of equality of results'. The National Programme for the

Development of Education (White Paper) approved by the government in 2001 clearly documents the emphasis on equality of results and justifies the compensatory actions:

> Ensuring truly fair access to educational opportunities...Nevertheless the demand for fair provision of educational opportunities means much more than overcoming material obstacles, i.e. inequalities in economic status, for example through a system of grants and supports. It is necessary to overcome disadvantages caused by different social-cultural levels and to introduce adequate compensatory mechanisms in order that the education system does not further reproduce existing inequalities.
>
> (White Paper, p. 18)

Many other extracts that could be quoted from this document call for the equality of results and criticise the selective nature of the Czech education system. Only some of the recommendations were projected into Education Act No. 561/2004. This act states, among the main principles for education in the Czech Republic: (1) equal access for all...without any discrimination based on any grounds such as race, colour, sex, language, belief or religion, nationality, ethnic or social origin, property, kith or kin, or the health condition or any other status of a citizen; and (2) consideration of the educational needs of an individual. In this act there are explicitly stated groups for which special treatment or different compensatory actions are to be applied:

1. § 13–14: Language of Instruction and Education of Members of National Minorities.
2. § 16: Education of Children, Pupils and Students with Special Educational Needs (this category covers mentally and physically disabled; students with learning and behavioural disabilities; socially disadvantaged students; students in institutional education ordered or protective education imposed; and asylum seekers).
3. § 17: Education of Gifted Children, Pupils and Students.

These quotations from the Education Act (2004) demonstrate that there are more targeted groups recognised in the official documentation than was the case before 1989. These groups are considered to be somehow disadvantaged or requiring special treatment that is specified partly in this act, but more thoroughly in other documentation at a lower legislative level (e.g. regulations, recommendations, conceptions, etc.). In this documentation there is also another relevant group that is not mentioned – gender. We will therefore also describe the PEPs targeted at equalising education opportunities for boys and girls. At the lower legislative level many programmes and political measures are defined for Roma students. Even though they are not mentioned as a specific group in the Education Act, they are the group that have been most affected by PEPs in the Czech Republic since 1989.

Prior to 1989 there was a strong emphasis on the assimilation of the Roma people, while today it is integration and respect for their culture that is mainly stressed. Different programmes, political action and compensatory measures for Roma students could be hidden under different labels – for example programmes for students of national minorities or compensatory action for socially disadvantaged students, where many of these are accounted for by Roma students, and so on. Because of the overlapping nature of the categories defined in the Education Act, we have decided to structure our text according to specific categories, which are defined at the lower legislative levels and that correspond with the groups actually perceived in schools and groups defined as a separate population by the numerous items of research. Those groups are arranged in order of importance in regard to PEPs in the Czech Republic:

– Roma people;
– national minorities;
– asylum seekers;
– students with learning and behavioural disabilities;
– gifted pupils;
– gender – girls and boys.

Roma people

After the 1989 political changes, the Roma were recognised as a nationality for the first time in 1991; until that time they were referred to as citizens of gypsy origin, and the purpose of government policy was the assimilation and acculturation of this social group, living at 'a low socio-cultural level'.

In the population censuses of 1991 and 2001 the Roma people could espouse their Roma nationality. To the surprise of the majority, there were not many who declared themselves to be of Roma ethnicity (32,903 in 1991 and 11,746 in 2001).

The fact that Roma did not espouse their nationality surprised many people, including politicians. We now offer a few explanations. The first is that the assimilation of the socialist regime was 'successful'. The second is that the Roma were afraid officially to declare their own nationality, for various reasons. Legal discrimination appeared in 1993. The Czechoslovak Republic had split into two independent countries and the Czech National Council adopted the controversial Act No. 40/1993 Coll., on the Acquisition and Loss of Citizenship of the Czech Republic. Roma people had to apply for Czech citizenship in spite of the fact that they had been born in the country. Finally, Roma people do not recognise the difference between nationality and citizenship. They commonly fill in official documents as Czech, Slovak or Hungarian nationality depending on the place where they were born; they simultaneously refer to themselves as Roma or gypsies.[1] It is the life style of Roma elites to publicly declare their own nationality; its members are conscious of the impact of this act.

Currently, according to S. 3(2) of The Charter of Fundamental Rights and Freedoms and S. 2 of Act No. 273/2001 Coll., a Roma person is anyone who declares him/herself to be of Roma nationality. Current legislation does not resolve the conditions of the declaration. The act guarantees Roma people the right to education and to receive information in their own language, the right to develop their culture, the right of association of members of a national minority and the right of participation in dealing with matters concerning Roma people.

After the Roma started to leave the Czech Republic in large numbers in 1997, the Governmental Council for Roma Community Affairs was established and in the same year The Report on Roma Communities (the so-called Bratinka Report) was adopted by the government. Since then, information on applying government resolutions on the integration of Roma communities and the policy concept of Roma integration are regularly updated. In 2001, the Government Council of the Czech Republic for National Minorities was established. This includes 12 national minorities; the Roma have three deputies on this council.

The Roma issue is now being resolved by two Councils: the Council for National Minorities and the Council for Roma Community Affairs (both are only consultative authorities and not legislative). There are certain special advisory bodies under both the Ministry of Education, Youth and Sports (MoEYS) and the Ministry of Labour and Social Affairs (MoLSA) in charge of these affairs.

The advisory bodies explain this split as a consequence of the separation of the Roma ethnic identity between the subjective and personal declaration of nationality and the objective identification of an individual as a member of the Roma community by the rest of the population. One should realise that Roma people cannot expect any support from their country of origin. From our point of view, this dichotomy is the product of conflict between the conceptualisation of national identity by the Roma and that of national identity by the rest of the population. According to current legislation, the Roma cannot be required to waive their right to national identity and, simultaneously, they cannot be considered as a homogeneous nation. Considering the Roma as a complex set of communities makes it possible to see them as a population comprising various sub-ethnic and social groups with specific needs. This point of view allows their needs and difficulties to be dealt with efficiently.

In the former Czechoslovak Socialist Republic, the Act on the Common Education system of 1948 then in force did not allow education in the Roma language. The purpose of the policies applied was the education of gypsy citizens, their assimilation and acculturation. In the 1960s specialised classes for the children of settled Olach Roma (*Vlachike*) were set up to make it easier for these children to adapt to the school environment.

Formally, Education Act No. 561/2004 guarantees equal access to education for all citizens regardless of their nationality. Special primary schools were abolished, and in their place now exist the so-called elementary practical schools within the special schools. Romani children may or may not belong to a group of children, pupils or students with special educational needs. A Romani child may be considered as disadvantaged in terms of social position. Social disadvantage in the Czech Republic, under a special legal regulation, means a family environment of low social and cultural status, a risk of pathological social phenomena, institutional education ordered or protective education imposed, the status of asylum seeker and a party to asylum proceedings.

If there is such child in a class or in a study group, the head teacher of the relevant school may, with the consent of the relevant Regional Authority, create the job of teaching assistant. The minimum requirement for this post is the successful completion of basic school, being at least 18 years old, having no criminal record and completing a course of basic teaching skills consisting of 80 training hours.

For children from socially disadvantaged backgrounds, the municipalities, unions of municipalities or a region may, with the prior consent of the regional authority, set up preparatory classes. These are intended for children for whom it is presumed that inclusion in such a class may balance out their development. A preparatory class may be set up if there are at least seven eligible children, and it may consist of no more than 15 pupils. The decision to include pupils in a preparatory class is made by the head teacher following a recommendation in writing from the pedagogical–psychological advisor facility.

The idea of Roma teaching assistants[2] appeared for the first time in the Czech Republic in the 1990s. The idea of employing Roma assistants was supported by non-governmental organisations (NGOs) such as the Association of the Roma in Moravia (*Společenství Romů na Moravě*) and the New School (*Nová škola*). Until 1998, Roma assistants were employed by NGOs. Based on a 1998 Governmental Resolution, funds were for the first time allocated from the state budget to finance the salaries of Roma teaching assistants. From September 1997 until June 2000, the MoEYS tested the introduction of both teaching assistants and preparatory classes. The pilot projects were evaluated as being successful, and preparatory classes and teaching assistant posts began to be established on a regular basis pursuant to the Methodical Instruction by the MoEYS.

For the first time, the post of teaching assistant was stipulated by the Education Act of 2004. This act regulates the conditions under which teaching assistants can operate, the scope of their activities, remuneration and their required training and education. In 2005 there were 235 teaching assistants in the Czech Republic and for 2006 there were 318 posts created (for 328 individuals) upon request by regional authorities.

The initial role of a Roma assistant was to provide a link between the Roma community and the school. This has been partially abandoned by the current act as it does not require a teaching assistant to be a member of the Roma community. Formally, a school can therefore have a teaching assistant in its classes who will assist children in the teaching–learning process, but who may not be able to act as a go-between whose role is to mitigate the conflicting of two different cultural experiences. The benefit introduced by the act is the fact that a teaching assistant is recognised as a professional educational worker. However, as salaries for teaching assistants are quite low this limits the possibility of hiring people with higher professional qualifications as teaching assistants and it de-motivates current teaching assistants in their efforts to obtain higher qualifications. This fact may limit the positive effect of assistants on the education of pupils.

Preparatory classes[3] were developed contemporally with the post of teaching assistant. The first preparatory classes were established as early as 1993 – they were established in nursery schools, primary schools and in special primary schools. As in the final year of pre-school, education in preparatory classes is provided free of charge. Textbooks and other educational aids for children in preparatory classes and in the first year of primary school are also provided free of charge. This legal regulation applies only to preparatory classes and pre-schools established by the state, the regional government, the municipality or the union of municipalities. This regulation is aimed at supporting the integration of children from socially disadvantaged backgrounds and enabling pre-school education for children from small villages, where it is difficult to provide preparatory classes for financial reasons.

The first evaluation of the efficiency of preparatory classes was carried out by a team from the Faculty of Humanities at Charles University, in Prague (Bolf *et al.*, 2003). The team conducted quantitative research in 103 schools operating preparatory classes according to the data provided by MoEYS, which was accompanied by qualitative research in three to four schools in selected locations. The data from the years 1999–2003 were analysed.[4]

The difference between Romani and non-Romani children in the lower grades is relatively small; the differences start to become apparent in the higher grades, in which the problems of Romani children become more serious. These children often have learning difficulties and have to be transferred to special schools. Roma families attribute low priority to the higher grades as they usually do not plan to send their children to study at a secondary school. We also believe that this is the result of Roma parents' inability to help their own children with their homework at higher levels. The research disproved the proposition that Roma families intentionally choose practical (special) schools. It showed that the preparatory class programme is more efficient if the school does not focus on the pupil alone, but co-operates with the family as well. The involvement of Roma assistants or in-field social workers may significantly contribute to the success of the programme.

The research confirmed that preparatory classes helped children in overcoming specific difficulties relating to school education, improved children's attitude towards the school, reduced absenteeism and positively influenced school results. This research, and later the study by I. Gabal (2006), showed that setting up preparatory classes in practical (special) schools is not recommended. Children leaving preparatory classes in practical schools are three times more likely to be sent to special schools in comparison with children from other preparatory classes. This type of preparatory class may also become a factor contributing to the ethnicisation of schools.

A negative aspect of pro-Roma programmes is the fact that the so-called ghettoised schools are of significantly lower quality. This has very negative impacts on the integration of Romani children and their further education. Preparatory classes should be a tool for overcoming segregation. They should be established at schools not frequently attended by Romani children, but they are instead established in areas with a strong Roma population.

Other education programmes for improving the relationship with education and for increasing schooling time are 'The school with a whole-day programme/community school' (Vik and Vrzáček 2005) and the Step by step (SBS) programmes.

Initially, the Open Society Funds (OSF) in Prague and the Charles Stewart Motte foundation (ChSM) supported community education and its establishment in the Czech Republic. The first community project was called *Poryv*, and its purpose was to offer community-oriented activities in three primary schools. Schools should be an open place for community meetings and they should help to resolve the problems of community members. Schools also ran leisure activities and clubs for whole families. In 2006, the NGO 'New School'[5] set up a two-year project, Support for community schools, in order to initiate community education in four ethnically mixed schools. Considering that the programme was positively evaluated, the ChSM foundation decided to support the community education project 'Varianty – intercultural education' for three years. This is financed by the European Union (EU) and the state budget for the Czech Republic – EQUAL. There are currently eight community schools in the Czech Republic, three of which are active in areas with a high density of Roma population and children from socially disadvantaged backgrounds.

Gabal (2006, p. 66) provides a report from five schools supported by MoEYS. A pilot project was introduced with the aim of verifying the efficiency and financial requirements of the programme. The selected schools should not be exclusively Roma schools, but some of them could be viewed as Roma schools due to the high proportion of Romani children. In this case, the majority would leave these schools and the quality of education provided would decrease.[6]

Step by Step is an educational programme developed by an NGO for nursery schools and primary schools. This programme supports the inclusion of children with special needs, emphasising an individual approach to the child and co-operation with the child's family. Step by Step in the Czech Republic provides around 60 pre-schools, 36 mainstream schools and 6 special schools. Through this network the SBS Programme Foundation supports 12,586 children in total, including 1335 children with disabilities, and minority children. The project requires relatively high funding and a change in the attitude of teaching staff.

The Czech Republic's move into the EU had a great influence on its legislation. The Czech Republic had to comply with European standards, in particular with regard to disadvantaged people. The Czech Republic has joined the international initiative of eight European countries termed the Decade of Roma Inclusion: 2005–2015. The annual Decade Report provides information about fulfilling the National Decade Action Plan.

In the framework of Decade, MoEYS prepared the Project Concept of Early Care Provided to Children from Socio-Culturally Disadvantaged Environments, which was adopted by governmental resolution. The purpose of the early care concept is to increase the number of Roma pupils in mainstream schools. The Concept involves supporting and implementing programmes aimed at socially disadvantaged families. The Ministry of Education has planned to do away with the Concept of Early Care and was due to publish the results of the pilot scheme in August 2007.

The Ministry of Education sees the need to develop guidelines for drawing up the preparatory class curriculum, which is the task of the Research Institute of Education (*VÚP*). The Institute will draw up a methodology for observing and evaluating the individual development of children and their individual educational progress in pre-school education conditions. The outcome of the project should be a methodology handbook for teachers. This MoEYS programme aimed at supporting the integration of the Roma community should help to achieve these goals.

The other tool for integration is the System project (SIM: Centres for Integration of Minorities). This was inaugurated in 2006 and is run by the Institute of Educational and Psychological Counselling (IPPP) and financed by MoEYS and European Social Fund (ESF). The purpose of the pilot project is to establish a support system for the care of socially disadvantaged pupils. Besides providing aid for their clients, the Centres provide systematic monitoring, research activities and support for teachers and teaching assistants, as well as their professional in-service training.

It may be said that the legal provisions were created by the alarming situation of the Roma in the Czech Republic and its entry into the EU. The Czech

Republic has to confront new conceptions of rights and requirements related to the new reality. The implementation and evaluation of new measures should be profitable and should provide new knowledge, but the application of these measures runs up against an array of problems. The basic problem is an ambiguous definition of the target population: when does one consider that a child is a Roma? Who comes from a socially disadvantaged environment? Who is 'mentally retarded'? Co-operation with local institutions is difficult, too. At the same time, the MoEYS has no executive power over schools and it cannot directly influence the existing practices established within schools. Its current function is more to monitor the existing status, and to introduce legislative changes and changes in the curriculum via an advisory service.

The Office of the Government Council for Roma Community Affairs suggests carrying out panel discussions in the Committee of the Roma Decade, which should clarify controversial indicators and help pilot the annual evaluation of the targeted programmes. For this, it is planned to use qualitative and quantitative research methodologies.

On the legislative level, Roma-related issues are approached from a nationality as well as a social group perspective. Provisions concerning Roma affairs are often provisions for persons with special educational needs. It could be said that this is the consequence of the current social development. The Roma population has lived on the outskirts of society and involuntary assimilation is gradually erasing its identity, mother tongue and cultural identity. For many Roma their original language has lost its value and they do not feel that it is important to learn and use their own language as a language of instruction or to use its written form for official purposes. The common opinion of the Czech majority is that the Roma should use Czech language because they are residents of the Czech Republic and they are not able to use the Roma language any more, so it is not necessary to be active with regard to supporting the official use of the Roma language.

It should be stressed that even though the new Education Act of 2004 abolished special primary schools, with their replacement by elementary practical schools, Roma pupils have not disappeared from them and they continue to follow compulsory education at elementary practical schools in large numbers. These schools are focused on partially mentally handicapped children and on those with education problems. Possibly the new teach-in programmes of integration for teachers, multicultural education and information to parents about education difficulties will represent a departure from this complicated situation.

Currently, society is trying to rectify the injustices of the past – at least at the legislative level. The government of the Czech Republic and the MoEYS are making efforts to ensure that effective legislation provides for equal access to education, and are backing various integration and compensatory programmes.

National minorities, foreigners, asylum seekers

Individuals speaking mother languages other than Czech are classified by law into three basic categories: members of national minorities, persons with the status of asylum seeker and refugees, and foreigners. Each of these groups has its own particular paragraph in the new Education Act. The Government Council for National Minorities, the Government Council for Human Rights and the bureaus of the MoEYS, MoLSa and Ministry of Culture (MC) safeguard the rights of these inhabitants.

The first Council for National Minorities was formally established in 1968; the current Council for National Minorities was constituted by a government resolution in 2001. The rights of members of ethnic minorities are grounded in the Constitution of the Czech Republic and in the Charter of Fundamental Rights and Freedoms. Twelve national minorities are represented in the council, each having between one and three deputies.

On condition that 10 per cent of the inhabitants of a particular municipality declare membership of a national minority, a committee for national minorities is set up there. The members of these minorities have the right to be educated in their mother tongue at nurseries, primary schools and lower and upper secondary schools. The municipality, the regional authority or the ministry ensure education in the minority language. Education in the language of a national minority may be also organised by a union of municipalities or by a municipality. The minority members must nevertheless learn Czech. Classes for minority students in the lower and upper secondary school (the so-called *základní škola*) can be inaugurated with a minimum number of ten pupils. Pre-school or basic school teaching in the language of the national minority may be initiated provided that each class has on average at least 12 children claiming to be members of the national minority.

Poles are just one minority in the Czech Republic, with their own education system supported by the Czech Government. The Bulgarian minority has primary schools with Bulgarian as the teaching language under jurisdiction of the Bulgarian Embassy. Other nationalities run various classes in their respective languages. The EU criticises the Czech Republic for the fact that the largest minority – Slovak – does not have enough support from the state. However, the ratification by the charter of regional and minority languages has given the Slovak minority almost the same rights as Poles.

Approximately 52,000 Polish minority members live in the Czech Republic, most of whom (80 per cent) have settled in Těšín (Silesia). This region is on the border with Poland, where Poles account for 10 per cent of the population.

Traces of the Polish school system dating from the First Republic have been found in Czech (Silesian) lands. The right to use Polish as a teaching language at school was written into the 1948 Education Act – an exception based on the idea of a Slav brotherhood. A network of nurseries, basic schools and upper secondary schools has now been set up in the Silesian region. There are currently 26 nurseries, 26 basic schools and 1 high school at Český Těšín with Polish as the language of instruction; 5 nurseries, 1 basic school and 3 upper secondary schools with Czech and Polish as the teaching language; 2200 pupils study in Polish primary schools.

According to current legislation, children of asylum seekers and refugees are considered as children with special educational needs, and more specifically as socially disadvantaged children. School principals may, with the consent of the relevant regional authorities, establish the position of teaching assistant for classes or study groups where a child, pupil or student with special educational needs is educated. They have the right to be educated in pre-school classes.

Foreigners residing legally in the Czech Republic have access to education under the same conditions as citizens of the country, including education in special or protective institutions. People who are not citizens of the EU must prove the legitimacy of their residence in the Czech Republic no later than the date on which they begin their education.

Regional authorities, in co-operation with the founder of the schools, ensure that foreigners can attend free preparation for their inclusion into basic education, including learning the Czech language and support in learning their mother tongue.

The current legislation does not allow foreign residents (whether permanent or not) and refugees unpaid education in nurseries, pre-school classes or private schools offering courses in art and leisure activities. Nonetheless, it is known that access to pre-school education considerably helps pupils to adapt to the school environment and to integrate into Czech society. The sensitive issue is that of access to education for foreigners lacking a residence permit and who live illegally in the Czech Republic.

Considering that the Czech Republic has ratified the Convention on the Rights of the Child, it is not possible to deny their right to education. As previously stated, one of the roles of education is to integrate and prevent social exclusion. To deal with this problem, the Committee for the Rights of Foreigners developed the scheme 'Suggestion', created by the Czech Republic Government Council for Human Rights and due to be rolled out in 2006, for equal and effective access to education and school services for foreigners. This Suggestion should lead to a change in the curriculum, as it does not specify to which groups the amendment shall be applied.

In addition, much legislation will have to include the Vietnamese, who represent a fairly large group of foreigners. They have almost fulfilled their quota for classes with Vietnamese as the teaching language in the western part of Bohemia and in Prague. Given that they are not citizens of the Czech Republic, not having national minority status but only that of foreigners, they have limited access to education, even though it is estimated that there are 17,500 of them living in the Czech Republic (the true number is certainly greater).

Democratisation and social equality in the Czech Republic have made considerable strides forward through the adoption of the Charter for Regional and Minorities' Languages, but much still remains to be done.

Pupils with specific learning and behavioural disabilities

Pupils with specific learning and behavioural disabilities (SLBDs) make up the largest group of pupils with special educational needs. In addition, this group commands historically significant attention in the Czech elementary education system. For both reasons, diagnostic, pedagogical and corrective procedures for pupils with specific learning disabilities (SLDs) (and to a lesser extent for pupils with specific behavioural disabilities – SBDs) are elaborated in significant detail in both documentation and school practices.

SLDBs (early developmental disabilities) began to attract attention in school counselling psychology in the latter half of the 1970s. The system of counselling centres offering psychological services to schools was set up at that time. Diagnostics and care for pupils with SLDs gradually became their main agenda. In the 1990s, teachers became fully aware of SLDs. This was due to both the higher quality of initial teacher training and greater attention given to this topic during in-service teacher training, and also because of the overall transformation of professional and general public discourse about education.[7] SLDs (especially dyslexia, dysgraphia, dysorthography and dyscalculia) came to be perceived as a disadvantage for pupils independently of their intelligence or diligence. It was concluded that the pupils involved needed more sensitive educational handling. In similar fashion, SLDs came to be perceived as manifestations of improper and socially insensitive behaviour, independent of intelligence.

On the other hand, this change of discourse led to a certain inflation in the expert definition of SLDs. Since the latter half of the 1990s, there has been a significant increase in the number of pupils diagnosed with SLDs. It was debated whether this increase was due to improved diagnostic tools, increased awareness of the diagnosis or a real change in pupil populations. Unfortunately, research that would enable evaluation of the validity of these alternative explanations is not available.

According to the education legislation in force, pupils with SLDs and SBDs are grouped among those with special educational needs. Current legislation defines this group of pupils and makes schools responsible for offering them special educational care. Its concrete form is today further elaborated in various regulations and public notices such as Public Notice No. 73/2005 Sb. on the education of children, pupils and students with special educational needs and particularly talented children, pupils and students (amended 19 March 2007), and the Methodical Directive of the MoEYS Ref. No.: 13 711/2001-24 concerning educating pupils with specific learning or behavioural disabilities. These determine how SLBD diagnostics should be performed, how pupils with SLBDs are classified within the education system and how the school should treat them. The policies are quite rigid, and they support school practice. In actual fact, to a significant extent care for pupils with SLBDs conforms to the officially formulated requirements and recommendations. The public notice and methodical directive above, therefore, are not simply formal documents with little influence on everyday school life. This also illustrates the fact that SLDs (and to a lesser extent SBDs) are a long-established topic in Czech education.

In accordance with the above-mentioned documents, pupils suspected of having specific learning and behavioural disabilities are examined in pedagogical–psychological counselling centres (PPCCs) or special educational centres (SECs). These centres were originally part of a major, unified network. However, since 1989, this network has been reduced. Today, there are 58 PPCCs and 108 SECs for a total of 1,494,180 elementary and secondary school pupils. Apart from these supporting counselling centres, the use of school psychologists employed directly by the schools is increasing within a project called V.I.P., which has been developed by the IPPP (www.ippp.cz). The aim of this project is to support school psychologists and special educationists from a financial, organisational and methodical standpoint. Their involvement enhances the effectiveness of care for pupils with SLBDs. However, school psychologists have to face a number of difficulties, among the most serious of which are limited financial resources and an ill-defined division of responsibilities between the psychologist, school management and pedagogical–psychological counselling places.

Pupils are recommended for examination in pedagogical–psychological counselling centres and special educational centres either by the teacher or directly based on the request of parents (i.e. the school does not have the right to have the child examined). SLD diagnostics include tests of intelligence, vision and hearing analyses, or tests of other faculties and abilities, and the analysis of school performance.

After the examination, a report is drawn up which the legal guardian can submit to the school. If a pupil is diagnosed with SLBDs, further decisions follow concerning the form of his/her integration within the education system. Pupils with SLDs and SBDs can attend special schools, specialised classes in regular schools or they can be integrated on an individual basis into regular classrooms. Individual integration is the most frequent form. At the primary level of education, specialised classes with a small class size are relatively frequent. According to the public notice, classes for pupils with SBDs should consist of 6–12 children based on the level of disability. Classes for pupils with SLDs should consist of 10–12 children in primary school, and 12–14 children in lower secondary school. In the timetable of these classes, 1–2 hours are set aside for improvement of SLDs and SBDs. These classes are usually taught by specially trained teachers, or teachers who graduated from educational courses accredited by the Ministry of Education. In the school year 2005/2006, 7965 pupils with SLDs and SBDs attended specialised classes at the elementary education level, that is 0.85 per cent of all pupils.

Individual integration of pupils in regular classes involved 41,346 pupils in the school year 2005/2006, that is 4.5 per cent of all pupils. Individual integration involves creating an individual study plan for each pupil, which is drawn up on the basis of the results of examinations and in collaboration with the child, parents, school management, teachers, school counsellor and representative of PPCCs or SECs. The individual study programmes become a part of pupils' personal school portfolio. The programme determines how teachers should work with the pupil during individual classes/subjects – what compensation aids can he/she use; what tasks/homework he/she should be assigned to do; how much extra time should be allotted for performing tasks/homework; what forms of knowledge and skill testing should be used; and how his/her performance should be evaluated and classified. The individual study programme is usually updated once or twice during the school year, and the school counsellor or other designated school employee ensures that it is followed.

Educational practice towards pupils with SLDs differs according to the subject being studied and the degree of disability. In all cases of SLDs, pupils receive longer time to solve tasks, or the tasks are shortened. For classification, verbal evaluation based on the individual evaluation norm is more often used than in the case of other pupils. The education legislation in force requires, however, that verbal evaluation is transferable to regular grades. This goes against its very purpose.

With respect to tasks and assessing knowledge and skills, two privileges are granted in the case of dyslexia: (1) pupils are not called on to read aloud in front of others; alternatively, they use aids such as a reading window when reading; and (2) pupils do not write long dictations, but they complete gap-fill exercises. This second method is also used for pupils with dysorthography. In the case of dysgraphia, tolerance is shown with respect to graphic appearance, and pupils can use sound recording devices or copy notes from fellow pupils and they are not usually tested using the written form, and so on. Finally, in the case of dyscalculia, errors in the use of mathematical examples are tolerated and vivid illustrations are used to fixate the mathematical imagination.

In the special schools – and usually also in the specialised classrooms – teachers are directly trained in the correct educational approach for pupils with SLDs. Teaching therefore involves procedures that respect special educational practices for working with pupils with SLDs. In schools with individually integrated pupils, the school counsellor or person in charge of special education ensures that correct procedures are followed in individual subjects of study. They advise teachers of individual subjects how to work with pupils with SLDs. In schools with larger numbers of integrated pupils, internal differentiation of schooling is usually also used. For some subjects (most often Czech, mathematics and foreign languages), pupils with SLDs are usually taken out of their respective classes and they learn in small groups under the supervision of a special education teacher.

In addition to provisions that are integrated directly into schooling, pupils with SLDs are also usually entitled to corrective and compensation exercises. In those schools with a large number of pupils with SLDs, the special-education teacher leads these exercises; in other schools, children undertake exercises in the PPCCs or SECs. The exercises are not focused on the school curriculum, but on removing the very causes of disabilities and improving the abilities necessary for successful learning.

The Czech elementary education system of care for pupils with SLDs, and to a lesser extent with SBDs, is of a relatively high level. Most teachers have a good knowledge of SLDs. In each school, there is a special counsellor who is familiar with SLBD syndromes as well as educational procedures. Furthermore, each school collaborates with PPCCs or SECs, which not only perform SLBD diagnostics, but also offer methodological support. However, in spite of the relatively functional system, the effectiveness of help for pupils with SLBDs always depends on the attitude and collaboration of the people involved – teachers, parents, school management, school counsellor and psychologist – who are not infallible as individuals.

Gifted pupils

The approach to 'particularly gifted' pupils as a group was changed in Czech schools in the 1990s. Prior to 1989, the education system was based on the idea of the unified school, which paid little attention to the special needs of any groups of students, especially gifted students. The Education Act of 1984 was the first to define their status. Some measures were formulated for these pupils, in terms of their differentiation both inside and outside classrooms, such as transfer to schools or classes with extended teaching in some subjects and the individual educational programme. However, those opportunities did not mean any specific changes in the teaching approach for gifted students, except in regard to providing a broader or deeper range of subject matter. Within inner differentiation, pupils could participate in competitions in different subjects, usually called Olympic Games, in maths, physics, and so on. The legislative and practical activities focused on improving the quality of care for gifted students (in the sense of a more specific approach based on the psychological characteristics of this target group) have started to appear since the 1990s, for example the Centre for Talent (MENZA).

Nowadays, particularly gifted students are considered as pupils with special educational needs according to the 2004 Education Act. The specific procedures on how to treat these pupils are defined by Ministry Regulation No. 73/2005 (amended in 2007). This regulation specifies how to deal with particularly gifted students. If psychological tests show that pupils have above-normal talents (IQ above 130), they can then benefit from individual integration. In that case an individual educational programme is created that prescribes how teachers should treat this student, which tasks the student should be assigned to do, how school performance should be assessed and marked and so on. The programme is drawn up in collaboration with the child, parents, school management, teachers, school counsellor and representative of the PPCC or SEC. The programme is adjusted regularly and its implementation is inspected.

Individual educational programmes are used to provide particularly gifted pupils with more difficult tasks or extra activities that teachers prepare, or that use materials provided by outside institutions. The programme may also include lessons that the pupils would normally learn in a higher class. Nevertheless, internal differentiation in Czech schools is not very common. The method that applies to these pupils mainly involves jumping a class, provided they pass a psychological test.

The current Education Act also contains external educational differentiation for the education of gifted students, and some new special schools for these pupils have been provided within the Czech education system. This initiative is supported by curriculum reform that allows schools to prepare their programmes according to their own special orientation. In particular, students with particularly special talents are directly targeted by these schools. They face many problems in standard schools – they have excellent results in some subjects, while they fail in others and are usually less adaptable in regard to social issues. These schools are specialised in dealing with particularly gifted students. Nevertheless, such schools are rare in the Czech education system and their utilisation is not trouble-free.

The Czech education system has only recently started to pay attention to particularly gifted students. These students are defined as a group with special educational needs. This means that schools should treat these children in special way. However, this is not very often the case in Czech schools because most teachers are not prepared for working with these gifted students. Talented students with high school motivation usually choose to transfer to the lower *gymnázium*. In the case of students with low school motivation, the specific educational techniques are not usually used. Some of these children may be lucky enough to study at schools specialising in teaching gifted students, but there are only few of these and they are mostly private schools with admission fees. Other children attend standard primary schools (so-called basic schools). Except for some innovative schools, standard primary schools cannot usually make special cases of pupils identified as being gifted.[8] Many pupils studying at multi-year *gymnáziums* have no special talent. In the Czech Republic there are 1472 high schools and 685 schools providing the lower level of secondary education, which means that students in multi-year *gymnáziums* are usually not particularly gifted, but do attain a good academic level.

Women/girls and men/boys in Czech schools

The Constitution of the Czech Republic guarantees equal access to education for all citizens regardless of sex. Following the political changes in 1989 the legislation concerning the school system was modified. As a result, the Czech education system formally ensures equal opportunities for boys and girls.

Gender inequalities in education were completely marginal in the mid-1990s. The change came as the Czech Republic prepared to move into the EU. Gender equality is one of the priorities of the EU, and therefore the question of equal opportunities of women and men in the Czech Republic, including within the education system, had to be dealt with. The Czech government charged the Ministry of Labour and Social Affairs with this agenda and established the Government Council for Equal Opportunities for Women and Men. Since 1998 the report 'Government procedures and priorities for promoting equal opportunity for women and men' has been published annually. This document includes tasks to be carried out in the following year that are designed to improve gender equality in Czech society.

Based on this government document, the MoEYS has produced the document 'Ministry of education procedures and priorities for promoting equal opportunity for women and men'. Around 25 tasks per year are formulated, dealing with different issues of gender equality in education. Some of these are related to the percentages of females and males employed in the ministry, or how gender equality is presented in the media; others are related to certain teaching practices that have direct influence on school life.

The policy of gender equality in education is based on the general legislation that guarantees equal treatment for women and men and on the special act called the Methodological Directive of the Minister of Education. This directive urges school boards and teachers to build equal opportunity for girls and boys, helping them to 'think outside the gender stereotype box' and respect gender equality in teaching approaches. The Methodological Directive was published in 2000 and its amendment is expected in 2009. The current version is too general – it is of no use as a guide for teachers and does not provide any criteria for inspecting (e.g. by the Czech School inspectorate). This leads to an absurd situation: a democratic education system formally providing equal treatment for boys and girls, while situations of real, profound gender inequality sometimes remain.

Czech and international educational research[9] regularly identifies gender differences in Czech schools. This can be seen in several areas, mainly in (1) unequal percentages of female and male students at different levels and different types of schools; and (2) unequal educational results between girls and boys.

On average, girls obtain significantly better marks than boys in all school subjects and at all levels of school. However, girls' results in external evaluations (these are mainly tests created by external institutions) are worse than, or on a par with, boys' results. This is particularly true in maths and science. The contradiction between school results and external tests comes from the different approaches adopted by teachers towards girls and boys. Girls attain higher grades than boys because they are, or are seen to be, more studious and obedient than boys. Teachers and students are also aware of the different criteria used for assessing girls and boys. It is a generally accepted assumption that the way girls learn is based on memorising, while boys prefer to use logic. Girls' results are seen as tedious and mechanical; the value of the results they obtain is perceived as being lower. The differences in awareness of girls' and boys' skills and between their ambitions arise from that approach. Boys, more then girls, are supported (by teachers and by peers) in their self-confidence and skills concerning the decisions they take about their educational and professional career.

The next gender-determined element in Czech schools is that subjects and fields of study are perceived and interpreted through gender stereotypes. According to these stereotypes, boys have more affinity with technical and natural scientific subjects, while women are more attracted to the humanities, including activities that involve caring for others. This is noticeable in the curriculum and in textbooks,[10] but also in the approaches and ways of thinking of teachers and pupils. We can still hear statements today such as 'Girls don't have a head for maths'.

The above issues led to relatively deep gender segregation in the education system. Typical educational paths are conditioned by gender, in combination with high selectiveness and low accessibility. These paths appear at the level of school subjects in primary schools, become worse in high schools and reach their zenith in tertiary education. As an illustration of gender segregation in secondary schools, we can use the percentages of boys and girls in the academic year 2005/2006. In the first year of mechanical engineering school, 98 per cent of students were boys, while in nursing school 91 per cent were girls.

The support that the Ministry of Education gives to the idea of gender equality in education is focused mainly on teachers. They know that gender stereotypes exist, accept the value of equal opportunity for women and men in education and learn some procedures to help minimise the influence of stereotypes on their own teaching. Foreign experience shows that such efforts are necessary. Nevertheless, this objective has not been successfully implemented in schools. One cannot really speak about active and effective promotion of gender equality in the Czech education system. The measures promoted by the Ministry of Education and other educational institutions are mainly formal statements of intent, without any real value or impact.

Conclusion

This chapter has provided a brief description of PEPs in the Czech Republic based on the targeting of specific groups. For each group we have shown the political measures being applied and the overall assessment of the current status of teaching practices. In very general terms, we have compared the state of these groups and the programmes implemented within them. Special measures for physically and mentally handicapped pupils (a subject beyond the scope of this project) and for pupils with specific learning and behavioural disabilities are well developed at state level in official documents, and these function well in practice. This is due to a long tradition of targeting this population, a well-developed support structure during the period of socialist Czechoslovakia and a long tradition of research in the field.

For the Polish minority there is also a well-developed education system that also has a long tradition. On the other hand, other national minorities in increasing numbers do not have special national schooling, for many reasons. For example, the Slovak minority has attempted to open Slovak schools, but the members of this minority preferred to stay in Czech schools. As a result, the Slovak school in Karviná was closed through lack of students. The other large national minority, the Roma, can now receive education in their own language, but because of their low numbers (as officially declared in the population census) – and also policy documents stating that the Roma do not need their own education system, this has not really happened.

The policies described above for other targeted groups are still under development and they are only just beginning to be implemented. We are far from being able to analyse the results of these policies and, in particular, the effects of these changes on the targeted groups, since the history of the policies implemented is still very recent. This can be understood in the context of the large transformation of education that was begun in 1989.

Generally, four stages in this transformation can be identified. The main aim of the early years following the political changeover in late 1989 was to immediately redress the shortcomings in education caused by the totalitarian regime. De-ideologisation of the legal documents including curricula programmes and de-monopolisation of state education were among the most important tasks in the first stage, known as deconstruction (early 1990s), when the trend of 'negating the past and restoring the "status quo ante" ' was pursued. The second stage was characterised by 'partial stabilisation' (late 1990s) when further amendments to the Education Act were prepared, but most of the political measures applied were *ad hoc* measures limited by their lack of a systematic approach and long-term strategy. Discussions about the future of national education were started at this time and came to a head in the next stage, called reconstruction, when the 2001 White Paper was prepared and approved by the government, followed in 2004 by the new Education Act. The stage following reconstruction is referred to by J. Kotásek (2005a, 2005b) as implementation, and this is the phase in which we currently find ourselves. Many changes codified in the new Education Act (e.g. the major curriculum reform) are still to be implemented (for more details, see Greger & Walterová 2007; Kotásek, Greger & Procházková 2004).

According to J. Kotásek (2005a, b), the real long-term reforms of the Czech education system are just starting to be implemented. As far as PEPs are concerned, we believe that their development is lagging slightly behind the overall development. For example, in the case of Roma people experts agree that the Czech government was not very interested in issues relating to the education of the Roma in the early years after 1989, and they usually place the beginning of the official policy targeted at Roma education in October 1997, when the government adopted the so-called Bratinka Report. The results of the first large-scale research concerning the situation of the Roma population in the Czech Republic were published in August 2006, following which the great public debate on education started in the media. The discussions mainly focused on the need to prepare a long-term project that would connect educational as well as social policy measures. Even the foundation of a special institute was proposed. It can be stated, therefore, that we are somewhere on the way to reconstruction and formulation of the new policy.

While government preoccupation with the situation of the Roma Community is said to date from 1997, the important role of NGOs since the early 1990s must be stressed. They put this question on the agenda and began actions (e.g. Roma assistants) that were later implemented and supported by the state. The NGOs stood in for the state in the early years of the transformation and they are still driving the most significant elements of progress. In the case of the education of Romani children, NGOs run many progressive programmes (e.g. mentoring) and they also influence policy formulation. The leading role of NGOs is also apparent in the case of programmes targeted at equal opportunity for women and men and in those for gifted students.

The other major influence on the current status of PEPs in the Czech Republic is international organisations, especially the EU. The major impact of the EU is seen particularly in improved legislation in the post-communist countries. The Czech Republic, like other countries, had to prepare new legislative documentation, in particular with respect to disadvantaged groups (including national minorities, gender, the disabled, etc.) and to cope with discrimination. This was one of the criteria to be fulfilled for accession to the EU that took effect on 1 May 2004. This, according to many experts, has led to a better quality of legislation in the 'New Member States' as far as the respect for minorities and disadvantaged groups is concerned, and is in many ways better than the legislation of the 'Old Member States'.

Davidová, Lhotka and Vojtová (2005) point out that the Council of Europe recommendation no. 1557 (2002) states that 'the Roma must be treated as an ethnic or national minority group in every member state, and their minority rights must be guaranteed' but some member states, such as France and Greece, do not legally recognise the concept of a national minority at all and some other member states do not consider the Roma as a national minority (e.g. Italy and Spain). These are among the arguments the authors use to justify the progress of legislation for all groups in the post-communist countries. Nevertheless, the reality and practice lag far behind the legislation.

The role of the EU is nowadays strengthened through European social funds. The programmes for disadvantaged groups and for combating educational inequality are largely financed from these sources. Various NGOs working in the field are mainly financed from these sources, and the question asked is: what will happen after this funding ends? There is a great danger that this third sector (NGOs) will weaken and gradually disappear.

In describing the groups defined in this report, we have not devoted a special section to socially disadvantaged families. Even though they are defined at the beginning of the Education Act, programmes for the socially disadvantaged are described under the section of the Act entitled "Romas". In many cases the programmes described above (teaching assistants and preparatory classes) are largely directed towards the Roma, since Czech documentation, as well as recommendation no. 1557, considers the Roma as having a double-minority status. The Roma are an ethnic community and most of them belong to socially disadvantaged groups. Even though socially disadvantaged students are an important group that should be targeted by political measures, the proper definition of the term and of the programmes for implementation has been insufficiently developed.

This description and critical analysis of the current stage of the development of PEPs in the Czech Republic are brief indeed, and deal only with general characteristics. They show only the major trends in the development of priority education policies and describe the programmes currently applied by the official authorities. The various local reforms deriving from teachers' initiatives and from those of other individuals that are of considerable significance have not been explored here.

Notes

1. Seven years ago the Personal Data Protection Act (Act No. 101/2000 Coll.) came into force in the Czech Republic, and it is now prohibited to collect personal data such as those on ethnicity.
2. We have obtained most information about the teaching assistant from Wagner (2006): *Thematic Report – Teaching Assistants for Children, Pupils and Students with*

Special Educational Needs-Social Disadvantage. We have been informed that the report is based on background materials sent to the Ministry of Education.

3. Most of the information presented here was obtained from the Report on Roma Decade 2005–2015 published for the year 2006.

4. The total number of preparatory classes in 2006/2007 was 146; 102 classes were established in primary schools, 44 in special schools. A total of 1713 pupils were educated in these classes.

5. New School is an NGO, which from 1996 has been encouraging the education of minorities; MoEYS, MoLSA and MC also support it.

6. The education level of schools is measured by the number of pupils accepted in secondary schools.

7. The Czech Dyslectic Society should also be credited for this. It is a part of the European Dyslectic Society and it includes psychologists and special educators specialising in SDLs.

8. We can use as an illustration the number of courses in the Faculty of Education concerning the teaching of students with different kinds of 'problems leading to failure' and gifted students. Much more attention is paid to students with SLBD or other problems than to gifted students. This means that teachers are not so well prepared to work with this target group.

9. Mainly international research – PISA, TIMSS, CivEd – and Czech research – Gender in Transition Moments in the Czech Educational System (2005), CERMAT (Centre for Educational Evaluation) research and projects, Kalibro projects, etc.

10. Most textbooks in Czech schools are based on strong gender stereotypes. We can see evidence of this and their influence in the curriculum, in examples and exercises, in pictures and in language. These findings are confirmed by a study from the Institute for Research in Education (2005) and the handbook for the evaluation of gender correctness of textbooks (Czech Republic: Ministry of Education, Youth and Sports, 2005).

Bibliography

Scientific documents

BOLF Š., HŮLE D., LÁBUSOVÁ A. & STEINER J. (2003). *Monitoring efektivity přípravných ročníků* [Monitoring of Efficiency of Preparatory Classes]. Prague: Faculty of Humanities, Charles University in Prague.

DAVIDOVÁ E., LHOTKA P. & VOJTOVÁ P. (2005). *Právní postavení Romů v zemích Evropské unie* [Legal Status of Roma people in the EU countries]. Prague: Triton.

GABAL I. (2006). *Analýza sociálně vyloučených romských lokalit a absorpční kapacity subjektů působících v této oblasti* [Analysis of Socially Excluded Roma Localities and Communities and the Absorption Capacity of Subjects Operating in the Field]. Prague: GAC.

GREGER D. & WALTEROVÁ E. (2007). 'In Pursuit of Educational Change: Transformation of Education in the Czech Republic'. *Orbis scholae*, vol. 1, no. 2, pp. 15–38.

HANLEY E. (2001). 'Centrally Administered Mobility Reconsidered: The Political Dimension of Educational Stratification in State-Socialist Czechoslovakia'. *Sociology of Education*, no. 74, pp. 25–43.

KOTÁSEK J. (2005a). 'Vzdělávací politika a rozvoj školství v České republice po roce 1989 – 1. Časť [Education policy and the education system development in the Czech Republic after 1989 – 1st part]'. *Technológia vzdelávania*, no. 3, pp. 7–11.

218   *Czech Republic*

KOTÁSEK J. (2005b). 'Vzdělávací politika a rozvoj školství v České republice po roce 1989 – pokračovanie' [Education policy and the education system development in the Czech Republic after 1989 – continuation]. *Technológia vzdelávania*, no. 4, pp. 7–11.

KOTÁSEK J., GREGER D. & PROCHÁZKOVÁ I. (2004). *Demand for Schooling in the Czech Republic (Country Report for OECD)*. Paris: OECD. Report available on the Internet: <http://www.oecd.org/dataoecd/38/37/33707802.pdf> (consulted on July 18, 2008).

KREIDL M. (2006). 'Socialist Egalitarian Policies and Inequality in Access to Secondary and Post-Secondary Education: New Evidence Using Information on Detailed Educational Careers and Their Timing'. *Sociológia/Slovak Sociological Review*, vol. 38, no. 3. Document available on the website of the California Center for Population Research: <http://repositories.cdlib.org/ccpr/olwp/CCPR-058-05/> (consulted on July 18, 2008).

MATĚJŮ P. (1993). 'Who Won and Who Lost in a Socialist Redistribution in Czechoslovakia?' In *Persistent Inequality. Changing Educational Attainment in Thirteen Countries*. Boulder, CO: Westview Press, pp. 251–271.

MATĚJŮ P. & STRAKOVÁ J. (2005). 'The Role of the Family and the School in the Reproduction of Educational Inequalities in the Post-Communist Czech Republic'. *British Journal of Sociology of Education*, vol. 26, no. 1, 2005, pp. 15–38.

SHAVIT Y. & BLOSSFELD H. P. (1993). *Persistent Inequality. Changing Educational Attainment in Thirteen Countries*. Boulder, CO, San Francisco, CA and Oxford: Westview Press.

ŠTECH S. (2008). De la justice statistique à la justice libérale le cas d'une société 'post-égalitaire' [From statistical justice to liberal justice: the case of a 'post-egalitarian' society]. Proposal for a presentation at the seminar *Repenser la justice dans le domaine de l'éducation et de la formation* [Rethinking justice in the field of education and training], Lyon, May 15–17, 2008 (INRP). Document available on the Internet: <http://ep.inrp.fr/EP/colloques/colloque_repenser_justice/communication_stanislav_stech/view> (consulted on July 18, 2008).

UHEREK Z. & ČERNÍK J. (2004). *Výzkumné zprávy a studie o integraci cizinců na území České republiky* [Research reports and studies on the integration of foreigners in the Czech Republic]. Report available on the Internet: <http://www.cizinci.cz/files/clanky/100/vyzkum.pdf> (consulted on August 25, 2008).

VALDROVÁ J., SMETÁČKOVÁ I. & KNOTKOVÁ-ČAPKOVÁ B. (2005). 'Handbook for Evaluation of Gender Correctness of Textbooks'. In B. KNOTKOVÁ-ČAPKOVÁ (ed.), *Yearbook of Department of Gender Studies 2003/2004*. Prague: Faculty of Humanities, Charles University, pp. 176–193.

VIKV. & VRZÁČEK P. (2005). *Stav komunitních škol v České republice* [State of community schools in the Czech Republic]. Document available on the Internet: <www.komunitnivzdelavani.cz> (consulted on July 18, 2008).

VOCILKA M. (1997). Integrace sociálně a zdravotně handicapovaných a ohrožených dětí do společnosti [Integration of socially and medically handicapped children into society]. Praha: ÚIV.

WAGNER M. (2006). *Thematic Report – Teaching assistants for Children, Pupils and Students with Special Educational Needs-Social Disadvantage*. Report available on the Internet: <http://www.vlada.cz/scripts/detail.php?id=22727> (consulted on July 18, 2008).

Legal references and official or administrative documents

CZECH REPUBLIC: MINISTRY OF EDUCATION, YOUTH AND SPORTS (2001). White Paper. National Programme for the Development of Education in the Czech Republic.

CZECH REPUBLIC: MINISTRY OF EDUCATION, YOUTH AND SPORTS (2004). Act No. 561 of 24 September 2004 on Pre-school, Basic, Secondary, Tertiary, Professional and Other Education (the Education Act).

CZECH REPUBLIC: MINISTRY OF EDUCATION, YOUTH AND SPORTS (2005). *Handbook for Evaluation of Gender Correctness of Textbooks.* Document available on the Internet: <www.msmt.cz> (consulted on August 25, 2008).

CZECH REPUBLIC: MINISTRY OF EDUCATION, YOUTH AND SPORTS (2006). *Koncepce integrace cizinců* [Long-term plan for integration of foreigners].

Romania

8
Romania: A System in Evolution, Searching for Its Conceptual References

Calin Rus

Introduction

The goal of this chapter is to present a critical analysis and situate within their context the priority education policies (PEPs) in Romania. This analysis allows for the identification of the main approaches and theoretical options grounding or legitimising these policies, of the main target groups concerned as well as the description of the origins and of the evolution of these policies, taking into account administrative, financial and pedagogical issues.

No doubt, there is a need for this type of policy in the Romanian education system, related to the key social inequalities that are transposed in educational inequalities and demand compensation through specific educational policies.[1]

The existence of these inequalities has been acknowledged in official documents for only a few years, and this acknowledgement has only recently resulted in measures aimed explicitly at reducing the inequalities. Thus, although the concept of 'priority education policy' does not appear as such in the legislation, the emergence of the term 'priority education area' is noted in some official documentation,[2] without an explicit definition. Moreover, there is no analysis and systematic evaluation of the impact of the policies and measures already implemented to reduce the inequalities and address the specific needs of certain groups. However, such an analysis seems even more needed now, when important educational reforms are envisaged.

We could identify four categories of target groups of PEPs according to the definition given in this book (whether they are labelled as 'priority' in the official documentation or not):

- children with special educational needs[3] and gifted children;[4]
- children belonging to national minorities;

- Romani children;
- children living in rural areas.

Thus, we will start with a description of the evolution of the Romanian education system, from 1989 to the present period, as a reference framework for understanding the evolution of PEPs, while the following sections will analyse the education policies concerning the four categories of target group identified. The section on policies targeting the Roma, which are particularly important in the Romanian context, is more elaborate. It starts with an outline of the social and cultural differences justifying these policies – as they result from statistics and research on this topic – and continues with the presentation and analysis of the evolution of certain key elements of these policies, such as the reserved places, the school mediators or desegregation. Special attention is further given to the adaptation of the priority education zone (ZEP) to the Romanian context, a pilot experience of the Institute of Educational Sciences. Finally, the current education policy documents, including the strategies and the reform plans, are analysed with the aim of pointing out the ways in which they reflect the requirements of promoting equality in the education system.

The education system and its evolution, from communism to the post-EU accession period

A series of fundamental changes was initiated in the education system in 1990, after the fall of the totalitarian communist regime. Included among the most important of these were: (1) eliminating the Marxist ideology background from school programmes; (2) the introduction of religion as a school subject at all levels of primary and secondary education; and (3) the formulation of a new set of measures allowing national minorities' children to study in their own language. Nonetheless, apart from these 'emergency measures' (Iosifescu *et al.*, 2001), the system has remained hyper-centralised, with an overloaded curriculum placing emphasis more on knowledge transmission than on critical understanding and on development of competences. A group of recognised experts (Vlasceanu et al., 2002) analysing this evolution spoke about a 'reparation phase' followed by a 'phase of alternatives confrontation'.

A new Education Law was adopted in 1995; plans proposing a new perspective on the curriculum were revealed in the same year.[5] However, a wider reform was initiated only in 1998 (Marga, 1998, 2000). We are, according to Vlasceanu and his collaborators (2002), in a 'phase of systematic construction'. Officially, this reform aims at reducing the emphasis on knowledge acquisition, in favour of a focus on children's personal development. More in theory than in practice, it has also given more freedom and responsibility to teachers and schools. However, the reform has not been completed due to both a change of government and to the incapacity of the ministry to reform one key element: the teacher training system (the opposition of universities to this reform has also contributed to this failure). However, despite hesitations, steps backwards and contradictory messages sent to schools and teaching staff by educational authorities, a number of transformations have been achieved in several areas (Crişan *et al.*, 2006; Vlasceanu *et al.*, 2002). Thus, even though Ministry of Education maintained control over the major part of the curriculum, through the 'national curriculum' schools received the right to use a proportion of the teaching time (now around 25 per cent) for educational activities directly related to local needs (and parents must be involved in the choice of contents). Moreover, a transfer of responsibilities from the ministry to local authorities has been overseen and the opening of the in-service teacher training system has been initiated. If during the 1980s education reforms were strongly influenced by the World Bank, from 2000 to 2001 the dominant external influence became that of the European Union.[6] More recently, priority has been given to 'quality of education', legislation having being adopted in 2006 on this topic,[7] together with a set of specific structures and procedures.

Unfortunately, these changes giving the impression of permanent instability were carried out through isolated second-level documentation (usually orders from the ministry) and were not integrated into a clear, coherent and transparent vision.[8] Indeed, certain paragraphs in the current education legislation have been formulated in such a way that they have generated, unwittingly, situations of exclusion, through the fact that they did not envisage the situation and the practical situations of members of certain groups.[9] Moreover, the legislation itself has seen, over the past decade, no fewer than 28 changes, all labelled as 'reform',[10] but always lacking an explicit and real vision.

Special attention should be paid in this context to the progressive establishment, despite conflicts and resistance from both politicians and the majority public opinion, of a set of measures targeting 'national minorities'.[11] These measures are based on a tradition dating back to before the nationalist communism of the 1980s, and their adoption has been promoted both by requests from the national minorities' organisations, created or reactivated since 1990, and by external pressure, such as that from the Organization for Security and Co-operation in Europe (OSCE) High Commissioner for National Minorities and that connected with the adoption within the framework of the Council of Europe of the Framework-Convention–for the Protection of National Minorities. The implementation of this system, allowing for the use of national minorities' languages in education, can in fact be as a priority education policy and will be described in more detail in the following section.[12]

Thus, the system takes into account the specific needs of children belonging to national minorities, but very little information on the national minorities is presented in the mainstream curriculum, targeting all children. Only in 2007, on the order of the Minister of Education, following requests from several NGOs active in the field of education,[13] were plans adopted for the inclusion of elements concerning national minorities – as well as of that of a wider perspective on cultural diversity – in school programmes for all pupils. It remains to be seen in what measure this order will be followed up and implemented in the context of the revision of school programmes.

A legislation package for the reform of education was launched under public debate in 2007, by the Ministry of Education. However, its adoption by parliament has been postponed in the context of the signature in March 2008 of the National Pact for Education and of the change of government following the elections in late 2008. In our view, this proposal for changing education legislation does not reflect a coherent vision on the role of the education system in current Romanian society, while some of its provisions contradict recent measures taken by the ministry, including those for disadvantaged or vulnerable groups and those for national minorities. On the contrary, the National Pact for Education mentions that the signatories commit themselves to 'reject improvisations', and to elaborate, within 18 months, a 'coherent and unitary strategy' on the reform of the education system.

Education policies for children with 'special educational needs' and for gifted young people

The meaning of the label 'children with special educational needs' is not clearly specified in official documentation. However, two perspectives can be distinguished: a restricted perspective, associated with the 'special education system', and a wider perspective, associated with the 'promotion of an inclusive school'.

There is a definition of 'children with special educational needs' in the legislation on handicapped children and adults,[14] but it is far from being clear in our opinion. If this category was to be imposed in the field of education, other terms are used by institutions and in legal texts in other fields: the Authority for Child Protection refers to *dizabilitate*, while the National Authority for Handicapped Persons refers, obviously, to 'handicap'. In the initial form of the Law of Education (1995) there is a chapter on 'Special education'. In the modified form of this law, published in 2003, the title of this chapter has changed to 'Education for children and young people having special educational needs'. However, with regard to the actual content, differences are minor and references are still made to 'mental, physical, sensorial and language, socio-affective and behavioural deficiencies'. The text also mentions that expert commissions will define the 'type and degree of handicap'. The meaning of 'socio-affective deficiencies' is not explained and their evaluation depends on the interpretation given by these commissions.

For several years now, a reform has been envisaged for the special education institutions, within the framework of a wider reform focused on child protection policies, centred on the idea of 'integration', but with an ambiguous meaning:

- conceiving 'special education' as aimed at the 'education, instruction, recuperation and social integration' of children with 'special educational needs';
- mentioning that the 'school integration of children with special educational needs' is realised in 'special' schools or classes, or in ordinary school units, including those providing education in national minority languages, based on parents' request;
- insisting on the 'integration in mass schools of children having special educational needs', as a priority of current educational policies.

The content of priority policies targeting children with special educational needs relates to the conditions of age of pupils, profile and employment of teachers, curriculum contents, conditions of study, as well as an additional medical, psychological and material support. In the case of children with special educational needs, education is compulsory until age 10 or 11, according to their situation. Special schools offer not only an adapted curriculum, specialised psychological and psycho-pedagogical support, or equipment taking into account the specific needs of the child, but also access to a free meal and free school supplies. It is this additional offer that influenced parents from disadvantaged communities, often Roma, to ask for the registration of their children in these schools, while their learning difficulties are related only to their socio-economic disadvantage. This is not current practice, but NGOs[15] and even educational authorities (as specified in the justification of a PHARE project) acknowledge the overrepresentation of Romani children in special schools (12 per cent of the children in these schools are Roma, according to estimates from the Ministry of Education[16]).

The priority stated in the recent documentation from the ministry, particularly that connected with EU-funded projects or with those funded by various international agencies, is the integration of children with special educational needs in mainstream schools, by providing them with support teachers, psychologists and psycho-pedagogues. In this context, special schools are expected to continue their responsibilities towards children with 'severe deficiencies', but also by becoming resource centres with the mission to assist schools in integrating children with special educational needs. This process is not yet accomplished, and there are major differences between counties in this respect.

Mention is also made of 'integrated education' and the promotion of inclusion and of an 'inclusive school'. The conceptual references of these trends are to be found in United Nations Educational, Scientific and Cultural Organization (UNESCO) documentation.[17] It will be noted that, in education legislation, the use of 'special educational needs' is rather superficial, aiming at introducing a 'politically correct' vocabulary, but without real substantive changes, while the idea promoted by UNESCO aims at overcoming the divisions between children with 'deficiencies' and the rest (the 'normal' ones), as well as the labelling effects, in an approach recognising a continuum and a diversity of educational difficulties.

There is also a second, and wider, meaning of the notion of 'children with special educational needs'. This is made explicit, for instance, in the definition given by the National Network on Information and Co-operation for the Community Integration of Young People and Adults with Special Educational Needs (RENINCO):[18]

> special educational needs may derive from handicaps, negative environment conditions affecting human development, or other types of disadvantage, temporary or permanent, preventing the achievement of educational and social levels equivalent with those of children and young people of similar age.

This perspective, compatible with the approach suggested by UNESCO, opens the possibility of including in this category – and therefore envisaging similar educational policies for – children included within special education, children having learning difficulties due, for example, to a specific family situation,[19] as well as Romani children, whose multiple disadvantages will be described below. This perspective is reflected, in most cases implicitly, in the documentation and actions of the Ministry of Education in the framework of several PHARE projects, where the central concept becomes that of 'inclusive school', as described below.

By using this extended perspective on 'special educational needs', one can argue that gifted children can also be included in this category. Their 'specific needs' have been recognised recently through the adoption, directly by parliament, of legislation on this matter[20] that came into effect in January 2007. The adoption of this legislation was the result of a strong and effective lobby by a group of NGOs. One of the arguments used in this debate was the fact that in some countries, children labelled as 'gifted' are considered being within the category of 'children with special educational needs' and their situation therefore justifies the implementation of specific educational policies.[21]

The provisions of this legislation include the right of these children to special assistance, allowing them to valorise and develop their capabilities. They are now being offered the opportunity to follow an adapted curriculum, or even to finalise their studies over a shorter timespan than other children (differentiated curricular pathway). The legislation also mentions an additional and specific training, as well as a special status for teachers working with gifted children and youth, together with the establishment of specialised structures within the education system: a National Centre for Differential Training and local differential training centres.

The legislation also specifies the creation of 'educational units for gifted young people, capable of high achievement'. This corresponds to a paragraph in the education legislation that, since its adoption in 1995, mentions in the chapter on high school the opportunity to create 'special classes for the pupils having exceptional abilities and achievement'. But the legislation on gifted young people, capable of high achievement, does not set any limitation to a specific level of education, while not specifying the nature of these units. This emphasis on the constitution of separate classes and school structures represents a trend opposed to the promotion of inclusion, as is the case for special education. Taking into account its recent adoption, we do not yet have any data on the impact of this legislation.

There are, thus, at least three reasons for analysing jointly, in the same section, these two categories of policy:

– according to the wider approach, gifted children have 'special educational needs';
– in both the case of gifted children and that of children targeted by the special education system, the differences are situated at the individual level (and not at cultural or social levels);
– there are similarities in the content of the PEPs for the two groups.

The system of education in regard to the languages of national minorities

National minorities can be considered as a target for PEPs in Romania. The system established in the 1990s in this respect has been based, since its start, on linguistic criteria and not on the more problematic one, of ethnic affiliation. Thus, in theory, the system is open to all children whose parents opt for an education in a minority language. However, some recent measures perturb this approach, although these changes are not explicit and are not explained in official documents.

Taking into account the specific local situation, parents belonging to national minorities have the choice of three options:[22]

– Education in a national minority language: all subjects (except Romanian language and literature and, for certain levels, history and geography) are taught in the minority language.

- Partial education in a national minority language: some subjects, chosen by the school in consultation with parents – choice often depending on the availability of teachers speaking the respective language – are studied in the minority language, while others are studied in Romanian.
- The study of a national minority language: additional, optional, hours are dedicated to teaching the minority language. Pupils from different classes in a school can come together to follow these courses, for which written demand from parents is also required.

A recent change concerns the inclusion in this context of other optional subjects: history of the respective minority and 'culture and traditions' of the respective minority.

These options are not conditioned by demographic criteria, by stating a specific ethnic affiliation or by the educational background of the children concerned. A pupil having followed school in Romanian can, at the beginning of each school year, be transferred (based on a written demand from parents or tutors) to a class or school with tuition in a minority language, or vice versa.

This system has allowed for the establishment of classes with tuition in several minority languages. According to the statistics published by the Ministry of Education, during the school year 2004–2005, tuition in minority languages was available in Hungarian (1545 school units or sections with tuition in this language, with 181,887 pupils registered[23]), German (140 units or sections), Ukrainian (19 units or sections), Serbian (33 units or sections), Slovak (28 units or sections), Czech (3 units or sections), Croatian (3 units or sections) and in Bulgarian (1 unit). There are also schools with partial tuition in Turkish and Croatian, while teaching of a minority language is carried out in 1031 schools for the following languages: Hungarian, German, Ukrainian, Russian, Turkish, Polish, Bulgarian, Serbian, Slovak, Czech, Croatian, Greek, Romani and Armenian.

During the school year 2004–2005, 13,446 teachers were employed in this framework, of which 12,032 taught in Hungarian or the Hungarian language.

Among the current issues under discussion regarding this type of education policies, we list the following:

- difficulties of less numerous minorities in gaining access to textbooks for all subjects at reasonable prices;
- the reduction in some areas of the number of children registered in the schools or sections with tuition in a minority language (due both to parents opting for Romanian language schools and to demographic downturn), which is threatening the existence of these schools and sections (a minimum number of registered children is stipulated to maintain these);

- questioning of the quality of Romanian teaching in the schools situated in compact, rural Hungarian communities;
- questioning at the political level on the adoption of legislation on national minorities, one of the provisions in the current draft concerning the management of these schools by organisations representing the minorities outside of the education system.

Beyond certain descriptions of the system and the analysis of statistical data, there are few studies on the way these policies function (Liga Pro Europa, 2005, 2006; Rus, 2003). More in-depth analyses are worth conducting, for example on the access and achievement in higher education among young people having followed basic education in a minority language; or on the registration of children without a German ethnic background in schools with teaching in German, in the context of the marked decrease in the numbers of the German minority, a major proportion of them having emigrated to Germany over recent decades.

Educational policies targeting Romani children and young people

Differences and socio-cultural inequalities reflected in the educational system

Roma have the status of a national minority and benefit thus, at least in theory, from the educational policies described in the previous section. However, in our opinion their case deserves special attention. It is indeed a special case in the landscape of intercultural relations in Romania and, with some variations, at European level. Romania is the country with the largest Roma population in Europe and with a wide diversity of communities, some maintaining a traditional life style with others being almost completely assimilated; some having a similar socio-economic status to the majority population, while most live in extreme poverty (Cace & Vlădescu, 2004; Berescu & Celac, 2006; Rus, 2002, 2006, 2007a). Moreover, in this case, the socio-economic and cultural differences are also associated with strong and persistent prejudices and negative attitudes, of a racist nature, of the rest of the population against the Roma.

Several national-level studies have confirmed the existence of these negative attitudes, while outlining a trend towards improvement over the past few years in some areas. Thus, a study published in 2007, based on data from late 2006, indicates that 70 per cent of Romanians are opposed to measures such as the forced segregation of Roma, as suggested by extremists and supported by statements such as 'Roma are not able to integrate in society'. This type of measure was opposed by only 57 per cent of Romanians three years previously. Similarly, 69.3 per cent reject the idea that there should be public places, restaurants, shops and so on where access by Roma should not be allowed, while 60 per cent shared this opinion in 2003. These results show, despite the positive trends, that the persistence of prejudices and rejection of Roma is still strong and widespread throughout the population.

If the social distance between Roma and non-Roma remains much greater than between any other ethnocultural groups (36 per cent of non-Roma do not want Roma neighbours, according to the same 2007 study), it is half of that recorded in 2003. Some positive trends have also been pointed out by a study ordered by the government's Department for Interethnic Relations with regard to attitudes concerning Roma culture and identity. More than two-thirds of the population of Romania (68.5 per cent) agree with the idea that the state supports the cultural identity of Roma, as opposed to only 43.7 per cent in 2003. The percentage of the population accepting the principle of public support for the teaching of the Romani language in school remains similar to that recorded three years previously (45 per cent in 2006; 46.2 per cent in 2003).

Roma are also perceived as the group most exposed to risks of discrimination. For instance, 61.5 per cent of Romanians indicate that, if they were employers, they would not employ Roma, justifying this decision with arguments such as 'they are dirty and they steal'. However, as in 2003, 53 per cent of those in 2006 opposed increased public support and assistance to Roma. Moreover, an increase in opposition to positive measures can be observed: 38.9 per cent of Romanians in 2006, compared with 26 per cent in 2003, rejected the idea of reserved places for Roma in high schools and universities.

This is the context framing the analysis of educational inequalities between Roma and non-Roma. Despite the increase in the number of Roma attending school, from around 138,000 in 1990 to around 250,000 in 2007 according to estimates from the Soros Foundation,[24] a recent study funded by the same organisation[25] shows that 23 per cent of Roma have never attended school (while only 2 per cent of non-Roma are in this situation); 27 per cent of Roma have only completed the four years of primary education (11 per cent of non-Roma); and while only 33 per cent of Roma have completed the eight years of general education, the proportion of non-Roma in this category was 24 per cent. Ninety-five per cent of Roma (but only 60 per cent of non-Roma) did not complete high school. According to data from the 2002 census, 25.6 per cent of Roma do not have literacy skills, while only 2.6 per cent of the whole population lack this basic competency.[26] Attendance in pre-school education is four times higher for the whole population than in for Roma; Roma represent 80 per cent of children not attending school (Surdu, 2002).

Although the situation has improved in recent years, statistics from 2005–2006 on school participation for Romani children show consistently large inequalities (see Table 8.1).[27]

Table 8.1 School participation of Romani children in Romania

Level of education	Roma pupils (N)	Proportion of pupils who attended at previous level (%)
Pre-primary	12,427	–
Primary	38,670	–
Lower secondary	21,586	56
High school	1,011	5
Vocational education	2,718	13
Total	76,412	–

Not only is the number of Romani children attending pre-school education low, but only a little over half of those attending primary education continued to the next level, while only a small proportion of the latter followed on to high school or vocational education. This shows a high level of dropping out, even before the end of compulsory education, associated with high rates of school failure and lower educational achievement. As specified in the previous section, the proportion of Romani children registered in special schools is higher than that in the education system overall. This can be linked mainly to the fact that some Roma parents prefer to see their children benefit from the advantages offered by the special schools system (a free meal, additional allowances for school supplies, etc.).

Only in 1998 did the educational authorities begin to acknowledge the existence of these inequalities, and the first official document on this issue was published in 1999.

'Positive action' policies targeting Roma

Indeed, since the late 1990s the Ministry of Education initiated a set of educational policies targeting Roma, initially labelled 'positive discrimination' and more recently 'positive action'. Several of these policies have their origin in previous initiatives within the education system, but above all in pilot projects initiated by NGOs. Two phases can be identified in this evolution. The first started in 1998 with the designation of professor Gheorghe Sarau, linguist and specialist in Roma issues, in charge of this matter within the General Directorate for Education in Minority Languages of the Ministry of Education. The second, begun in 2002, is associated with the implementation by the General Directorate for Pre-university Education of a large-scale project supported by the PHARE Programme of the European Commission. We will review here the policies in the first phase, by structuring them in several categories.[28]

Before describing the positive measures, it is also worth mentioning a set of social measures initiated by those in charge of Roma issues and which take into consideration the needs of disadvantaged Roma communities, but are presented as being addressed in relation to all children, without specifying Roma as target group. Such is the case in the distribution among the schools of the monthly allowance for children under the condition of regular school attendance,[29] or of the snack offered to all primary school pupils.[30]

Two categories of positive measures focus on access to education. The first category concerns young Roma who have dropped out from school, and concerns two types of special class.[31]

The first is that of 'catch-up classes' (from 2005 termed 'second chance classes for primary school'[32]), established for children who have not completed primary school and are over 11 years old, where the focus is on ensuring the rapid acquisition of literacy, with the option of following an adapted curriculum (the four years of primary school can be completed within two years). Often, the establishment of such classes has initially resulted from NGO projects or has been supported by NGOs. Between 1999 and 2004 the framework for these classes has represented the programme for fighting marginalisation and the social and professional exclusion of young people who have dropped out of compulsory education without acquiring minimal competences needed to access the labour market.[33] Since 2005, classes of this type, around 100 in total, have been inaugurated in the framework of the PHARE programme described in the following section.[34]

The second is the 'second chance' class at lower secondary level. This type of class has its origins in a project of Centre Education 2000+, an NGO member of the Soros Network. Both Romani and non-Romani children attend such classes, but with the emphasis on Roma who have finished primary education but have dropped out from secondary school. They then have the option to follow an adapted and reduced curriculum, combined with vocational training, allowing them directly to achieve a professional certificate. The curriculum in these classes does not include specific cultural elements, but often the pupils can choose to study the Romani language and are given opportunities to participate in cultural activities offered by various NGOs, usually connected with Roma folklore and traditions, aiming at reinforcing the self-esteem. This hypothesis, which is claimed to facilitate the integration of specific cultural elements aimed at helping develop the children's self-esteem, while diminishing the effects of stigmatisation and increasing the chances of school success, has been supported by NGOs, both those involved in the 'Roma movement' (militating for emancipation and affirmation of Roma as a nation and as a national minority) and the non-Roma NGOs working on this issue.

The other major category of policies aimed at improving the access to education of young Roma concerns the reservation of places for Roma in universities and high schools. This type of measure[35] was initiated by the Ministry of Education in the early 1990s. Initially, this concerned certain pedagogical high schools, which at that time provided initial training to primary school teachers. During the university year 1992–1993, this was continued with the reservation of the first ten places in social work at the University of Bucharest, followed later in the decade by a similar measure in several other universities having social work sections. More recently the number of places has been increased, while other universities and other specialisations have also joined the programme. Thus, in 1998 only 8 large universities received 20 places each for specialisation in social work, while during the year 2007–2008 the ministry financed 454 places[36] for Roma in 48 universities,[37] the number of places ranging between 1, for artistic universities,[38] and 60, for Babes-Bolyai University in Cluj. The largest increase in the number of places was during the year 2002–2003, when 390 places were allocated in 26 universities, following the adoption in 2001 of the Governmental Strategy for the Improvement of the Situation of Roma. The implementation of such a system was justified partly by the fact that the number of Roma university students was extremely low, but chiefly due to the fact that Roma young people had very poor prospects in the admission exams for high schools and universities. This is therefore an access provision: once enrolled in university, Roma students are treated like all others, must follow the same courses together with their non-Roma colleagues, and pass the same exams. Of course, the diploma received will not mention the student's ethnic background, and will carry the same value as that awarded to others. Registration for these places must include, besides the usual documentation and a request to be included as a Roma student, a certificate of ethnic affiliation provided by either a civic or political Roma organisation.

If at initial implementation the system faced a number of resistances and difficulties, these have been overcome with time and its effectiveness demonstrated. Thus, initially, several universities received insufficient requests to occupy all available places, and situations of abuse were also identified: non-Roma young people declared a Roma origin to gain access to these places. At present, several generations of young Roma have been able, thanks to this system, to complete their university education and contribute in this way to the development of a new Roma elite and to a significant strengthening of the Roma emancipation movement. But, beyond these immediate positive effects, such measures also represent an official acknowledgement of the fact that the situation of Roma is of special importance in Romanian society and that it cannot be improved purely through either social measures or the existing system for national minorities (Rus, 2007a).[39]

Based on the success in the implementation of the system of reserved places in universities,[40] since 2004 a similar system has been established for high schools. Thus, following requests, for high school class two supplementary places can be added for Roma candidates. During the first year of implementation of this system the number of Roma candidates was low, but over the following years 1500–2000 young Roma benefited from this measure, one third of them coming from Bucharest (Sarau, 2006).

Another important category of educational policies targeting Roma is represented by what can be called the support system for the teaching of the Romani language. Roma can benefit, as may all other national minorities, from a system allowing for the teaching of all or a part of the subjects in minority languages, or the teaching of Romani as an optional subject. The choice between these options depends on the availability of teachers with the necessary linguistic competences, and on the demands of parents. In the case of Roma the implementation of these measures has been delayed, and for a long time considered impossible, for several reasons, including:

- the important differences between dialects spoken by various Roma communities and the ongoing standardisation of the Romani language;
- the lack of pedagogical material, of publications for both children and teachers;
- the very low number of Romani speakers with the required teaching qualification;
- the low level of information for and awareness of Roma parents on the existing opportunities, and of the benefits these can bring to their children.

Despite these difficulties, in great measure due to the efforts of Ghoerghe Sarau in his double capacity as linguist specialised in the Romani language and inspector for Roma at the Ministry of Education, a well-structured set of PEPs, adapted to current practicalities, has been elaborated by the Ministry of Education with the aim of supporting Romani language teaching. This includes, more precisely:

- administrative measures allowing, through a temporary exemption, young Romani speakers who have completed high school to be employed as Romani teachers, under the condition of following an intensive summer training course organised by the ministry and registering for two years of distance training;
- the option of starting classes in Romani at any time during the school year;
- the employment in each county of an inspector for Roma; in more than half of the counties Roma teachers have been employed full-time in such positions, while in the remainder previously employed inspectors have been employed part-time; identification of those schools deemed suitable for the inauguration of Romani language classes is included among the tasks of these inspectors;
- the publication by the ministry of textbooks and pedagogical material needed for the teaching of the Romani language.

Some of these measures promoted by the ministry (intensive summer training and distance training, publications, training of inspectors) were implemented purely on account of the ongoing partnership and support offered by UNICEF, several other international organisations and Romanian NGOs. This system has functioned since 1999 and has led to a gradual increase in the number of children registered in Romani language classes, from 780 in 1998–1999 to 16,925 in 2003–2004. It should be mentioned that Romani classes have been instigated not only in communities speaking a Romani dialect close to standard Romani, but also in those speaking different dialects and even in some where Romani is not spoken in the family home. This could be interpreted as a trend of returning to the affirmation of a Roma identity in communities recently assimilated. Moreover, in 2005 a new version of the curriculum for the optional course on Roma history and traditions was approved through the orders of minister concerned. This subject is also taught by parental demand, but is far less popular than Romani language classes.

Another policy initiative of this set of positive measures targeting Roma is the employment of Roma school mediators, with the aim of facilitating better communication between schools and Roma communities. Its origin is in a pilot project co-ordinated by the Intercultural Institute of Timisoara and the Roma organisation Romani CRISS, implemented between 1996 and 1998 in partnership with the Institute for Educational Sciences and two French partners, with the support of the Council of Europe. The success of the pilot scheme, which led to a significant reduction in the school drop-out rate among Romani children in targeted communities (Rus & Gheorghe, 1998), led to the adoption of school mediators by the Ministry of Education. In the first phase, the ministry allowed only schools themselves to employ mediators, accepting even those having only the first eight years of compulsory education and giving them general guidelines for their work, through a job description adopted in 2000. However, the ministry had not planned a budget to pay mediators' salaries (justifying this by the fact that mediator is not a formal position according to education legislation). Thus, the use of school mediators has remained marginal and is dependent on isolated support provided by NGOs. A new development in this field, which will be detailed below, was initiated in 2003 with the support of the European Commission.

Finally, another initiative by the Ministry of Education, inspired by projects and proposals from civil society, concerns both the training of non-Roma teachers in promoting intercultural education and elements of Roma history and culture. This corresponds to a real need, as teachers generally have little knowledge of this topic and familiarity with the Roma historical and cultural background can represent a pedagogical asset and generate more positive attitudes towards Romani children and parents (Rus, 2007b). Since 2001, in partnership with various NGOs and their associated financial assistance, implementation of this programme, designed to cover all regions of Romania, has been inconsistent. In 2006 the programme oversaw the training of a team of trainers expected to continue such activities in teacher training centres in their respective counties. However, the scheme's follow-up is in doubt as this programme has not been clearly co-ordinated with the other ministry initiative, the PHARE programme, described in the following section, and with the recent changes in the in-service teacher training system.

The policies implemented in the framework of this first generation of positive measures targeting Roma can be divided into three categories according to the emphasis placed on the cultural dimension:

- social policies that do not take into account the cultural dimension or consider this dimension as secondary, even if a considerable section of the beneficiaries are Roma;
- policies focused on the promotion and development of the specific Roma cultural identity, explicitly targeting Romani children and young people and related to the existing educational policies for national minorities;
- policies focused on the intercultural dimension, aiming at promoting intercultural education, at training teachers to work with mixed classes including Roma and non-Romani children, and at improving the relations between school, Roma families and wider communities.

Access to education by children from disadvantaged groups, with a focus on Roma

An important moment in the promotion of more equality in education was the initiation of a series of reforms aiming at producing a more 'inclusive' education system. This corresponds with the launching by the Ministry of Education during the school year 2002–2003 of a number of macro-projects co-funded by the ministry and the European Commission, in the framework of the PHARE programme. These projects deserve an analysis in relation to the PEPs, not only due to their focus on disadvantaged groups, Roma and 'children with special educational needs', but mainly because, on the one hand, their implementation, with a large institutional mobilisation and the use of procedures expected to be reproduced and scaled-up, has determined a change in the functioning of educational authorities and of the schools concerned, and, on the other, they have been the direct origin of a set of educational policy changes and of changes in the legal framework of this field.

The elaboration of these projects is affirmed as being connected with the implementation of the national Strategy for the Improvement of the Situation of Roma, adopted by the Romanian Government in 2001 following wide consultation with Roma organisations. However, when analysing the vocabulary and the conceptual references in the project documents, in comparison with those in the Strategy, a relatively weak correspondence will be noted. But, if the framework of the Strategy is largely overcome by the approach of the PHARE programme, the actions in these projects rely in large part on experiences in the first generation of positive measures, described above.

It should be mentioned that the title of this section is taken from the first of the series of three projects, while the title of the other two, the 'focus on Roma', no longer appears. However, Romani children continue to be mentioned as a main target group, together with children with 'special educational needs'.

The general objectives of these projects are to improve access to education for disadvantaged groups and to promote an inclusive education, with a special focus on Roma and pupils with special educational needs, in order to combat social exclusion and marginalisation and to promote human rights and equality of opportunities. The three phases of the project were initially designed to achieve this objective through similar activities covering, initially 10 counties, 14 counties in the second phase, and the remaining 18 Romanian counties in the third phase. Although in general the approach and the main activities have been similar in the three phases, conceptual and methodological adjustments can be identified. Thus, for example, the concept of 'inclusive education' has become the central element of the approach, while the cultural dimension and the intercultural approach have declined in importance.

Leaving aside the funding of local projects submitted by selected school inspectorates, the activities have been focused on:

- support provided to school inspectorates for the elaboration and implementation of county strategies for improving the access to education of disadvantaged groups, with special attention paid to Roma and the inclusion of children with special educational needs in mainstream schools;
- the elaboration, organisation and monitoring of training programmes for school inspectors (those responsible for pre-school, primary and special education, as well as the inspector for Roma), school principals from pilot schools, teacher trainers, teachers in pilot schools and members of the Roma communities wishing to become primary school teachers or school mediators;
- the development of curriculum and pedagogical resources;
- support for community participation in education;
- the creation of a framework for supporting the integration of children with special needs in mainstream schools.

Starting with the second phase, as will be explained further, a new line of work has been added: the identification of all cases of educational segregation, in close co-operation with school inspectorates, NGOs and other stakeholders, as well as support for local actions for identification and implementation of effective desegregation measures.

Each school inspectorate has been required to elaborate its own strategy for improving access to education of disadvantaged groups through a participatory procedure, involving Roma NGOs, local and regional authorities, special education institutions and representatives of schools situated in disadvantaged communities. In relation to this strategy, in each county pilot schools have been identified and these have received funding to improve educational conditions, at both material and pedagogical level.

At county level, besides the work on improving the situation in pilot schools, activities are aimed at:

- increased participation of children from disadvantaged communities in pre-school education;
- encouragement of children of disadvantaged groups to complete compulsory education and improve their educational achievement;
- registration in 'second chance classes' of young people who have dropped out from school before the end of compulsory education;
- integration within mainstream schools of children with special educational needs, and the transformation of special schools into resource centres to provide psychological and pedagogical support for children with special needs registered in mainstream schools.

The concept that became the core of these projects, 'inclusive school', is a novelty for the Romanian education system and has evolved under the influence of suggestions made by international experts during the initial phases. This approach has not been used previously as a possible solution for the educational difficulties experienced by Romani children. On the one hand, this approach is compatible with the conclusions and recommendations formulated in the framework of various projects on this topic by NGOs: for instance, regarding the importance of changing school climate, teaching methods and school–community relations, as well as regarding the idea of making school an institution that promotes respect for diversity. On the other hand, this conceptual option is opposed, although not explicitly, by the approaches emphasising the cultural dimension, the development of a positive cultural identity of Romani children as a way to compensate for the lack of self-esteem, often generated by the social environment. This approach of 'inclusive schools' tends to give less visibility to the ethnic dimension and to the intercultural perspective, while associating Romani children with children having special educational needs based on biological or psychological problems.

These projects had an essential role in raising the awareness of national and regional educational activities of the existence of unacceptable inequalities in terms of access to quality education and of the need to overcome the risks of perpetuating social exclusion generated by restrictive rules (which have not considered the possibility of school drop-out).

Another important contribution of these projects concerns the strengthening of the position and the institutionalisation of Roma school mediators. As described in the previous section, the employment of Roma school mediators, adopted by the Ministry of Education following pilot initiatives of the non-governmental sector, did not receive appropriate institutional and financial support. An interesting development has been seen in this matter by the implementation of this series of PHARE projects. Thus, in order to benefit from support in the framework of the projects, each pilot school was required to identify and employ a school mediator. The training and salary of the mediators for a year were covered by the budget of the project, and some measures were taken to ensure the continuation of the work after the end of the project. In this way, over 200 mediators were trained and employed during the three phases.

The solution initially envisaged to cover the salaries of the school mediators employed in the framework of the project was to transfer their contracts to local authorities. However, this appeared problematic, particularly in the poorest communities, where often the local budget lacked resources. Facing these challenges of implementation, the ministry had to initiate changes concerning the status, institutional affiliation and training of school mediators.

Measures have therefore been taken to recognise school mediators as auxiliary pedagogical staff, which gave rise to the option of paying their salary from the budget of the education system. Moreover, a ministerial order issued in July 2007 clearly specifies the criteria (of three categories: educational, socio-economic and cultural) allowing a school to request a position of school mediator, together with the administrative details of the employment contract, the monitoring and evaluation of the work done and the specific responsibilities. This new system also allows for the employment of school mediators by the county-based resource centres, recently established. This way, professional mediators can offer their services to the most disadvantaged schools, those that usually have the greatest needs and for which the financial support of a mediator position from the local budget is the most problematic. This new system also allows schools corresponding to the newly defined criteria to employ a mediator directly.

Another positive change brought by these new norms concerns the training of mediators. In the early phases, relatively long-term training was carried out as part of the project and the post-project option envisaged was a dedicated section in pedagogical high schools, implying five years of study, barely accessible for young Roma coming from disadvantaged communities. On the contrary, the new formula allows for the possibility of training mediators through a shorter vocational training period, more flexible and appropriate not only for initial training but also seen as professional reconversion of those individuals who had already completed high school. Access to these courses is also open to those who have completed eight years of school, under the condition that they register at the same time to continue their secondary education.

It should also be mentioned that the employment and training of mediators in this new perspective are not conditioned by an ethnic affiliation, but knowledge of 'the language and of the culture of the local community' is recommended. Moreover, the ministerial order no longer refers to 'Roma school mediator', as in previous documents, but talks about 'school mediator', which, at least in theory, allows the employment of school mediators by schools with pupils from other disadvantaged groups, not only Roma.[41] This document also mentions that schools corresponding to the defined criteria will be designated as 'priority education areas'.[42]

Desegregation

Since the first years of the 21st century, Roma organisations – and especially the organisation Romani CRISS – have raised the issue of segregation of Romani children in schools.[43] This corresponds to a previous consensus of the most important Roma organisations and leaders on the promotion of school integration of Romani children at all levels, since the early 1990s (when the trend was towards establishing separate educational institutions with teaching in minority languages, as demanded particularly by the Hungarian minority but supported also by other minorities).

Educational authorities have not followed up the complaints of Romani CRISS or those of several international NGOs and have denied the existence of this phenomenon. Thus, at regional and local levels, numerous educational authorities and school principals did not view school segregation as discriminatory, and justified it as being a measure for the benefit of both Romani and non-Romani children.[44] It was during the implementation of the first phase of the PHARE project described above, in the school year 2003–2004, that senior officials of the Ministry of Education were confronted with the reality of segregation and became convinced that action was required.

Thus, in April 2004 the Ministry of Education issued a notification on school segregation. This document, the first issued by the ministry on this matter, specifies that

> segregation in education represents a severe form of discrimination ... ,
> [it] implies the physical separation, intentional or non-intentional, of
> Roma from other children, in schools, classes, buildings and other facilities, making that the number of Roma children is disproportionally
> higher that the that of non-Roma, in comparison with the proportion
> of Roma children of school age in the total of the school-age population
> in that area.

The ministry

> forbids the establishment of pre-school, primary or secondary classes containing exclusively or mainly Roma pupils. This way of constituting classes is considered as a form of segregation, what ever explanation is given to justify it.

Moreover, the notification not only recognises segregation as a form of discrimination and forbids it, but goes further by promoting desegregation measures and requiring school inspectorates to 'revue the situation in all schools in which the number of Roma children is disproportionally higher that that of the non-Roma' and to initiate 'action plans aiming at eliminating segregation'.

However, the implementation of the measures specified in the notification has not been without difficulties and misunderstandings. Several school inspectorates have not given to the ministry the required statistics and action plans, while others responded that in their county there were no segregation cases, without providing further details. A phone enquiry carried out by the ministry among schools during the school year 2004–2005 pointed out that the information on the notification has not been passed on to schools by certain school inspectorates and that many teachers were not aware of it. Situations of segregation continued to be identified by NGOs, as well as those where Roma parents wishing to register their children in ethnically mixed schools were sent to the segregated schools in their neighbourhoods.

In this context, desegregation has become one of the priorities of the second phase of the macro-project implemented by the ministry with the support of the PHARE programme. This decision led not only to a series of local successes in the limitation of segregation phenomenon, but also to an important progress in education policy in this respect. Thus, in July 2007 an order was issued by the Minister of Education on the prevention of segregation and on promoting desegregation. The order explicitly forbids segregation of Romani children, but also includes a methodology and indicators that school are required to use to evaluate their current situation and to evaluate plans to combat segregation. However, even if the provisions of the order were intended to have been implemented from the school year 2007–2008, its impact remains problematic due to a lack of adapted training of inspectors, school principals, school mediators and other staff categories involved in this process.[45] These training needs have been signalled by representatives of a group of NGOs working in this field and which has been consulted during the process of elaboration of the order and of its methodological annexes. The Ministry of Education recently obtained additional support for action on this matter from the Roma Education Fund, a structure associated with the Roma Inclusion Decade,[46] which shows the will to advance and expectations of improved implementation of the existing policies.

The Priority Education Area

An attempt to advance – in the Romanian context– the concept of Priority Education Area (which in Romania has the initials ZEP, as in French) as an option for consideration in regard to future education policies is due to a project from the Institute of Education Sciences,[47] supported by UNICEF.

This initiative is based on the results of research on the school situation of Romani children, published in 2002 by the Institute of Educational Sciences and the Institute for Research on the Quality of Life, which shows important inequalities between the schools having a higher number of Romani children and other schools, inequalities manifested in the quality of the material and human resources available, as well as in the drop-out rate.

The pertinence of this approach in the Romanian context has been tested within the framework of a project implemented from 2002 to 2005 in a school in Giurgiu, a small town 60 kilometres south of Bucharest.

The targeted school corresponds to a large extent with the set of criteria defined by the project:

- community-related criteria

  - a community in a situation of extreme poverty, with a large number of families struggling for subsistence, with a very low level of education and job integration and precarious housing conditions;
  - a large concentration of Roma;
  - a reserved attitude towards the school by a section of the community, particularly from the Roma.

- school-related criteria

  - a drop-out rate of almost 10 per cent;
  - a large number of children not attending school in the school catchment area;
  - a figure of around 5 per cent of pupils having repeated the year;
  - a high level of school failure, particularly among Roma children;
  - a large proportion of pupils with learning difficulties.

In terms of teaching staff the situation appears better, with only one teacher in 23 without pedagogical qualification, good stability, satisfactory level of certified qualification and a balanced age distribution. This situation has been judged as favouring the process envisaged.

The main activities were preceded by the gathering of information on the school and the community, as well as by interviews with teachers, with the aim of giving their perspective on the problems of the school, on the current legal framework and curriculum, as well as on the identification of the training needs of the teaching staff.

In this context, the activities focused on two general objectives:

- increasing the level of school participation and reducing the risks of school drop-out for children facing learning difficulties and for those with a disadvantaged socio-economic background, with special attention given to Romani children;
- ensuring the acquisition of basic competencies by the Romani children and by the majority of those from disadvantaged socio-economic back-grounds who had dropped out of school before the end of compulsory education.

While targeting the overall population of the school, activities focused particularly on the needs of three disadvantaged groups:

- children between 11 and 16 years of age who had never attended school or who had dropped out of school at least one year previously; a catch-up class at primary level was inaugurated for this group;
- children who had dropped out of school during lower secondary educa-tion or at the end of primary education at least two years previously; a catch-up class at secondary level was inaugurated for this group;
- children at major risk of school failure due to a disadvantaged socio-economic situation, children under 11 years of age not attending school or children who had dropped out of first grade less than two years previ-ously; they were integrated in ZEP classes functioning in parallel with the regular classes in the school.

The main activities concerned were:

- the design of curriculum materials adapted for the three target groups;
- the training of teachers and of the school principal, mainly in two areas:

  - raising of awareness regarding the approach of a 'learning school', of an intercultural approach[48] and on the importance of partnership, with a focus also on management of change, project management and organisational communication;
  - development of competencies in using innovative didactic strategies for implementation of the adapted curriculum, with the aim of increas-ing the motivation of pupils to learn and to facilitate the learning process.

- identification of pupils for each of the special classes;
- provision for all children of a warm meal and of material support for those from disadvantaged socio-economic background;

- rehabilitation of schools and provision of equipment, including IT;
- establishment a resource centre for literacy and other training for parents and adults in general, as well as counselling of children and their families.

The adapted curriculum elaborated for the three categories of classes (primary catch-up class, secondary catch-up class and ZEP class) is a simplified curriculum, with more practical elements and oriented towards the development of the key competencies specified in European documentation.[49] It also encouraged work in interdisciplinary projects and integrated approaches, such as history/geography or sciences, up to the sixth grade.[50] For the catch-up classes, the content has been structured as two years per cycle, rather than four, as the systems normally requires. This adapted curriculum has been approved by the Ministry of Education.

The implementation of these changes has faced a series of difficulties, which has limited their impact. Thus, the renovation of school buildings, the responsibility of the local authorities, has been delayed due to administrative problems and to poor co-operation with local authorities during the initial phase of the project. However, the changes have, in large measure, been achieved and their implementation continued after the end of the project. The issue of providing a warm meal for all children, appreciated as very important by teachers and parents, could only be supported for one year. The immediate consequence of this was an increase in the rate of drop-out and class repetition, after a reduction in both of these indicators during the school year when the free meal was provided. Four new teaching positions were established, one being for a Roma teacher to teach Romani language and work in parallel as a school mediator. However, this person remained in school for only one year.

Despite these challenges, positive outcomes have been achieved, particularly through the establishment of the three ZEP classes, the two primary catch-up classes and the two lower-secondary catch-up classes. Without these, the children integrated in these classes would have faced serious risk of social exclusion. Additionally, recognition of the resource centre, which allowed over 250 members of the community to attend educational and informational activities, the development of teachers' competencies and the improvement in the general educational conditions, should be given.

The weakest point of the project was, in our opinion, its limited impact on educational policies. The design of a special curriculum for catch-up classes, validated by the Ministry of Education, represents, without doubt, an important step towards making the education system more accessible to those who had dropped out of school, and better able to provide pedagogical and administrative answers in limiting the risks of exclusion, taking into consideration the specific situations of disadvantaged children. This curriculum must now, however, be revised and adapted to the recent reorganisation of secondary education and to the extension of the compulsory education period to ten years. Besides, much remains to be done regarding the definition of clear proposals for public policy changes, based on clear criteria, accompanied by a corresponding financial commitment and using mechanisms that can be reproduced in different situations where their presence is needed. Despite these limitations and the fact that the proposed approach does not facilitate its clarification in the Romanian context, the ZEP remains as an option for future policies, as we will show below.

Priority education policies targeting rural areas

The disadvantaged situation of children and young people living in rural areas is clearly demonstrated by studies on this topic, not only from a socio-economic point of view but also with respect to education. Since 1990, the drop-out rate (often associated with the employment of children in agriculture or households, in the context of subsistence agriculture with a low level of productivity) has risen more steeply in rural than in urban areas, and a significantly lower participation in upper secondary education (high schools or vocational schools) has been recorded. Participation in higher education is even lower. Moreover, there is a lower level of teacher qualification and a greater fluctuation in teacher numbers while, in general, a lower quality of the education is offered in rural schools than in the urban environment.[51]

In this context, taking into account the strong political support represented by the singling out of rural education as a priority for governmental programmes since 2001, and a series of projects implemented since 1999 by the Ministry of Education and the Institute of Education Sciences, a wide-ranging programme aiming at reducing these inequalities in education has been launched with the support of the World Bank. Among the measures taken in this context, the most important include free school transportation for children from isolated disadvantaged communities and the option of scholarships for high school or university studies. The long-term special project of the ministry, currently under implementation, includes the following work areas:

- rehabilitation of school infrastructure;
- improvement of material conditions in rural schools (equipment, pedagogical resources, etc.);
- training of teachers from rural schools;
- provision of additional financial support and other incentives for teachers accepting a stable position in rural areas;
- strengthening of school–community partnerships in rural areas.

These priority policies for rural areas are much more rigorous and coherent: they have a clear and explicit conceptual background; they rely on complex diagnostic studies, using both statistical data and qualitative and participatory approaches; they include well-structured evaluation mechanisms, as well as impact studies; and, additionally, they benefit from a large material support, compatible with the size of the disadvantage identified.

Perspectives in a changing education system

The policies described above deserve a more in-depth analysis, both regarding their theoretical background and their fundamental assumptions, explicit or implicit, and regarding their implementation and impact. What these policies have in common is without doubt the fact that they aim to promote equity, equality of opportunities and social inclusion through education, in a perspective of access to education as a fundamental right.

It is obvious that some policies have just been elaborated and their implementation has started only recently. Such an analysis should take into account the dynamics of this process, as well as the complexity of the political and social context.[52]

We are indeed looking at a very dynamic field, with continuous changes in education policies, large-scale projects and political influences from outside the education system that impact the education of disadvantaged groups. Such is the case of decentralisation, the implementation of various sectoral strategies, including a new system of funding for schools, the establishment of a social protection system aiming at fighting social exclusion, rural development policies, implementation of the Strategy for the Improvement of the Situation of Roma, or policies on combating discrimination. Moreover, additional changes are envisaged for the future. Some new initiatives concern the Roma, such as the co-operation of the Ministry of Education with the Council of Europe, the framework offered by the Roma Inclusion Decade or the projects supported by the Roma Education Fund (focused explicitly, at least at statement level, on impacting education policies). Other initiatives take a wider perspective on development, such as new programmes for rural development or some sections of the Operational Programme on Human Resources Development, co-funded by the European Commission through the European Social Fund.

An important issue in regard to these policies concerns the hesitations between ethnic labelling associated with policies targeting national minorities and 'inclusion', without ethnic or cultural references. In some cases confusions exist between needs related to a socio-economic disadvantage and the specific needs related to cultural differences. Similarly, an analysis is needed on the founding principles of policies for national minorities: are they actually based on language or on ethnic affiliation? This dilemma is reflected by the names give to structures of the Ministry of Education: the Directorate for Education in the Languages of National Minorities includes an office for Romani language and programmes for Roma. A sensitive issue is also represented by the procedures used to collect statistical data about Romani children while avoiding the negative effects of hetero-identification and encouraging an open affirmation of ethnic and cultural identities.

Finally, as evident from the facts presented above, educational authorities seem to be more concerned with the implementation of projects than with the elaboration, monitoring and evaluation of public policies, which should actually be their main task. This trend may be connected with an insufficient internal capacity for management and reform, as well as with a lack of resources, and is stimulated by the current system that allows the attracting of additional project-based funding from the EU and other agencies. A fragmentation of the various policies and projects may also be noted, together with a tendency to adopt special programmes, combined with a grudging acceptance of the principles behind these initiatives in mainstream education policies.

It is nevertheless a fact that significant progress has been made in recent years, in terms of the wider impact of the macro-projects initiated by the ministry, of the integration of some ideas emerging from the PEPs into mainstream policies, at least at discourse level, as well as of the promotion of a real and sustainable consultation and co-operation between educational authorities and the most experienced civil society structures.

An important mark of progress, announced by the ministry in 2007 but not yet accomplished, would be the inauguration of a national-level database facilitating the identification of inequalities in education for different groups. Moreover, the indicators defined in the framework of the desegregation or the criteria formulated for the employment of school mediators can be seen as the seed of a more structured approach in this field and of a more coherent definition of realistic and effective PEPs.

Finally, the recent debates around the National Pact for Education confirm our conclusions. They give more public visibility to the issues targeted by the priority education policies and contribute to moving the emphasis towards a strategic approach, better structured and able to provide medium-term guidance for the ongoing reform processes.

Acknowledgements

The author thanks Daniel Frandji, David Greger and César Birzea for their suggestions and comments.

Notes

1. This need has also been acknowledged at political level. For example, according to the Government Programme 2001–2004 (social-democrat government): 'taking into account that, because of their life condition, certain categories of population ... do not have access to basic education, they will benefit from educational protection and support programmes: special education for the handicapped; compensatory programmes for the persons excluded from a normal social life'. The Government Programme 2005–2008 (centre-right government) mentions 'the extension of the network of structures called *second chance*', as well as the 'reconstruction of the education system in rural areas'.
2. For example, in the documentation of the PHARE project of the Ministry of Education and Research on Access to education of disadvantaged groups, in the Orders of the Minister of Education and Research from July 2007, which will be

analysed later in this chapter, or in the statements of the Romanian Presidential Administration in the context of the debate on the future of the education reform (minutes of the second meeting of the Presidential Commission for the analysis and elaboration of policies in the field of education and research – 13 September 2007), as well as in the National Pact for Education, signed by all parliamentary political parties and by the President on 5 March 2008.

3. The legal definition of handicapped children and adults (Romanian Parliament, Law 448/2006) is not clear, but seems to be taken as a reference in educational documents. It mentions additional educational needs connected with 'individual deficiencies' or 'learning difficulties'.

4. Category defined in the legislation on gifted young people, capable of good performance (Romanian Parliament, Law 17/2007).

5. In the context of a project funded by the World Bank.

6. Both through references to European processes and documents (Bologna Process, Lisbon Strategy, etc.) and through the implementation of macro-programmes with financial support and according to the procedures of the European Union.

7. The Law 87/2006 on quality assurance in education.

8. This evaluation is supported by the conclusions and recommendations of several studies (Iosifescu *et al.*, 2001; Vlasceanu *et al.*, 2002; Crişan *et al.*, 2006), as well as of various seminars on this topic.

9. Such is the case of the provision stating that the last year of pre-school education is compulsory, without taking into account the costs which must be covered by the families, or the initial formulation of Article 20 of the law, providing access to completion of primary education only for young people under 14 years of age, while many Roma young people who have abandoned school or have never attended it did not have any means of reintegrating into the education system or accessing vocational training.

10. According to a statement by the president during the signature of the Pact for Education by representatives of unions and NGOs, on 10 March 2008.

11. This term, not explicitly defined in the legislation, should be understood in the spirit of the Framework-Convention for the Protection of National Minorities, from the Council of Europe.

12. It should be mentioned that general studies on the status of the education system and of the reform (Iosifescu *et al.*, 2001; Vlasceanu *et al.*, 2002) do not address this topic.

13. Several Roma NGOs (Romani CRISS, Amare Rromentza, 'Together' Agency), the Intercultural Institute of Timisoara, Project for Ethnic Relations and Save the Children Romania.

14. Law 448/2006, Article 5, point 12.

15. Romani CRISS, in several reports, 'Pro Europe' Ligue, in a report on the implementation by Romania of the commitments made in relation with the Framework-Convention for the Protection of National Minorities, or the Resource Centre for Roma Communities and the Open Society Institute in the EUMAP report 2007.

16. Project reference document 'Access to education for disadvantaged groups' RO03/551.01.02.

17. Salamanca Statement and Action Framework for Special Educational Needs, adopted by the World Conference on Special Educational Needs: access and quality, Salamanca, Spain, 1994, UNESCO.

18. RENINCO Statutes, Article 5. Available online at http://www.reninco.ro, accessed on 15 July 2009.

19. An issue increasingly addressed in current public debates is that concerning children whose parents spend at least several months per year working abroad.

20. Law 17/2007 concerning the education of gifted young people, capable of a high level of achievement.

21. A 1997 study carried out by the Institute of Educational Sciences (Stanescu & Jigau, 1997) outlined the conceptual framework of the approach and made a comparative analysis at European level.

22. Of course, there is also the option, made by many, to choose Romanian language schools.

23. According to data from the 2002 census, 1,434,377 Romanian citizens declared their affiliation to the Hungarian minority, that is around 6 per cent of the overall population.

24. EU Monitoring Access Program, Open Society Institute, Budapest.

25. Roma Inclusion Barometer, 2007, Soros Foundation Romania.

26. Other studies estimate that the proportion is around 40 per cent (Surdu, 2002; Zamfir & Preda, 2002).

27. Source: National Statistical Institute, 2005. It should be mentioned that of the 60,256 Romani children attending primary and lower-secondary schools, 1662 were in special schools.

28. This categorisation is not explicit in official documentation but results from the analysis.

29. This measure is no longer implemented following a court decision which considered that this conditioning was hindering access to a constitutional right.

30. The pertinence of the inclusion of this measure in relation to the Roma issue can be justified by the presence in the section 'Education' of the Government's Strategy for the Improvement of the Situation of Roma of the following provision: 'stimulating access to education through offering a free meal to all children in primary and secondary cycles'.

31. These classes are not included in the Law of Education but have been established by order of the minister.

32. Order of the Minister of Education 5160/6.10.2005.

33. Order of the Minister of Education 4231/18.08.1999.

34. Order of the Minister of Education 5160/6.10.2005.

35. A system similar to the quota system used in other countries. The system was a novelty, without no corresponding item in the educational policies of the communist regime.

36. An increase from the 415 places in 26 universities in the previous year.

37. All public universities in Romania except Marine University of Constanta.

38. These universities have the lowest number of students in general.

39. It is obvious that the creation of an elite is not a solution in itself for the current inequalities and that it is not a risk-free process. However, taking into consideration the initial situation, with a quasi-total absence of Roma from the level of society's elite, it is easy to understand why a large consensus could be built on this matter at the level of civil society, of specialists and of politicians, at least at the beginning of the process. Currently, there are more and more voices arguing against these measures, in the debates on the reform of education and especially in the debates on discrimination against Roma. It is true that no systematic study has yet evaluated the impact of these policies. Such an evaluation implies several challenges, such as that resulting from the fact that nothing requires young

Roma, having entered university, to maintain the affirmation of their ethnic affiliation.

40. Every year there have been increases in the number of candidates, in the number of places and in the number of young Roma graduating and becoming involved in Roma organisations or benefiting from positive measures in the field of employment of Roma in public administration.

41. The list of criteria contains a mix of general statements with references to national minorities, without naming any, and of explicit references to Roma communities.

42. As will be explained further, the meaning given to 'priority education area' is not clearly specified and one may consider that it is in a process of crystallisation in the Romanian context, but risks being different from the meaning given to it in Western European countries where it is used.

43. This was part of a wider regional trend, supported by the European Roma Rights Center of Budapest, and by other organisations connected to the network of foundations established by George Soros.

44. The inauguration of classes taught in Romani has not been considered as segregation and is supported by certain Roma activists. There is currently only one school, in a village with a large majority of Roma in the West of Romania, where there is teaching in Romani at primary school level.

45. Only those directly involved in the last phase of the PHARE project have been trained on this matter.

46. See the website of Roma Inclusion Decade 2005–2015: <www.romadecade.org> (accessed 15 July 2009).

47. The Institute of Education Sciences is a public institution, part of the education system, under the supervision of the Ministry of Education.

48. See the works of the Council of Europe on this topic for references.

49. Documents concerning the implementation of the Programme 'Education and Training 2010'.

50. While in the usual national curriculum there is a division by scientific field from the fifth grade.

51. This results from the very rigorous studies carried out by the Institute of Educational Sciences (Jigau, 1996, 2000) and by the Centre Education 2000+ (Radulescu & Crisan, 2002), as well as from reports by the Ministry of Education.

52. This dynamics will probably manifest itself in the near future in relation to the target groups of the priority education policies. Thus, there will soon be a need for priority education policies targeting migrant children, taking into account that Romania increasingly becomes, as do other EU member countries, a country of net immigration.

Bibliography

ANDREESCU G. (2005). *Naţiuni şi minorităţi* [Nations and Minorities]. Iaşi: Polirom.

BERESCU C. & CELAC M. (2006). *Locuirea şi sărăcia extremă. Cazul romilor* [Housing and Extreme Poverty. The Roma Case]. Editura Universitară Ion Mincu.

CACE S. & VLĂDESCU C. (co-ord.) (2004). *Starea de sănătate a populaţiei Roma şi accesul la serviciile de sănătate* [The state of health of the Roma and access to health services]. Editura Expert.

CRIŞAN A., DVORSK M. & RADULESCU E. (2002). *Studiu de impact asupra dezvoltarii invatamantului rural* [Impact Study on the Development of Rural Education]. Centrul Educatia 2000+, Centrul de Asistenta Rurala.

CRIŞAN A., IOSIFESCU S., IUCU R. & NEDELCU A. (2006). *Patru exerciţii de politici educaţionale* [Four Exercises on Educational Policies]. Bucutresti. Centrul Educaţia 2000+.

CONSTANTIN T. (1996). *Minoritatea romilor – de la investigaţii constatative la intervenţie socială.* In *Adrian Neculau şi Gilles Ferréol, Minoritari, marginali, excluşi* [The Roma Minority – from investigations to social intervention]. Iaşi: Polirom.

COZMA T., CUCOŞ C. & MOMANU M. (1996). *Educaţia copiilor de ţigani: reprezentări, ipoteze, dificultăţi* [The education of gypsy children: representations, hypotheses, difficulties]. In Adrian Neculau şi Gilles Ferréol, Minoritari, marginali, excluşi. [The Minority, the Marginal, the Excluded]. Iaşi: Polirom.

IONESCU M. & CACE S. (2006a). *Politici publice pentru romi. Evoluţii şi perspective* [Public Policies for the Roma. Evolutions and perspectives]. Editura Expert.

IONESCU M. & CACE S. (2006b). *Politici de ocupare pentru romi* [Job Insertion Policies for the Roma]. Editura Expert.

IOSIFESCU S. *et al.* (2001). *Proiectul de Reformă a Învăţământului Preuniversitar – Management educaţional pentru instituţiile de învăţământ* [The proposed reform of pre-university education – Management educational institutions for teaching]. Bucharest: Institut des sciences de l'éducation et ministère de l'Éducation nationale.

JIGAU M. (co-ord.) (1996). *Invatamantul in zone defavorizate. Strategii si alternative educationale* [Education in disadvantaged areas. Strategies and educational alternatives]. Bucharest: Institutul de Stiinte ale Educatiei.

JIGAU M. (co-ord.) (2000/2002). *Rural education in Romania. Conditions, challenges and development strategies.* Bucharest: MarLink Publishing.

JIGAU M. & SURDU M. (co-ord.) (2002). Participarea la educatie a copiilor romi. Probleme, solutii, actori [The Participation in Education of Roma children. Problems, Solutions, Actors]. Ministerul Educaţiei şi Cercetării, Institutul de Ştiinţe ale Educaţiei, Institutul de Cercetare a Calităţii Vieţii, UNICEF Romania.

LIÉGEOIS J.-P. (2007). *Roma in Europe.* Strasbourg: Council of Europe.

MARGA A. (1998). *Guidelines for the Reform of Education in Romania.* Bucharest: Ministry of National Education.

MARGA A. (2000). *Anii reformei 1997–2000* [The years of reform 1997–2000]. Cluj: Editura Fundatiei de Studii Europene.

POLEDNA R., RUEGG F. & RUS C. (co-ord.) (2002). *Interculturalitate. Cercetări şi perspective româneşti* [Interculturality. Romanian research and perspectives]. Presa Universitară Clujeană.

PREDA M. (2002). In Cătălin Zamfir şi Marian Preda (co-ord.) *Romii în România.* [Roma in Romania]. Editura Expert.

RUS C. (2002). Relaţiile interculturale in Romania – O perspectiva psihosociologica [Intercultural Relations in Romania – A Psycho-Sociological Perspective]. In RUDOLF POLEDNA, FRANÇOIS RUEGG & CALIN RUS (co-ord.) *Interculturalitate: cercetari si perspective romanesti* [Interculturality: Romanian Research and Perspectives]. Cluj: Presa Universitara Clujeana.

RUS C. (2003). Traduire l'interculturel en Roumanie [Translating the Intercultural in Romania]. In ALINE GOHARD-RADENKOVIC, DONATILLE MUJAWAMARIYA & SOLEDAD PEREZ (co-ord.) *Intégration des 'minorités' et nouveaux espaces interculturels* [Integration of 'minorities' and new intercultural spaces]. Berne: Peter Lang.

RUS C. (2006). Multiculturalism, Interculturality and Minority Rights: From West to East and back. In R. POLEDNA, F. RUEGG and C. RUS (eds) *Interculturalism and Discrimination in Romania. Policies, Practices, Identities and Representations.* Berlin: LIT Verlag.

Rus C. (2007a).Problematica romilor şi reforma asistenţei sociale în România [The Roma issue and the social assistance reform in Romania]. In Ana Munteanu şi Juliane Sagebiel (co-ord.), *Practici in Asistenta Sociala* [Practices in social assistance]. Romania – Germania. Iaşi: Polirom.

Rus C. (2007b). Discours discriminatoire et préjugés à l'égard des Roms dans un cours en ligne [Discriminatory discourse and prejudice with regard to the Roma in an online course]. Communication at the International Congress of Intercultural Research, Timisoara, September 2007.

Rus C. & Gheorghe N. (1998). La scolarisation des enfants roms: la formation continue des enseignants travaillant avec des enfants roms [Schooling of Roma children: in-service training for teachers working with Roma children]. Institutul Intercultural Timisoara and the Council of Europe.

Rus C. & Pepenel V. (2006). Drama-based education for the empowerment of Roma parents and young people. Experiences of Timisoara Roma Youth Centre. Institutul Intercultural Timisoara.

Sarau G. (1990). Contributions à l'histoire des recherches portant sur la langue et le folklore des tziganes de Roumanie [Contributions to the history of research into the language and folklore of the gypsies of Romania]. 'Revue Roumaine de Linguistique', Bucharest: Editura Academiei Române, Vol. XXXV, No. 2 (March–April), pp. 117–131.

Sarau G. (2006). Experienţa românească privind învăţământul pentru rromi şi predarea limbii materne rromani în perioada 1990 – 2005 [The Romanian experience concerning education of the Roma and teaching the Romani mother tongue, 1990–2005]. Bucharest: Ministerul Educaţiei şi Cercetării.

Stanescu L. & Jigau M. (1997). Strategii organizatorice de educatie a copiilor capabili de performante superioare: scolare si extrascolare. Bucuresti [Organisation strategies for the education of children capable of high achievement: in school and out of school]. Institutul de Stiinte ale Educatiei.

Surdu M. (2002). Educaţia şcolară a populaţiei de romi [School education of the Roma population]. In Cătălin Zamfir şi Marian Preda (co-ord.) *Romii în România*. [Roma in Romania]. Editura Expert.

Vlasceanu L. et al. (2002). *School at the Crossroads. Change and continuity in the compulsory education curriculum.* Iaşi: Polirom.

Voicu B. (2001). Sustenabilitatea unor soluţii de relansare a învăţământului rural: descentralizarea şi marketizarea [Sustainability of certain solutions to relaunch rural education: decentralisation and marketing] în *Calitatea Vieţii*, nr. 1–4/2001.

Voicu M. (2007). Toleranţă şi discriminare percepută. [Tolerance and perceived discrimination]. In Gabriel Bădescu, Vlad Grigoraş, Cosima Rughiniş, Mălina Voicu & Ovidiu Voicu (co-ord.). *Barometrul incluziunii romilor* [The barometer of Roma inclusion]. Fundaţia pentru o Societate Deschisă.

Zamfir C. & Preda M. (co-ord.) (2002). *Romii în România*. [Roma in Romania]. Editura Expert.

Legal references and NGO reports

Etnobarometrul Rural (2006). Fundatia pentru o Societate Deschisa Romania.

European Commission (2002). EU Support for Roma Communities in Central and Eastern Europe. European Commission.

Liga Pro Europa (2005). Raport privind implementarea de către România a Convenţiei-cadru pentru protecţia minorităţilor naţionale [Report on the

Implementation by Romania of the Framework-Convention for the Protection of National Minorities]. Tîrgu-Mures: Liga Pro Europa.

LIGA PRO EUROPA (2006). Discriminarea rasială, etnică şi lingvistică în judeţele Alba, Bihor, Braşov, Caraş-Severin şi Sălaj. [Racial, Ethnic and Linguistic Discrimination in Alba, Bihor, Braşov, Caraş-Severin and Sălaj Counties]. Tîrgu-Mures: Liga Pro Europa.

OECD (2007). Politici in educaţie pentru elevii în situaţie de risc şi pentru cei cu dizabilităţi din europa de sud est. Romania [Synthesis Report and Chapter 8 Romania in *Education Policies for Students at Risk and those with Disabilities in South Eastern Europe: Bosnia-Herzegovina, Bulgaria, Croatia, Kosovo, FYR of Macedonia, Moldova, Montenegro, Romania and Serbia*]. OECD.

OPEN SOCIETY INSTITUTE (2007). Equal Access to Quality Education for Roma. Romania. Monitoring Report 2007. EU Monitoring and Advocacy Program. Education Support Program. Roma Participation Program. Open Society Institute. Budapest.

ROMA EDUCATION FUND (2007). Advancing Education of Roma in Romania. Country Assessment and the Roma Education Fund's Strategic Directions. Roma Education Fund.

Advancing Education of Roma in Romania. Country Assessment and the Roma Education Fund's Strategic Directions. Roma Education Fund 2007.

Calitate si echitate in invatamantul romanesc. Raport pentru Biroul International de Educatie, 2004. Ministerul Educatiei si Cercetarii [Quality and equity in the Romanian educational system. Report for the international bureau of education, 2004. Ministry of Education and Research].

Climatul interetnic în România în pragul integrării europene. Departamentul pentru Relatii Interetnice, Guvernul Romaniei, 2006 [The interethnic climate in Romania on the verge of European integration. Department for interethnic relations, Romanian Government, 2006].

Discriminarea rasială, etnică şi lingvistică în judeţele Alba, Bihor, Braşov, Caraş-Severin şi Sălaj. Liga ProEuropa, 2006 [Racial, ethnical and linguistic discrimination in the counties of Alba, Bihor, Braşov, Caraş-Severin and Sălaj].

Equal Access to Quality Education for Roma. Romania. Monitoring Report 2007. EU Monitoring and Advocacy Program. Education Support Program. Roma Participation Program. Open Society Institute. Budapest.

Etnobarometrul Rural 2006 [The Rural Ethno-barometer 2006], Fundatia pentru o Societate Deschisa Romania.

HG 430/2001 privind aprobarea Strategiei Guvernului României de îmbunătăţire a situaţiei romilor [Government's decision concerning the approval of the government's strategy for improvement in the situation of the Roma].

HG 829/2002 Planul naţional antisărăcie şi pentru promovarea incluziunii sociale, Guvernul României [National Plan Anti-Poverty and for the Promotion of Social Inclusion, Romanian Government].

Legea învăţământului, nr 84/1995 actualizata cu modificarile ulterioare la 20.07.2006. Parlamentul României [Education law No. 84/2005, Updated with further amendments on 20 July 2006 by the Romanian Parliament].

Legea privind asigurarea calităţii educaţiei. Nr. 87/2006. Parlamentul României [Law on ensuring the quality of education No. 87/2006. Romanian Parliament].

Notificare Nr 29323/2004 a Ministerului Educatiei si Cercetarii privind interzicerea segregarii scolare a copiilor romi [Notification No 29323/2004 of the Ministry of Education on the prohibition of educational segregation of Roma children].

Ordin privind interzicerea segregării şcolare a copiilor romi şi aprobarea Metodologiei pentru prevenirea şi eliminarea segregării şcolare a copiilor romi. Ministerul Educaţiei şi Cercetării. Cabinet Ministru. Nr 1540. 2007 [Order on the prohibition of educational segregation of Roma children and approval of the methodology for the prevention and elimination of educational segregation of Roma children. Ministry of Education and Research].

Ordin privind normele de încadrare şi de activitate ale mediatorului şcolar. Ministerul Educaţiei şi Cercetării. Cabinet Ministru. Nr 1539. 2007 [Order on the employment and activity standards of school mediator. Ministry of Education and Research].

Pactul Naţional pentru Educaţie. Administraţia Prezidenţială, martie 2008 [The National Pact for Education. Presidential Administration, March 2008].

Politici in educaţie pentru elevii în situaţie de risc şi pentru cei cu dizabilităţi din europa de sud est. Romania [Summary report and Chapter 8 Romania in *Education Policies for Students at Risk and those with Disabilities in South Eastern Europe: Bosnia-Herzegovina, Bulgaria, Croatia, Kosovo, FYR of Macedonia, Moldova, Montenegro, Romania and Serbia*] OECD, 2007.

POS-DRU Programul Operaţional Sectorial Dezvoltarea Resurselor Umane 2007–2013. Ministerul Muncii, Familiei şi Egalităţii de Şanse, 2007 [The operational sectoral programme for the developement of human resources 2007–2013, Ministry of Labour, Family and Equal Opportunity, 2007].

Raportul Comisiei Prezidenţiale pentru Analiza şi Elaborarea Politicilor din Domeniile Educaţiei şi Cercetării, Administraţia Prezidenţială, 2007 [Report of the Presidential Commission for the analysis and elaboration of education and research policies. Presidential Administration, 2007].

Raport privind implementarea de către România a Convenţiei-cadru pentru protecţia minorităţilor naţionale. Liga ProEuropa, 2005 [Report on the implementation by Romania of the framework-convention for the protection of national minorities].

Recensământul populaţiei 2002, Institutul Naţional de Statistică [2002 Population Census. National Statistics Institute].

Strategia de dezvoltare a învăţământului preuniversitar, Ministerul Educaţiei Naţionale, 2000 [Development strategy of pre-university education, Ministry of Education and Research].

Strategia Postaderare, 2007–2013 a Ministerului Educatiei si Cercetarii [Post-accession strategy 2007–2013 of the Ministry of Education and Research].

Information and documents regarding certain projects have been obtained by meetings or interviews with Aurora Ailincai, Costel Bercus, César Birzea, Elisabeta Danciu, Nicolae Gheorghe, Daniel Grebeldinger, Delia Grigore, Mihaela Jigău, Margareta Matache, Edita Nagy, Valentin Pepenel, Liliana Preoteasa, Gheorghe Sarau, Eugen Stoica and Mihaela Zatreanu.

Sweden

9
Sweden: Priority Education Policies in Times of Decentralisation and Individualisation

Guadalupe Francia and Lázaro Moreno Herrera

Introduction

The Swedish education system[1] has a long tradition of policies of educational equity (Wildt-Persson & Rosengren, 2001). The transition from a parallel education system[2] based on the division of social classes to a highly uniform system giving equal access to all children can be considered the starting point and the foundation of educational equity policies in Sweden. From 1962, with the introduction of a free public common school based on the idea of a 'school for all', a centralised policy of homogeneity to reduce educational differences between social classes and between sexes has dominated the Swedish educational system (Isling, 1980; Richardson, 2004; Utbildningsdepartementet, 1995).

Although the creation of common public schools can be regarded as an instrument of equity, such a policy for equality by homogenisation has led to injustice and inequality. While it led to raising the educational level of the Swedish population, this homogenisation failed to reduce differences between groups and has functioned as an instrument of legitimisation of differences in the academic achievement of students (Sjögren, 1995; Wallin, 2002). In addition, this policy has especially hampered the integration and achievement of ethnic minorities (Sjögren, 1995; Lahdenperä, 1997).

However, this uniformity was interrupted by decentralisation and the introduction of free choice established by the neo-liberal reforms of the late 1980s. The replacement of the concept of equality with the concept of equity in the legal texts introduced by this reform can be seen as a measure to ensure the acceptance of differences in the educational system. In these documents, free choice is even presented as an instrument to ensure an equitable education (Wallin, 2002; Francia, 2005). By the same logic, this neo-liberal policy considers the funding of private schools by the state as a mechanism to ensure plurality, quality and even equity in the education system. It emphasises the development of free choice and individualisation to match education to the needs and interests of children. Regarding the development of priority education policies (PEPs) for educational equity in Sweden, one can identify three major paths. The first form of PEP is designed for children with physical and mental disabilities. The second, which started as early as the 1960s, is that involving children of the Sami minority.[3] The third concerns PEP for immigrants. These include measures to promote language learning and integration of ethnic minorities in Swedish society (INCA, 2007; Skolverket, 2007a).

Priority education policies to reduce inequalities and injustices in Sweden are characterised by compensatory perspective legitimising of the strengthening of economic, education and human resources in unfavourable educational contexts. According to B. Lindensjö and U. P. Lundgren (2002) a compensatory perspective characterised the Swedish educational policy from the 1970s, when the struggle for educational equality began to be associated with a policy of redistribution of resources for the most disadvantaged students as well as introducing the concept of fairness in the discourse of educational policy.

The analysis of the PEP that we present in this chapter is limited to that targeting children of neighbourhoods affected by segregation, and the so-called Individual Programme. These PEPs aim to tackle disadvantage through the school system or targeted action programmes offering more resources to the groups mainly affected by educational failure in Sweden. The choice of the first type of PEP is motivated by the over-representation of children living in segregated neighbourhoods in the statistics for academic failure. The second type of PEP has been chosen because of the specific aim of the individual programme. It works as compensation to the school, giving special pedagogical support to students who have not acquired the formal competency necessary to begin the upper secondary school.

Strategies of educational equity

In agreement with the National Education Act (Utbildningsdepartementet, 1997), educational equity presupposes respect for the diversity of students and at the same time, achieving a level of satisfactory education for all citizens. To guarantee the right to fair education, Swedish school has general features that provide both equal standards and free choice for all students. To give readers a better understanding of PEP in Sweden we will present some general aspects that we consider important for the analysis of equity in the Swedish education system.

The integrated school without repetition

The Swedish school system is organised as a common public and free system. The National Education Act (Utbildningsdepartementet, 1997), the school ordinance (Utbildningsdepartementet, 1994a) and the national cur-riculum for compulsory school (Utbildningsdepartementet, 1994b) stipulate the educational support measures for students failing to attain the national objectives. In school practice, repeating a school year is rarely used as a strategy against educational failure. According to V. Dupriez and X. Dumay (2004), the educational systems of the Scandinavian countries are more suc-cessful in the fight against educational failure by using a school system for all children up to age 16. The practice of repeating a school year is often replaced by compensatory measures to help children at risk of educational failure.

Free education and distribution of resources

The National Education Act (Utbildningsdepartementet, 1997) established free education throughout the public school system. Access to free educa-tion is guaranteed regardless of gender, place of residence and the social and economic conditions of the child. The Swedish school features a free design in the broad sense, i.e. not limited only to access to school, but also involv-ing expenses for school materials, school meals and appropriate pedagogical and medical support for the pupils. This broad conception of free education also extends to private schools financed by the state. This funding requires private schools to ensure access for all children (Francia, 2005).

The National Education Act (Utbildningsdepartementet, 1997), the school ordinance (Utbildningsdepartementet, 1994a) and the curriculum of com-pulsory schooling (Utbildningsdepartementet, 1994b) state the need to accept variations and differences in the distribution of economic resources to ensure the adaptation of education to the specific needs of students.

Despite the regulations on the distribution of economic resources for students with special needs, the decentralisation of education, resulting from the neo-liberal reform of the eighties, has led to observed differences between municipalities in the possibilities of aid for students who require special support (Skolverket, 2007b).

The subjects 'Mother tongue tuition' and 'Swedish as a second language'

As an equity strategy, the National Education Act (Utbildningsdepartementet, 1997) established the right of students with foreign backgrounds to receive education in the subjects 'Mother tongue tuition'[4] and 'Swedish as a second language'[5].

According to statistics from The Swedish National Agency for Educa-tion (Skolverket, 2007b), the teaching of Mother tongue tuition included 15 per cent of all students in Sweden during the 2005–2006 academic year. The cities of Stockholm, Gothenburg and Malmö account for most of the students participating in this teaching. In the group of pupils entitled to receive education in the language of origin, Somali-speaking students record the highest participation (72.8%), followed by Albanian-speaking (67.6%), Arabic (66.5%), Persian (64%), Turkish (58.7%) and Kurdish (55.9%).[6] Those participating the least are English-speaking (49.8%) and Finnish-speaking (42.5%) students; 6.8 per cent of students received instruction in the subject 'Swedish as a second language' during the school year 2005–2006. In the group of students entitled to receive instruction in 'Swedish as a second language', students who speak Somali record the highest participation (70.8%), followed by Turkish-speaking students (63.4%), Kurdish (62.2%), Arabic (60.5%), Albanian (57.7%) and Persian (41.9%). Those participating the least are English-speaking (22.8%) and Finnish-speaking (22.3%) students (Skolverket).

A report by The Swedish National Agency for Education (Myndigheten för skolutveckling, 2004a) shows that students of foreign origin who follow the subject 'Swedish as a second language' are more affected by educational failure than those who study Swedish as a first language. The report also showed that only a small proportion of these students has recently arrived in Sweden. This report also recorded negative attitudes among students and parents towards the subject 'Swedish as a second language', which is often associated with discrimination and stigma.

Control over education

The transfer of the power of education from the state to municipalities and schools has led to differences in the interpretation of curriculum objectives and criteria for national qualification between schools. These differences are quite considerable: they may limit a fair standard of education at the national level (Francia, 1999, 2007a, 2007b; Gustafsson, 2006; Skolverket, 2004a, 2004b, 2004c). In addition, research shows that national targets are negotiated by schools and municipalities in relation to the social, religious and ethnic background, and gender of the children (Gustafsson, 2004; Högdin, 2007; Francia 2007a, 2007b). These negotiations risk reducing the level of demand of curricular aims with regard to the socially and ethnically marginalised. This trend, created by the low expectations of teachers towards the success of these groups of students or the desire to avoid conflicts with religious and ethnic minority parents in school, threatens equity at the expense of these students.

Policy documents regulating the Swedish education system limit the required national examinations to English, mathematics and Swedish. At the same time, they limit themselves to these three subjects as the requirement for approval to begin upper secondary school. This limitation has created a tendency to intensify education in these subjects, but at the expense of other disciplines. In order to post positive statistics, schools tend to concentrate their economic and pedagogical resources on the teaching of mathematics,

English and Swedish. In some cases, schools reorganise the normal schedule of lessons to provide extra training, which they hope will prevent students' failure in these three subjects. However, this is a practice at school level that is not stipulated in the policy documents regulating the education system at national level. On the contrary, it may be interpreted as a strategy for teachers to facilitate the entry of students to the upper secondary school and a strategy to prevent educational failure in the statistics of The Swedish National Agency for Education (Francia, 1999; Skolverket, 2001).

Because of the considerable differences regarding the interpretation and implementation of core curricular objectives at national, municipal and school level, the former Social Democratic government commissioned a revision of national curriculum and programmes of studies for the system of national tests. This revision has resulted in a report (Utbildningsdepartementet, 2007) proposing an increase in the control of academic achievement by introducing the national tests in the third, sixth and ninth years of compulsory schooling. In an interview with the newspaper *Dagens Nyheter* (Wijnbladh, 2007), the Conservative government Minister for Schools, Jan Björklund, also stressed the need to introduce national tests in all theoretical subjects.

Targeted PEP strategies

Although the Swedish education system could be regarded as one of the most effective with regard to academic achievement (Dupriez & Dumay, 2004), the percentage of educational failure is still considerable. Despite the fact that Sweden spends a considerable proportion of its GNP on education,[7] the recent statistics of The Swedish National Agency for Education (Skolverket, 2007c) show that 11.4 per cent of pupils in the later years of lower-secondary school lacked the formal skills required to start high school in spring 2007.

According to the Organisation for Economic Co-operation and Development (OECD) (2005), the increasing ethnic inequality should be seen as the 'Achilles heel' of the Swedish education system, students of foreign origin being overrepresented in the figures of educational failure. Sweden shows considerable variation between the results of foreign students and students of ethnic Swedish origin in the Programme for International Student Assessment (PISA) and Trends in International Mathematics and Science Study (TIMSS) evaluations.

These inequalities in relation to school success were behind our choice of PEP to improve the percentage of academic achievement and educational equity in the education system in Sweden. To exemplify these types of PEP, we will continue to make a presentation focused on children of the neighbourhoods affected by segregation and PEP targeted on students in the so-called individual programme.

PEPs focused on children in neighbourhoods affected by segregation

Priority education policies focused on children affected by suburban segregation are aimed at improving the educational situation of children in these marginalised areas.

The analysis of this PEP presented in our report includes the periods 2003–2005 and 2006–2007. Preventive in character, this PEP proposes a support policy for schools in segregated neighbourhoods. This PEP specifically targets children of foreign origin failing at school. These strategies also focus on children of foreign origin failing national objectives but living in non-segregated neighbourhoods.

According to The Swedish National Agency for Education (Myndigheten för skolutveckling, 2003a), this targeting strategy for priority education has been motivated by the poor academic outcome of students living in these neighbourhoods, as well as the unfavourable economic situation of the schools located there. This PEP mainly targets students born outside Sweden or children born in Sweden but whose parents were born abroad.

In the PEP strategy plan *Etnicitet, måluppfyllelse, utanförskap* [Ethnicity, goal fulfilment, exclusion] dated 2001, The Swedish National Agency for Education (*Skolverket*) specifically emphasised the failure of children of foreign origin in these segregated neighbourhoods and the need to positively change their educational situation. The action plan suggested focusing on the teaching of language in the subjects 'Swedish' and 'Swedish as a second language' (Myndigheten för skolutveckling, 2003b).

In 2003 the Social Democratic government required the Swedish National Agency for Education to restructure in order to separate responsibility for monitoring and supervising schools and municipalities from that of educational support to schools and towns. To this end, it set up a new organisation, The National Agency for School Development, and restricted the function of The Swedish National Agency for Education to control duties (Myndigheten för skolutveckling, 2003b). The new organisation came into force in early 2005.

Because of this administrative restructuring plan, the implementation of the *Etnicitet, måluppfyllelse, utanförskap* PEP was halted before it was completed. At the same time, Government Order U2003/1157/S gave The National Agency for School Development the responsibility for developing a PEP for children of foreign origin in segregated neighbourhoods (Myndigheten för Skolutveckling, 2003b).

To materialise this PEP, the National Agency for School Development has developed two educational support plans to improve the educational situation of neighbourhoods affected by segregation: the first for the period 2003–2005 and the second for the period 2006–2007.

In Government Order U2003/1157/S, the former Social Democratic government implemented a PEP including measures of educational support in areas affected by social and ethnic segregation in the period 2003–2005. This order highlights the needs of school development strategies. However, it also indicates the existence of factors outside the school in the failure of children of foreign origin, such as socio-economic status, levels of parental education, unemployment and length of residency in Sweden. The educational strategies established by this ordinance are mainly concentrated in the development of Swedish as a second language, mother tongue tuition and bilingual education (Myndigheten för skolutveckling, 2003b).

The Swedish National Agency for Education (Myndigheten för skolutveckling, 2003b) focuses on the positive attitude of municipalities and schools to these PEPs even if these resources are limited. These municipalities and schools appreciate the potential of continuing education for teachers offered by these actions in helping deal with the causes of student failure.

After an assessment of the 2003–2005 PEP, the former Social Democratic government intended to continue with its proposed strategies. In the proposed national budget for 2005 (Finansdepartementet, 2004), the government stipulated the development of experimental four-year bilingual education in the final grade of school (years 7–9) in selected schools in disadvantaged neighbourhoods. This was done on the strength of the success encountered by the 2003–2005 strategies for bilingual teaching in grades 1–6. The government also decreed an increase in economic resources for teaching the mother tongue. These resources were intended as the basis for development of a website about the teaching of the mother tongue (*Tema modersmål*) created by the National Agency for School Development. (Finansdepartementet, 2004).

In November 2005, the National Agency for School Development presented the plan *Bättre resultat och mins-kade skillnader – planering för mångfaldsarbetet* 2006–2007 [Better Results and Reduced Differences – Planning for the Work on Diversity 2006–2007], stating that the actions of the PEP focused on children affected by suburban segregation during the period 2006–2007 (Myndigheten för skolutveckling, 2005a).

Educational failure interpreted as a result of residential and ethnic segregation

The evaluation reports of the National Agency for School Development (Myndigheten för skolutveckling, 2003b, 2004b) on the preliminary result of the PEP for the period 2003–2005 refer to the effects of selected socio-economic and ethnic segregation to explain the situation of education in disadvantaged neighbourhoods. These areas are defined as enclaves of immigrants in Swedish society with disadvantaged social and economic conditions. However, these reports (Myndigheten för skolutveckling, 2003b, 2004b) emphasise that it was important not to be limited to a socio-economic explanation of educational failure, and to include the role of ethnic segregation and racial inequality in the analysis of the poor situation of pupils in these neighbourhoods. The National Agency for School Development highlights the existence of scientific research showing that the ethnic segregation of disadvantaged neighbourhoods does not mean the identification of an ethnic group in particular. On the contrary, this ethnic segregation involves a group of people with diverse life experiences and ethnic backgrounds, including very few people of ethnic Swedish origin. Ethnic segregation of neighbourhoods is a consequence not only of the socio-economic situation of their inhabitants, but a selection based on the racial characteristics of people. Persons of foreign origin with physical traits that are different from those of citizens of Nordic origin are often affected by residential segregation.

Given the negative effects of ethnic segregation, the National Agency for School Development stressed the need for PEP actions to develop teachers' and principals' understanding of the mechanisms of this negative stigma to ethnic background and change attitudes towards marginalised groups. This department also proposes that for PEPs targeting children of foreign origin, the educational action be adapted to the complex needs of students from neighbourhoods affected by segregation (för Myndigheten Skolutveckling, 2003b, 2004b).

The National Agency for School Development refers to the risk of associating academic failure with children of foreign origin. In order to avoid the tendency to define a child of foreign origin as a child with special needs in terms of educational support, the ordinance from the government requires that PEP targeted actions be based on a conscious evaluation to distinguish which types of students in the 'child of foreign origin' category are affected by educational failure, and why. It also proposes an analysis of the effects of categorisation in relation to the risk of stigmatising children (Myndigheten för skolutveckling, 2003b, 2004b).

During the period 2006–2007, the PEP plan *Bättre resultat och mins-kade skillnader – planering för mångfaldsarbetet* 2006–2007 stated that the PEP measures to improve academic achievement concern only ethnic segregation. The plan for 2006–2007 states that the PEP includes neither sexual segregation nor geographical segregation of neighbourhoods. However it stressed that priority support actions should be based on the need to assist students and not on the mere fact of their foreign origin (Myndigheten för Skolutveckling, 2005a).

The measures and financing of PEPs targeting children in segregated neighbourhoods

The politico-administrative and educational opinions and beliefs characterising the PEPs analysed present the actions required by training teachers, head teachers and municipal officials, and for sharing these positive educational experiences. According to the National Agency for School Development (Myndigheten för skolutveckling, 2003b, 2004b, 2005a), this PEP action is based on three fundamental principles: the prominence of curricular objectives and educational outcomes, long-term planning; the idea that the success of development work takes time and requires the influence and participation of teachers, principals, parents and students.

In this PEP, the National Agency for School Development notes that school segregation is primarily a social problem rather than a school problem. It also stresses that the PEP action should be carried out in collaboration with other development projects initiated by other government and municipal agencies in ethnically segregated neighbourhoods (Myndigheten för Skolutvec-kling, 2005a).

According to the National Agency for School Development (Myndigheten för skolutveckling, 2005a), the local perspective of municipalities must be taken into consideration because of the decentralisation of the education system that establishes the responsibility of municipalities on educational outcomes for students. This decentralisation limits the responsibility of the state in the development of educational objectives and monitoring work of the municipalities regarding the success of these objectives. In addition, the 2006–2007 PEP plan (Myndigheten för skolutveckling, 2005a) stressed that the support of the National Agency for School Development is limited to signing contracts for strategies to support the municipalities and the inventory of needs. In other words, this support is concentrated on the analysis stage of needs. The responsibility for this governmental organisation must be assessed as regards the capacity to assist municipalities in organising these PEP strategies. However, it is the municipalities that are responsible for monitoring and evaluation, and it is up to them to demonstrate improved academic performance in the final report.

The choice of municipalities participating in this PEP is based on the percentage of educational failure for students enrolled in the ninth class. During the period 2003–2005, 15 municipalities and 24 schools were chosen. Seven of these municipalities are also involved in the programme of priority assistance to disadvantaged neighbourhoods in large cities (*Storstadsprogrammet*), and nine were already in the project of development dialogue initiated by The Swedish National Agency for Education in the early 2000s. For the period 2006–2007, this department (Myndigheten för Skolutveckling, 2005a) chose 32 municipalities. The selected municipalities receive at least 18 per cent of children of foreign origin and attain an academic achievement of 75 per cent or less. Fourteen of these municipalities are located in the Stockholm area; 12 municipalities had already participated in the 2003–2005 PEP plan. The 2006–2007 supporting action plan includes approximately 100 schools at the compulsory and upper secondary level.

The 2006–2007 PEP also stressed the need for municipalities to develop their own strategies. This primarily concerns municipalities that do not have a significant number of foreign pupils. These municipalities, which tend to concentrate children with foreign backgrounds in certain schools, show a high percentage of educational failure among these students. This is the case for small and medium-sized municipalities with no economic and human resources to help schools in need of support (Myndigheten för skolutveckling, 2005a).

The priority assistance of PEPs targeting children from neighbourhoods affected by segregation is concentrated on the development of language education of pupils with foreign backgrounds. These priorities relate to the school subjects 'Swedish', 'Swedish as a second language' and 'mother tongue tuition' for children of foreign origin, as well as to the teaching of other subjects in the language of origin of these children, especially maths, reading and writing. This action also includes collaboration with the library in relation to the above-mentioned subjects (Myndigheten för Skolutveckling, 2005a).

This PEP (Myndigheten för skolutveckling, 2005a) focuses on support for educational processes and agreement with municipalities for development dialogues as a means of action.[8] The development dialogue method was chosen because of the good results that these strategies had shown in earlier educational development actions. PEPs targeting children affected by suburban segregation also include the development and updating of training for teachers and head teachers. Action related to PEPs for the period 2003–2005 was mainly concentrated in the educational training of school staff working in the early years of compulsory schooling. The plan of the PEPs for the period 2006–2007 also includes setting up a network for exchange of educational experience in which all schools and municipalities may participate. The plan also stipulates the development of training on the question of diversity of school employees in the National Agency for School Development (Myndigheten för skolutveckling, 2003b, 2004b, 2005a).

From a theoretical perspective, PEPs targeting children from neighbourhoods affected by segregation begin by arguing that student learning is more effective when the contents of various school subjects are taught in the language that students master best, which, for most students, means their mother tongue. The plan for the period 2006–2007 (Myndigheten för skolutveckling, 2005a) confirms that the possibilities of teaching subjects in the students' original language are limited because of the lack of teachers with the ability to teach bilingual students, or to speak and write in languages other than Swedish and English. The Swedish National Agency for Education considers the increase in the teaching of school subjects in the original language as an effective strategy for academic success. To this end, the National Agency for School Development has economic resources for professional teacher training for higher education graduates of foreign origin. Around 100 'academics' of foreign origin are expected to receive teacher training for two years. These scholars work as human resources for children with a language other than the original Swedish. This assistance will include targeted support for such children in mainstream education or individual education support in the original language, or to help children of foreign origin with their homework. These academics can work together with teachers to provide bilingual education in different school subjects (Myndigheten för skolutveckling, 2005a).

The plan for the period 2006–2007 also provides strategies for developing the competence of other categories of municipal and school employees, for example the heads of the municipal administration and vocational assistants.[9] To this end, days of teacher training on diversity are suggested, bringing together school teachers, principals, municipal leaders and developers; as well as days of teacher training on reading development for teachers and librarians. The plan also organises education exhibitions in Stockholm, Gothenburg and Malmö for pupils in the final class of compulsory school and upper secondary school in order to stimulate them to pursue higher education. The National Agency for School Development takes the same responsibility to create opportunity for interaction between researchers and teachers on the issue of diversity at university (Myn-digheten för skolutveckling, 2005a).

The plan for the period 2006–2007 also has economic resources to stimulate schools showing forms of efficient and innovative work. These schools, known as 'Schools of ideas' (*Idéskolorna*), must be schools that have succeeded in developing new methods and forms of educational work. This educational innovation must be effectively integrated into the regular schools and provide positive results in the long term. The National Agency for School Development selected 80 Schools of ideas for the year 2007.

The selection criteria for Schools of ideas relate to the effective work of these schools in relation to a holistic vision of learning; in the relationship between child and school staff and children's relationships with each other; in the co-operation of the school with parents and local society; and in language and communication. These Schools of ideas are to receive visits from staff of other schools wishing to train to work effectively and benefit from their ideas. They must present their work on a website and they are required to answer questions about their forms of work (Myndighe för skolutveckling, 2007b).

For 2004 the total budget for the National Agency for School Development (Myndigheten för Skolut-veckling, 2005b) was 335 million crowns (about 36 million euros). Of this total, 3.5 million were set aside for the priority education activities of nursery schools and recreational schools in the neighbourhoods affected by segregation, while 22.7 million were allocated to priority education measures related to children and youth in these segregated neighbourhoods. There was also an increase in economic resources for actions relating to equity and diversity, from 8.7 million crowns in 2003 to 19.3 million during 2004.

As regards the year 2005, the total budget for the National Agency for School Development (Myndighe för skolutveckling, 2006) was 341 million crowns. Of this, 42.2 million were used in relation to measures of educational priority for children and young people in segregated neighbourhoods.

According to the National Agency for School Development (Myndigheten för skolutveckling, 2005a), the total sum of money intended for the actions of the plan for the period 2006–2007 was 225,300,000 million crowns. Among other activities, it redistributes the economic resources to support the development of the dialogue process (63 million crowns); the development of the quality of education in the mother tongue, Swedish as a second language and reading (54 million crowns); the development of upper secondary schools (19 million crowns) and the Schools of ideas (16 million crowns); support for development activities (20 million crowns); support for the municipality of Malmö (10 million crowns); and external support activity for the development of the dialogue process (10 million crowns).

The results of the PEP for children of neighbourhoods affected by segregation

The National Agency for School Development (Myndigheten för skolutveckling, 2005c, 2006) refers to evaluations confirming the success of the PEP with respect to strengthening the work of pre-schools. These assessments also consider the measures to improve working conditions for the language development of children as being effective. In addition, they underline the effectiveness of the measures to develop co-operation between pre-schools and compulsory schools and that between libraries and compulsory schools. Furthermore, the development dialogues have resulted in positive effects on the training and ability of school personnel regarding the teaching of Swedish as a second language. According to this agency (Myndigheten för skolutveckling, 2005c), work with development dialogues has also assisted municipalities in considering their needs and the necessary steps to improve the educational situation of students at risk of educational failure.

The National Agency for School Development (Myndigheten för skolutveckling, 2005a, 2005c 2006, 2007b) considers that the Schools of ideas project contributed to the dissemination of positive experiences on the work of the schools with the national curriculum objectives. An evaluation of the Schools of ideas project (Gisselberg, Maraldi & Lindblom, 2007) shows that this project has helped develop academic work on the ethnic diversity of schools. At the same time the evaluation noted that teachers in some Schools of ideas paradoxically lacked knowledge on the problem of, and research into, diversity. The annual meetings of the Schools of ideas organised by the National Agency for School Development were positively assessed by the schools.

Even though one of the fundamental principles of this PEP is the emphasis on curricular objectives and educational outcomes, The National Agency for School Development (Myndigheten för skolutveckling, 2005a, 2005b, 2005c) underlines the difficulty of establishing the effects of the PEP with respect to improving the academic achievement of foreign students in the neighbourhoods affected by segregation. This agency (Myndigheten för skolutveckling, 2003b, 2004b, 2005a) also emphasises the need for long-term planning and urges one to keep in mind that the success of development work takes time.

In this way, we can see a certain amount of ambivalence on the part of the National Agency for School Development regarding the possibilities of assessing the effects of this PEP in the educational outcomes of children in areas affected by segregation. In addition, it should be noted that The National Agency for School Development, on their website dedicated to teaching the mother tongue (för Myndigheten Skolutveckling, 2007c), refers to sociological research problematising the use of students' school results as an instrument for measuring the effectiveness of schools in neighbourhoods affected by segregation. This research (Stigendal, 2001) gives an example of the efficiency of a school in a suburban marginalised area that is working to improve the competency of teachers to appreciate and enjoy the benefits of the ethnic diversity of students. Although this research does not reject the students' results in the form of marks as a measurement of success, it highlights the work of the schools in developing forms of active student and parent participation as an important variable in the analysis of the academic achievement of schools in marginalised areas.

Although we agree with the problematisation of student grades as the only strategy for measuring the success and effectiveness of schools, it seems essential not to underestimate the role of the educational performance of children from marginalised neighbourhoods in the analysis of this PEP. Insofar as the poor academic outcome of students living in these areas remains a central focus of this PEP, we consider the analysis of the percentage of students reaching the national target to be very important.

For this purpose, and to follow the development of academic municipalities participating in the actions of PEP developed by The National Agency for School Development, we have selected the municipalities that participated in the PEP during the periods 2003–2005 and 2006–2007. These municipalities were Botkyrka, Gothenburg, Huddinge, Haninge, Malmö, Stockholm and Örebro.

From the statistics of The Swedish National Agency for Education[10] (Skolverket 2007d), we can see a downward trend in the percentage of pupils of foreign origin born outside Sweden, both in selected municipalities and at national level during the period 2002–2006.[11] At the same time, these statistics for the period 2002–2006 (Skolverket 2007d) show some increase in most municipalities, and at national level, of the percentage of pupils of foreign

Table 9.1   Success rates of students in compulsory schooling tests

Municipality	Students attaining school objectives in 9th grade, 2002 (%)	Students attaining school objectives in 9th grade, 2006 (%)	Evaluation of students' success, comparing 2006 with 2002 (%)
Botkyrka	68	64	−4
Gothenburg	74	73	−1
Haninge	59	64	+5
Huddinge	75	78	+3
Malmö	68	67	−1
Stockholm	72	74	+2
Örebro	70	74	+4
National average	75	76	+1

Source: Statistics from The Swedish National Agency for Education (Skolverket, 2007d).

origin born in Sweden.[12] The municipalities of Haninge and Huddinge, however, recorded a small decrease in this group of students.[13]

At the same time, if we analyse the statistical results from the years 2002 and 2006, there was a degree of variation as regards pupils' results. Three municipalities (Huddinge, Haninge and Örebro) showed some improvement in the percentage of students who attained the academic goals. Four municipalities (Botkyrka, Gothenburg, Malmö and Stockholm) experienced some reduction in the percentage of students attaining the national objectives. The national average showed a small improvement (see Table 9.1).

If we therefore compare the figures for the percentage of children of foreign origin and those for students' progress, we can see that some municipalities recorded a decrease in the proportion of pupils attaining the objectives of compulsory school, although the percentage of foreign children born outside of Sweden decreased. This is the case for the larger cities of Malmö and Gothenburg.[14] The municipality of Botkyrka, with an increase in the percentage of pupils of foreign origin born outside of Sweden, also shows a considerable number of failures.[15] The municipalities of Haninge and Huddinge, which show an increase in the academic success of students, also register a considerable decrease in the percentage of pupils of foreign origin born either in Sweden[16] or outside Sweden.[17] The municipality of Örebro also shows some improvement in students' academic achievement, even though it also shows a decrease in numbers of students of foreign origin born outside of Sweden and an increase in numbers of those of foreign origin born in Sweden. The larger city of Stockholm also shows an improvement in results even though it does not show any change in the number of pupils of foreign origin during the period 2002–2006.

At the same time, if we compare the figures for educational failure in these municipalities, we can see that the percentage of academic achievement continues to be low in the municipalities of Botkyrka (64%), Haninge (64%) and Malmö (67%) in relation to the national average (76%). The municipalities of Gothenburg (73%), Stockholm (74%) and Örebro (74%) recorded very similar figures to those at the national level, while the municipality of Huddinge (78%) recorded a figure slightly higher than the national average.

The Schools of ideas were chosen for their innovative work with diversity but, taking into account the academic performance of students, the criteria used by The National Agency for School Development for selecting some Schools of ideas as examples of school practice may be called into question. For example Hulstaskolan in the municipality of Stockholm was chosen as a School of ideas during the period 2005–2007. However, the percentage of educational failure in that school continued to increase. According to statistics from The Swedish National Agency for Education (Skolverket 2007d), the percentage of students in that school reaching national targets had fallen from 41 per cent in 2003 to 36 per cent in 2006. Another example is Annerstaskolan, located in the municipality of Huddinge, whose percentage of success dropped from 60 per cent in 2003 to 52 per cent in 2006 (Skolverket, 2007d). The same situation was noted for Internationella Skolan in Nacka municipality, in which the percentage was down from 64 per cent in 2003 to 46 per cent in 2006 (Skolverket, 2007d).

We are aware that it is difficult to explain the direct relationship of the PEP to the figures recording school success/failure in these municipalities. However, we consider that these figures allow us to gain some idea of the current educational situation of these municipalities and schools involved in PEP plans during the periods 2003–2005 and 2006–2007.

An evaluation of the results of the 2006–2007 PEP is planned for 2008. An expert academic from the higher education centre Mälardalens högskola will be in charge, and the evaluation report will be presented in December 2008. However, the budget proposal for 2007 did not grant the economic resources to allow The National Agency for School Development to continue with this PEP to the same extent as previously. The National Agency for School Development received economic resources to implement and strengthen a PEP to help pupils of foreign origin recently arrived in Sweden. Given the considerable differences between municipalities as regards the opportunity to provide an equitable education for these children, the National Agency for School Development (Myndigheten för Skolutveckling, 2007d) is in the process of developing a PEP plan particularly targeted at these groups of children of foreign origin. The strategies of this plan are intended primarily to inform municipalities and schools of the rights of children recently arrived in Sweden to receive an equitable education. They aim to ensure a quality introduction to school for all children of foreign origin that have recently arrived in Sweden. These strategies emphasise the training and the ability of school staff regarding the teaching of Swedish as both second language and mother tongue, the relation between the school and families and the individualisation of educational support for these children.

Priority education policies for the Individual Programme

The Individual Programme

The Education Reform of the 1990s stipulated three years of schooling at upper secondary level for all pupils who have finished compulsory school, whichever upper secondary programme they choose. This prolongation of the upper secondary school aims to make access to further studies easier, whatever the programme choices the pupils make. This reform has even stipulated the creation of one programme target for pupils who leave compulsory school without the necessary qualification to begin upper secondary school (the Individual Programme).

This programme provides special education for pupils lacking the necessary qualifications to enter one of the national programmes of the upper secondary school. Even though the Individual Programme comes within the aegis of the upper secondary school, it provides help and education support for pupils to reach the compulsory school competence necessary for basic eligibility for secondary school.

As a consequence of the compulsory school's failure to provide eligibility for secondary upper school, the number of pupils enrolled in the individual programme is significant. According to the Swedish National Agency for Education (Skolverket, 2003, 2004), foreign-background pupils, those with hyperactivity and concentration problems and those with Asperger's syndrome are overrepresented in this programme. The number of pupils enrolled on the Individual Programme may differ significantly between municipalities – as many as 20 per cent of the total number of pupils in certain municipalities.

Even if the majority of the pupils on the Individual Programme lack the necessary qualification to begin upper secondary school, this group is heterogeneous as far as their level of knowledge is concerned.

According to the Swedish National Agency for School Development (Myndigheten for Skolutveckling 2007e), a certain proportion of Individual Programme pupils are said to be 'tired of school'; in other words, they have lost the motivation to continue studying. Other pupils have this motivation but they have considerable learning difficulties that demand limited or prolonged educational support. However, some pupils on the Individual Programme have reached the compulsory school competency necessary for basic eligibility for secondary school but they have dropped out of the national programmes in upper secondary school.[18] Another category of pupils has chosen the Individual Programme while waiting for a place on a better programme (Myndigheten för Skolutveckling, 2007e).

According to the statistics from the Swedish National Agency for School Development (Myndigheten for Skolutveckling 2007e), the proportion of pupils in the Individual Programme was 7.4 per cent of the total number attending upper secondary school in the academic year 2005–2006; 14.5 per cent of the pupils in the first academic year of upper secondary level followed these programme courses.

Fifty-seven per cent of pupils on the Individual Programme were boys and 43 per cent girls; 37 per cent of pupils were born outside Sweden or had parents born outside Sweden. This shows an overrepresentation of foreign-background pupils on the Individual Programme, taking into consideration the fact that only 15 per cent of the total number of pupils in upper secondary school have a foreign background.

PEP strategies for the Individual Programme

Even though the Individual Programme was created as a strategy to cope with pupils' learning problems, scientific research (Hultqvist, 2001) shows it to be inefficient as far as this goal is concerned. It does not succeed in giving pupils the compulsory school competency necessary for basic eligibility for other secondary upper school programmes. According to statistics from the Swedish National Agency for Education (Skolverket, 2007b), only 38 per cent of pupils beginning the Individual Programme in autumn 2004 had access to upper secondary school in autumn 2005. The degree of success differs between municipalities. Small municipalities are more successful than the big cities like Stockholm and Gothenburg. Pupils on the Individual Programme more often interrupt their studies as compared with pupils on other programmes: 27.9 per cent in the Individual Programme and 7.3 per cent in other programmes. According to the Swedish National Agency for School Development (Skolverket, 2007e), the percentage of pupils starting the Individual Programme in 2002 and having completed upper secondary school for four years was only 19.1.

At the same time, a research study (Broady 200) shows differences concerning the efficacy of this programme, in terms of its success in giving pupils the compulsory school competency necessary for basic eligibility to other programmes in secondary upper school. The Individual Programme has, to a large extent, failed to give the educational support required for foreign-background pupils in Sweden who had never attended compulsory school. In contrast, this programme was more efficient regarding pupils who had come directly from Swedish compulsory school.

According to Broady (2000), the failure of the Individual Programme as an equity strategy is a consequence of the upper secondary school reforms implemented in the 1990s. These reforms, which stipulated three years of schooling at upper secondary for all pupils, have increased the academic content of the curriculum subjects, in particular Swedish, English and mathematics. This importance attached to academic subjects for all pupils has negatively affected the chances of educational success for young people in socially and ethnically disadvantaged groups.

In order to make the Individual Programme more efficient, the Government proposed to increase economic resources for the year 2004. The government proposal for the year 2005, 'Knowledge and quality – eleven steps for the development of the upper secondary school', pointed out the need to improve the educational quality of the Individual Programme. This proposal even stipulates that this programme must be full-time, and not part-time as previously. This limitation in instruction time has hindered pupils in receiving an equitable education, in comparison with pupils on other programmes. In order to help municipalities increase instruction time, the government awarded an annual economic grant of 425 million Swedish crowns (Utbildningsdepartment, 2004). This government proposal ordered the Swedish National Agency for School Development to draw up a plan for the development of the educational quality of this programme with the following goals: develop the competency of the educational work carried out by the municipalities and schools regarding the quality of education; support the municipalities in planning full-time instruction for the Individual Programme; stimulate the dissemination of positive and effective experiences concerning the educational quality of the Individual Programme; and follow up the municipalities' work regarding the organisation and funding of the Individual Programme (Utbildningsdepartementet, 2004).

Having a remediation goal, the PEPs concerning the Individual Programme function as compensatory action aimed at the educational success of pupils who do not have the necessary qualifications to start upper secondary school. One of the more important strategies of the PEPs for the Individual Programme is the development of the teaching skills of teachers and head teachers. To this end, the Swedish National Agency for School Development has created a website providing educational material, as well as reports and conferences organised on this subject. Two websites have been created as meeting places for the municipal authorities of 191 municipalities. A national conference on 'Pupils who recently have immigrated to Sweden' and another on 'School Development' have been organised. Nineteen 'regional networks' aimed at stimulating the exchange of educational experiences have been created and funded by the Swedish National Agency for School Development. The staff in charge of these networks have also received further educational training at university level (Myndigheten för Skolutveckling, 2007e).

The Swedish National Agency for School Development (Myndigheten för Skolutveckling, 2007e) points out the impossibility of measuring the short-term effects of these PEPs concerning pupils' academic results within the Individual Programme. However, the municipalities are favourable to the organisation of conferences and meeting places as strategies for the development of educational competencies.

According to the Swedish National Agency for Education (Skolverket, 2007e), the Individual Programme can function as a possible support for pupils at an individual level, but this programme contributes to segregation in compulsory and upper secondary school at national level. The number and the quality of hours of instruction on this programme still differ significantly from one municipality to another, even though an improvement in the length of instruction time has been recorded in the majority of municipalities. In some municipalities, the Individual Programme has become a place where the compulsory school or the municipalities can transfer pupils considered problematic instead of taking responsibility for their learning.

Segregation, decentralisation and individualisation

The PEPs of the Swedish National Agency for School Development analysed in this rapport focus on the development of the formal competencies of teachers, head teachers and municipal officials, and on the dissemination of positive teaching experiences. However, it is difficult to measure the direct effects of these PEPs on the educational failure of children from socially and ethnically underprivileged groups over the short term. At the same time, it is necessary to give some thought to the consequences of choosing to have PEPs target only those groups and programmes that are most affected by educational failure.

Sweden has a long tradition of equity strategies targeting children of foreign background, without any positive result. A research study on structural segregation in Swedish society shows that even education systems tend to reduce groups and individual differences to cultural differences that are not clearly defined and established. This structural segregation often tends to develop diversity-based educational policies limited to schools with a number of pupils of foreign background instead of developing a general diversity policy for all schools. This policy of diversity has often pointed out the shortcomings of pupils of foreign background and the problems in learning Swedish. Insofar as these children are considered as 'exceptions', they have often been the main or exclusive target of PEPs.

Targeting children of foreign background is problematic because it conceals a reproduction process of the social and educational inequalities and a domination of ethnic minorities by the Swedish majority. The Swedish diversity policy has often used an essentialist discourse concerning cultural differences that limit individuals' and groups' behaviours deterministically. The use of categorisations and stereotypes regarding the different ethnic groups is an instrument often used during periods when the education system is affected by claims for both efficiency and reduction of economic resources (Integrations- och jämställdhetsdepartement, 2006).

The choice of PEPs that stipulate improvement in language teaching strategies for children of foreign background is based on educational research. This research shows the positive effects of mother tongue education and teaching Swedish as second language. However, this educational vision is never questioned in the PEP plans that target children from disadvantaged and segregated neighbourhoods. Even though an evaluation (Myndigheten för Skolutveckling, 2004a) of the curricular subject 'Swedish as second language' calls into question the existence of a curricular subject with goals that target only this category of pupil, this PEP does not question the existence of different syllabuses and evaluation criteria for different pupil groups.

Measures whose target is to develop the instruction of different curricular subjects in the pupils' mother tongue can be seen as a strategy for improving pupils' learning of educational content. However, mother tongue education is a strategy that targets the more disadvantaged social and ethnic groups, for example children whose mother tongue is a language such as Somali, Albanian or Arabic. In contrast, minorities that are more integrated into Swedish society do not take part in mother tongue education to the same extent. A more in-depth discussion on the effects of the expansion of teaching different curricular subjects in pupils' mother tongue is therefore necessary, starting out from an analysis of pupils' social class and mother tongue. More thought needs to be given to the risks of PEP strategies that aim to promote equality via an organisational and educational separation of pupils from socially and ethnically disadvantaged groups.

In the PEP plans for the periods 2003–2005 and 2006–2007, the measures implemented are focused more on reducing educational failure as a result of ethnic segregation than that as a consequence of the interaction of ethnicity with social class and gender. This ethnic segregation discourse has consequently encouraged development strategies focused on the teaching of the academic subjects 'Swedish as second language' and 'mother tongue'. However, the fact that these strategies have not been problematised prohibits thinking about the risks of deeper stigmatisation of the most disadvantaged social groups.

The restriction of the support provided by the Swedish National Agency for School Development to the stage of analysing the needs for the 2006–2007 PEP is justified by the decentralisation of the education system, because the municipalities are responsible for the improvement of pupils' academic results. As a result, the role of the state in this PEP is restricted to providing support for municipalities during the period of organisation of these improvement strategies. This means that the municipalities, and not the state, are responsible for the success or failure of these PEPs.

The PEP plans that target children from segregated neighbourhoods during the periods 2003–2005 and 2006–2007 refer to the negative consequences of school decentralisation, when they point out the existence of considerable differences between the economic municipal resources targeting the education of the children with foreign backgrounds. However, they lack deeper consideration of the consequences of the interpretation and the way national goals are adapted to the pupils' social class at the school level.

This thinking is all the more important because the decentralisation of the school in Sweden implemented by the neo-liberal reform of the 1990s is likely to create different goals for different social and ethnic groups. Research studies (Skolverket 2004b, 2004c, 2006; Perez Pietro, Sahlström, Calander, Karlsson & Mia Heikkilä 2003) in fact already show a tendency to increase segregation and inequalities in the Swedish education system concerning the decentralisation process. A considerable variation has been recorded regarding the scope of the access of different municipalities to economic and human resources ensuring equitable education.

J.E. Gustafson's research study (2006) shows, for example, the increase in school segregation and inequalities concerning the resources made available to school staff since 1992.

This research argues that schools and disadvantaged suburbs have less scope for guaranteeing an equitable education in keeping with the declaration of the rights of the child. It also shows that the percentage of teachers with formal educational training and the pupil–teacher ratio have dramatically decreased since the 1990s.

Even though pupils' academic results are a variable that is problematic in use (Gustafsson, 2006), they do allow some kind of understanding of what is happening with pupils' standard of knowledge. To this end, a research study by the Swedish National Agency for School Development (2006) shows that decentralisation and privatisation of the Swedish school system has increased the variation between schools regarding pupils' academic results and educational segregation.

The extreme tendency to individualise can be considered as a form of decentralisation of the Swedish education system, because it means transferring responsibility for learning from teachers to the pupils. However, this strategy of equity based on extreme individualisation, a child-driven curriculum, free choice and educational flexibility is likely to increase, rather than reduce, the differences in academic results between various school groups.

M. Dovemark's research (2004) shows, for example, that the individualisation of teaching on the basis of a child-driven curriculum that has characterised the Swedish education system has seldom been problematised in Sweden. This vision, based on the exaltation of flexibility and free choice, limits the role of teachers to supporting and helping pupils' independent work. However, this extreme individualisation only deepens the differences in attitudes of various social groups to school work. Given that pupils are responsible for their own learning, they tend to make choices concerning school work and curricular goals depending on the level of their social class. In addition, research by the Swedish National Agency for School Development (Vinterek, 2006) confirms that since the 1990s individualised school work has increased at the expense of teaching addressed to all the pupils in the classroom. This explosion of individualised work as a teaching method has not allowed for any variation in teaching forms in Swedish schools.

The vogue for individualisation has resulted in reducing the direct contact that teachers have with their pupils during the learning process, which in turn has led to a deterioration in the pupils' learning environment and has not been seriously questioned by educational research in Sweden. The goal of the use of individualisation at school level is also diffuse and unclear. In addition, the results of individualisation are difficult to evaluate.

Conclusions

The PEP plans of the Swedish National Agency for School Development are based on research studies that stress the need to pay heed to the special effects of the process of ethnic stigmatisation in the development of segregation in disadvantaged neighbourhoods. However, the concentration of political and pedagogical action concentrated on the question of ethnic segregation also carries risks.

The strategies that aim at equality in results via the organisational and educational separation of pupils have failed to reduce the differences in academic results between pupils. The introduction of a special syllabus for teaching 'Swedish as second language' aiming to guarantee a good command of the Swedish language for some groups of pupils of foreign background is likely to increase the level of discrimination that affects these pupils. Similarly, the existence of the Individual Programme, as a compensatory strategy providing eligibility for upper secondary school, has not succeeded in guaranteeing equality in results for children who leave compulsory school without the necessary qualifications to start upper secondary school. This programme is likely to act as a kind of 'dumping ground' for pupils considered as 'problematic' or 'difficult' in compulsory or upper secondary school.

The PEPs targeting groups and programmes analysed in our report do not take into account the negative effects of the extreme decentralisation and individualisation of the Swedish education system. They run the risk of ignoring the combined effects of social class, gender and ethnicity on educational failure. Neither do they take into consideration the negative effects of a perspective that aims to limit education policies for diversity to pupils of foreign background only, instead of developing a general diversity policy for all pupils in the Swedish education system.

We are lacking an analysis of the effects of individualisation and decentralisation related to the social class and gender of pupils of foreign background and to those on the Individual Programme. Consequently, the PEPs analysed in this chapter are nothing more than another example of the tradition based on cultural ethnic differences, dominant in Swedish education policy over the last 20 years. For this reason, even these PEPs are also likely to fail in attaining the goal of educational equity in Sweden.

Acknowledgements

We would like to thank Donald Broady (University of Uppsala) for his critical reading of the French version of this text.

Notes

1. The Swedish public school system consists of the compulsory school and other forms of optional education. Compulsory education includes school, Sami school and compulsory school for the mentally handicapped. Schools that are optional are pre-school class, upper secondary school, municipal adult education and education for mentally handicapped adults (Skolverket, 2007a).
2. The parallel system of education previously included the folk schools (*Folkskolan*) created in 1842 to provide literacy classes and schools for privileged social groups (*Realskole*). It also included schools for girls and a considerable number of private schools. The parallel system disappeared in 1962 with the introduction of the common school (*grundskola*) for all children irrespective of social origin and sex. The introduction of the common public school resulted in a considerable reduction in private schools and the disappearance of girls' schools during the 1970s (Richardson, 2004).
3. The Sami are an indigenous minority that live in the territory of Lapland shared between Sweden, Norway, Finland and Russia. This minority speak the Sami language as the language of origin.
4. Students with mother tongue other than Swedish are entitled to study their language in compulsory school and upper secondary school. These children also have the right to support in their original language in learning other subjects, if required. Participation in studying the language of origin is voluntary, but municipalities are obliged by law to organise such education (Skolverket, 2007a).
5. Students whose mother language is not Swedish are entitled to learn Swedish as a second language as a school discipline. The introduction of a school subject specially designed and reserved for these groups of children is aimed at helping these pupils to develop their language, as well as being daily means of communication for appropriating knowledge in the subjects taught at school. A curriculum has been specially created for this subject (Skolverket, 2007a).
6. It will be observed that minorities speaking Somali, Arabic, Kurdish, Turkish and Persian are affected more by segregation in Swedish society than the Finnish and English minorities. A report by The National Integration Agency (Integrationsverket, 2004) shows that foreigners of African and Asian origin are affected by structural discrimination in their working life. Employment levels of these ethnic groups are lower than those of other ethnic groups, irrespective of the time spent in Sweden, education, marital status and gender.
7. The share of GNP for the education sector in 2004 was 8%. Of the total GNP for education, the highest percentage (35%) was given to compulsory education (SCB, 2006).
8. The Swedish National Agency for Education (Myndigheten för Skolutveckling, 2007a) describes development dialogues as conversations in which different views are respected. These dialogues are based on the exchange of ideas and experiences between people involved in school practice (school head teachers, teachers) and academic researchers. These dialogues also enable the dissemination

of these experiences to school practice and scientific knowledge between schools participating in these meetings.

9. Each school has a vocational assistant responsible for informing students about the choice of studies and professions (e.g. choice of subjects at secondary level).

10. These statistics from The Swedish National Agency for Education were obtained with the statistical model established by SALSA. This model aims to analyse the academic performance of pupils in municipalities and schools with attention given to their social and ethnic composition (Skolverket, 2007d). The analysis by this model also takes into account the effect of value added, estimated impact of gender, place of birth and ethnicity of students and the educational level of their parents.

11. The percentage of the national average for pupils of foreign origin born outside Sweden was 9% and 7% for 2002 and 2006, respectively.

12. The percentage of the national average for pupils of foreign origin born outside Sweden was 5% and 6% for 2002 and 2006, respectively.

13. The percentage of pupils of foreign origin born outside Sweden in the municipalities of Huddinge and Haninge was 14% and 13% for 2002 and 2006, respectively.

14. The percentage of pupils of foreign origin born outside Sweden in the municipality of Malmö was 27% and 20% for 2002 and 2006, respectively; the corresponding figures for Gothenburg were 18% and 13%, respectively.

15. The percentage of pupils of foreign origin born in Sweden in the municipality of Botkyrka was 29% and 31% for 2002 and 2006, respectively.

16. The percentage of pupils of foreign origin born outside Sweden in the city of Haninge declined by 8% to 6% and 14% to 13% during the period 2002–2006; and in the municipality of Huddinge from 9% to 8% during the same period.

17. The percentage of pupils of foreign origin born in Sweden in the municipalities of Haninge and Huddinge decreased from 14% to 13% during the period 2002–2006.

18. Upper secondary school consists of 17 national programmes, which last for 3 years. All programmes provide broad instruction and basic eligibility to further education at the higher education level. Upper secondary courses comprise national programmes, specially designed programmes and Individual Programmes

Bibliography

Scientific documents

BROADY D. (2000). 'Inledning [Introduction]'. In D. BROADY (ed.), *Skolan under 1990. Sociala förutsättningar och utbildningsstrategier* [The School during the 1990s. Social conditions and education strategies]. Sociology of Education and Culture Research Rapport. Nr 27 SEC, ILU Uppsala universitet. Retrieved February 16, 2008 from: http://www.skeptron.uu.se/broady/sec/archives.htm.

DOVEMARK M. (2004). *Ansvar – flexibilitet – valfrihet. En etnografisk studie om en skola i förändring* [Responsibilty – flexibility – free choice. An ethnographic study about a school undergoing change]. Göteborg: ACTA (Göterborg Studies in Educational Sciences 233).

DUPRIEZ V. & DUMAY X. (2004). 'L'égalité dans les systèmes scolaires: effet école ou effet société?' [Equality in education systems: an effect of schooling or of society?]. *Les Cahiers de recherche en éducation et formation*, no. 31.

FRANCIA G. (1999). *Policy som text och som praktik. En analys av likvärdighetsbegreppet i 1990-talets utbildningsreform för det obligatoriska skolväsendet.* [Policy as text and as practice. An analysis of the equity concept in the Education Reform for the compulsory school during the 1990s]. Doctoral dissertation. Stockholm: Pedagogiska institutionen, Stockholms universitet.

FRANCIA G. (2005). 'La marche ver l'équité en Suède' [The pursuit of equity in Sweden]. In M. DEMEUSE *et al.* (eds), *Vers une école juste et efficace. Vingt-six contributions sur les systèmes d'enseignement et de formation.* [Towards fair and efficient schooling. Twenty-six contributions to the analysis of learning and training systems]. Brussels: De Boeck Université (Économie, société, région), pp. 25–46.

FRANCIA G. (2007a). 'Religiösa friskolor, en fråga om rättvisa' [Religious Indepedent School, a question of justice]. In J. BERGLUND & G. LARSSON (eds), *Religiösa friskolor i Sverige: Historiska och nutida perspektiv* [Religious Independent Schools in Sweden. A historical and modern perspective]. Lund: Studentlitteratur.

FRANCIA G. (2007b). *The Negotiation of the Right of the Child to Education in the Name of Religion.* Paper presented to the conference *Religion on the Borders: New Challenges in the Academic Study of Religion.* Södertörn: Södertörn University College, April 19–22, 2007.

GISSELBERG K., LINDBLOM S. & MÅRALD G. (2007). *Utvärdering av projektet Idéskolor för mångfald. Delrapport 2* [Evaluation of the Project School of Ideas for Diversity] Partial Report 2]. Umeå: Umeå Center for Evaluation Research (ECER). August 2007. Retrieved October 7, 2007 from: http://ideskola.skolutveckling.se/pdf/Delrapport2.pdf.

GUSTAFSSON, K. (2004). *Muslimsk skola, svenska villkor* [Islamic schools, Swedish conditions]. Doctoral thesis. Umeå: Boréa Bokförlag.

GUSTAFSSON, J. E. (2006). *Barns utbildningssituation* [Children's educational situation]. Stockholm: Rädda Barnen.

HULTQVIST, E. (2001). *Segregerande intergrering: en studie av gymnasieskolans individuella programmet* [Segregative Integration: a research study of the Individual Programme at the upper secondary school]. Stockholm: HLS förlag.

HÖGDIN, S. (2007). *Utbildning på (o)lika villkor: om kön och etnisk bakgrund i grundskolan* [Differences in education: About gender and ethnicity at the Compulsory School]. Stockholm: Institutionen för socialt arbete, Stockholms universitet.

INCA (2007). *Country description: Sweden.* Retrieved May 10, 2007 from: http://www.inca.org.uk/index.html.

ISLING, Å. (1980). *Kampen för och mot en demokratisk skola* [The Struggle for a Democratic School]. Stockholm: SOBER Förlag.

LAHDENPERÄ, P. (1997). *Invandrarbakgrund eller skolsvårigheter?: En textanalytisk studie av åtgärdsprogramme för elever med invandrarbakgrund* [Foreign Background or School Problem? A study of text analysis about educational support programmes for Foreign Background pupils]. Stockholm: HLS.

LINDENSJÖ, B. & LUNDGREN, U. P. (2002). *Utbildningsreformer och politisk styrning* [Education Reforms or political steering] Stockholm: HLS Förlag.

OECD (2005). *Equity in Education Thematic Review. Country Note.* Retrieved September 2007 from: https://www.oecd.org/dataoecd/10/5/35892546.pdf.

PRIETO, H., SALHSTRÖM, F., CALANDER, F., KARLSSON, M. & HEIKKILÄ, M. (2003). 'Together? On Childcare as a Meeting Place in a Swedish City'. *Scandinavian Journal of Educational Research*, 47, no. 1, pp. 43–62.

RICHARDSON, G. (2004). *Svensk utbildningshistoria: skola och samhälle förr och nu* [Swedish Education History: school and society before and today]. Lund: Studentlitteratur.

SJÖGREN, A. (1995). 'En "bra" svenska, från rimligt krav till försvarsmekanism' ['Good' Swedish, reasonably demanding for a defence mechanism]. Contribution to the IMER conference *Det mångkulturella Sverige efter år 2000*. *Forskning och framtidsvisioner* [Multicultural Sweden after the year 2000], October 26–27, Lund (Sweden).

STIGENDAL, M. (2001). *Framgång – vad är det? Mötet mellan innanförskap och utanförskap i skolan* [What is success? Meeting between inclusion and exclusion in the school]. Lärarutbildningen. Regionalt utvecklingscentrum. Malmö: Malmöhögskolan. Retrieved September 25 2007 from: http://webzone.lut.mah.se/projects/MS1/upload/download.asp?file=40109100303859.

VINTEREK, M. (2006). 'Individualisering i ett skolsammanhang' [Individualisation in the school context]. *Forskning i fokus*, no. 31. Retrieved September 25, 2007 from: http://www.skolutveckling.se/sok/?q=Vinterek+individualisering&btnG=S%C3%B6k&output=xml_no_dtd&client=default_frontend&num=10& proxystylesheet=securesearch.

WALLIN, E. (2002). 'Jämlikhet, likvärdighet och individer i undervisning' [Equality, Equity and individuals in education]. *Pedagogisk Forskning i Sverige*, vol. 7, no. 3, pp. 200–209.

WIJNBLADH, O. (2007). 'Nationella prov i flera ämnen' [National examinations concerning several curricular subjects]. *Dagens Nyheter*. Retrieved May 3, 2007 from: Document available from: http://www.dn.se/DNet/jsp/polopoly.jsp?d=147& a=645802.

WildT-PERSSON A. & ROSENGREN P. G. (2001). 'Equity and Equivalence in the Swedish School System'. In W. Hutmacher, D. Cochrane & N. Bottani (eds), *In Pursuit of Equity in Education. Using International Indicators to Compare Equity Policies*. The Netherlands: Kluwer, pp. 299–321.

Official documents

FINANSDEPARTEMENTET [SWEDEN: MINISTRY OF FINANCE] (2004). *PROP. 2004/05:1. Budgetpropositionen för 2005*. [Budget Proposal]. Retrieved May 10, 2007 from: http://www.temaasyl.se/Templates/Page.aspx?id=301.

INTEGRATIONSVERKET [SWEDISH NATIONAL INTEGRATION BOARD] (2004). *Integrationsverkets årsredovisning 2004* [Swedish National Integration Board's Annual Report]. Retrieved October 7, 2007 from: http://www.temaasyl.se/Templates/Page.aspx?id=301.

INTEGRATIONS-OCH JÄMSTÄLLDHETSDEPARTEMENTET [SWEDEN: MINISTRY OF INTEGRATION AND GENDER EQUALITY] (2005). SOU 2005:56. *Det blågula glashuset – strukturell diskriminering i Sverige.Utredningen om strukturell diskriminering på grund av etnisk eller religiös tillhörighet* [The blue and yellow glass house – structural discrimination in Sweden. Research study into structural discrimination because of ethnicity and religion]. Official report by the Swedish Government. Retrieved April 15, 2007 from: http://www.regeringen.se/sb/d/5073/a/46188.

INTEGRATIONS-OCH JÄMSTÄLLDHETSDEPARTEMENTET [SWEDEN: MINISTRY OF INTEGRATION AND GENDER EQUALITY] (2006). SOU 2006:40. *Utbildningens dilemma Demokratiska ideal och andrafierande praxis*. Rapport av Utredningen om makt, integration och strukturell diskriminering Stockholm 2006 Rapport av Utredningen om makt, integration och strukturell diskriminering Stockholm 2006 [The Education Dilemma: democratic ideas and discriminative practice. Report by the commission for research into integration and structural discrimination. Stockholm 2006]. Retrieved October 7, 2007 from: http://www.regeringen.se/content/1/c6/06/17/98/1fb66fa9.pdf.

Myndigheten för Skolutveckling [Swedish National Agency For School Development] (2004a). *Kartläggning av svenska som andraspråk.* Dnr 2003:757 [Territories and measures that must be prioritised in the Education system]. Retrieved May 15, 2007 from: http://www.skolutveckling.se/digitalAssets/116334_ defkartlaggmars04.pdf.

Myndigheten för Skolutveckling [Swedish National Agency For School Development] (2004b). Delrapport 2, 2004-11-23. Dnr 2003:639. *Mångfald och likvärdighet Uppdrag att stödja kommunernas arbete med att förbättra utbildningsvillkoren i områden präglade av mångfald och social utsatthet.* [Partial Report 2003-12-01 Dnr 2003: 639 Support mission for municipal work in order to improve educational conditions in disadvantaged neighbourhoods]. Retrieved May 5, 2007 from: http:// www.skolutveckling.se.

Myndigheten för Skolutveckling [Swedish National Agency For School Development] (2005a). *Bättre resultat och minskade skillnader – planering för mångfaldsarbete 2006–2007* [Better results and reduced differences – planning for diversity work 2006–2007 Dnr 2005:177]. Retrieved May 5, 2007 from: http://www. skolutveckling.se/digitalAssets/86450_mangfaldsplan2006_2007.pdf.

Myndigheten för Skolutveckling [Swedish National Agency for School Development] (2005b). *Årsredovisning 2004* [Annual Report 2004]. Retrieved October 7, 2007 from: http://www.skolutveckling.se/digitalAssets/114944_ arsredovisning_2004.pdf.

Myndigheten för Skolutveckling [Swedish National Agency for School Development] (2005c). *Uppdrag till Myndigheten för skolutveckling att arbeta för för-bättrad förskole- och skolsituation i segregerade områden. Slutrapport. 2005-12.02* [Commission of the Swedish National Agency for School Development to improve the pre-school and school situation in segregated neighbourhoods. Final Report 2005-12.02]. Retrieved October 7, 2007 from: http://www.skolutveckling.se/ sok/?q=stigendal&output=xml_no_dtd&client=default_frontend&num=10& proxystylesheet =securesearch.

Myndigheten för Skolutveckling [Swedish National Agency for School Development] (2006). *Årsredovisning 2005* [Annual Report 2005]. Retrieved October 7, 2007 from: http://www.skolutveckling.se/digitalAssets/114945_ arsredovisning2005_msu_webb.pdf.

Myndigheten för Skolutveckling [Swedish National Agency for School Development] (2007a). *Dialoger brygger broar och bryter barriärer* [Dialogues build bridges and destroy barriers]. Retrieved October 7, 2007 from: http://www. skolutveckling.se/innehall/mangfald_likvardighet//utvecklingsdialoger/Mer_om_ dialoger/.

Myndigheten för Skolutveckling [Swedish National Agency for School Development] (2007b). *Idéskola för mångfald* [School of Ideas for Diversity]. Retrieved October 7, 2007 from: http://ideskola.skolutveckling.se/index.php.

Myndigheten för Skolutveckling [Swedish National Agency for School Development] (2007c). *Tema modersmål* [Subject Mother Tongue]. Retrieved October 7, 2007 from: http://modersmal.skolutveckling.se/projekt/index.php?module= htmlpages&func=display&pid=10.

Myndigheten för Skolutveckling [Swedish National Agency for School Development] (2007d). *Förslag till Nationell strategi för nyanlända barn och ungdomar* [Proposal for a national strategy for foreign background children and young people who have recently arrived in Sweden]. Retrieved October 7, 2007 from: http://www. skolutveckling.se/innehall/mangfald_likvardighet/nyanlanda/nationell_strategi/.

MYNDIGHETEN FÖR SKOLUTVECKLING [SWEDISH NATIONAL AGENCY FOR SCHOOL DEVELOPMENT] (2007e). *Slutredovisning av uppraget om kvalitetsutveckling inom gymnasieskolans individuella program.* Dnr 2006:16 [Final Report on the commission developing the quality of the Individual Programme at upper secondary school]. Retrieved July 23, 2008 from: http://www.skolutveckling.se/digitalAssets/116594_Slutredovisning_IV-uppdraget.pdf.

SCB (2006). *På tal om utbildning 2006* [About Education 2006]. Retrieved July 25, 2007 from: http://www.scb.se/statistik/_publikationer/UF0527_2006A01_BR_UF07ST0601.pdf.

SKOLVERKET [SWEDISH NATIONAL AGENCY FOR EDUCATION] (2001). *Den hägrande framtiden...? Regeringsuppdrag 'Konsekvenser av de nya behörighetsreglerna till gymnasieskolan' – slutrapport* [Attractive future. Government mission 'Consequences of the new regulation concerning eligibility for the upper secondary school']. Retrieved May 15, 2006 from: http://www.skolverket.se.

SKOLVERKET [SWEDISH NATIONAL AGENCY FOR EDUCATION] (2003). *Bättre grundskolebetyg för både pojkar och flickor* [Better final marks at compulsory school for boys and girls] Pressmeddelande, 2002-12-18. Retrieved December 18, 2002 from: http://www.skolverket.se/.

SKOLVERKET [SWEDISH NATIONAL AGENCY FOR EDUCATION] (2004a). *Utan fullständiga betyg – varför når inte alla elever målen?* [Pupils who leave compulsory school without the necessary qualifications to start upper secondary school. Why don't all children reach the National Education Goals? Report 202]. Retrieved August 25, 2008 from: http://www.skolverket.se/.

SKOLVERKET [SWEDISH NATIONAL AGENCY FOR EDUCATION] (2004b). *Handlingsplan för en rättssäker och likvärdig betygssättning.* Dnr. 00-2004:556 [Action plan for an equitable grading process according to the law]. Retrieved May15, 2006 from: http://www.skolverket.se/content/1/c4/07/76/Handlingsplan_betygssattning.pdf.

SKOLVERKET [SWEDISH NATIONAL AGENCY FOR EDUCATION] (2004c). *Allmänna råd och kommentarer. Likvärdig bedömning och betygssättning* [General guideline and comments]. Retrieved August 15, 2006 from: http://www.skolverket.se/sb/d/208/a/218;jsessionid=DC10BF23632707744A0BACB8108AB928.

SKOLVERKET [SWEDISH NATIONAL AGENCY FOR EDUCATION] (2006). *Vad händer med likvärdigheten i svensk skola? En kvalitativ analys av variation och likvärdighet över tid.* Rapport 275:2006 [What is happening to equity in the Swedish School? A qualitative analysis of variation and equity over time. Report 275, 2006]. Retrieved September 30, 2007 from: http://www.skolverket.se.

SKOLVERKET [SWEDISH NATIONAL AGENCY FOR EDUCATION] (2007a). [The Swedish Education system]. Retrieved September 15, 2007 from: http://www.skolverket.se/sb/d/376.

SKOLVERKET [SWEDISH NATIONAL AGENCY FOR EDUCATION] (2007b). *Descriptive data on pre-school activities, school-age childcare, schools and adult education in Sweden 2006.* Swedish National Agency for Education report no. 283. Retrieved April 15, 2007 from: http://www.skolverket.se/sb/d/356/a/1326.

SKOLVERKET [SWEDISH NATIONAL AGENCY FOR EDUCATION] (2007c). *Andelen behöriga till gymnasieskolan är den lägsta på tio år.* Pressmeddelande, 2007-2008-14 [The percentage eligible to start the upper secondary school is the lowest for the last ten years]. Retrieved August 15, 2007 from: http://www.skolverket.se/sb/d/203/a/9642.

SKOLVERKET [SWEDISH NATIONAL AGENCY FOR EDUCATION] (2007d). *SALSA databas* [SALSA database]. Retrieved October 7, 2007 from: http://salsa.artisan.se/.

SKOLVERKET [SWEDISH NATIONAL AGENCY FOR EDUCATION] (2007e). *Kommuner har satsat på de individuella programmen* [The municipalities have invested in the Individual Programme]. Retrieved May 15, 2007 from: http://www.skolverket.se/sb/d/1707/a/9247;jsessionid=C2FE6510DEE28302ECE3F3BFCB92D7C8.

UTBILDNINGSDEPARTEMENTET [SWEDISH MINISTRY OF EDUCATION AND RESEARCH] (1994a). SOU 1994:1194, *Grundskoleförordning* [National education ordinance]. Retrieved October 7, 2007 from: http://www.riksdagen.se/webbnav/index.aspx?nid=3911&bet=1994:1194.

UTBILDNINGSDEPARTEMENTET [SWEDISH MINISTRY OF EDUCATION AND RESEARCH] (1994b). *Läroplan för det obligatoriska skolväsendet, förskoleklassen och fritidshemmet-lpO 94* – [Curriculum for the Compulsory School System, the Pre-School Class and the Leisure-time Centre]. Retrieved September 30, 2007 from: http://www.skolverket.se/sb/d/468/a/1841.

UTBILDNINGSDEPARTEMENTET [SWEDISH MINISTRY OF EDUCATION AND RESEARCH] (1995). SOU 1995:109. *Likvärdig utbildning på lika vilkor. Slutbetänkande av Friskolekommittén* [Equitable education with equal conditions. Final Report of the Independent School Commission]. Official report of the Swedish Government. Stockholm: Fritzes offentliga publikationer.

UTBILDNINGSDEPARTEMENTET [SWEDISH MINISTRY OF EDUCATION AND RESEARCH] (1997). SKOLLAGEN [National Education Act] (SFS 1997:1212). Retrieved October 7, 2007 from: http://www.riksdagen.se/webbnav/index.aspx?nid=3911&dok_id=SFS1985:1100&rm=1985&bet=1985:1100.

UTBILDNINGSDEPARTEMENTET [SWEDISH MINISTRY OF EDUCATION AND RESEARCH] (2004). Regeringens proposition 2003/04:140.*Kunskap och kvalitet – elva steg för utvecklingen av gymnasieskolan* [Goverment Proposal 2003-2004:140. Knowledge and Quality – eleven steps for the development of the Upper Secondary School]. Retrieved September 25, 2007 from: http://www.skolverket.se/content/1/c4/79/67/prop.pdf.

UTBILDNINGSDEPARTEMENTET [SWEDISH MINISTRY OF EDUCATION AND RESEARCH] (2007). SOU 2007:28. *Tydliga mål och kunskapskrav i grundskolan – Förslag till nytt mål och uppföljningssystem* [*uppföljningssystem* [Clear national educational goals and compulsory knowledge levels. A proposal on the new national goals and the evaluation system]. *Official Report of the Swedish Government*. Retrieved September 17, 2007 from: http://www.regeringen.se/sb/d/108/a/81428.

10
General Conclusion: Priority Education Policies in Europe, from One 'Age' and One Country to Another

Jean-Yves Rochex

What can we conclude[1] from this first phase of our work? What lessons, what basics for analysis and what questions can we draw from reading and confronting the eight country case studies, and the presentations they contain of the 'priority education policies' (PEPs) implemented in each of the eight countries involved in our study?

It has already been said that one of the first difficulties of our undertaking, which is also one of the first lines of thinking for gaining a better grasp of PEPs and how they are changing in Europe, is in the use of, or failure to use, the very term *priority education policies* (or its corollaries) in our eight countries; it is concerned as much with the diversity of measures and approaches that the authors of these eight chapters have brought together, presented and analysed under this term, as with the slightly different uses that this diversity has led them to make of the common definition that we had been given at the beginning of this collective work. The very terms *priority education policies* or *positive discrimination policies* are in everyday use, and even correspond to political and/or administrative categories in those countries involved in the study where these kinds of concerns and political measures are most long-standing, whether what is involved is a clearly labelled policy (as is the case in France, Belgium and Portugal) or a burgeoning of highly diverse measures, grouped together into what appears to be a concept or an umbrella term. It is not the case in other countries, such as Romania or the Czech Republic, which came later, and in different socio-political contexts, to the implementation of measures targeting categories of population considered as being 'at risk'. As far as these countries are concerned, these approaches and the measures they include were grouped together under the heading PEPs by the authors who present and analyse them in the chapters that they devote to them, but it does not correspond to a class of politico-administrative actions, the latter being rather thought of and designated, according to the terms of the European invitation to tender that we answered and also according to the now dominant categories in inter- or supra-national organisations such as the European commission, in terms of 'educational policies adapted to the needs of groups at risk'.

So it is not surprising that the teams working in the various countries did not make exactly the same use of the common definition that we had initially decided upon for PEPs as being

> policies aiming at acting on educational disadvantage through targeted measures or action plans (whether targeted on socio-economic, ethnic, linguistic or religious, regional or educational criteria or breakdowns) by offering to provide the populations determined in this way something extra (or 'better' or 'different').

In addition to the fact that educational disadvantage is open to many definitions, the attentive reader will have noticed – to give just one example: the area of handicap – that educational policies and institutions aimed at population categories defined according to criteria of the nosographic or medical type, a field which we had initially regarded as not coming within the scope of our study, have nevertheless been included by the authors of certain chapters of this book, who told us that they were unable in their analyses to separate this field and the changes within it from those relating to other population categories targeted by policies and measures perhaps more easily identifiable as concerning PEPs.

It seems to us that this should be seen not as an inconsistency, a failure to pose the problem correctly or a kind of waste product that should be eliminated or reduced to a minimum, no more than the symptom of the inanity of the comparative approach that we are trying to implement, but rather as an invitation and an opportunity to better think through our purpose, to better analyse what PEPs, their changes and their contradictions are in the various national and international, social and historical contexts, in which we can observe them and analyse how they are developed and implemented. This is why we felt it was necessary not to limit our comparative approach to a synchronic point of view without putting into perspective, and giving us a chance to interpret the changes, convergences and divergences observed via a diachronic point of view. It must be made clear from the start that such a diachronic point of view, if it is to attempt to describe and understand how and why this type of policy appears and changes, arises and is argued as targeting such and such an objective and as answering such and such a problem at various times and in various contexts, has nothing to do with a unilateral, historicist or developmental point of view that would aim at highlighting general laws and processes extending their empire beyond national and social borders and histories and not being affected by these. Quite the reverse: it aims at promoting a dynamic, comparative analysis taking into consideration the socio-historical contextualisation of the processes and political measures being studied, without ignoring the weight and the influence of supranational policies and institutions (on this point, cf. Dubar, Gadea & Rolle, 2003; Mons, 2007).

PEPs: From one period and one context to another

It is obviously not possible in this conclusion to give an exhaustive history and archaeology of PEPs and the concepts and problems which their promoters took as a starting point, from the compensatory education policies begun in the United States in the mid-1960 (cf. Little & Smith, 1971; Robert, 2007) to the present day. It is nevertheless worthwhile recalling that those European countries who were first to set up this type of policy were countries in which the economic development of the 'thirty glorious years' and the social model which accompanied it (the welfare state model) could not be dissociated from a proactive educational policy, aiming to raise the educational level of the new generations by setting up a mass education system and providing widespread access to secondary education. Dynamism and economic progress, transformation and social advancement processes, and educational democratisation seem to move forward in step with each other, while the transition from a segmented and elitist education system towards a unified system based on merit (the comprehensive school model) seems to be one of the essential conditions for social progress and a reduction in both educational and socio-economic inequality of destiny.

The welfare state crisis and the emergence of compensatory policies

A first source of disillusionment appears fairly early on when the facts make it obvious that the unification of the education system and the opening up of secondary education, far from reducing the social inequalities of educational development and success, rather bring about a reconfiguration of these, putting off the most visible manifestations to higher levels of the curriculum, while making them more trying for individuals and families. The topic of 'learning difficulties' then becomes a subject of social debate, concerns and public policies to differing degrees from country to country (Isambert-Jamati, 1985; Ravon, 2000). In countries (the United Kingdom, Sweden, France, Belgium, of those involved in our study) where basic schooling is available for all, there then emerged the first educational policy measures explicitly aiming at fighting against educational inequality and learning difficulties; among these measures were the creation of *Educational Priority Areas (EPAs)* in the United Kingdom in the late 1960s, the first compensatory measures taken in Sweden in the 1970s, and the creation of priority education zones (ZEPs) in France and later in Belgium, in the early and late 1980s. These generic or targeted measures can consequently be regarded as an answer to both the completion of the comprehensive school model's implementation in the countries concerned and its insufficiency in relation to the hopes for democratisation that it had so strongly raised. These measures, aimed at ensuring there were no more, or many fewer, people left out of social and education progress, were at that time greatly inspired by a political ideology to fight against inequality, based on a principle of compensation (which was nevertheless at the heart of theoretical and political debates, to which we will return later) and directed, according to variations in how the issue was stressed from one country to another, at the middle or working classes and at linguistic and/or ethnic minorities.

Nevertheless, the sources of disillusionment with regard to the ideology of progress specific to the 30 glorious years obviously do not relate only to education systems and policies. They concern at least as much, if not more, economic and social transformations: the move from situations of full employment and social security systems associated with them to situations where unemployment, poverty, precariousness and 'social insecurity' have returned and have set in on a long-term basis (Castel, 2003); the working class are, in particular, victims of this but they are radically transforming all social backgrounds and the social imagination of the countries involved. These transformations are increasing not only social inequality but also forms of regional inequality related to them; they greatly contribute to an increasing socio-economic polarisation of the social space, and to a con-centration – also on the increase – of populations that are most greatly affected by the phenomena of poverty and precariousness, and of socio-economic and educational difficulties in certain zones of this social space, particularly in many urban districts and areas (generally suburbs or outlying districts; sometimes inner city areas). Political concerns and measures con-cerning these social regions and the schools that are either in these regions or that take in local children and teenagers consequently assert themselves; these concerns mean that PEPs are thought of, following the example of the 'urban renewal' policies on which they are dependent (Garrec, 2006), as area-based policies, combining various modes of targeting aimed at reaching the populations who suffer most from the difficulties and social contradic-tions of the time (unqualified or poorly qualified working-class populations, which are to a large extent also immigrant populations, or those resulting from immigration).

PEPs and their contexts

The compensatory approach seems, then, to bring relative coherency to the three modes of targeting population categories (mainly defined from soci-ological categories related to educational criteria), regions and schools or networks of schools. The first PEPs were aimed explicitly at reducing educational inequality, and to achieve this target the population categories suffering most from it, and the regions (primarily urban) and schools where these population categories are in the majority, or where their concentration poses specific problems. They are sometimes perceived or presented as laboratories for educational and social policies, and for new modes of collaboration between the school and its environment (the 'district' or 'community', according to the various political and cultural traditions) heading, beyond even the territories and schools involved, towards educational democratisation (certain French researchers [CRESAS, 1985] were to speak of the EPA policy as a 'laboratory for social change in education'). Such relative coherency seems to characterise the first PEPs implemented in England, Sweden, France and Belgium and, a little later, in Portugal; these are countries that differ notably on issues such as families' right to choose a school, the amount of centralisation or decentralisation, the relative importance attached to interpretations of what educational inequality leads to in terms of classes and social environments and/or in terms of cultural, ethnic or linguistic minorities, or the socio-historically determined relationship between the school and its environment.

But as of the 1970s, this relative coherency did not fail to raise various political and scientific questions and controversies: in particular, critical sociological standpoints questioned the very prospect of compensation and the disadvantagement point of view, which were at that time the foundations of English and North American policies (cf. *inter alia* Bernstein, 1975; Isambert-Jamati, 1973), and stressed that the goal of democratisation could not be exempted from taking into account the role played in the creation of educational inequality, by the way the education system works, how it constructs and transmits educational culture, no more than it could not be based on an approach to populations and regions that is unaware of, or undervalues, their potential resources. Other work came later to highlight and question changes in political views and objectives, which tended now to be defined in terms of the fight against social exclusion rather than the fight against inequality, a change that we will return to later. It should also be remembered here that the compensatory view came under another type of criticism at this time, particularly in the United States, from promoters of the idea of community control over school, or even of 'community schools', which involved promoting projects and achievements that served the development of the community and its assumption of responsibility for itself, and not just the development of education, a position that was often associated with a political posture asserting that the dominant political authorities and groups have little to gain from implementing a radical change in education (Little & Smith, 1971; Isambert-Jamati, 1973). This criticism hardly seems to have modified North American compensatory policies, whereas the reform of standards and work on the effectiveness of schools and teaching, assigning as they did predominant importance to the endogenous processes of producing educational efficiency – in which work and reform sociologists played only a minor role – was, at the end of the 20th century, to reconfigure these policies from the outside (Robert, 2007).

To return to the countries in our study, it was later and in other political and social contexts that those countries we have not yet mentioned came to adopt and implement policies aiming at reducing educational inequality and the targeted measures which we regarded as concerning PEPs. In 1974, both Portugal and Greece emerged from a period of military dictatorship. The democratisation of political life and social and economic change meant that their education systems faced several challenges: transforming educational culture after years or even decades of authoritarianism or anti-educational culture; reducing educational inequality by encouraging access to secondary education and by extending compulsory schooling; and allowing more widespread access to primary schooling from beginning to end, which a major proportion of children from working-class environments still did not manage to complete until the final decades of the 20th century. They had to take up these challenges simultaneously (unlike the countries we have already mentioned), and at a time of profound transformation of their national and international contexts, particularly affecting migratory processes. As for the Czech Republic and Romania, their return to democracy after the collapse of the 'communist bloc' at the end of the 1980s led them not only to feeling a certain amount of distrust with regard to the central state, but also to radically question the structures (in particular the single school model) and the way their education systems used to function, identifying as they did with a totalitarian and standardising egalitarianism, indifferent to the diversity of pupils and families, and detrimental to their creativity and personal development. The reforms and debates relating to the educational system of these two countries, which cannot be dissociated from their joining the European Union, and recommendations and means of funding of the latter as regards educational policy, tended to assign as much, if not more, importance to questions of democratisation in the sense of freedom of individuals and families, of promotion and recognition of the diversity of individual, cultural or ethnic features, than to those postulated by another meaning of the term democratisation, which looks at the reduction in social and sexual inequalities impacting access to courses and educational success. These changes or tensions between the various meanings of the term democratisation obviously do not relate to the countries of the 'communist bloc' alone; they can be observed today, to differing degrees, in all the countries of our study, and within the European framework into which fit their educational policies and the methods by which they design and implement priority education policies, again very differently from country to country.

PEPs and new ways of regulating educational policies

To stress the increasing importance – though this be uneven from country to country – that the European framework is taking on in the definition, the changes and the implementation of PEPs and, more generally, in those of national educational policies, is to insist on the fact that the diachronic point of view adopted here cannot be restricted to PEPs or national policies alone, without referring them to the transformations which, at the end of the 20th century, affected educational policies and the conceptions and ideologies which inspired them, and to the coming of what the authors believe can be considered as new ways of regulating, a new frame of reference or a neo-liberal turning for educational policies,[2] nor without wondering to what extent PEPs, far from merely suffering the consequences of these, might contribute to these transformations and to this coming.

From the educating state model to that of the appraising state

The model on which educational policies in the 1970s were based – a regulatory model that C. Maroy (2006) describes as 'bureaucratico-professional', because it combines a role that is predominantly, even almost exclusively, that of the educational, rule-making state, standardisation of these rules allowing equal treatment and a high level of autonomy for teachers and their organisations, based on their professional expertise and know-how – came under fire in the following decades from apparently convergent criticism, though resulting from contradictory points of view. To 'leftist' criticism which reproached it for not having kept the promises or fulfilled the hopes of democratisation that 'progressive' reformers had attributed to it, 'conservative' criticism answered with a reproach for its lack of effectiveness in dealing with unemployment and the requirements of economic competitiveness, or with leading to a 'dumbing down' of what pupils learn. Both criticisms may converge to underline the rigidity of education systems and the difficulties they experience in changing. The legitimacy crisis of the old model was to hasten the arrival of new modes of regulation, supposed to meet the requirements of the period: the demand for efficiency and competitiveness, in a context of globalisation leading economies to move towards a 'knowledge economy', innovation and 'lifelong learning'; the demand for diversification to meet with the logic of the promotion of the individual and his/her personal development; and the demand for quality and differentiation faced with the exacerbation of educational issues and competition for the appropriation of education as an asset. Heavily promoted by supranational authorities, such as the European commission or the Organization for Economic Co-operation and Development (OECD), these new regulation modes will lead, in keeping with schedules and methods that will differ from one country to another, to the implementation of substantial reforms in most countries in Europe; this does not mean, however, that one may speak of a process for disseminating and applying a model that would make its presence felt without needing to be contextualised, translated and reconfigured to cope with the political and educational requirements and culture specific to each country.

And yet, without ignoring the diversity and the complexity of the reform processes in the various countries, it seems possible to extract from this the main trends and overall coherency that C. Maroy described and analysed in terms of arrangements between the quasi-market and the appraisal state models.[3] These two models are structured around certain main trends. In the countries where this was not the case, the freedom of choice of families can be seen to be considerably on the increase, these families being promoted to the rank of 'enlightened consumers' on what is looking more and more like a form of educational market. This increase goes hand in hand with increased autonomy now granted to schools, this 'local' level being presented as the most relevant unit for handling the difficulties and contradictions that the policies drawn up and run at official level would be inadequate or powerless to solve. Families' freedom to choose and schools' autonomy logically go together with increasing diversification of available training, between schools, but also within them; this diversification, in the name of the 'need' to take into account pupils' diversity, their characteristics and their 'needs', and of widening the range of choice offered to families, more or less openly questions the single school model and the integrated curriculum, to promote the diversity of syllabuses, courses of study, methods and curricula. As C. Maroy sums up, for its partisans, this quasi-market model in conjunction with a broader autonomy for schools, even with competition between them, should be able to encourage a greater diversity in the educational commodity offer, and thus better meet with the changing demand, thereby moving towards higher quality and greater effectiveness for the educational system.

But while this process helps to increase the impact and the role of those whose involvement was less significant or even on the sidelines (parents, communities and local authorities, public or private schools), these need, if they are to act in an enlightened way, tools to help them better compare and assess the educational commodities, and to better run, control and modify the nature and the quality of these commodities. The quasi-market model is then equipped and strengthened by the increase in external assessment concerns and measures. Measuring and comparing the value of pupils', schools' and even educational systems' performance requires the use of common tools and scales. Hence the implementation of what A. Vinokur (2005) calls 'an assessment, comparability, certification technology', showing the increasing importance and sophistication of national and international surveys aiming not only to provide better information for the 'decision makers' that are supposed to be all those involved from the social and institutional world, from the ministry down to the parents, but also to enable them to influence the educational offer and policies. The assessment instruments and the results (*evidence*), or even the classifications which they make it possible to obtain, are no longer mere knowledge tools but also become (if they were not initially so) tools and techniques for change, results-oriented control being added to, or even standing in for, rule- and procedure-oriented control. They are also tools for the transformation and standardisation (dumbing down, as their detractors would say) of contents and curricula, and contribute to redefining these in terms of skills and competencies, or even key competencies (Rychen & Salganik, 2001).

The model of the appraising state consequently aims at better control of both the educational 'commodity' and its various 'producers', in particular schools and their agents. It underlines the importance of processes that are internal, rather than external, to the educational systems, the schools or the professional practices, that it tends to regard as the main, or even the only possible, levers for action to improve effectiveness and quality and to fight against educational inequality or exclusion. This leads to a broader and stricter control of the teacher's work and of that of other school agents, both being required to be more accountable to the community, and to the preoccupation with promoting good practices and criticising and changing ineffective practices (*evidence-based policies*), with the risk of ignoring the impact of external constraints on performance and educational inequality, while stigmatising the teachers and the schools regarded as insufficiently efficient and making them feel guilty (Myers & Goldstein, 1998). But the concern to improve the quality of 'educational commodities', in order to better meet with the needs and changes of the economic world, is not without impact on the very design of these 'commodities' and their modes of production; and the trend today in European countries is more and more to reconsider and redefine the curricula and educational views in terms of competencies rather than of knowledge, a process that is also coming under fierce criticism from those who see in this a refocusing on short-sighted instrumental objectives to the detriment of what they believe must be a perspective for more ambitious reworking of the curriculum, from both the cultural and the social justice standpoints.

These main trends in the new modes of regulating educational policies are obviously to be found to differing degrees and under different guises in each country concerned. They are widely publicised and promoted by international authorities, and are reconfigured to suit national, political, administrative and cultural contexts, which are themselves changing. In very many countries they are accompanied by processes for recombining the competencies of the various levels of political and administrative decision making, and their relationships of dependence and interdependence, a process in which, from one country to another but sometimes within the same country, movements can be found intersecting towards greater decentralisation and a devolution of competencies and powers, hitherto the responsibility of the state, to other public or private authorities, above or below state level, and, conversely, movements towards greater central-isation, and an increase in the powers of control and decision making exerted by the state (for assessment, as we have seen but also for the cur-riculum and educational practices). Through its recommendations (for a critical analysis of these concerning the effectiveness and the fairness of education systems, cf. Demeuse & Baye, 2007), its programmes, its funding offers and procedures, the European Commission plays an increasing role in the development and implementation of educational policies and action plans, a role which may seem all the more important to those countries that have recently joined the European Union and/or are more dependent on its funding.

From the concept of equality to that of fairness:
Developments and controversies

The European Commission contributes notably to the reformulation and the redefinition of these policies, but also to the ideologies or philosophies that inspire them. European authorities have not only adopted the rhetoric and the problems of effectiveness and fairness and made them their own, but have also significantly contributed to promoting them. The relationship between these terms and those of equality and social justice is the subject of lively political and conceptual debate: certain analysts believe that the first are asserting themselves to the detriment of the second, while others hold that they are simply being reworked and gone into in more depth, which significantly broadens the range and the perspective.

So for the latter, the concept of fairness means that it has to multi-ply the references as regards educational justice, and to combine various non-contradictory manners and criteria, in order to give thought to and assess equality: equal access to teaching and to the educational offer; equal treatment (of resources) guaranteeing equivalent learning conditions for all pupils; equality of attainment (or results) aimed at seeing that all pupils gain equal mastery of the competencies and knowledge appropriate for a school level, an objective that is often reformulated in terms of access for all to a basic level and to attainments deemed to be fundamental in order to allow everyone to take an active part in society; and finally, equality of achieve-ment so that everyone has equivalent opportunities to exploit and develop the competencies and knowledge acquired during his/her schooling.

To these considerations for the various conceptions of equality, the con-cept of fairness adds a political objective of unequal distribution of resources for dealing with the disadvantages relating to inequality of resources and dispositions of families and individuals, the founding principle of prior-ity education policies, sometimes known as positive discrimination (on this concept of fairness and its consequences, cf. *inter alia* Grisay, 1984; Drælants, Dupriez & Maroy, 2003; Demeuse & Baye, 2005).

Authors who are critical with regard to the preponderance of this issue of fairness over that of equality underline that, while it has the advantage of going beyond a formal conception of equality to take into account equality of attainment (the perspective of equality of achievement scarcely having any concrete consequences), it is mostly to focus on the objective of attainment by all of a basic minimum level, of key competencies, or of a common minimum core of knowledge and competencies, according to the terms of the law on guidance voted for in France in 2005. These critics are not unaware that the achievement of such an objective – the guarantee of a minimum of knowledge and competencies for all, and in particular for the pupils who have most difficulties – may be counted as progress for a number of them who currently leave the education system without these attainments. But as educational commodities are also positional goods, whose relative value does not depend on their nature but on how 'distinctive' and unequally distributed between social groups and individuals they are, they stress that this improvement in terms of attaining a minimum level does not rule out an increase in inequalities concerning more advanced levels of the syllabus and more complex knowledge and competencies; nor, therefore, does it rule out a worsening of the relative position of pupils targeted by this objective of guaranteeing a basic level, in a context where competing stakes, and strategies involving over-schooling and competition in order to appropriate the most distinctive educational commodities, are exacerbated. This explains their criticism of a development of educational policies, particularly PEPs, in which they see the objective of fighting against inequality and the 'compensatory' perspective (which they may in addition criticise) fade away behind the issues of inclusion or the fight against social exclusion and behind the objective of guaranteeing the minimum of educational commodities necessary to integrate into a society whose inequality should from now on be regarded as out of the reach of political action, which could only correct the most unacceptable aspects of this and pacify the consequences and manifestations that are the most dangerous for social order.

A profusion of targeted programmes and uncertain policies

This development from a 'compensatory' perspective to an 'inclusive' one is noticeable from reading several of the chapters in this book. It goes hand in hand with what a number of their authors have also underlined, namely a significant change in the ways that PEPs are 'targeted', associating what seems to be a reduction in the targeting of regions with an increase in targeting specific categories of population; this subsumes the *groups at risk* formulation used by the European Commission, in particular in the drafting of the invitation to tender to which our research work was the response, but also the extension of the term *pupils with special needs* from the area of specialised education to that of priority education and the fight again exclusion. It is then a question of identifying the various categories of pupils not likely to benefit sufficiently from the educational offer and to be confronted with failure and discrimination, in order to modify this offer and to bring them the assistance and recognition that they need, and thereby ensure that they get the most out of school and avoid social exclusion. The regional dimension is consequently not greatly prevalent in the countries that have only recently adopted policies of the PEP type, while it seems to be retreating in countries where it was at the heart of the first era of PEPs, in favour of an approach in terms of categories of populations or individuals. To be more precise, what seems to be diminishing is the relative coherency between the three modes of targeting aiming not only at reaching populations through the regions in which they live and the schools where their children are educated, but also to mobilise resources and collective dynamics in favour of 'social change in education'.

Such diminishing coherency would work in favour of a proven trend towards dissociation between, on the one hand, a regionalised and 'partnership' approach aiming at helping underprivileged families and their children to better prepare them for the requirements of schooling, by means of early intervention programmes (such as the very significantly named *Sure start* programme) concerning what the English call *multi-agency working*, and on the other hand, an approach to, or targeting of, schools coming under a generic policy (i.e. not just 'priority' schools) of efficiency improvement and results-oriented control, very often considering each school independently of any interdependent relationship with other schools and with its social environment, and mainly, or even exclusively, stressing the internal factors and processes making up its educational performance. Is such a trend therefore not likely to reinforce the juxtaposition or cleavage between various types of programmes and measures, and also to result in paying less attention to relationships of interdependence (and not only of coexistence or successiveness) between, on the one hand, the modes of socialisation and family educational practices specific to various social backgrounds, in particular working-class backgrounds, and, on the other hand, the modes of development and transmission of school culture, the operating processes and professional practices that belong to educational system(s), meaning to the relational approach which, as of the 1970s, certain sociologists who were critical of the concept and the policies of compensatory education, like Bernstein in England or Isambert-Jamati in France, attempted to promote?

At all events, it is undeniable, upon reading the foregoing chapters, that we are today dealing with a multiplication not only of syllabuses that come under PEPs but also of categories of populations targeted by these programmes. The list of those targeted by the programmes presented and analysed by both our English and our Czech colleagues – who come from two countries who began implementing PEPs at very different periods and in very different contexts – bears witness to this. In addition to the 'conventional' modes of targeting and categories for this type of policies, which are pupils from socially underprivileged families and backgrounds, and/or national linguistic, cultural or ethnic minorities (with this second mode of categorisation undoubtedly tending today to gain ground over the first), there are other modes of targeting or categorisation that concern, for example, children of refugees or asylum-seekers; ill children with learning or behavioural difficulties, or with 'special educational needs'; gifted and talented pupils; those belonging to one or other gender (boys or girls, depending on the programme); and even 'any pupil at risk from disinterest and exclusion'. At the same time, the objectives and the 'social problems' that the programmes concerned aim to answer are becoming more diversified and are increasing in number: the fight against absenteeism or dropping out of school; the fight against violence at school and prevention of juvenile delinquency; assistance for parents; recognition and development of the individual potentials of 'different' pupils, and so on.

Such diversification and multiplication of the targeted population categories and the programmes designed for them significantly broaden the scope, the definition or even the aim of PEPs. The composite or even heterogeneous nature of the list of these categories and programmes poses new questions, for example, when one notes that there is a category – that of gifted and talented children – defined not by a disadvantage, but by what might seem to be, on the contrary, an advantage, that education systems might not be able to bring to fruition. The appearance of this category testifies to what may seem to be a modification (to which we will return later) of the very issue of priority education, which would then aim less at reducing educational inequalities related to social and cultural inequalities, than at allowing each pupil and each category of pupil, in particular those not sufficiently reaching the expectations of an education system regarded as excessively normative, to maximise his or her development and chances of educational success, taking into account his or her particular or specific characteristics. It may therefore seem logical to consider and deal with the various categories of pupils as though they were all part of the same overall issue, whatever the nature of the criteria (social, educational, medical or even genetic) from which these categories are built and are used, this overall issue coming under the heading of 'inclusive education', that is taking care to ensure that each pupil or category of pupils, whatever their characteristics, is taken in and recognised at school, and that the latter – and the policies which aim to facilitate its work – make it possible to develop his or her potential to the full. Such an issue can, without any doubt, when contrasted with 'disadvantagement' conceptions that very often support compensatory approaches, have the advantage of questioning and of attempting to change the way education systems work from the standpoint of their ability to facilitate learning for all, and to promote a more social and more dynamic conception of handicap, centred less on deficiency (motor, sensory or other) than on the way in which society and its institutions (in this case, school) endeavour, in spite of this, to provide the handicapped person with the situations, cultural tools and mediation likely to encourage his or her development by compensating for, or circumventing, the deficiency and its direct consequences to the greatest possible extent (for such a conception of handicap and the education of handicapped children, cf. Vygotski, 1994).

One may nevertheless wonder about the nature of the generalisation or unification which these issues bring to bear between the various categories to which they relate, their methods of social construction and the types of treatment or solutions they call on from the educational institution or from those that propose to make its action easier; and especially about the risk of naturalising the categories used in this way, which might result in regarding all of them as indicating *de facto* characteristics that 'go without saying', that one might find on a medical register, or even on a genetic register, to which the conceptions of 'donations' or 'talents' which certain children might benefit from rather than others refer. The risk here is not only one of undervaluing diversity and heterogeneity, or even the radically different 'nature' of the categories and criteria used, and the social and educational problems related to them, but just as much one of hiding or understating the need for questioning the social and education construction processes of these categories, those giving form and content to the characteristics of the pupils and the types of pupils, and to the 'special needs' they are said to have or the 'problems' they are said to pose, and to which education systems would have to answer. It is not only to deprive oneself of the critical distance and vigilance that a sociological posture maintains with regard to the categories of ordinary action, but also to impoverish its possible scope by seriously compromising its ability to grasp social reality in all its heterogeneity and with all its contradictions, over and above the first appearances and categories which are very often those as viewed by politicians and the media.

Examining PEPs and their developments shows that the risk of naturalisation concerns not only pupils, their characteristics or their 'needs', but just as much the educational and social problems that the measures implemented are meant to answer, and the temptation to use the most immediate, most general and most problem-laden formulation: violence at school, juvenile delinquency, language, social or cultural origin, and to attempt to deal with the most obvious and most immediate manifestations, to the detriment of longer-term social and education processes that give them form and content. Hence the multiplication of programmes and measures to match that of the population categories that they target, the 'needs' and the 'problems' they aim to answer; programmes that are fragmented, sometimes assessed, reiterated or modified very quickly or even 'agitatedly', as our English colleagues put it, under the influence of deadlines and of national or international political programmes, or even of NGOs or various lobbies.

Such a multiplication or fragmentation and such agitation often, as certain analyses in the foregoing chapters show, seriously compromise the development, implementation and follow-up of a more coherent long-term policy, aiming at attacking the fundamental and structural causes of educational and social inequality and exclusion, rather than their surface appearance.

Transversal topics and trends for PEPs in various countries

So what constitutes the programmes and measures of PEPs in our different countries? What do they aim to achieve and what are the main topics they deal with? To what developments do they bear witness? Over and above the fact that they appear hard to unravel, to what extent are they coherent and where do their tensions and contradictions lie? What questions do they encourage us to ask? We will attempt here to take initial stock of the main trends we have observed at this stage of our work. As these lines are being written, those trends are being analysed transversally and in more depth; the results of these analyses will be presented in another book to appear at a later date.

Pre-school education and early childhood

One of the first transverse topics that appear essential to scrutinise after reading the foregoing chapters is the assertion of the importance of work targeting early learners; the importance of this varies according to country, and it gives rise to programmes and measures that differ in kind and name according to the specific way in which early learners are dealt with from the social and institutional standpoints in each country. For example, in France, where the nursery school is practically compulsory, this type of programme will obviously not be considered in the same light as in England, in Greece or Portugal, where early learning is conceived as being less related to schooling. These early learning (or pre-school) programmes are based on the idea that early childhood is the best time to work on compensating for the disadvantages related to social and family situations, and to provide children with quality educational experiences preparing them as much as possible for the demands that school will place on them (*school readiness*) and to 'get off to a good start', according to the very meaningful name of the English programme *Sure start*. This has explicitly a preventive rather than a corrective aim, and associates measures of parental or maternal assistance for social or medical matters with those aiming at facilitating development and learning in the various fields of communication and language, affectivity and creativity, bodily activities, literacy and numeracy. These programmes generally refer to hypotheses and research results in the field of psychology. While many partners or service providers, and many different institutions, are involved in these programmes, and not just school professionals, the increased 'educationalisation' of their objectives and their contents, or even the professionalisation of multi-agency working, may have the unwanted effect of increasing the difficulty of involving families or communities in the conception and the implementation of measures and programmes that concern them to the greatest degree, or even of developing the idea of competition between the various service providers, from the public, charitable or private sectors.

Assessments (few in number) of this type of programme seem to show that they make it possible to obtain better short-term results for the children concerned, although the long-term benefits appear, in contrast, much less proven, much more fragile and even disappointing. These observations raise the question of knowing whether the logic of 'preparing for school' that is behind this type of programme has any effect on school in return, and whether lessons can be learnt and their findings implemented that would not only better prepare children for school, but also better prepare school for children and for helping them to succeed, especially those who are the least familiar with its demands and how it works. In other words, how, to what extent and in what conditions can this logic contribute to the transformation and the democratisation of school, making it more effective for the most underprivileged, and not just 'adapt' pupils better to education systems and to schools that might take only a marginal interest in questioning themselves and in changing, or do so only internally and endogenously, with a view to effectiveness that is more technical and instrumental that social and cultural? This question arises as much in connection with 'remedial' programmes and measures targeting older pupils, often pupils in the early stages of secondary school, as in aiming at curing, downstream, their learning and/or behavioural difficulties (violence, absenteeism, etc.).

Policies and programmes in favour of 'minorities'

A second transverse topic relates to measures aiming to encourage school integration and the success of pupils belonging to national linguistic, ethnic, cultural and even religious minorities, and to fight against the processes of segregation or discrimination of which they are particular victims. Alone among the countries in our sample, Romania has gone as far as to introduce quotas and a policy of reserved places for young Roma people in secondary schools or universities, to which previously they hardly had any access, thereby helping to create a new Roma elite and reinforcing this minority's emancipation movement. More generally, the measures taken in favour of various minorities can lead to the establishment of classes or special methods of dealing with newly arrived pupils (in particular for recently arrived immigrant children and/or for those who do not master the language of the host country) or, on the contrary, to help the integration of pupils belonging to these minority groups gain access to 'common' courses and measures, through various changes to teaching approaches or to the curriculum, instructions aiming to prohibit or restrict classes or schools in which these pupils are beginning to be over-represented, or recruiting and training 'mediators', sometimes from the communities concerned, whose function is to help with the dialogue between them and the school. These measures may also stress particular dimensions and aim at developing, asserting and enhancing specific identities (cultural, linguistic, ethnic, etc.) or, on the contrary, from a point of view more coherent with the concept of the 'inclusive school', promoting intercultural education for all, which would thereby target not only, nor even primarily, those pupils belonging to minority groups.

In all the countries of our study, this transverse topic devotes a large amount of space to language questions, providing the pupils concerned with means for learning or reinforcing the language of the host country (which is also the language in which most or all of the teaching is carried out), or even learning this language as a second language, as well as measures aiming at reinforcing pupils' mastery of their original language (which is sometimes just the language that their parents speak), so that it is recognised and valued, in and out of school, or even allow pupils (or the families) the choice of taking certain lessons in this minority language. Entwined within these linguistic and cultural questions and issues – and without it being possible to assess either their respective role or effects – are concerns and objectives of an 'instrumental' nature, aiming at facilitating learning of subjects on the curriculum, and cognitive and intellectual attainments, concerns and objectives of a 'symbolic' nature, aiming to restore or reinforce pupils' self-esteem and to contribute to the requalification of the original and/or family languages and cultures of origin. It remains the case that thinking on these language questions often seems to be carried out in very general terms, without reference to the diversity of the language skills mastered by the speakers and used by them in either of their languages ('original' language or 'host country' language), with hardly any references either to issues pertaining to the written culture, to its expectations and its cognitive and subjective effects. More generally, the topics involved here are also exposed to the risk, mentioned above, of 'naturalisation' of the pupils' categories and language or ethnic characteristics, or of the groups to which they belong, which may result in them being considered in isolation without linking them to the historical and social processes which give them form and content.

It is, in particular, the complex link between social relationships and linguistic, cultural or ethnic differences or characteristics that we are called on to investigate in more depth as we read the chapters on each country.

Our Swedish colleagues, for example, point out that the opportunity given to pupils of foreign origin to have lessons in their original language and lessons in Swedish as a second language is taken up to very different degrees by pupils according to their national, linguistic or social origin: less by pupils whose original language is English or Finnish, who also tend to be pupils from privileged backgrounds, and much more so by pupils whose original language is Somali, Arabic or Turkish, the vast majority of whom belong to social categories that have suffered from domination and segregation. In the same way, comparison of the chapters from both the Czech Republic and Romania shows that the Roma populations in each of these countries are not keen on asserting such an identity or on having their children taught in the Romany language.[4] These few examples obviously bring us on to the special features of the social configurations and the national histories of the various countries. We know, for example, that the dominant traditions of research into the sociology of education in France, Greece and Portugal reason more in terms of classes and social relationships (at the risk of eclipsing the ethnic or 'ethnicising' dimensions of the social and educational domination and segregation processes, as a number of more recent works stress), where their Anglo-Saxon counterparts are more comfortable reasoning in terms of ethnic or cultural minorities. It is also understandable that Romania and the Czech Republic, after their experience of Communist regimes, appear more reticent with regard to an egalitarian ideology and preoccupations, always suspected of awaking the spectres or vestiges of totalitarian egalitarianism,[5] and are more amenable to issues of difference recognition, respect and promotion of diversity. Similarly again, the fact that certain countries – such as France or the Czech Republic – do not authorise the production of ethnic statistics (which raises a complex issue that we will not explore here), or statistical reasoning of the type 'all other things being equal' resulting in not making foreign nationality or immigrant origin a targeting criterion for PEPs, because the educational performance and development of the pupils concerned do not significantly differ from those of their peers from the same socio-economic background (a reasoning and choice which are also subject to debate), raises tough theoretical and political issues.[6] On the one hand, they may lead to a reduction in the importance of the processes and feelings of segregation and discrimination felt by certain categories of population and certain districts or urban areas, and who are victims of such processes, and yet fail to prevent the topic of 'ethnicity', or even the processes and rhetoric of the 'ethnicisation' of social and educational questions, from increasingly asserting itself in political and social debate. On the other hand, this increasing assertion may contribute to the naturalisation of the categories it uses and to euphemising or diminishing the social relationships and the processes of domination and social inequality. To assert this is not necessarily to plead in favour of any particular stance in scientific or political debate, but leads one to think that the latter would doubtless gain from more effective work on elucidating the relations between social questions and 'ethnicity', between social relationships or disadvantages and cultural (or linguistic) differences or disadvantages, both in the analysis of social reality and its historical depth, and in that of the ideologies that found social and educational policies.

Teaching and curriculum measures and developments

The third transverse topic to emerge from our comparative study relates to teaching and curriculum measures and developments. The first dimension of this type of measure consists of actions or measures to reinforce educational action or individual support: extending school time, reducing the number of pupils in classes or grouping pupils together; support, remedial or assistance measures to help pupils in their work, inside or outside school; and tutoring or mentoring. The underlying point of view here tends generally towards individualisation, the aim being to help individuals to deal with school activities and requirements, without the questioning or the transformations concerned or implemented necessarily involving the 'what' and the 'how'. These reinforcement or support actions and measures often seem mainly focused on certain disciplines or certain contents considered as fundamental, at the risk of falling back on academic and utilitarian subjects. These disciplines are generally mathematics, national, minority or second languages, reading/writing and literacy. We note here once again that, while questions of language and written culture feature in many PEP programmes and measures, according to the information we have available these are generally introduced and discussed in terms of communication, more than via a 'cultural' or socio-cognitive approach, which, following the example of the work begun and developed by Jack Goody, considers language practices and written culture not only as means of communication, but also as tools for the development and transformation of ways of thinking and of the relationship between speech and the world (on this point cf., *inter alia*, Goody, 1979, 1994; Lahire, 1993; Olson, 1998; Bautier, 2001).

Side by side, or over and above reinforcement or support actions and measures, PEP programmes contain a number of other measures and projects based on a perspective for transforming or adapting teaching (in the broad sense of the term) or curricula. Such an objective may be thought about and argued in general terms of modernisation or teaching innovation; its promoters then call upon the need for developing pupils' participation, 'active methods', 'differentiated learning' and 'constructivist' or 'socioconstructivist' approaches whose contribution to better success for the 'targeted' pupils seems to go without saying and does not even need to be clarified and justified, either conceptually or empirically. The issue often remains, then, very general and lacking in precision; it attaches little or no importance to pupils' characteristics and difficulties, nor to the special features of the curricula and subject content. The point of view supporting this consequently appears more educational, or even psychological than didactic or sociological; at least it is based on an idea or a conception of the pupil as 'generic' and is, it seems, fairly insensitive to the questions put by certain sociologists to the 'new' or 'invisible' learning approaches (Bernstein, 1975, 2007; Perrenoud, 1995), approaches closer to the habitus, the educational practices and the values of the 'new middle-classes' than those of working-class backgrounds. A more sociological point of view leads one to think of PEP programmes not just from the point of view of modernising teaching, but from that of transforming school culture, curricula and the ways in which they are transmitted, which attempt to make them more socially and culturally relevant for the categories of population targeted, so that appropriating them is part of a dynamics of empowerment for these categories, in view of their living conditions and the struggles in which they are involved. Such a point of view rarely appears in the PEP programmes presented and analysed in the various chapters, perhaps because it may appear to be more ideological than pragmatic, but also because it is sometimes quite difficult for the analysts, on reading the political and administrative documents and reports giving an account of PEP programmes and how they are implemented, to perceive what are the curricular and educational concepts or ideologies on which they are based, and because there is not much research work, or even very little in certain countries, that makes it possible to go beyond this interpretation.

Where this type of research does exist, it has sometimes been able to highlight, as some of the chapters on the different countries show, a more or less unwitting and involuntary logic for the transformation of the curriculum and of teaching approaches, which goes against the stated aims pursued and tends towards a restriction of the curriculum offer and requirements, and of the activities and time available for learning, or at least for certain types of learning. This logic or this risk of restriction of the requirements and opportunities for learning seem to be determined in two ways. First, by the ways of dealing with assessments and with performance- and standards-driven running of schools or practices, which lead teachers and school staff to restrict their teaching to the content and types of activity that they know need to be assessed, and to modify their practices, more or less consciously, in order to teach more with a view to test results that for the broader cultural aims and objectives assigned to them by the education system, or which they assign (or would prefer to assign) to themselves. This logic, or temptation of 'teaching to the test' and of lowering requirements and tasks, apparently does not concern only pupils targeted by PEPs, but it undoubtedly concerns them all the more as it is determined and reinforced both by the 'disadvantagement' conceptions that teachers and school staff often have of these pupils, and by their concern to propose tasks and learning activities of which they can make a success, this success contributing to preserving a positive self-image and motivation.

Detailed analysis of the results of pupils educated in or outside EPAs in the national assessments that they undergo in French and mathematics, encourages one to think that EPA teachers have a strong tendency to favour training their pupils in parcelled-out and repetitive 'basic' competencies and technical subjects, to the detriment of richer and more productive competences from the intellectual and cultural standpoints, but more demanding and more difficult, with the risk of thereby unwittingly contributing to widening the social and educational gaps and inequalities which they are aiming to fight against, while making them much less visible for the pupils and their families. Such a logic involving restriction of the curriculum offer and its requirements may go hand in hand with an apparent improvement in pupils' 'careers' (e.g. with a reduction in the number of pupils having to repeat a school year and falling behind, or with an extension of school courses) that would hardly correspond to an improvement in their effective attainments but more to a lesser selectivity of criteria and assessment and guidance practices that they undergo. Several of the national reports show that this type of observation or question undoubtedly deserves greater attention if we are to avoid the illusions and disillusions that cannot fail to arise from what would turn out to be not so much a reduction in social inequalities as regards access to knowledge as a poorer visibility of these related to the use of inadequate or even deluding statistical criteria.

Impacting professional practices and modes of collaboration

The fourth transverse topic that is to be found in all PEP programmes studied in the eight countries involved in our study relates directly to the various professional agents in the education systems, and even to their 'partners'. PEP programmes have given rise, in certain countries, not only to the creation and professionalisation (or rather 'semi-professionalisation') of new functions or new 'trades' – mediators in charge of promoting and improving relations between school and families or communities; people exerting the responsibility of driving, following up and co-ordinating the actions and the programmes implemented and/or of assessing their effects; a number of people involved in assisting pupils with their work, or in parental assistance – and also to new ways of dividing up educational work between school, families and other institutions or organisations. The commonly shared assertion and goal that school must not fight a lone combat against inequality and exclusion, and must have its own actions reinforced by those of other educational protagonists, has led to the appearance of new modes of collaboration and exchange between school staff and those in other professional fields (housing, social work, town planning, health, etc.) or between the various professionals and the families, here too in a way that is differentiated according to the contexts and the traditions of the various countries. And yet these changes may be also be the bearers of potential conflicts or competition for competency (in both the legal and professional senses of the term) between the various protagonists of these new modes of collaboration and exchange; conflicts or competition in which are to be found many old or returning processes of occupational or social disqualification of some people by others.

A considerable percentage of budgets devoted to PEPs in the various countries has been aimed at increasing the number of professionals working with pupils, or in targeted regions and schools (in particular the number of school agents), to improving their career and pay, and to reducing the significant turnover affecting professionals working under the most difficult conditions in certain countries. Other resources have been devoted to increasing their competencies and ability to act in the contexts concerned, by means of initial or in-service training programmes and by producing and publishing teaching materials and media. Such measures are also caught up in the tension between specificity and genericity, between concern for taking the specific characteristics of the population categories or targeted regions into account in order better to adapt professional practices and the equipment they need, and that of ensuring that the methods of professional work in schools and with pupils involved in PEP programmes not only do not move away from the standard or from common law and deal with the same issues of knowledge, learning or socialisation as elsewhere, in 'ordinary' regions and with 'ordinary' or privileged pupils, but that they may provide information and prospects for improvement or transformation of the whole of the education system and all pupils. Therefore, to take just a few examples, in certain cases textbooks and teaching media can be prepared for pupils belonging to a minority group, or training courses to help school teachers and school agents improve their knowledge of the language and the culture of this group; while in other cases, like that reported by our Greek colleagues in connection with after-school tutoring programmes, a significant amount of the educational materials produced within the framework of a PEP programme has been much more broadly disseminated, to the extent of reaching all the teachers working on the same level of a course, while the programme in question was itself discontinued.

Finally, other budgetary measures and resources have aimed at promoting experience sharing (cf. 'the Schools of ideas' mentioned in Chapter 9), sharing competences and comparing practices, extending those believed to have proved their worth, even the more or less strict incentive to adopt and implement what the promoters of *evidence-based policies* consider as being 'good practices'. On this point, as on others, the measures taken within the framework of PEP programmes must be thought of in relation to changes in how school policies are regulated and in how schools, teachers and management staff are managed, increasingly encouraged, or even instructed, to give an account of their results and ways of doing things. The organisation and balancing of this seem to vary according to country, even within each of them, depending on time and place, between an approach of the prescriptive and impositional type, which may obey a top-down administrative logic or be the result of a less easily identifiable logic giving free rein to the quasi-market processes, and a 'participative' approach that stakes more on teachers' and school heads' involvement and collective capacity for development.

However these balances are struck, whether they are more or less stable and whatever the hesitations between these two types of logic that characterise the various countries, the question arises of the abilities of PEPs and their promoters – and also the educational research work on which they may be based – to equip the categories and the ways of thinking, the types of logic and the modes of action of agents from whom a democratisation of school and an improvement in its effectiveness are expected. Between regulation and the incentive to adopt and implement 'good practices' or types of action considered as relevant with scant regard for the diversity of contexts on the one hand, and a call for the mobilisation of those working in the field supposed to be able to devise projects and relevant action plans on the other, one may wonder whether the PEPs and the recommendations they carry have not had the effect of increasing the ability of schools and teachers to detect the learning and educational difficulties of pupils or categories of targeted pupils better and earlier, and thereby of increasing their concern for these pupils, more than of increasing (or increasing in the same proportions) their ability to prevent these difficulties or to cure them as soon as they appear. Such a hiatus, and the theoretical and pragmatic difficulties of which it is the symptom, could partly account for the lukewarm or disappointing results of PEPs in practically all countries where evaluations of their effects have been possible. As stated above, these questions call for a development in research and thinking relating both to the characteristics and the difficulties encountered by pupils or categories of pupils, the means of building the population categories targeted by these policies, and the 'risks' of which the pupils concerned would be the bearers, their 'special needs' or the way in which the actions and measures implemented propose answering them.

Assessing PEPs? Results and difficulties

The final transverse dimension that we will look at here relates to the possibilities and methods of assessing PEPs, and their effects with regard to the objectives aimed at or asserted. One is first of all obliged to concede that the available assessment data are very uneven from country to country, even almost non-existent in some of them, and, as a general rule, full of gaps, so that it is not possible to say confidently what their effects might be. Rather than evidence-based policies, *PEPs seem in general to be* no evidence-based policies. There may be several reasons for this state of affairs. First, the concern with assessing the dynamics and the effects of PEP programmes, and that of learning from the available data, where these exist, create and meet with a certain amount of reticence, both from the decision makers and officials and from those involved 'in the field', particularly when the available data appear disappointing and result in questioning the problems and the programmes implemented and in doubting their relevance. Here arise the questions of the uses, the failure to use and the possible misuse of the assessment data and research results by those involved politically or professionally, who, from the ministry to the classroom, are, like anyone involved in the social arena, more eager to consolidate the presuppositions of their action than to question them; also raised is the question of the possible modes of exchange and collaboration between these politicians and professionals, and those of research work or assessment, the objectivisation of the effects of the work of the one party by the work of the other potentially always leading to an attitude of reciprocal disqualification. The uneven knowledge of the effects of PEP programmes also results from the fact that the various countries in our sample do not all have equivalent institutions or statistical or administrative departments for this type of assessment, nor do they have the same traditions of surveys and data collection concerning pupils' careers, attainments or performance. So while certain countries have traditions and tried and tested public or private services for the assessment of educational statistics, and therefore reliable and robust data allowing synchronic and diachronic comparisons, there are other countries in which, for various historical reasons, this type of institution and investigation are not as well developed and tested, including some which, for example, do not have specific survey data and depend consequently on international surveys, tools and methodologies, to evaluate the performance and attainments of their pupils.

But the other reason that little, or not enough, is known about the effects of PEPs is because it is very difficult to know them. It is extremely difficult either to disentangle or isolate what might be the effects of the many programmes concerned with PEPs as a political or administrative category or that we have regarded as such, to such an extent that these programmes overlap and superimpose themselves in time and in space, targeting as they do the same regions or the same populations at the same time. Where assessments of these programmes exist, they are very often short-term, concerned more with deadlines and requirements of a political or administrative nature related to short-term instrumental objectives than with scientific criteria and constraints, and they scarcely make it possible to assess the effects and impacts of an overall policy. They are often centred on the various operation programmes, rather than on the impact of a comprehensive political approach. In contrast, when, as in France, data do exist for the comparative evaluation and assessment of the school careers and acquisitions of pupils on PEPs, as opposed to their peers who are not, it is quite difficult to determine whether one can ascribe the variations and changes thus noted to the policy implemented, since this policy came under an educational, political and socio-economic context which has kept changing, and also because it is impossible to know what the changes in the regions, schools and populations concerned would have been in the absence of this policy. The comparative approaches on which the available assessments of PEPs are based, however invaluable and essential these may be, provide only imperfect grounds for considering that their results assess and measure only the effects of the policies and how they are implemented.

In spite of their imperfections and their unevenness from country to country in our sample, the available assessment data concerning PEP policies and programmes turn out to be contrasted, not very convincingly and relatively disappointingly from the standpoint of the hopes and objectives of fighting against educational inequality or exclusion. While some positive and encouraging results have appeared in certain countries and for certain programmes, the majority appear fragile and not very long-lasting, such as the improvements noted in England for young children from underprivileged backgrounds and ethnic minority groups who had benefited from the early programmes, which seem to fade away with time and the movement of the children concerned through the various stages of their schooling. The limited value of some of these results is also, according to some analysts, concerned with the fact that political and administrative pressures to which schools, teachers and local managers are subjected sometimes lead to instrumental answers favouring the types of work, or types of tests and criteria, that will serve as yardsticks by which their actions and their 'effectiveness' are evaluated, and granting, *de facto*, more weight to the concern and the requirement to achieve results quickly than to more long-term strategies and perspectives of greater scope. Whatever the reasons, and in spite of certain encouraging results on a particular point or a particular programme, it is not possible, in any country, to state that the implementation of PEPs and programmes grouped together under that name has led to a substantial, durable and incontestable improvement in the educational system of the population categories involved (with the possible exception, in certain countries of so-called 'gifted children', a category for which we have no difficulty in agreeing is very different from the others), and to a noticeable and lasting reduction in educational disadvantagement and inequality, and the social consequences of these of which these categories are the victims. Undoubtedly, real progress has been accomplished in regard to the concern of ensuring that institutions and schools operate more democratically and are more accessible to the diversity of practices and 'cultures' of pupils, families and 'communities'. But this progress seems to have been validated by very few convincing external assessments. In addition, even if it were proved, this certainly invaluable progress would nonetheless not make it possible to state that priority education policies, in all their diversity and in the varied ways they are implemented, have allowed the education systems and social formations concerned to progress notably on the road to democratising access to knowledge and academic success, or even to fighting against social exclusion.

But while the assessment of PEPs in each of the countries of our study (or in major political and territorial entities such as the French community of Belgium) proves relatively disappointing, it may nevertheless cover and mask a certain amount of heterogeneity on certain sites or programmes. In fact, those studies and assessments that use indicators and a focal point in helping to grasp more detailed situations and processes show that there may exist a great disparity in results between the regions and the schools concerned by PEPs, or between the programmes implemented there. This kind of observation encourages us to go beyond analyses and overall assessments to gain a better understanding of to what extent and why certain programmes, certain regions or certain schools succeed better than others, and so go beyond the very general modes of description and categorisation of the aims pursued and the measures taken (such as, for example, mastery of the spoken or written language, intercultural education or even differentiated learning), going into more detail about the practices and ways of operating, and individual and collective mobilisation processes.

Several difficulties arise here. First is the fact that all countries do not have the same administrative facilities, the same practices or the same research traditions to carry out this type of survey, or to combine various quantitative and qualitative approaches and methodologies, aiming for better understanding of the social, institutional and educational processes that lead to the statistical observations made. Second, the fact is that such an undertaking is not easy to carry out, both for politico-administrative reasons, related to political deadlines and operations, and for scientific reasons inherent in the difficulties of getting different research approaches and traditions to communicate with each other. The problems and difficulties raised by the various modes of assessment of PEPs and the programmes implemented within them turn out to be even greater if one takes into account the fact that statistical reports showing that the performance or the behaviour of the pupils concerned has hardly improved, or that the gulfs that it was attempted to bridge still exist, or have even become greater, are sometimes in opposition to the feeling of satisfaction that the various actors involved – teachers, head teachers or even pupils and families – may feel, with regard to what they may perceive as an improvement in their work and study conditions, or how they relate to, or work with, others, in spite of the less encouraging statistical results, the relevance of which they may even go as far as denying. Here too, one can only stress the need for, and the difficulty in developing, research and assessment methods that could take the various points of view and experiences into account, combine approaches and methodologies and vary the focal points and time dimensions, without compromising on essential scientific thoroughness. This is tantamount to admitting that we are very far away from the oversimplification of certain conceptions of evidence-based policies or the identification and dissemination of 'good practices' and that the scientific and political stakes of the assessment of PEPs crystallise or refract those of educational research as a whole.

PEPs and their contexts: What conceptions, what political objectives?

While the relatively disappointing assessment that can be drawn from the available data necessarily leads one to question the bases and the relevance of PEPs, the conceptions and problems inspiring them and the ways in which they are implemented, not all the blame for this can be laid at the door of the PEPs themselves. Admittedly the observed effects of these policies have not turned out to be in keeping with the objectives or the hopes of their partisans and promoters, but the reasons for such a result are not only endogenous. First, one should remember the obvious fact that while school is not powerless against the social constraints and contradictions imposed on it by non-egalitarian social formations that have been worked upon by many processes of 'exclusion' and segregation, neither can it be regarded as being able, alone or even predominantly, to reduce these inequalities and to fight against or reverse these processes. It is advisable, nevertheless, to delve deeper into the analysis by stressing the fact that, in the majority of the countries of our sample, PEPs or, more generally, measures and policies aiming at increasing the effectiveness and the fairness of school systems have been implemented over recent decades at the very time when, outside of school, the social, economic or housing processes that lead to social inequalities, segregation and exclusion were gaining in force. It is as if, to use an expression used by Pierre Bourdieu, the states and politicians were asking their left hand, the school and social policies, to repair and stitch the damage caused by the political decisions and economic logic that their right hand has been taking, consecrating or encouraging (Bourdieu, 1993). Not only is it the case, even if the relevance of the programmes and measures that compose them were proved, that PEPs cannot be other than inadequate in coping with the structural constraints and contradictions of social formations, but their very action can only be opposed by developments in these social formations and the reinforcement of these constraints and contradictions, as can be seen in most of the foregoing chapters. Some authors add that their action can only be frustrated by the very transformations of educational policies and of the new modes of regulation that most European countries have adopted and implemented, each in its own way. According to these authors, such policies and new modes of regulation – the quasi-market model, the increase in families' freedom of choice, the increased autonomy of schools and increased competition, the processes of decentralisation or recombining of competencies as regards educational policies produce – can only produce a notable increase in inequality and segregation processes between districts and schools, even between classes, and the between the population categories who live there or who are educated there, that is these same inequalities and processes that PEPs are asked to combat and reduce.

Taking into consideration these contradictions between PEPs and the socio-economic and educational policies appropriate for what appears – in all the countries of our study and in the European Union of which they all are long-standing or recent members – to involve a progressive shift from an ideology and policies of the social democrat (related to a *welfare state* model) or communist type, backed by egalitarian rhetoric and objectives, towards an ideology and policies of the neo-liberal type, leads one to underline once more what seems to involve a change or successive shifts from the objectives assigned to, or expected of, PEPs. As we have seen, the first versions of the PEP in Europe were, three or four decades ago, backed by a compensatory aim asking the school and its staff to contribute to equalising academic development and performance by reducing or making up for the deficits that the pupils belonging to working classes or minority groups were believed to owe to their living conditions or modes of socialisation and the family practices specific to their environment. This issue was criticised by those who, following the example of Bernstein, reproached it for 'diverting the attention of the internal organisation and the educational context of the school and directing it towards the families and the children' rather than 'questioning or clarifying the social presuppositions implied in the social definition of legitimate knowledge or legitimate implementation of this knowledge' (Bernstein, 1975, pp. 252, 254). This type of criticism nurtured another conception of PEPs or policies aiming at fighting against educational inequality, as having to work towards the transformation of educational practices by better elucidating their presupposed cognitive and social stakes, and how these come to be written into social relationships and life experiences. This was perhaps a partly utopian conception in which the aims and hopes for the transformation and the democratisation of the school were thought of as being inseparable from the aims and hopes for the transformation and the democratisation of society, in a dialectic between endogenous and exogenous transformations.

Giving up on this egalitarian perspective, according to some; taking into consideration other principles and other models of social and educational justice, according to others, has meant that the perspective of a fight against exclusion is supplanting both the compensatory perspective and the critical perspective championed, *inter alia* by Bernstein. Political rhetoric now stresses the objectives of effectiveness and fairness, a development that, for some, signals the abandoning or at least the weakening of the objective of equality, or which, for others, makes it plural, more concrete and more pragmatic. At all events, it is clear that the prospect of a fight against exclusion primarily results in the objective of guaranteeing access to a minimum level of social, economic or cultural commodities for all. PEPs, as far as they are concerned, must contribute to providing such guaranteed access to the minimum level of educational commodities necessary for social integration. This objective seems to go hand in hand with a certain depoliticisation or desociologisation of educational questions, in the sense of a drop in the influence of the approaches of critical or conflictualist sociology, in favour of more 'technical', pragmatic or 'professionalising' approaches, leaving more scope for psychological and educational work and perspectives, with a to-and-fro movement that has the paradigms succeeding one another, or even opposing one another, rather than dialectising themselves by questioning and fuelling each other reciprocally. Certain analysts of this development will stress the fact that the objective of a guaranteed minimum in a society where segregation and inequality are increasingly prevalent, through lack of wanting, or being able to tackle the structural processes that produce them, may become a mode of management of those who are 'excluded from the inside' (Bourdieu, 1973), of consolation for the losers of social and educational competition (Goffmann, 1989), or even of social pacification of the consequences of this competition and market and domination mechanisms, while possibly having only very limited effects on the exclusion processes and situations, or even being doomed to fail to prevent or to attenuate them. Whether one agrees with this type of analysis, it *can* be agreed that the problem of exclusion has contributed to a refocusing of political objectives and concerns, from social relations and their transformation towards improving the situation of the people and categories of people who are most exposed to the risks of exclusion. In conjunction with the economic and social conceptions and ideologies, specific to the forms of contemporary individualism, this refocusing has paved the way for what today may seem to be a new objective, or a new age for PEPs, which are from now on invited to focus on the special or specific needs of increasingly numerous categories of pupils or populations and whose characteristics appear increasingly heterogeneous, and to lay down the objective, not just of preventing or repairing the exclusion of the most fragile but of recognising the diversity of talents and potentials of everyone in order to maximise their possibilities of educational and social achievement.

This brief summary of the conceptions and problems on which, from one period to another and using different methods from one country to another, priority education policies and their objectives have been based, and continue to be based in Europe, shows to what extent PEPs and their developments and contradictions are inseparable from the transformations of the ideologies and the social and educational policies of recent decades, and the modes of regulation that these have promoted and implemented. Consequently, while PEPs have undoubtedly failed to be the 'laboratory for social change in education' in the sense given to this term by those who used it in the 1970s or 1980s to summarise their hopes that these policies would contribute jointly to a transformation of school and society that would make them both more democratic and less unequal, they can nevertheless undoubtedly be regarded as having been one of the areas or laboratories in which ideological changes and new modes of regulation specific to postmodern or neo-liberal societies and policies took shape and were tested.

Notes

1. This conclusion has greatly benefited from the many discussions to which the first stage of our research work has given rise, both during the seminars involving the various national teams and within the co-ordinating team. The responsibility for it is, however, the author's alone.
2. Within the framework of this conclusion, we obviously cannot go into details as to these ways of categorising and of conceptualising the transformations in progress, nor even the differentiated methods with which they are implemented, contextualised and adapted by the various protagonists in the various countries. For a broader and more detailed view, the reader is referred, *inter alia*, to Whitty, Power & Halpin, 1998; Green, Wolf & Leney, 1999; Maroy, 2006; Mons, 2007; Derouet & Normand, 2007.
3. We will not deal here with the question of deciding whether they are two different models or two alternatives of the same model.
4. Along the same lines, Stefania Pontrandolfo, inquiring into the educational and social situation of the Roma in Melfi, a town in the Italian region of Basilicate, shows how 'the Melfi Roma are invisible', having made the 'choice' of keeping 'the meaning of their presence in the world as Roma' in the private arena, and out of the public gaze, an observation which is somewhat disturbing for an anthropologist, and which leads her to question the risks of 'over-ethnicizing' which both anthropological research and its backers (in this case the European commission) may be the bearers of (Pontrandolfo, 2004, forthcoming).
5. Ivan Bajomi et al. observe, in connection with Hungary, that 'concerns related to inequality of opportunity were far from present in the minds of those involved in educational policy during the first twelve years of post-Communism' (Bajomi *et al.*, 2006, p. 247).
6. As can be seen, for example, in the different points of view adopted on this question by the French and Flemish communities of Belgium.

Bibliography

Bajomi I. *et al.* (2006). 'Compétition scolaire et inégalités dans un arrondissement de Budapest' [Academic competition in a district of Budapest]. In C. Maroy (ed.), *École, régulation et marché. Une comparaison de six espaces scolaires locaux en Europe* [School, regulation and market. A comparison of six local education areas in Europe]. Paris: PUF.

Bautier É. (2001). 'Pratiques langagières et scolarisation' [Language practices and schooling]. Summary report. *Revue française de pédagogie*, 137, pp. 117–161.

Bernstein B. (1971). 'Enseignement de compensation' [Compensation teaching]. In *Langage et classes sociales. Codes socio-linguistiques et contrôle socia* [Speech and social classes. Socio-linguistic codes and social control]. Paris: Les Ed. de Minuit. Initial version in English: 'Education cannot compensate for society'. *New Society*, 1970, 387, pp. 344–347.

Bernstein B. (1975). *Classes et pédagogies: visibles et invisibles* [Class and pedagogies: visible and invisible]. Paris: CERI-OCDE.

BERNSTEIN B. (2007). *Pédagogie, contrôle symbolique et identité. Théorie, recherche, critique.* Québec: Presses de l'Université Laval. (French translation of the revised edition – London, Rowman & Littlefield, 2000 – of 'Pedagogy, symbolic control and identity. Theory, research, critique'. (London: Taylor & Francis, 1996).

BOURDIEU P. (dir.) (1993). *La misère du monde* [The misery of the world]. Paris: Seuil.

CANÁRIO R. (2003). 'Politiques de discrimination positive: perspective historique' [Positive discrimination policies: a historical perspective]. In ministère de l'Éducation nationale, *La discrimination positive en France et dans le monde* [Positive discrimination in France and in the world]. Proceedings of the International Convention in March 2002. Paris: CNDP.

CASTEL R. (2003). *L'insécurité sociale* [Social insecurity]. Paris: Seuil.

CRESAS (1985). *Depuis 1981, l'école pour tous? Zones d'éducation prioritaires* [Since 1981: schooling for all? Priority education zones]. Paris: INRP/L'Harmattan.

DEMEUSE M. & BAYE A. (2005). 'Pourquoi parler d'équité?' [Why speak of equity?]. In M. DEMEUSE et al. (ed.), *Vers une école juste et efficace. 26 contributions sur les systèmes d'enseignement et de formation* [Towards fair and efficient schooling. 26 contributions on teaching and training systems]. Bruxelles: De Boeck, pp. 149–170.

DEMEUSE M. & BAYE A. (2007). 'La Commission européenne face à l'efficacité et l'équité des systèmes éducatifs européens' [The European commission and the efficiency and equity of European education systems]. *Éducation et Sociétés*, 20, pp. 105–119.

DEROUET J.-L. & NORMAND R. (dirs) (2007). *L'Europe de l'éducation: entre management et politique* [Education in Europe: between management and policy]. Lyon: INRP.

DRÆLANTS H., DUPRIEZ V. & MAROY C. (2003). *Le système scolaire en communauté française* [The educational system in the French community]. Brussels: CRISP.

DUBAR C., GADEA C. & ROLLE P. (2003). 'Pour une analyse comparée des configurations' [Towards a compared analysis of configurations]. In M. LALLEMENT and J. SPURK (eds), *Stratégie de la comparaison internationale* [Strategy for international comparison]. Paris: Ed. du CNRS.

GOFFMANN E. (1989). 'Calmer le jobard: quelques aspects de l'adaptation à l'échec' [Calming the gullible: some aspects of adapting to failure]. In Centre culturel international de Cerisy-la-Salle, *Le parler frais d'Erving Goffmann*. Paris: Les Ed. de Minuit.

GOODY J. (1979). *La raison graphique.* Paris: Les Ed. de Minuit. French translation of *The Domestication of the savage mind.* Cambridge: Cambridge University Press, 1977.

GOODY J. (1994). *Entre l'oralité et l'écriture.* Paris: PUF. French translation of *The interface between the oral and the written.* Cambridge: Cambridge University Press, 1987.

GREEN A., WOLF A. & LENEY T. (1999). *Convergence and Divergence in European Education and Training Systems.* London: Institute of Education.

GRISAY A. (1984). 'Quels indicateurs pour quelle réduction des inégalités scolaires?' [What indicators for what reduction in academic inequality]. *Revue de la direction générale de l'Organisation des Études*, 9, pp. 3–14.

ISAMBERT-JAMATI V. (1973). 'Les 'handicaps socio-culturels' et leurs remèdes pédagogiques' ['Socio-cultural handicaps' and their educational remedies]. *L'orientation scolaire et professionnelle*, 4, pp. 303–318.

ISAMBERT-JAMATI V. (1985). 'Quelques rappels de l'échec scolaire comme 'problème social' dans les milieux pédagogiques français' [Some reminders on educational failure as a 'social problem' in French pedagogical environments]. In É. PLAISANCE (ed.), *'L'échec scolaire': nouveaux débats, nouvelles approches sociologiques* ['Education failure': new debates, new sociological apporaches]. Paris: Ed. du CNRS.

LAHIRE B. (1993). *Culture écrite et inégalités scolaires* [Written culture and educational inequality]. Lyon: Presses universitaires de Lyon.

LE GARREC S. (2006). *Le renouvellement urbain, la genèse d'une notion fourre-tout* [Urban renewal: genesis of a catch-all notion]. Paris: PUCA.

LITTLE A. & SMITH G. (1971). *Stratégies de compensation: panorama des projets d'enseignement pour les groupes défavorisés aux États-Unis* Paris: CERI-OCDE (translated from the English in the same year, *Strategies of Compensation: A Review of Educational Projects for the Disadvantaged in the United States*, same publisher).

MAROY C. (ed.) (2006). *École, régulation et marché. Une comparaison de six espaces scolaires locaux en Europe* [School, regulation and market. A comparison of six local school areas in Europe]. Paris: PUF.

MONS N. (2007). *Les nouvelles politiques éducatives. La France fait-elle les bons choix?* [The new education policies. Is France making the right choices?]. Paris: PUF.

MYERS K. & GOLDSTEIN H. (1998). 'Who's failing?' In L. STOOL & K. MYERS (eds), *No quick fixes: Perspectives on schools in difficulty*. London: Falmer Press, pp. 175–188.

OLSON D. (1998). *L'univers de l'écrit. Comment la culture écrite donne forme à la pensée.* Paris: Retz. French translation of *The World on Paper. The conceptual and cognitive implications of writing and reading.* Cambridge: Cambridge University Press, 1994.

PERRENOUD P. (1995). 'Les pédagogies nouvelles sont-elles élitaires? Réflexion sur les contradictions de l'école active' [Are the new learning approaches elitist?] Proceedings of the convention *Classes populaires et pédagogie* [Working classes and pedagogy], Université de Rouen, 1985 (taken from P. Perrenoud, *La pédagogie à l'école des différences. Fragments d'une sociologie de l'échec* [Pedagogy in the school of differences. Fragments of a sociology of failure]. Paris: ESF).

PONTRANDOLFO S. (2004). 'Alla ricerca dei rom di Melfi'. *Quaderni di sociologia*, no. 36, pp. 51–72.

PONTRANDOLFO S. (forthcoming). 'La construction d'une identité rom invisible. Ethnographie et histoire dans l'école de Melfi [The construction of an invisible Roma identity. Ethnography and history in the school of Melfi]'. *Revue française de pédagogie*.

RAVON B. (2000). *L' 'échec scolaire'. Histoire d'un problème public* ['Educational failure'. The history of a public problem]. Paris: In Press Éditions.

ROBERT B. (2007). *De l'apprentissage au changement. Les politiques scolaires de compensation en France et aux États-Unis (1965–2006)* [From learning to change. Compensatory education policies in France and the USA (1965–2006)]. Doctoral thesis (supervised by Agnès van Zanten), political science, IEP Paris.

RYCHEN D. S. & SALGANIK L. H. (eds) (2001). *Defining and Selecting Key Competencies*. Berne: Hogrefe & Huber.

VINOKUR A. (2005). 'Avant-propos', *Cahiers de la recherche sur l'éducation et les savoirs* ['Foreword', research notes on education and knowledge], special issue no. 1 ('Pouvoirs et mesure en éducation' [Powers and measure in education]), pp. 7–14.

VYGOTSKI L. S. (1994). *Défectologie et déficience mentale* [Defectology and mental deficiency]. Collection of texts (1924–1934) published under the direction of K. BARISNIKOV and G. PETITPIERRE. Neuchâtel: Delachaux et Niestlé.

WHITTY G., POWER S. & HALPIN D. (1998). *Devolution and Choice in Education. The School, the State and the Market*. Buckingham and Philadelphia: Open University Press.

Index

absenteeism, 6, 71, 108–9, 111, 115, 134, 166, 171–2, 202, 300
academic
  achievement, 259, 263, 266–7, 271–2
  ambition, 117, 175, 213
  attainments, 107
  background, 114
  characteristics, 102
  criteria, 114, 178
  democratisation, 107
  excellence, 5, 30, 33, 35–6, 39–40, 99, 117
  failure, 260, 266
  goals, 272
  improvement, 132
  inequality, 112
  knowledge, 10
  level, 211
  management, 2, 11, 98, 178, 208–11
  outcome, 264, 271
  performance, 6, 9, 132, 194, 267, 273
  results, 98, 276, 278, 279–80
  segregation, 58, 102
  subjects, 275, 278
  success, 60, 98, 104, 109, 161, 169, 172, 177, 268, 272, 312
  work, 270
accountability, 27, 42, 171
achievement, 24–5, 27, 29, 33, 128, 233, 240, 259, 263, 266–7, 271–2
  underachievement, 29, 33, 43, 77
affirmative action, 3
area (area-based approaches), 4, 12, 31, 35, 135, 139, 291
  See also EAZ (Education Action Zones); EPA (education priority areas); ZEP (zones d'éducation prioritaires); TEIP (Territórios Educativos de Intervenção Prioritària)
assessment
  external, 144, 295, 312
  internal, 144

international, 128
large scale, 39, 215, 233
national, 41, 128, 130, 307
overall, 105, 214, 313
performance, 16, 29, 133
pupil, 160
self, 174
student, 57, 128, 133, 157, 193, 263
systematic, 132
asylum seekers, 30, 197–8, 200, 205–6, 300

Belgium, 1, 5, 13, 55–80, 290, 291, 292
belief, 11, 266
benchmarking, 15
Bernstein (Basile), 7, 10, 11, 116–17, 177, 292, 299, 306, 316
Bourdieu (Pierre), 114, 117, 314, 316
Britain, 4
budget, 8, 33, 36, 56, 61, 64–5, 74, 76, 77, 79, 96, 103–4, 200, 202, 237, 241, 265, 269, 270, 273, 309

categorisation, 6, 16, 66, 95, 266, 277, 300, 313
citizenship, 103, 109, 198–9
  active, 198–9
cohesion, 93, 101, 172
  social, 93, 101, 172
Coleman report, 1
collaborative study, 1
colour, 197
community, 4, 11, 12, 25, 27, 31, 33–6, 55–6, 59–64, 66–9, 71–2, 78–9, 130, 132, 136, 139–41, 143–5, 158, 162–4, 166, 168, 170, 172, 174–6, 178–80, 191, 199, 201–4, 215–16, 228, 239–40, 242, 244, 246–7, 292, 296, 312
comparative analysis, 1–2, 5, 12, 290
comparative approach, 6, 16, 289, 311